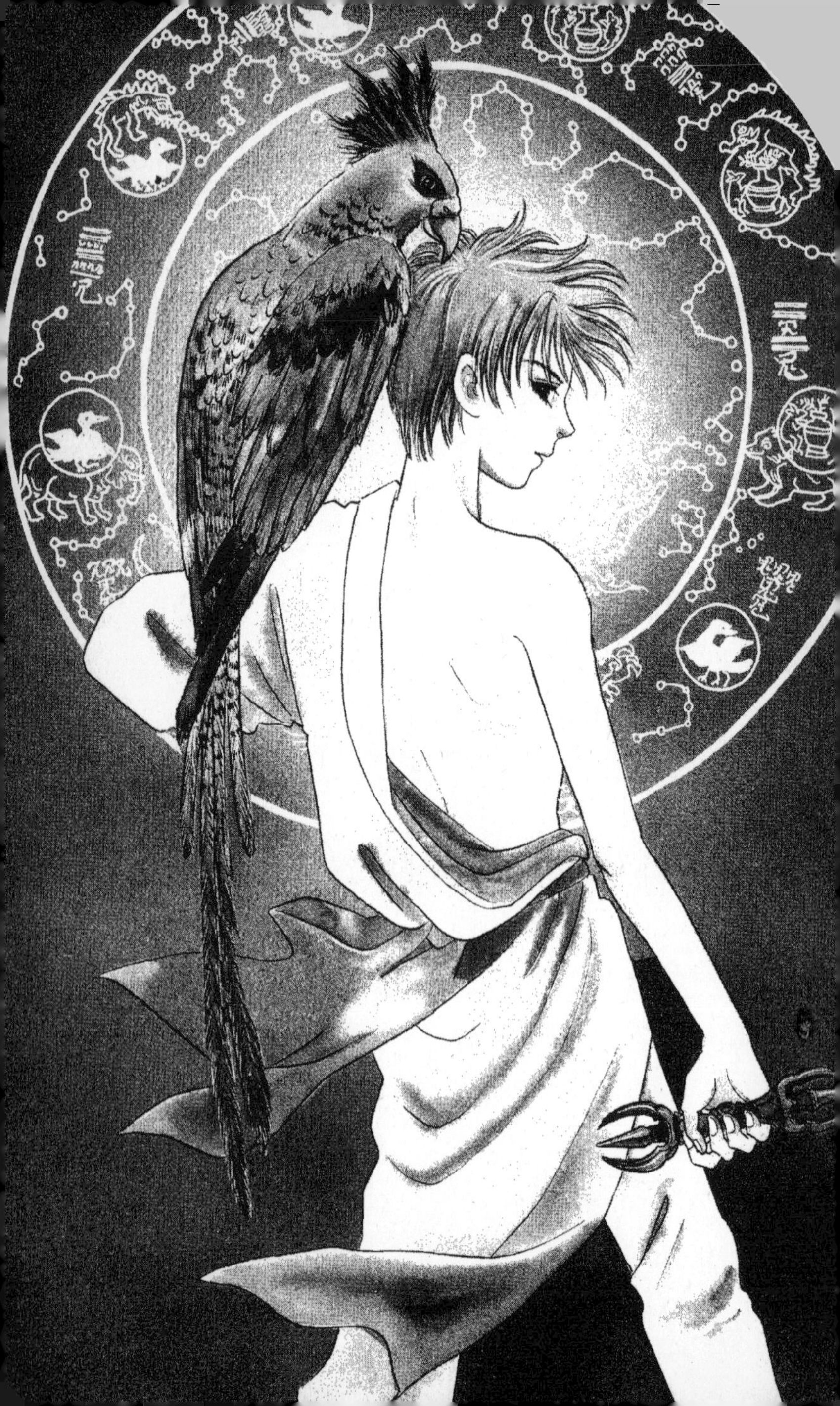

Genju no Seiza Volume 1
Created by Matsuri Akino

Translation - Mike Kiefl
English Adaptation - Christine Boylan
Retouch and Lettering - Courtney Geter
Graphic Designer - Jihye "Sophia" Hong
Cover Design - John Lo

Editor - Tim Beedle
Digital Imaging Manager - Chris Buford
Production Manager - Elisabeth Brizzi
VP of Production - Ron Klamert
Editor-In-Chief - Rob Tokar
Publisher - Mike Kiley
President and C.O.O. - John Parker
C.E.O. and Chief Creative Officer - Stuart Levy

A 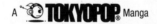 Manga

TOKYOPOP Inc.
5900 Wilshire Blvd. Suite 2000
Los Angeles, CA 90036

E-mail: info@TOKYOPOP.com
Come visit us online at www.TOKYOPOP.com

ISBN: 1-59816-607-7

First TOKYOPOP printing: August 2006
10 9 8 7 6 5 4 3 2 1
Printed in the USA

Genju no Seiza

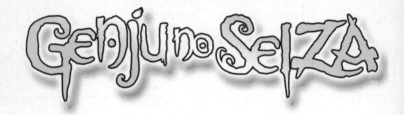

Volume 1

Created by
Matsuri Akino

TOKYOPOP®

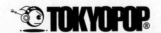

HAMBURG // LONDON // LOS ANGELES // TOKYO

Genju no Seiza

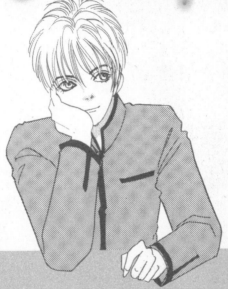

Table of Contents

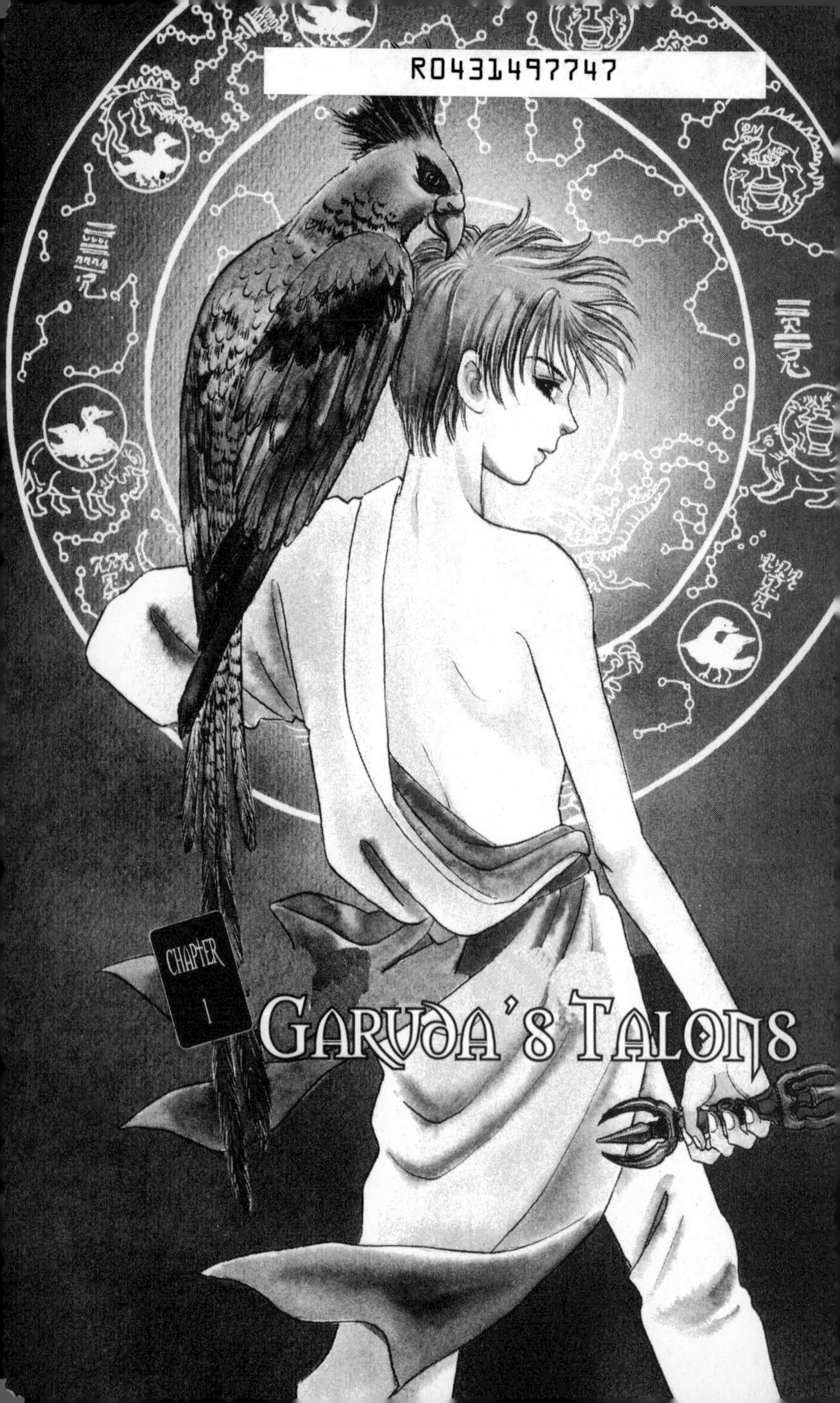
CHAPTER
1
GARUDA'S TALONS

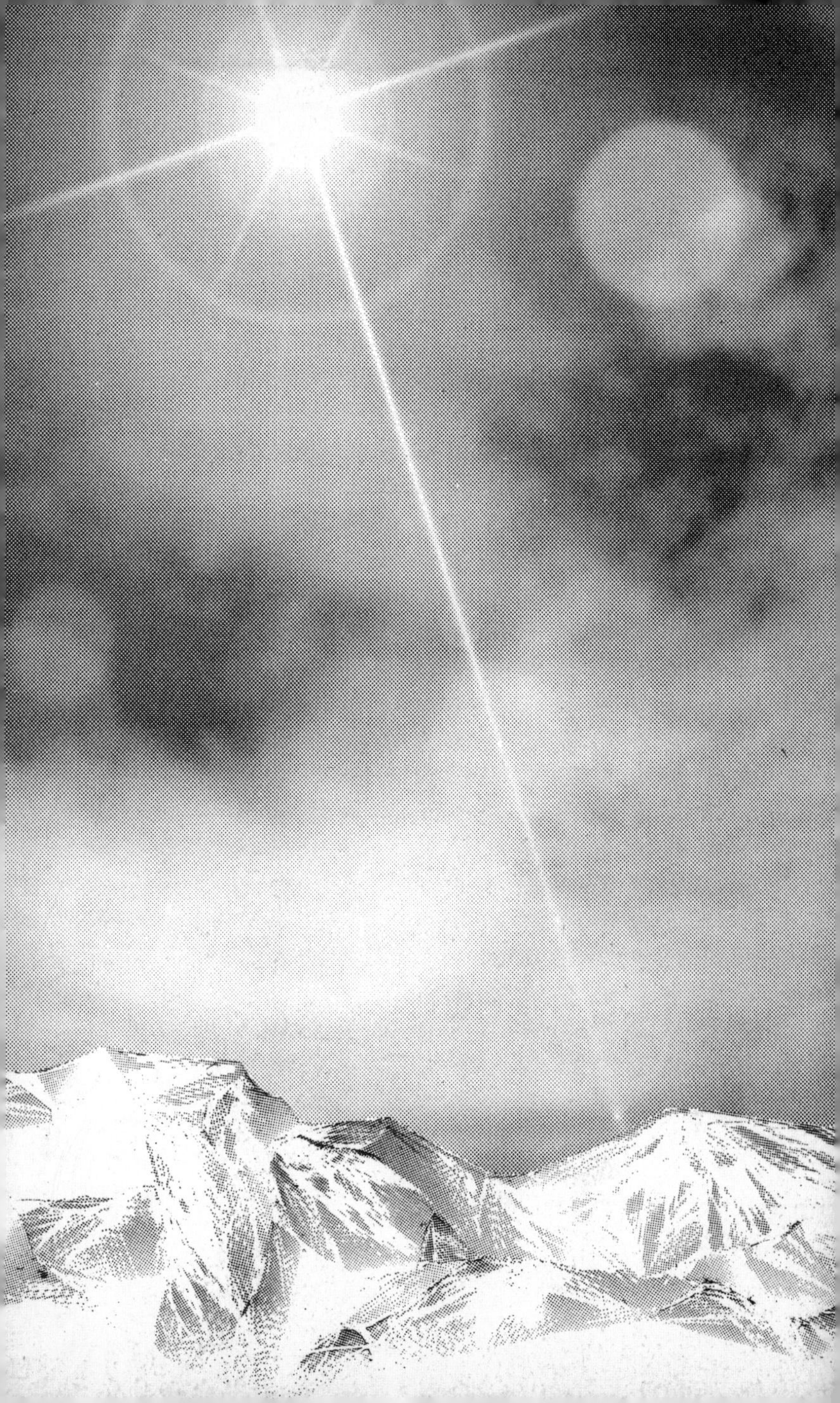

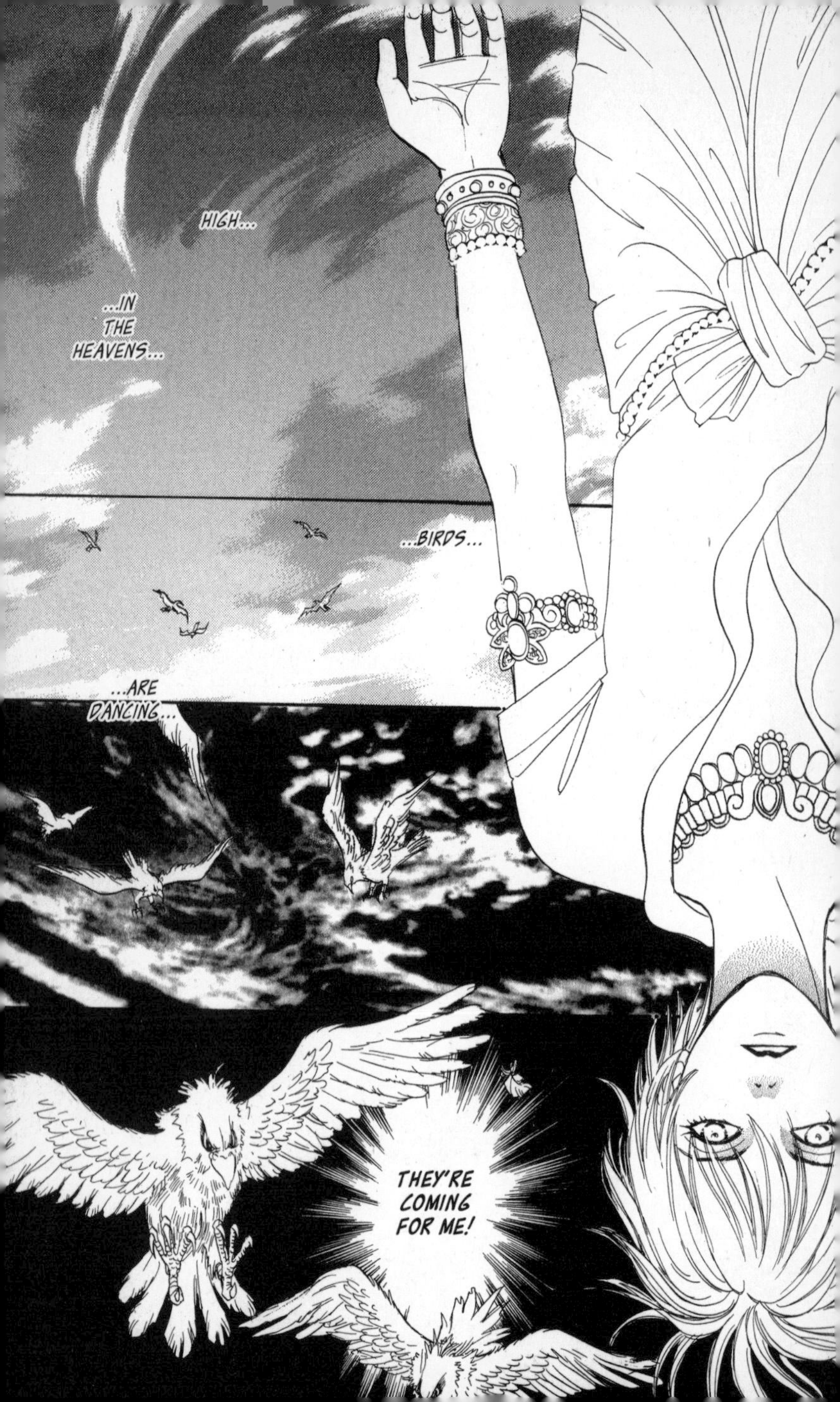
HIGH...
...IN THE HEAVENS...
...BIRDS...
...ARE DANCING...
THEY'RE COMING FOR ME!

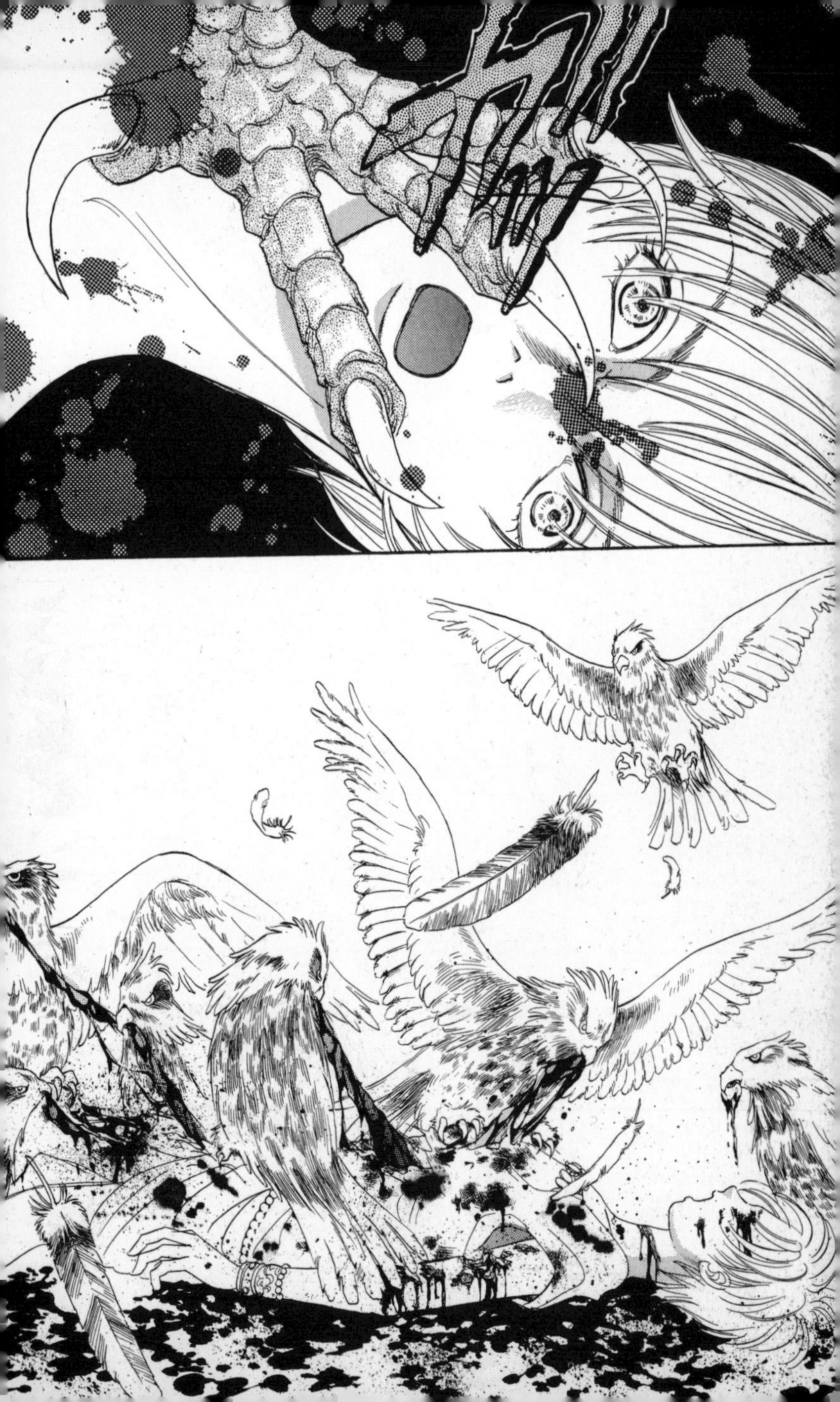

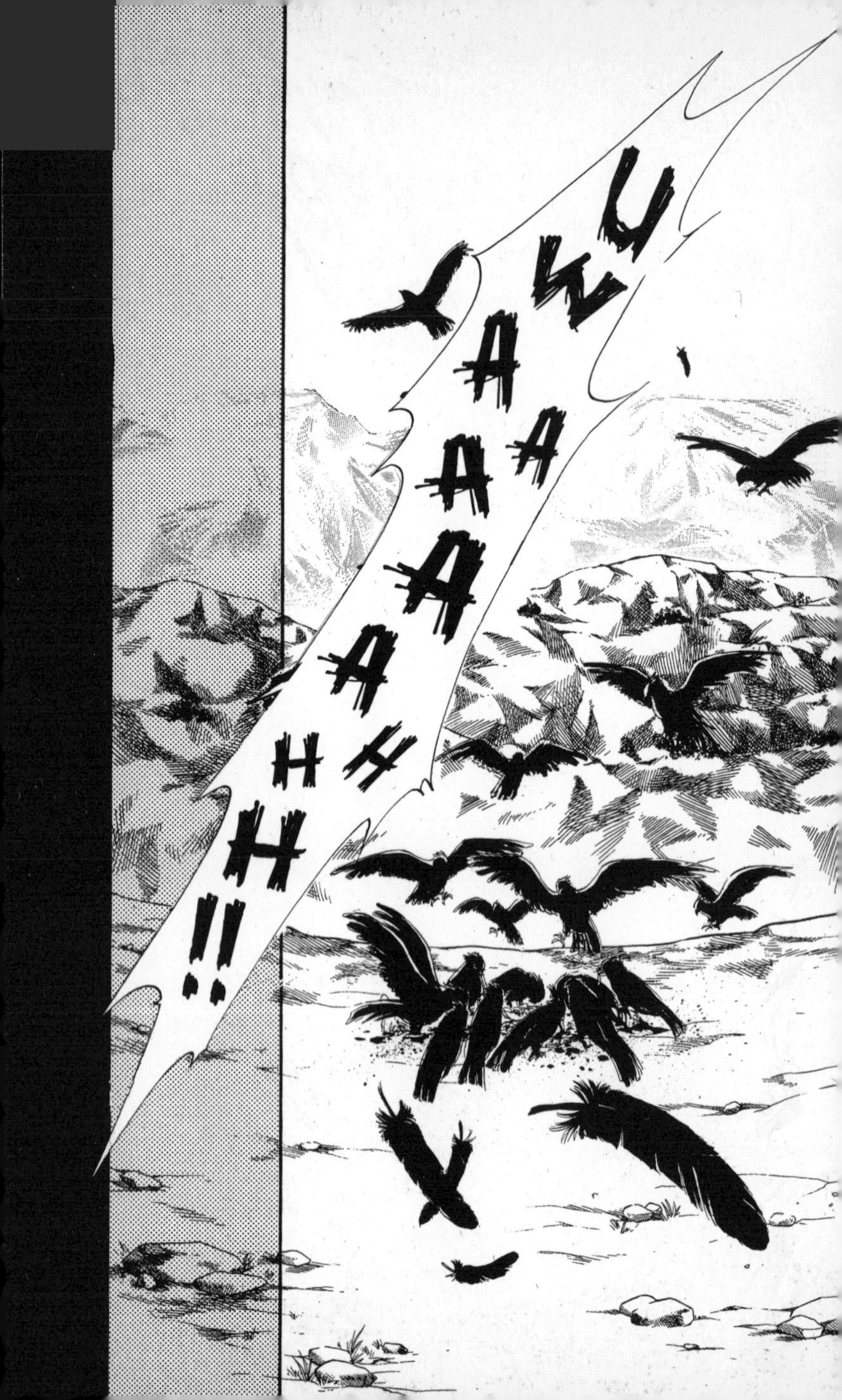
UWAAAAAHHH!!

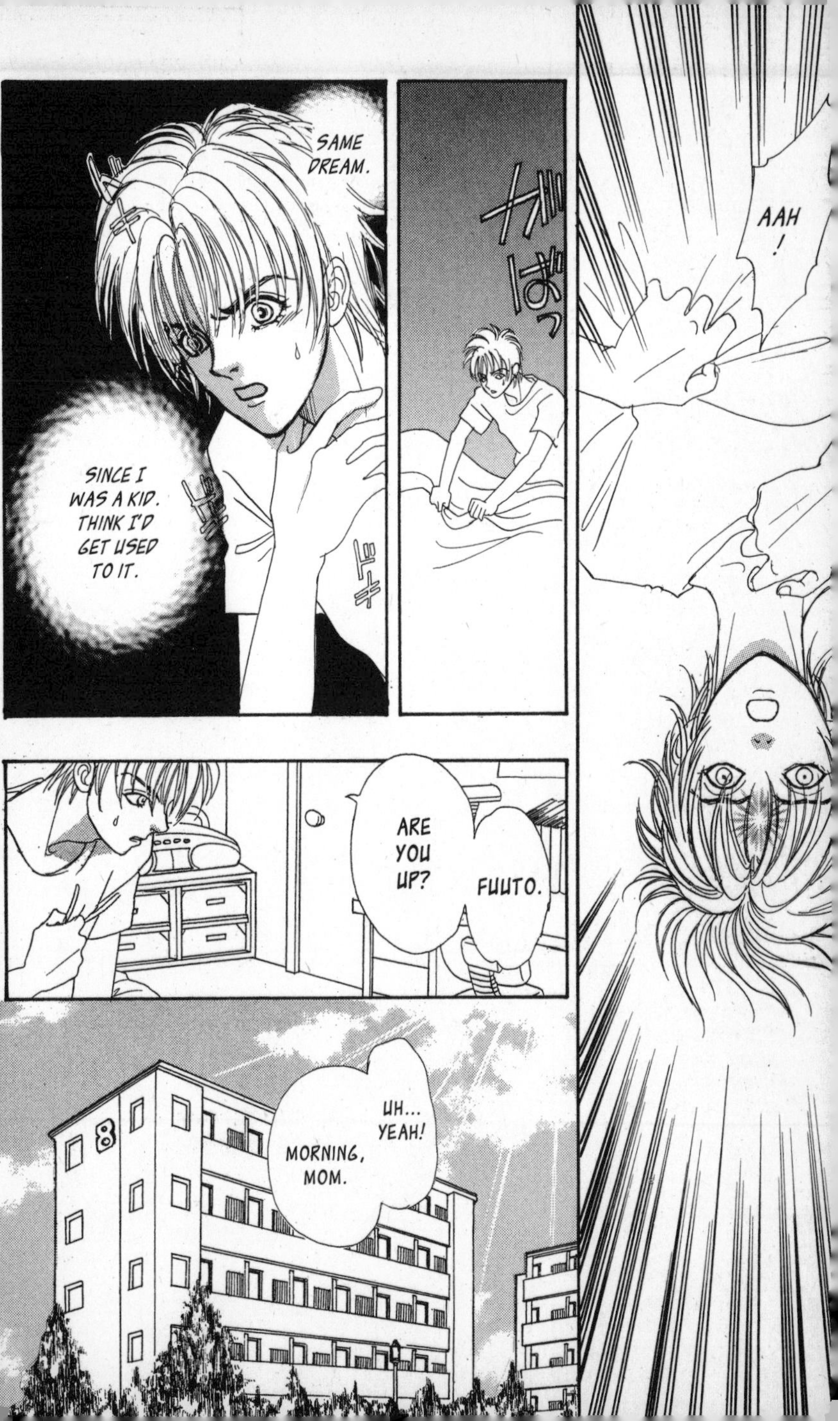
AAH!
SAME DREAM.
SINCE I WAS A KID. THINK I'D GET USED TO IT.
FUUTO.
ARE YOU UP?
UH... YEAH!
MORNING, MOM.

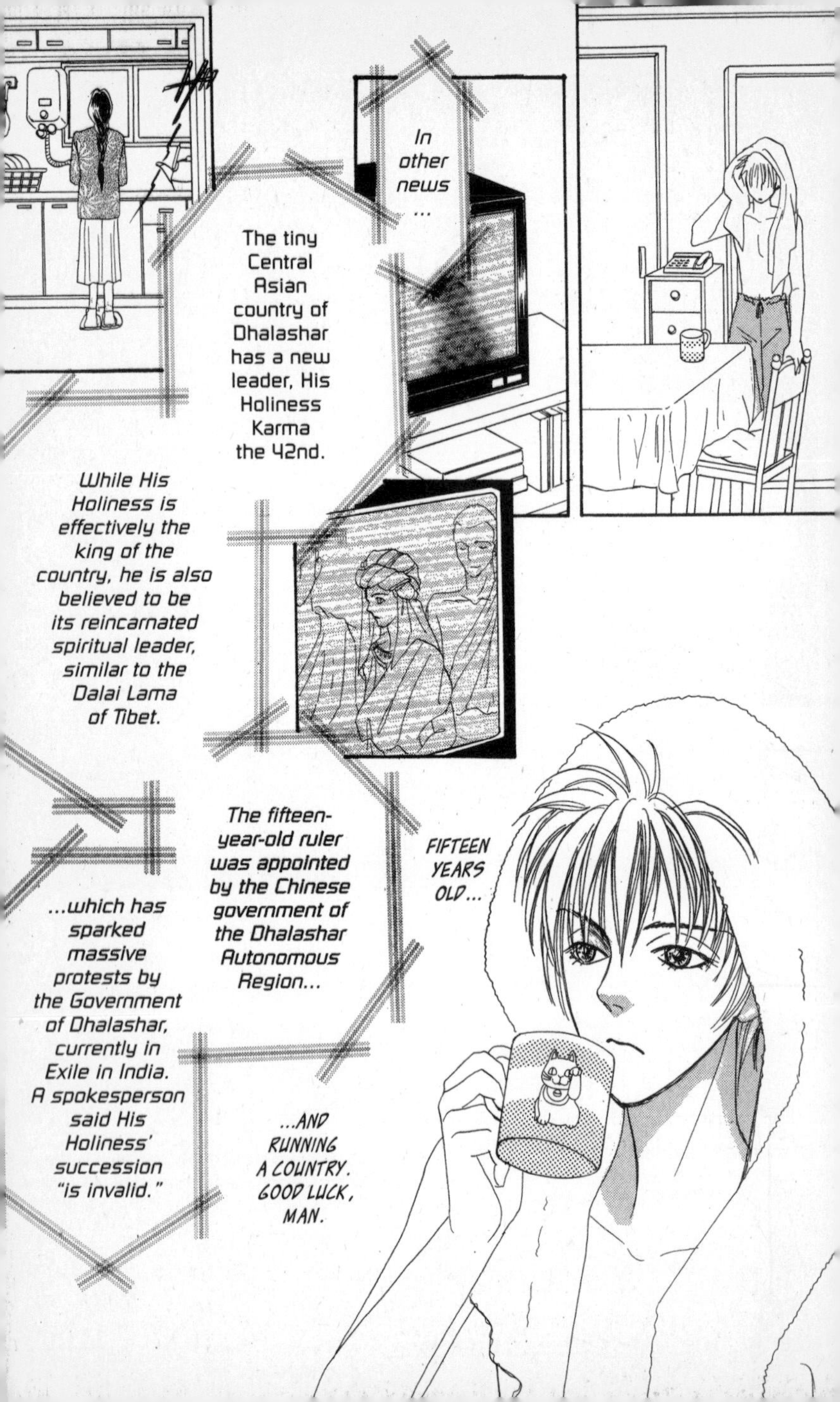
In other news ...
The tiny Central Asian country of Dhalashar has a new leader, His Holiness Karma the 42nd.
While His Holiness is effectively the king of the country, he is also believed to be its reincarnated spiritual leader, similar to the Dalai Lama of Tibet.
The fifteen-year-old ruler was appointed by the Chinese government of the Dhalashar Autonomous Region...
FIFTEEN YEARS OLD...
...which has sparked massive protests by the Government of Dhalashar, currently in Exile in India. A spokesperson said His Holiness' succession "is invalid."
...AND RUNNING A COUNTRY. GOOD LUCK, MAN.

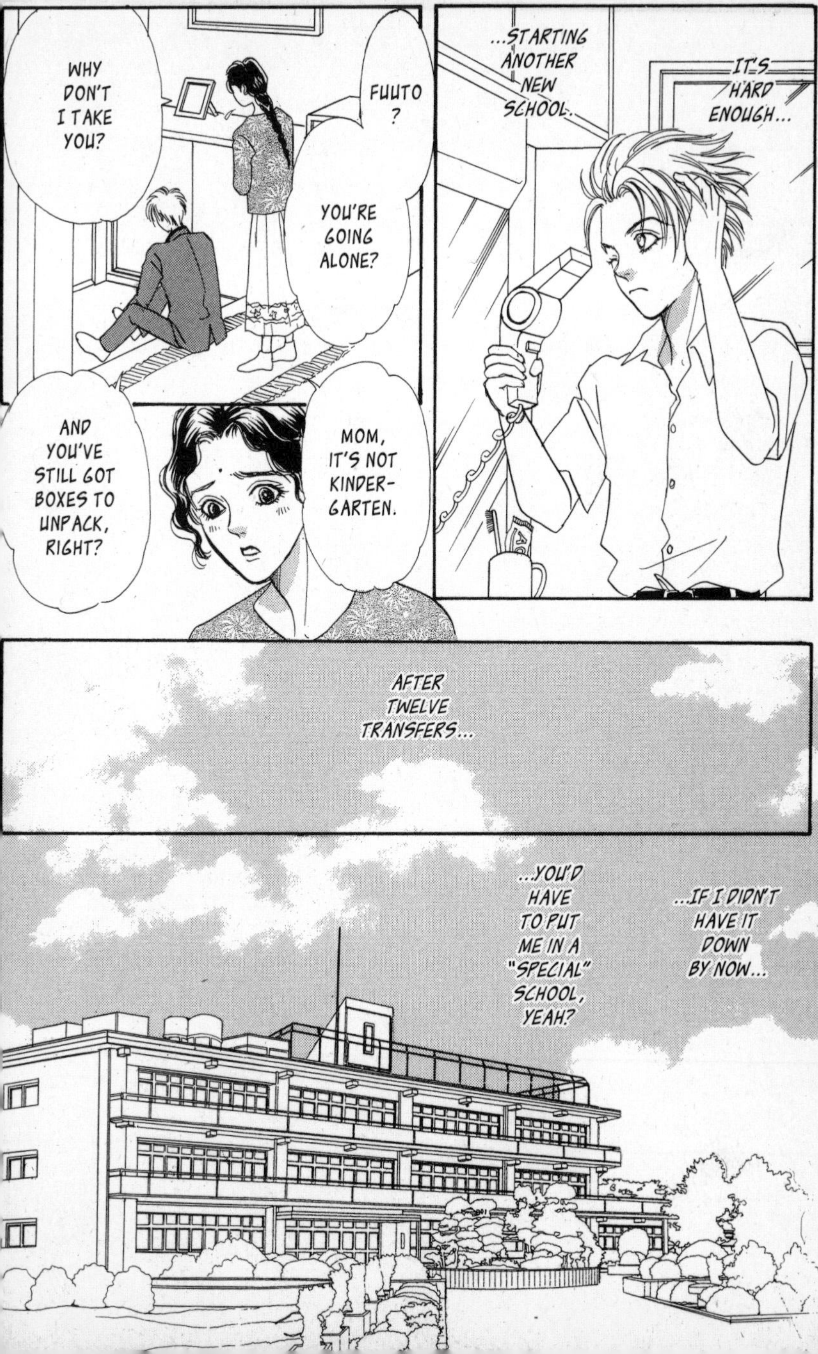
IT'S HARD ENOUGH...
...STARTING ANOTHER NEW SCHOOL.
FUUTO?
YOU'RE GOING ALONE?
WHY DON'T I TAKE YOU?
MOM, IT'S NOT KINDERGARTEN.
AND YOU'VE STILL GOT BOXES TO UNPACK, RIGHT?
AFTER TWELVE TRANSFERS...
...IF I DIDN'T HAVE IT DOWN BY NOW...
...YOU'D HAVE TO PUT ME IN A "SPECIAL" SCHOOL, YEAH?

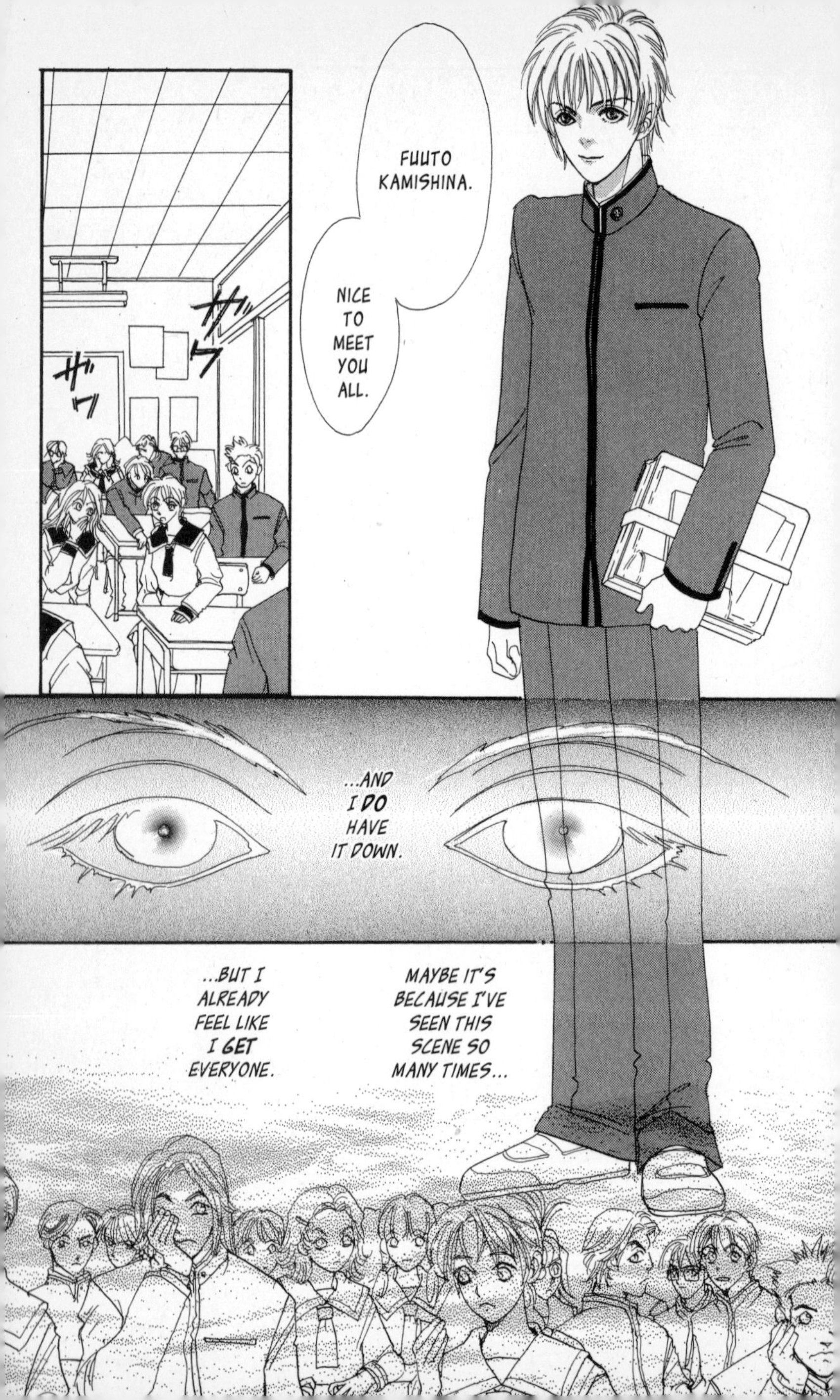

FUUTO KAMISHINA.
NICE TO MEET YOU ALL.
ザワ
ザワ
...AND I DO HAVE IT DOWN.
MAYBE IT'S BECAUSE I'VE SEEN THIS SCENE SO MANY TIMES...
...BUT I ALREADY FEEL LIKE I GET EVERYONE.

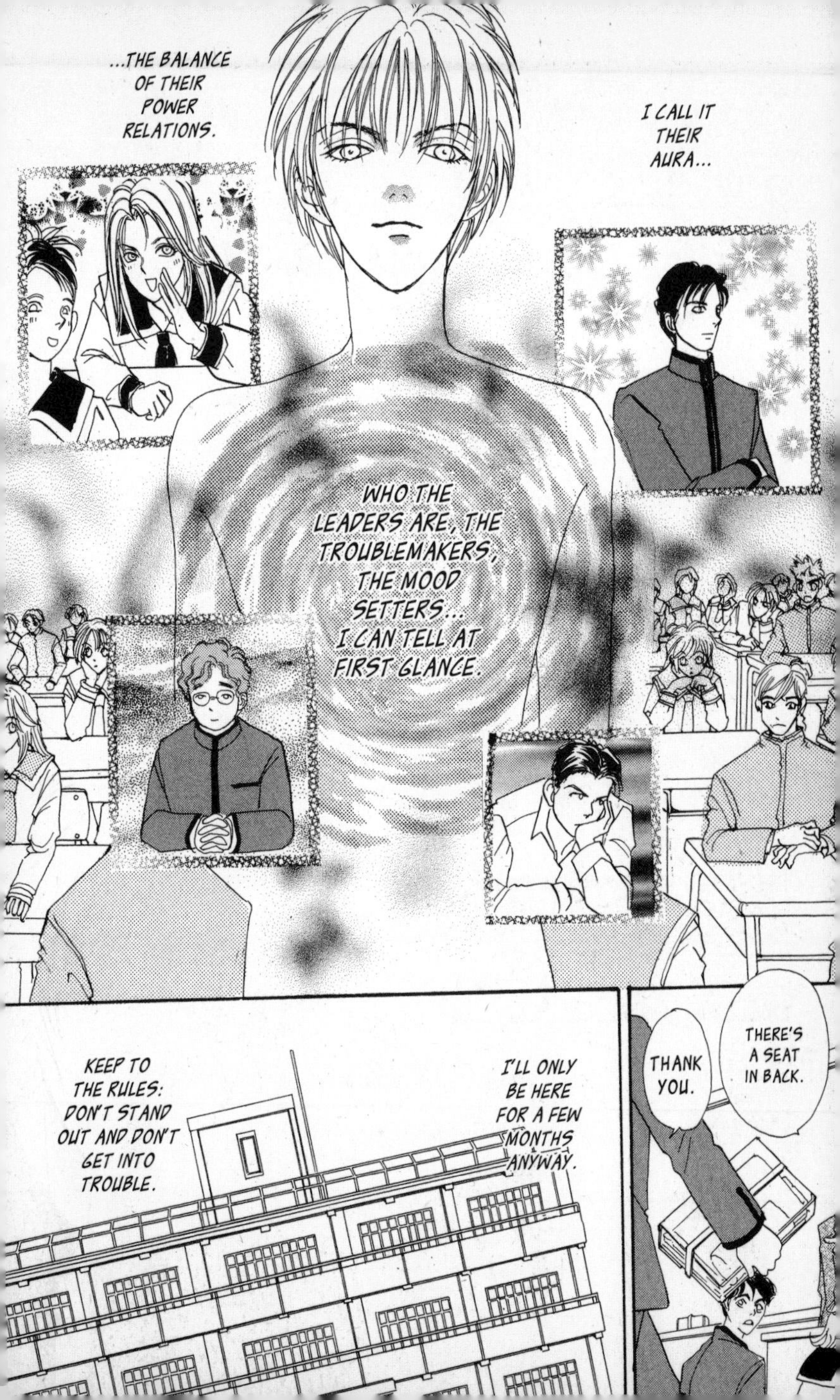
I CALL IT THEIR AURA...
...THE BALANCE OF THEIR POWER RELATIONS.
WHO THE LEADERS ARE, THE TROUBLEMAKERS, THE MOOD SETTERS... I CAN TELL AT FIRST GLANCE.
THERE'S A SEAT IN BACK.
THANK YOU.
I'LL ONLY BE HERE FOR A FEW MONTHS ANYWAY.
KEEP TO THE RULES: DON'T STAND OUT AND DON'T GET INTO TROUBLE.

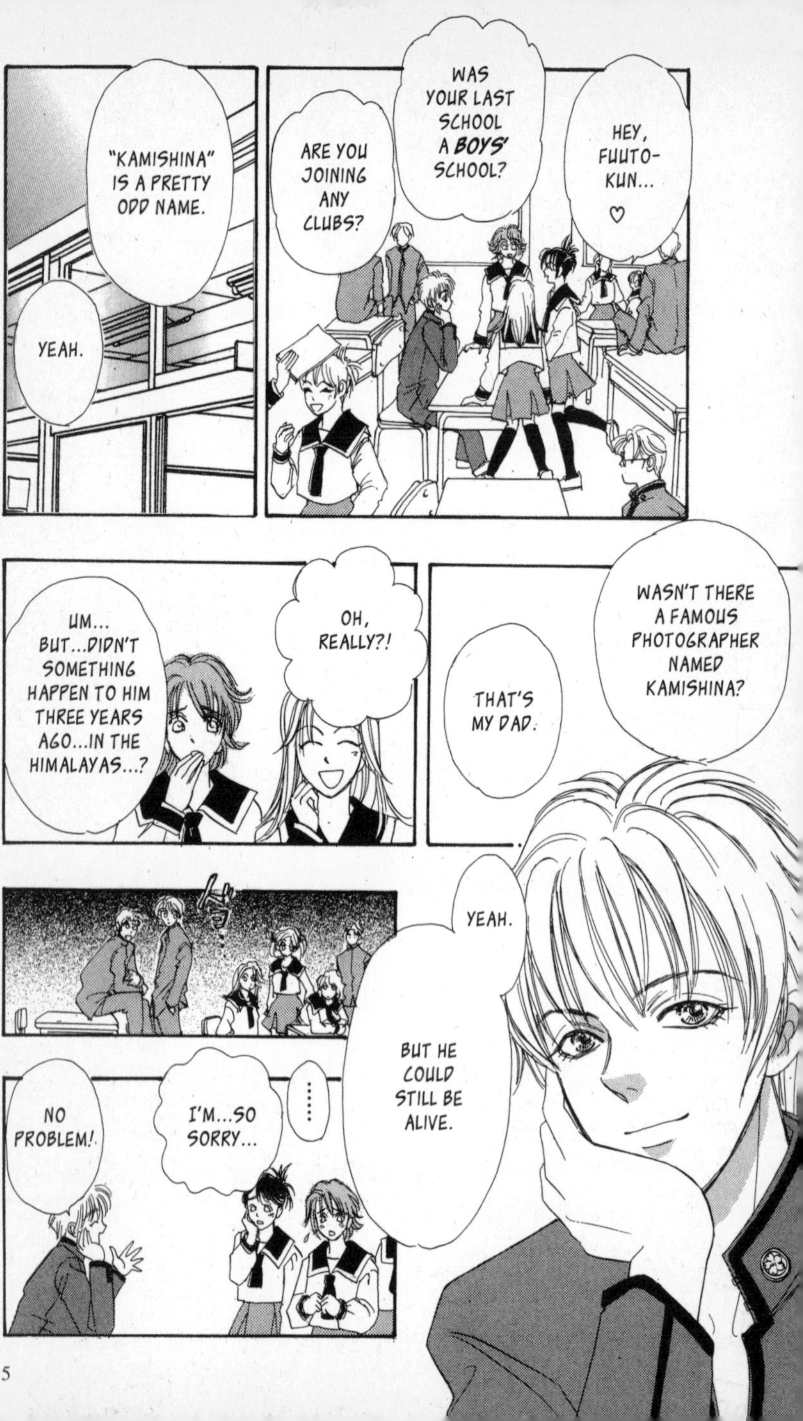
HEY, FUUTO-KUN... ♡
WAS YOUR LAST SCHOOL A **BOYS'** SCHOOL?
ARE YOU JOINING ANY CLUBS?
"KAMISHINA" IS A PRETTY ODD NAME.
YEAH.
WASN'T THERE A FAMOUS PHOTOGRAPHER NAMED KAMISHINA?
THAT'S MY DAD.
OH, REALLY?!
UM... BUT...DIDN'T SOMETHING HAPPEN TO HIM THREE YEARS AGO...IN THE HIMALAYAS...?
YEAH.
BUT HE COULD STILL BE ALIVE.
......
I'M...SO SORRY...
NO PROBLEM!

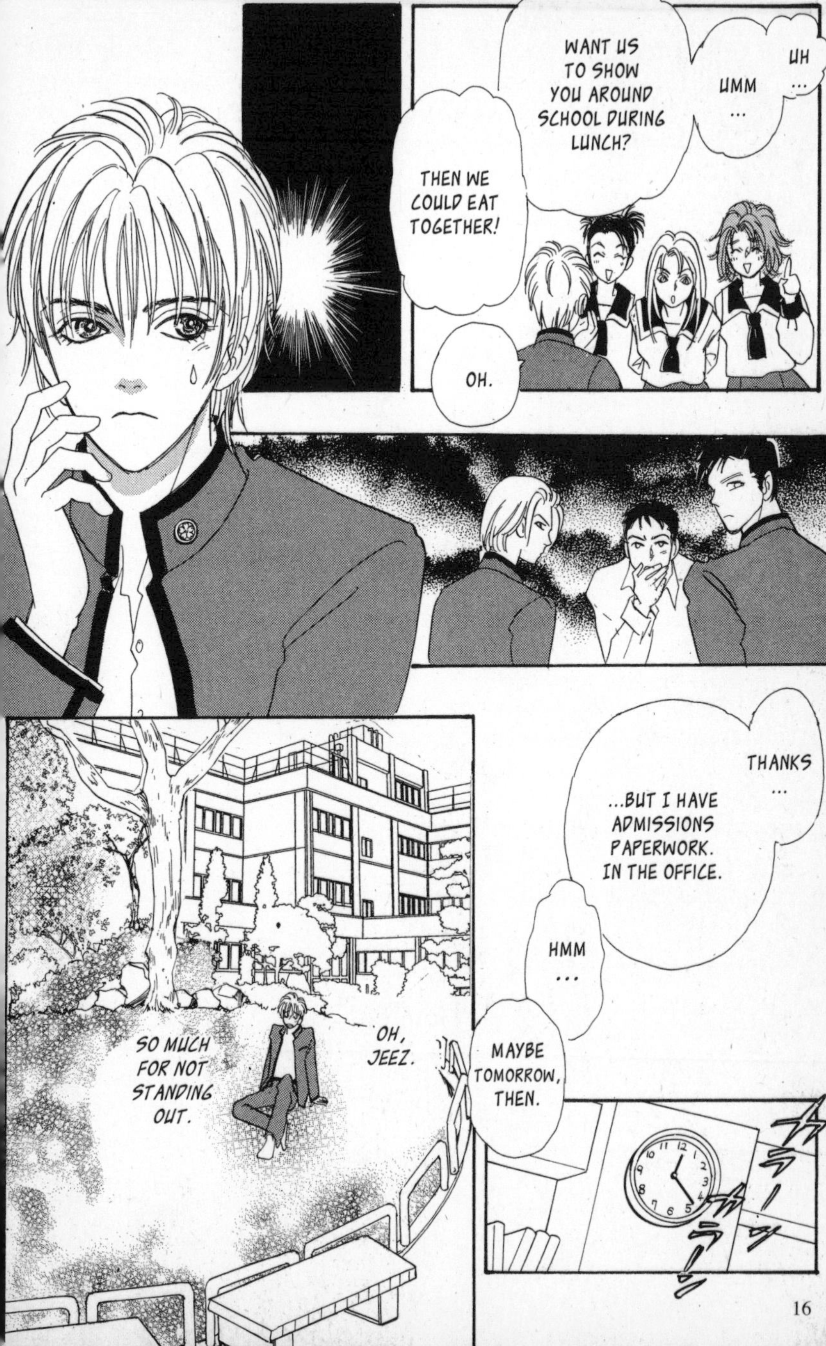
UH ...
UMM ...
WANT US TO SHOW YOU AROUND SCHOOL DURING LUNCH?
THEN WE COULD EAT TOGETHER!
OH.
THANKS ...
...BUT I HAVE ADMISSIONS PAPERWORK. IN THE OFFICE.
HMM ...
MAYBE TOMORROW, THEN.
OH, JEEZ.
SO MUCH FOR NOT STANDING OUT.

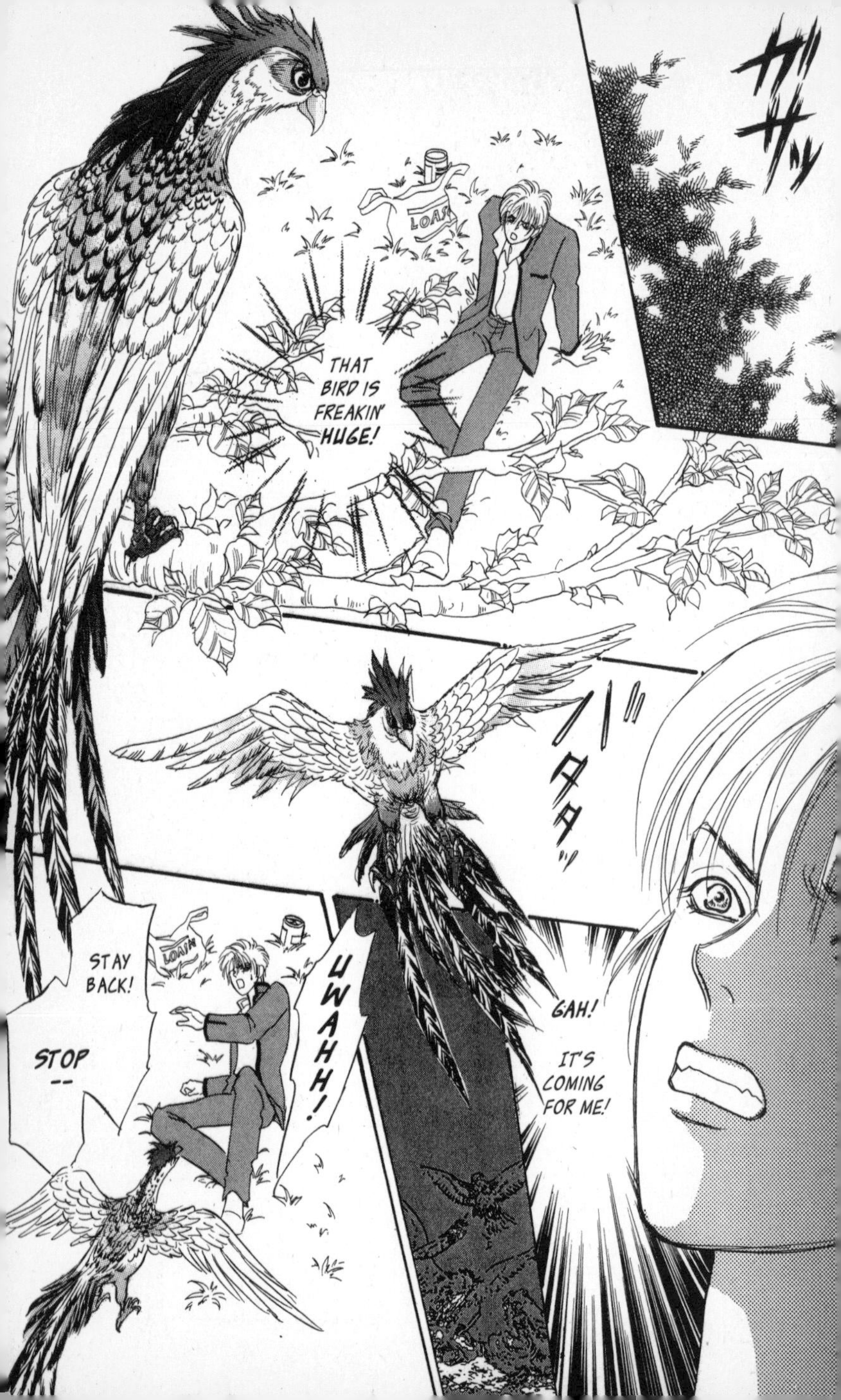
ガサッ
THAT BIRD IS FREAKIN' HUGE!
GAH!
IT'S COMING FOR ME!
バタタッ
UWAHH!
STAY BACK!
STOP --

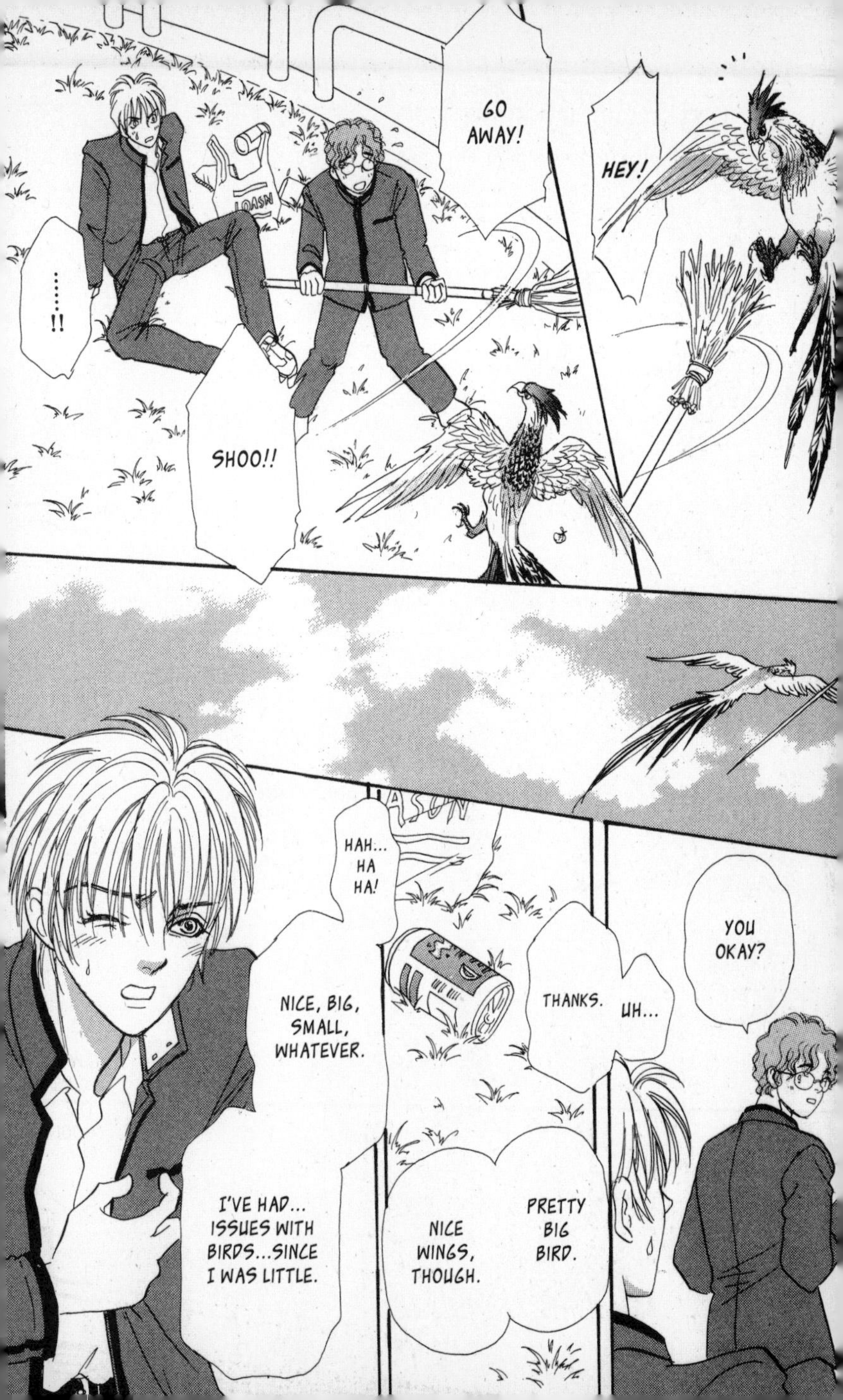
HEY!
GO AWAY!
SHOO!!
……!!
YOU OKAY?
UH...
THANKS.
PRETTY BIG BIRD.
NICE WINGS, THOUGH.
HAH... HA HA!
NICE, BIG, SMALL, WHATEVER.
I'VE HAD... ISSUES WITH BIRDS...SINCE I WAS LITTLE.

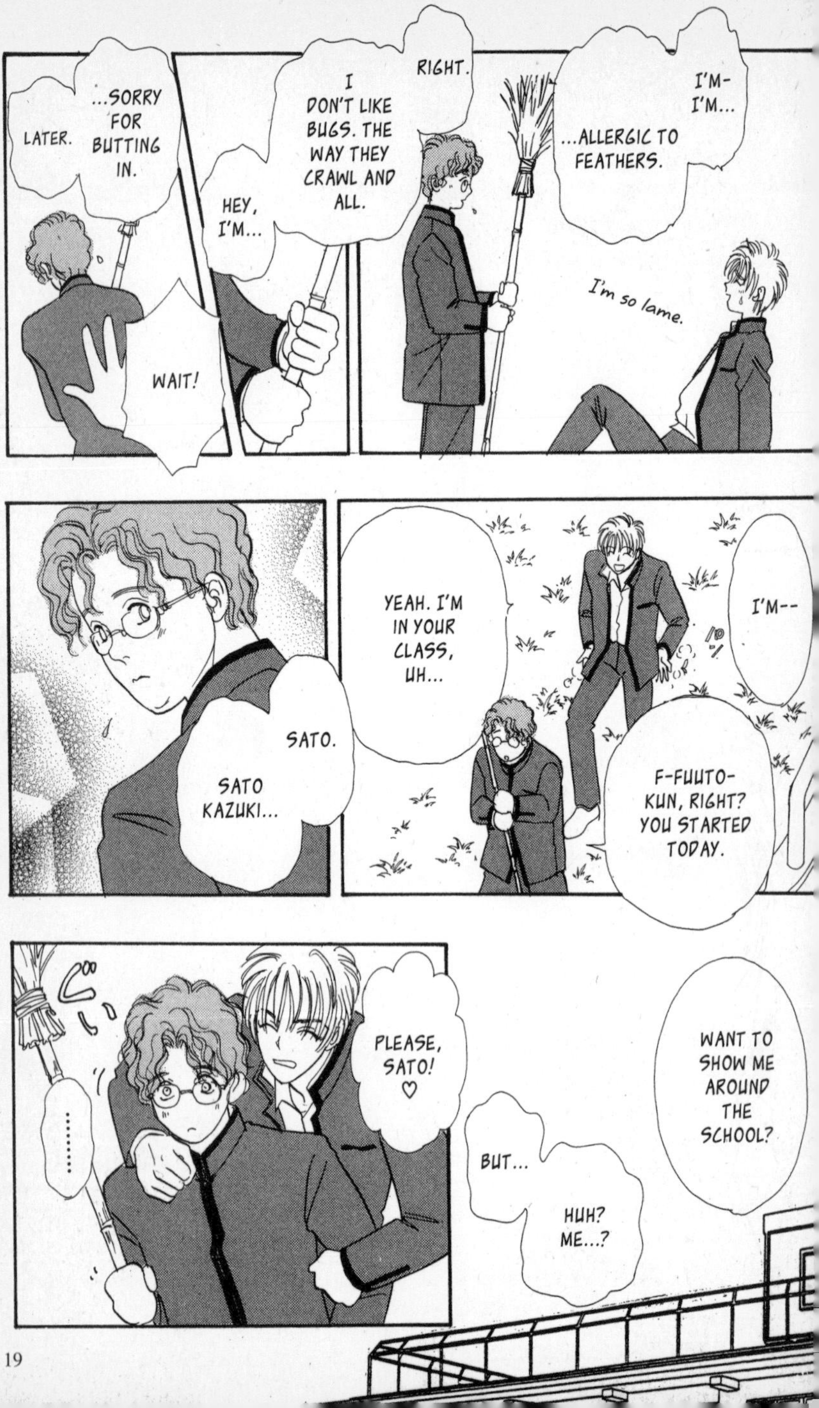
I'M- I'M...
...ALLERGIC TO FEATHERS.
I'm so lame.
RIGHT.
I DON'T LIKE BUGS. THE WAY THEY CRAWL AND ALL.
HEY, I'M...
...SORRY FOR BUTTING IN.
LATER.
WAIT!
I'M--
F-FUUTO-KUN, RIGHT? YOU STARTED TODAY.
YEAH. I'M IN YOUR CLASS, UH...
SATO.
SATO KAZUKI...
WANT TO SHOW ME AROUND THE SCHOOL?
HUH? ME...?
BUT...
PLEASE, SATO! ♡
....

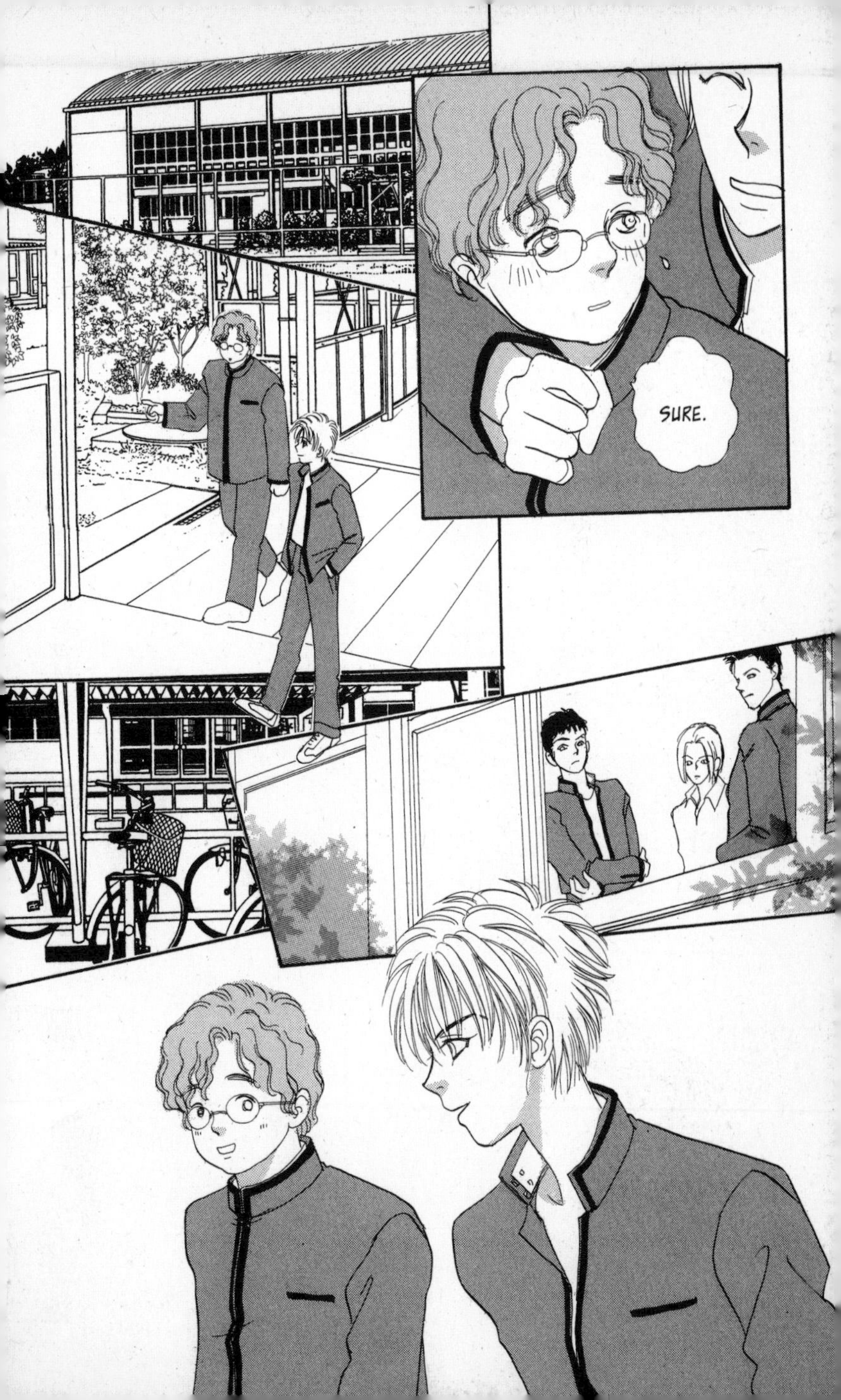
SURE.

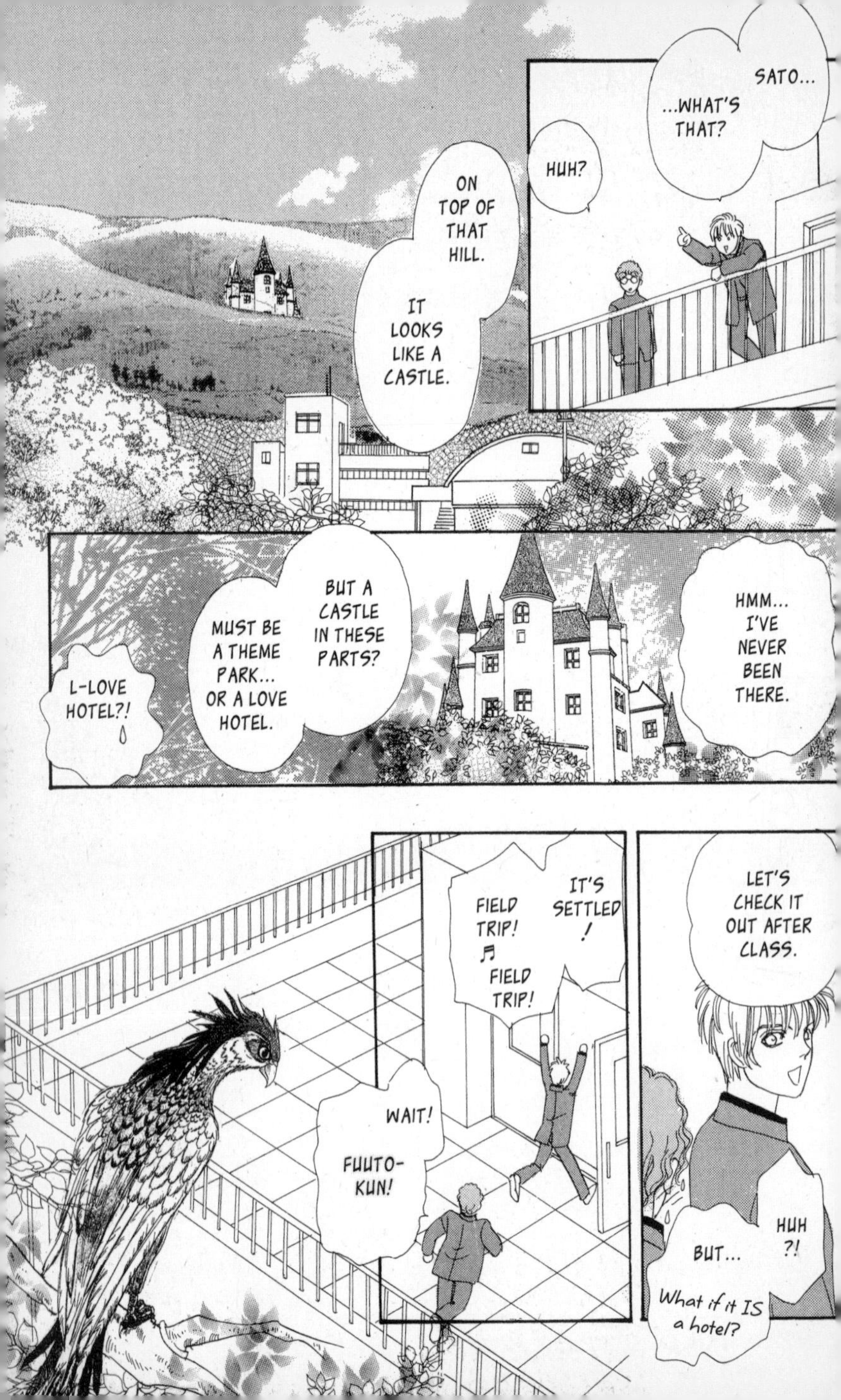
SATO...
...WHAT'S THAT?
HUH?
ON TOP OF THAT HILL.
IT LOOKS LIKE A CASTLE.
HMM... I'VE NEVER BEEN THERE.
BUT A CASTLE IN THESE PARTS?
MUST BE A THEME PARK... OR A LOVE HOTEL.
L-LOVE HOTEL?!
LET'S CHECK IT OUT AFTER CLASS.
HUH ?!
BUT...
What if it IS a hotel?
IT'S SETTLED!
FIELD TRIP! ♬ FIELD TRIP!
WAIT!
FUUTO-KUN!

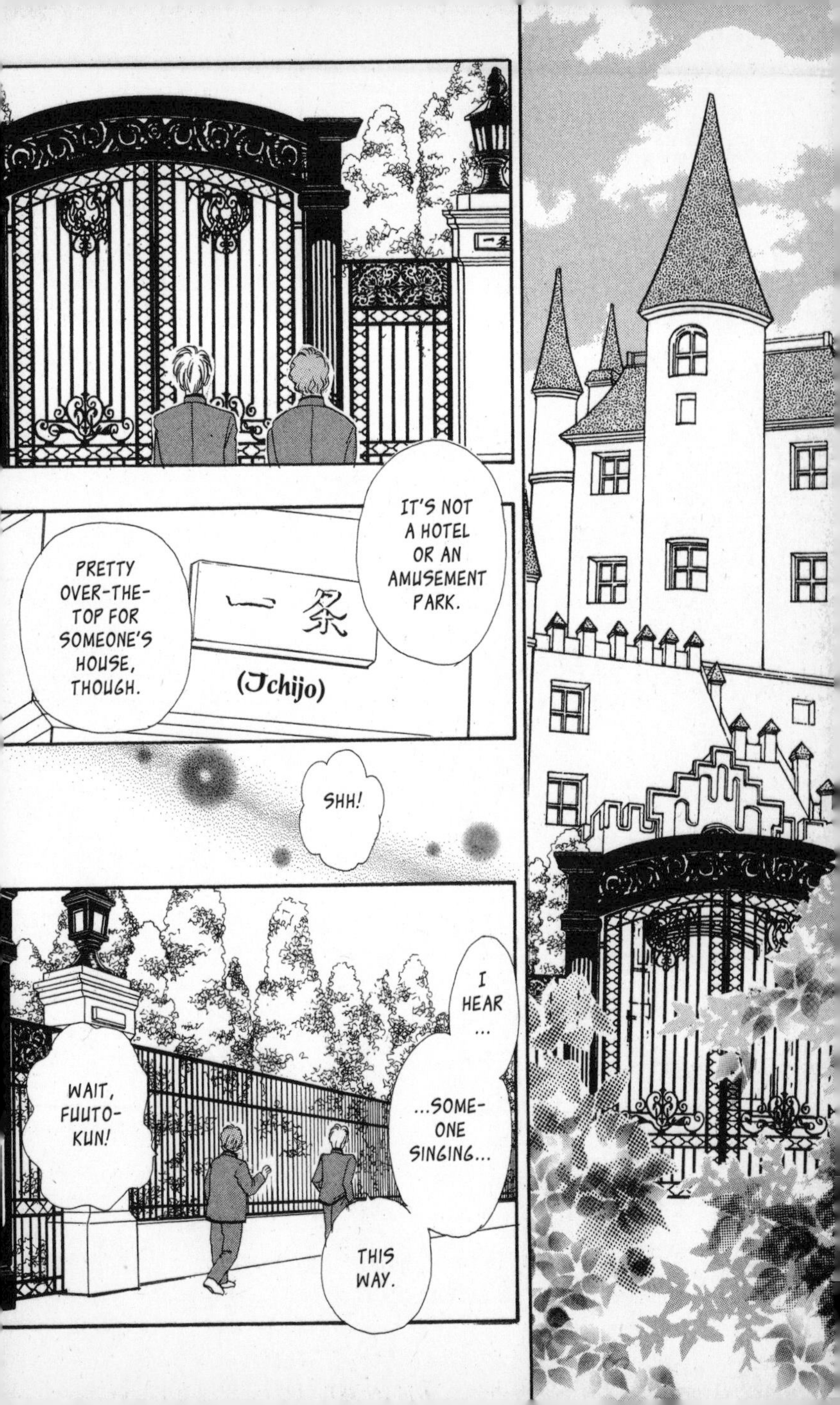
IT'S NOT A HOTEL OR AN AMUSEMENT PARK.
一条
(Ichijo)
PRETTY OVER-THE-TOP FOR SOMEONE'S HOUSE, THOUGH.
SHH!
I HEAR ...
...SOME-ONE SINGING...
THIS WAY.
WAIT, FUUTO-KUN!

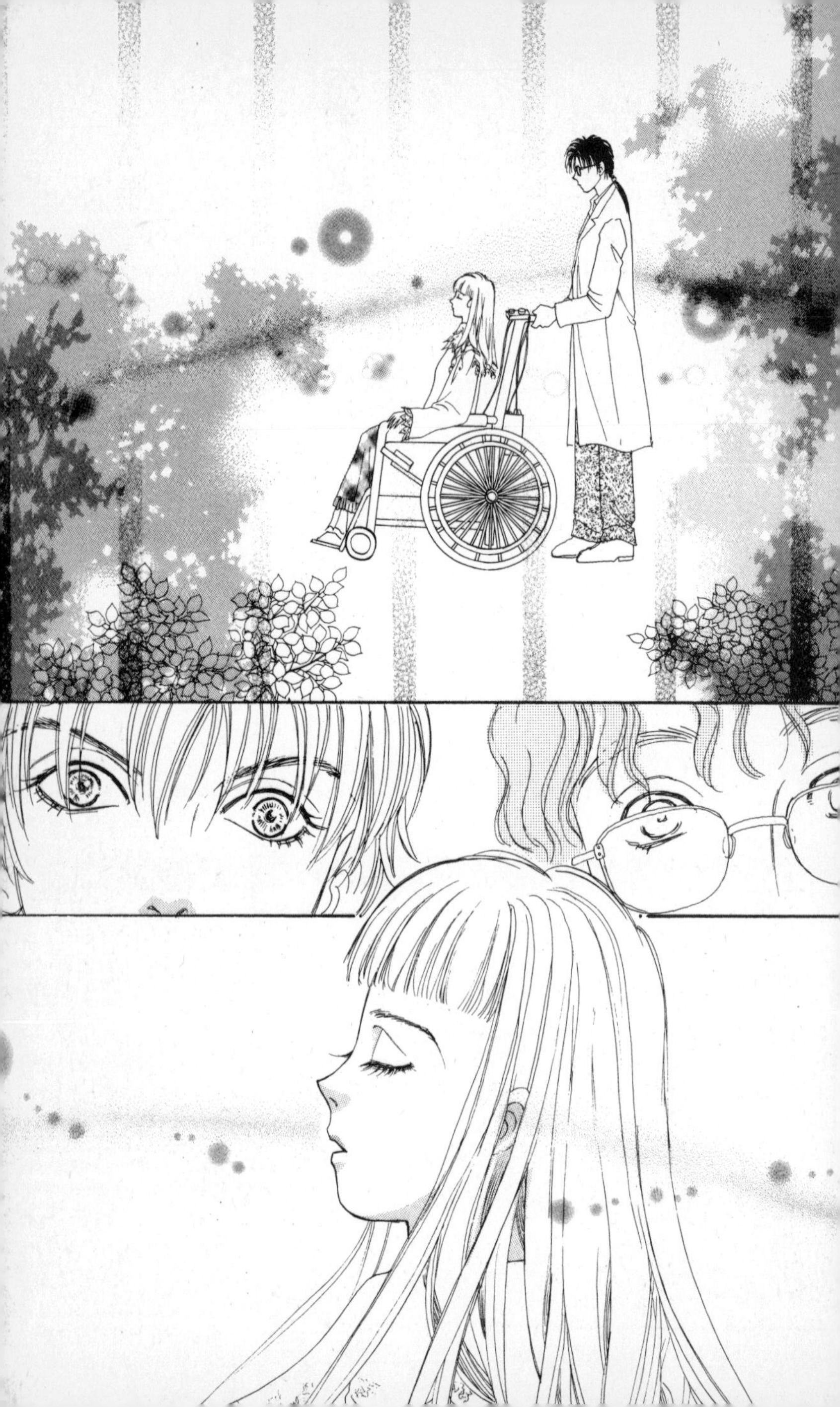

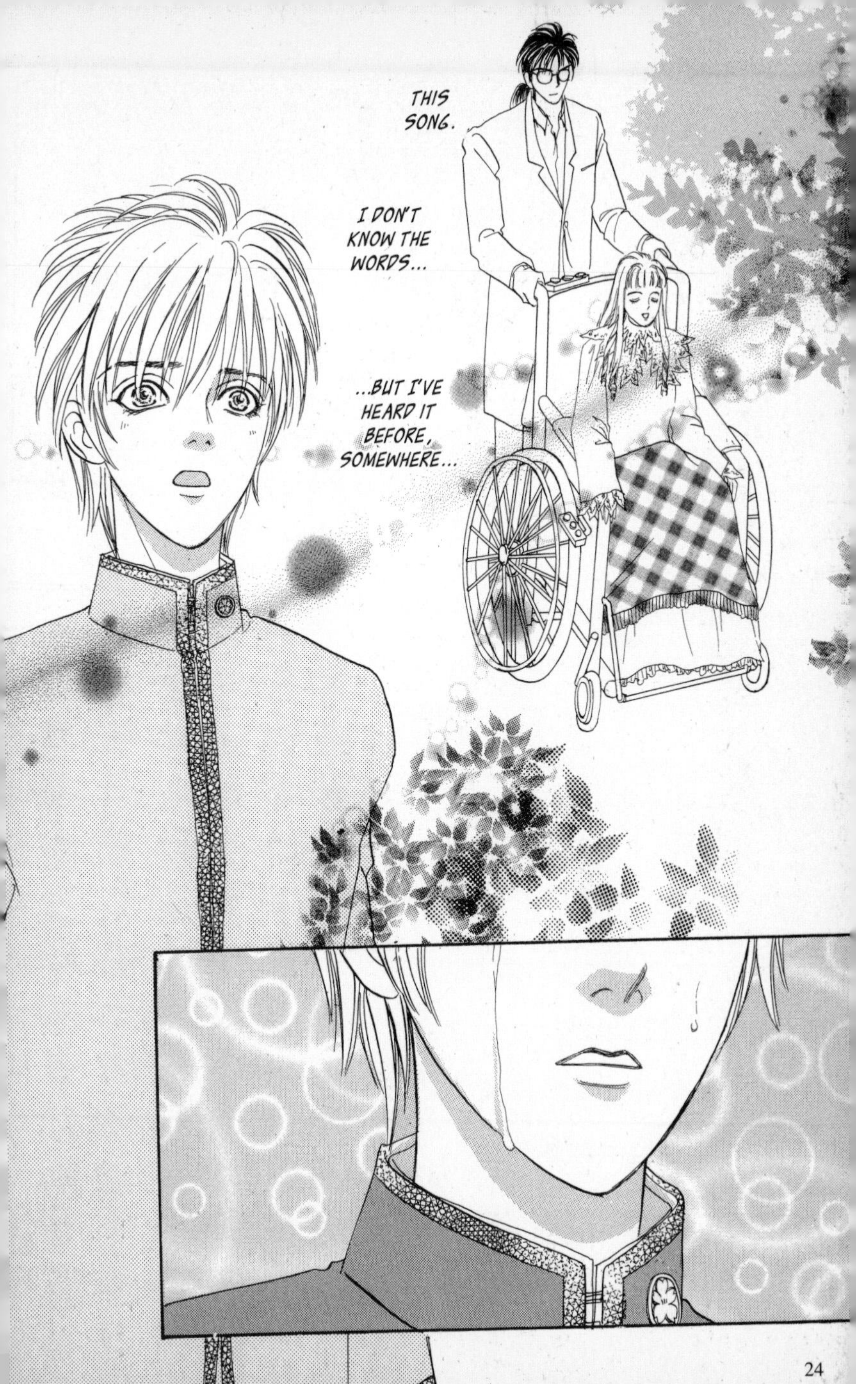
THIS SONG.
I DON'T KNOW THE WORDS...
...BUT I'VE HEARD IT BEFORE, SOMEWHERE...

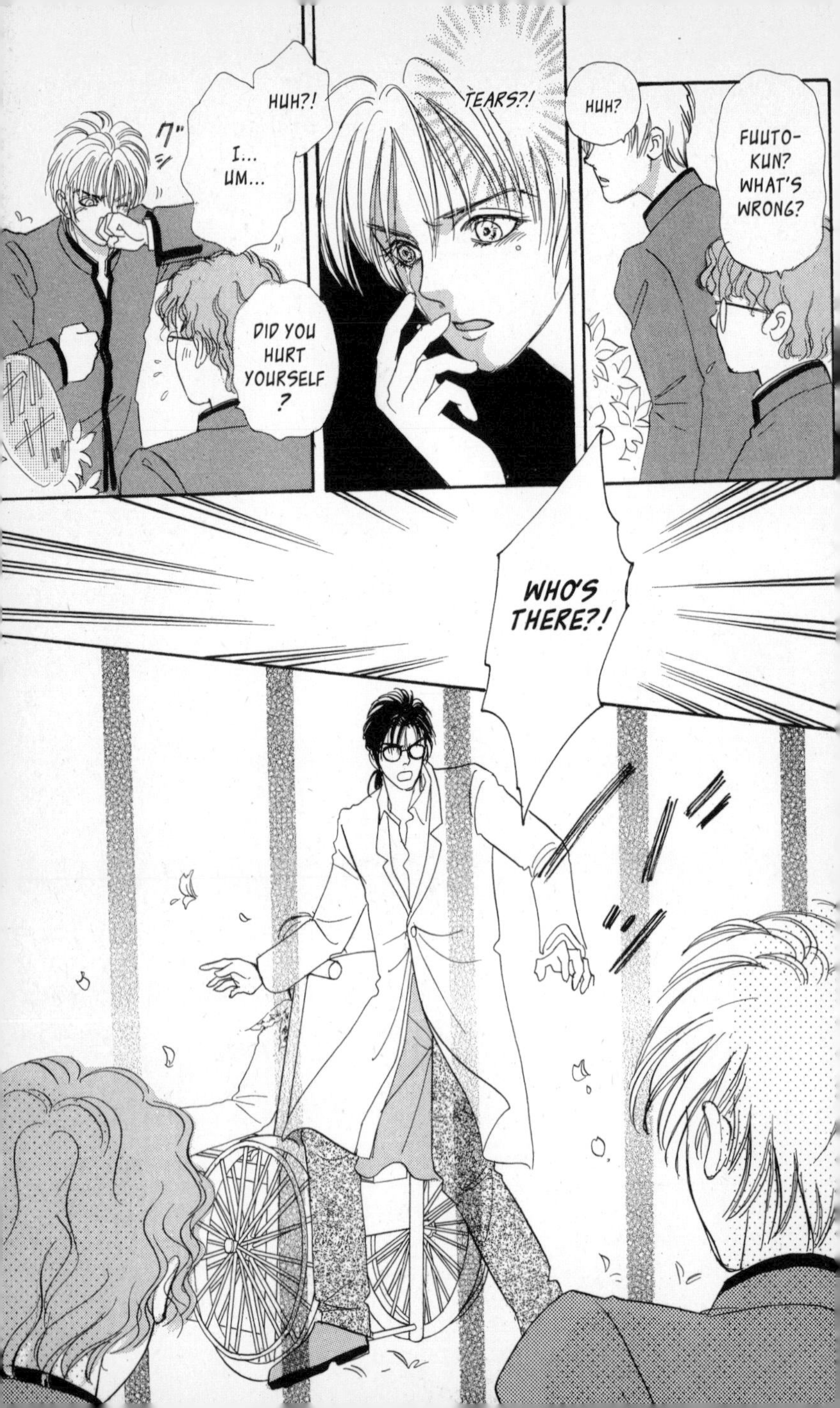
FUUTO-KUN? WHAT'S WRONG?
HUH?
TEARS?!
HUH?! I... UM...
DID YOU HURT YOURSELF?
WHO'S THERE?!

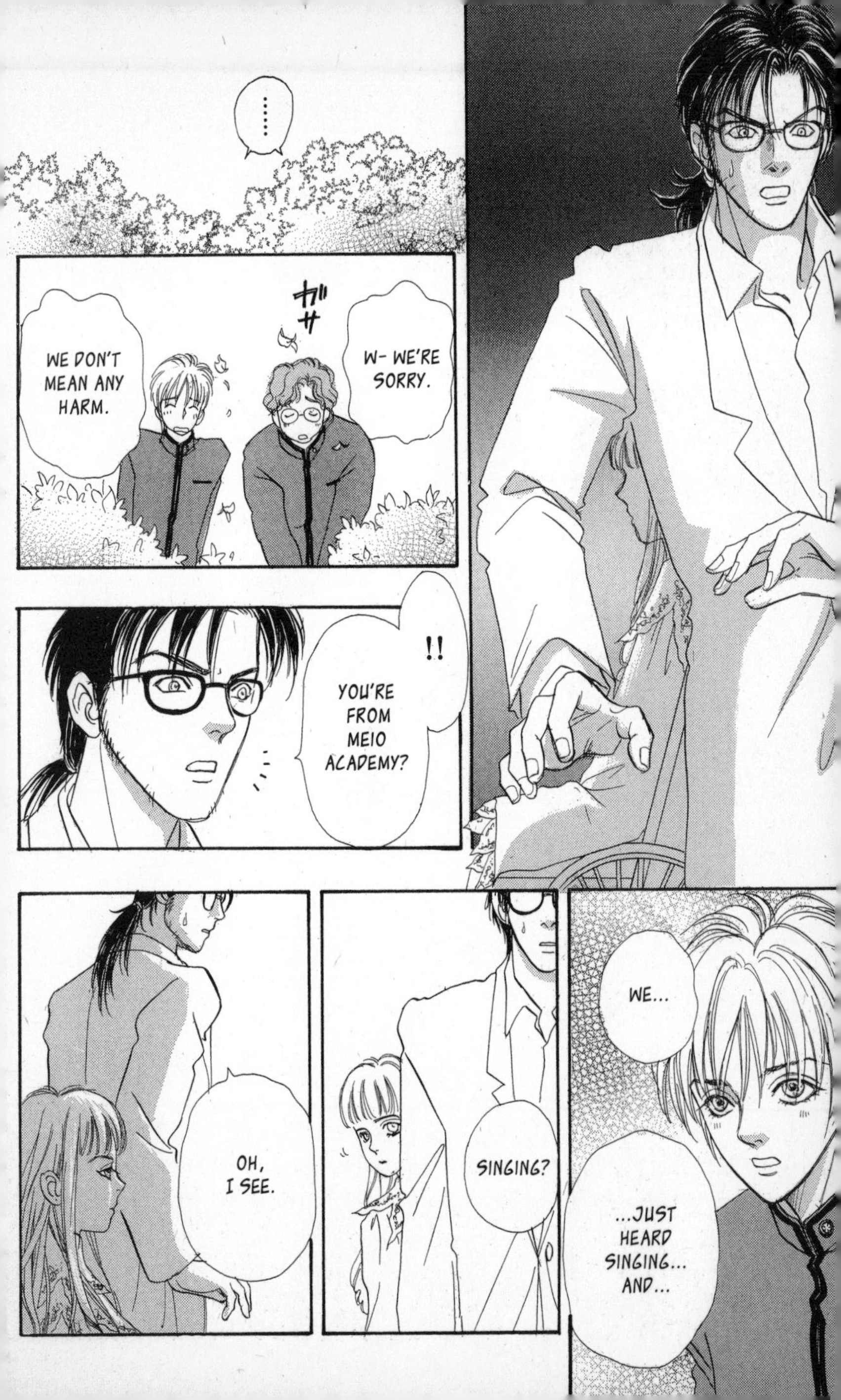
......
W- WE'RE SORRY.
ガサ
WE DON'T MEAN ANY HARM.
!!
YOU'RE FROM MEIO ACADEMY?
WE...
...JUST HEARD SINGING... AND...
SINGING?
OH, I SEE.

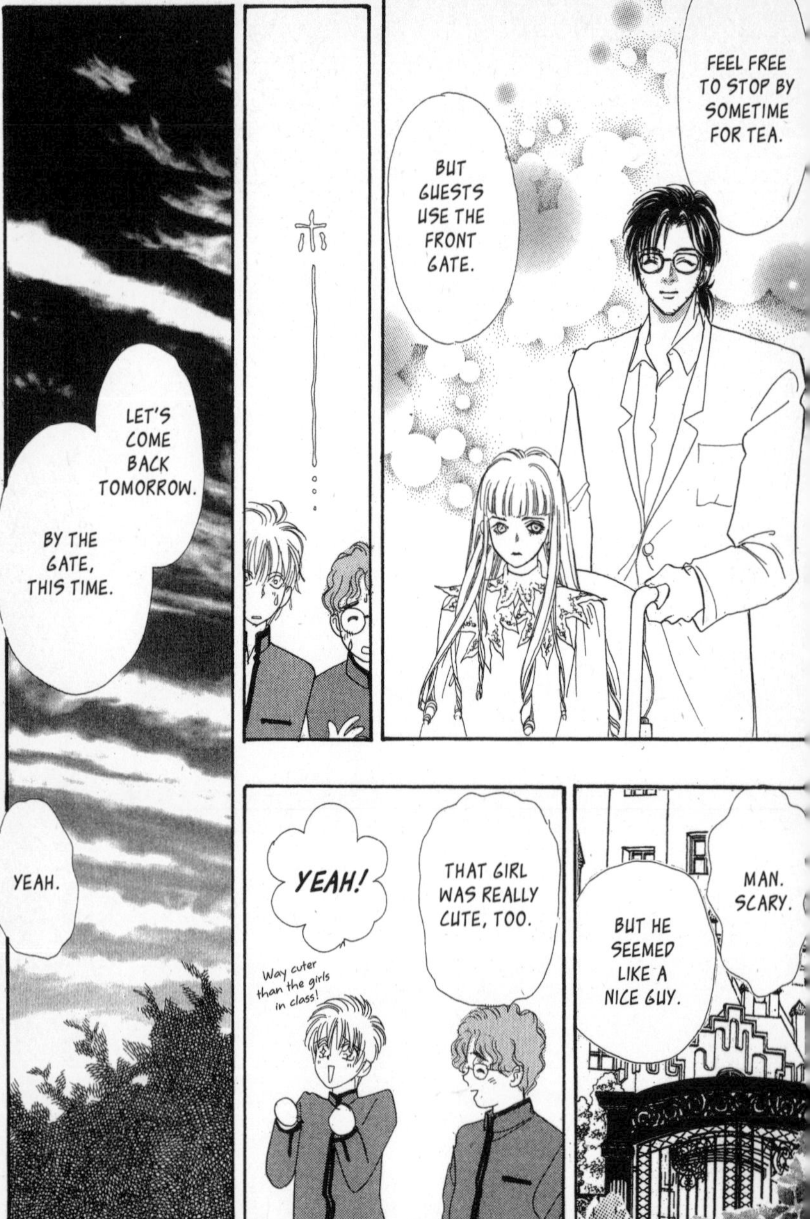
FEEL FREE TO STOP BY SOMETIME FOR TEA.
BUT GUESTS USE THE FRONT GATE.
MAN. SCARY.
BUT HE SEEMED LIKE A NICE GUY.
THAT GIRL WAS REALLY CUTE, TOO.
YEAH!
Way cuter than the girls in class!
LET'S COME BACK TOMORROW.
BY THE GATE, THIS TIME.
YEAH.

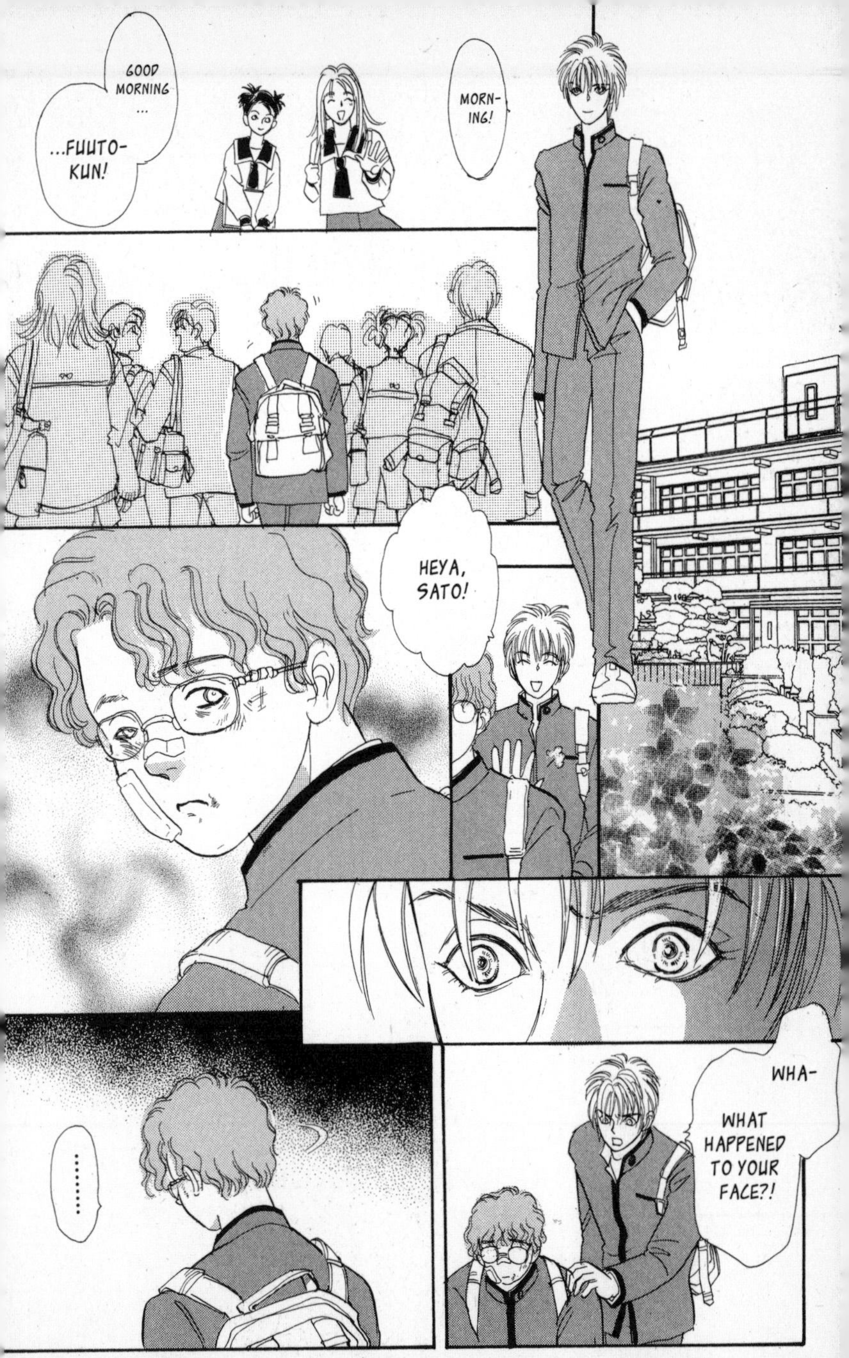

MORN-ING!
GOOD MORNING ...
...FUUTO-KUN!
HEYA, SATO!
WHA-
WHAT HAPPENED TO YOUR FACE?!
....

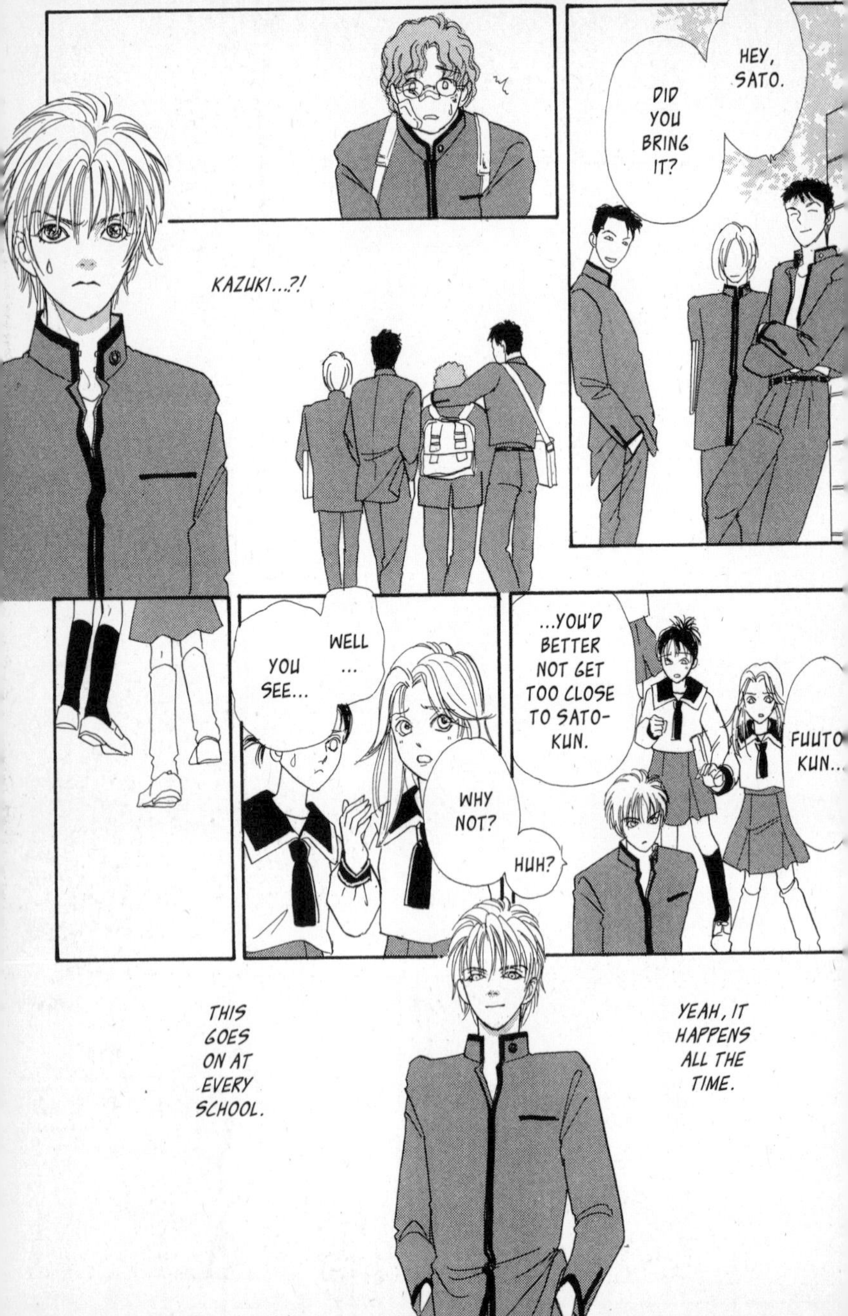
HEY, SATO.
DID YOU BRING IT?
KAZUKI...?!
FUUTO KUN...
...YOU'D BETTER NOT GET TOO CLOSE TO SATO-KUN.
WELL ...
YOU SEE...
WHY NOT?
HUH?
YEAH, IT HAPPENS ALL THE TIME.
THIS GOES ON AT EVERY SCHOOL.

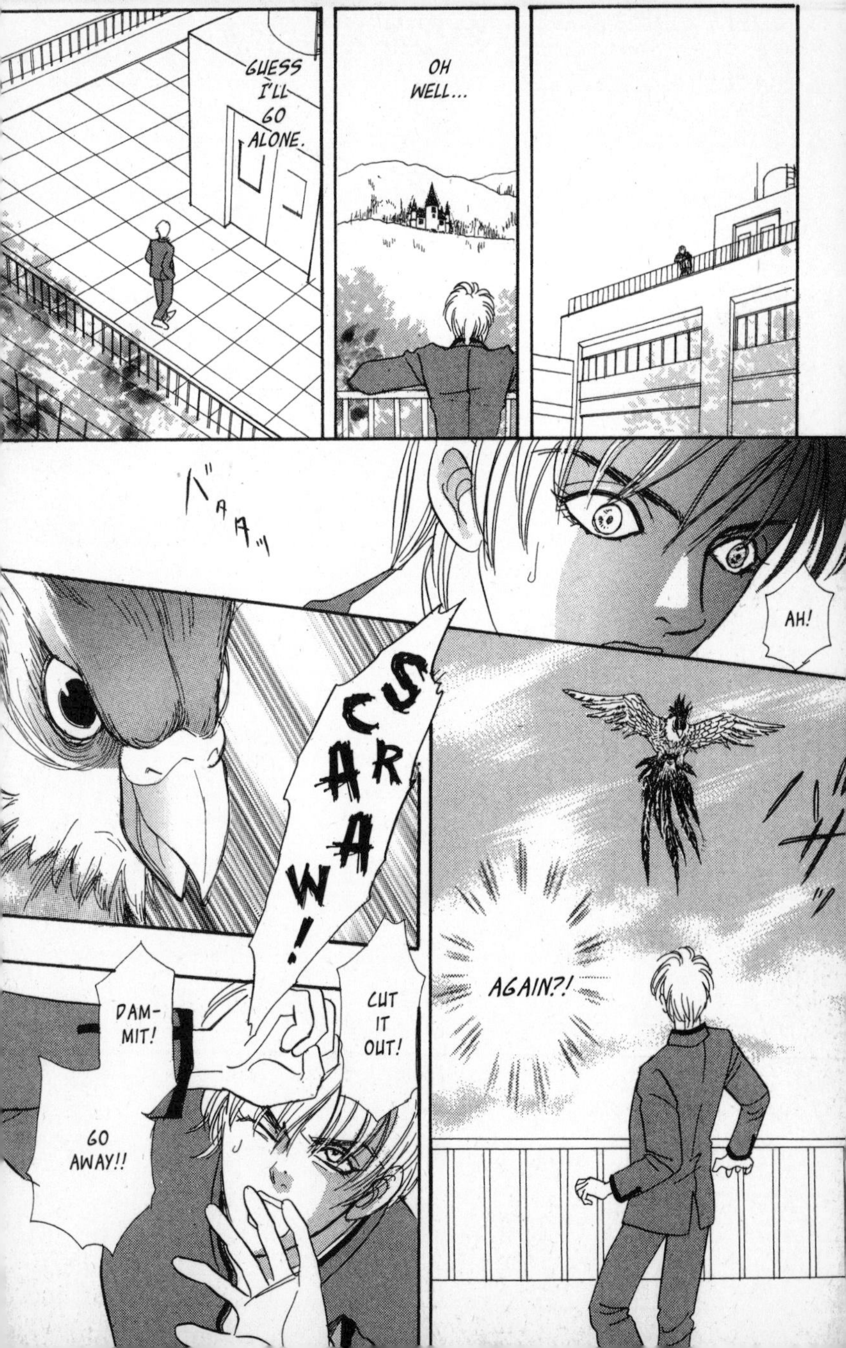
OH WELL...
GUESS I'LL GO ALONE.
AH!
バAAッ
AGAIN?!
SCRAAW!
CUT IT OUT!
DAM-MIT!
GO AWAY!!

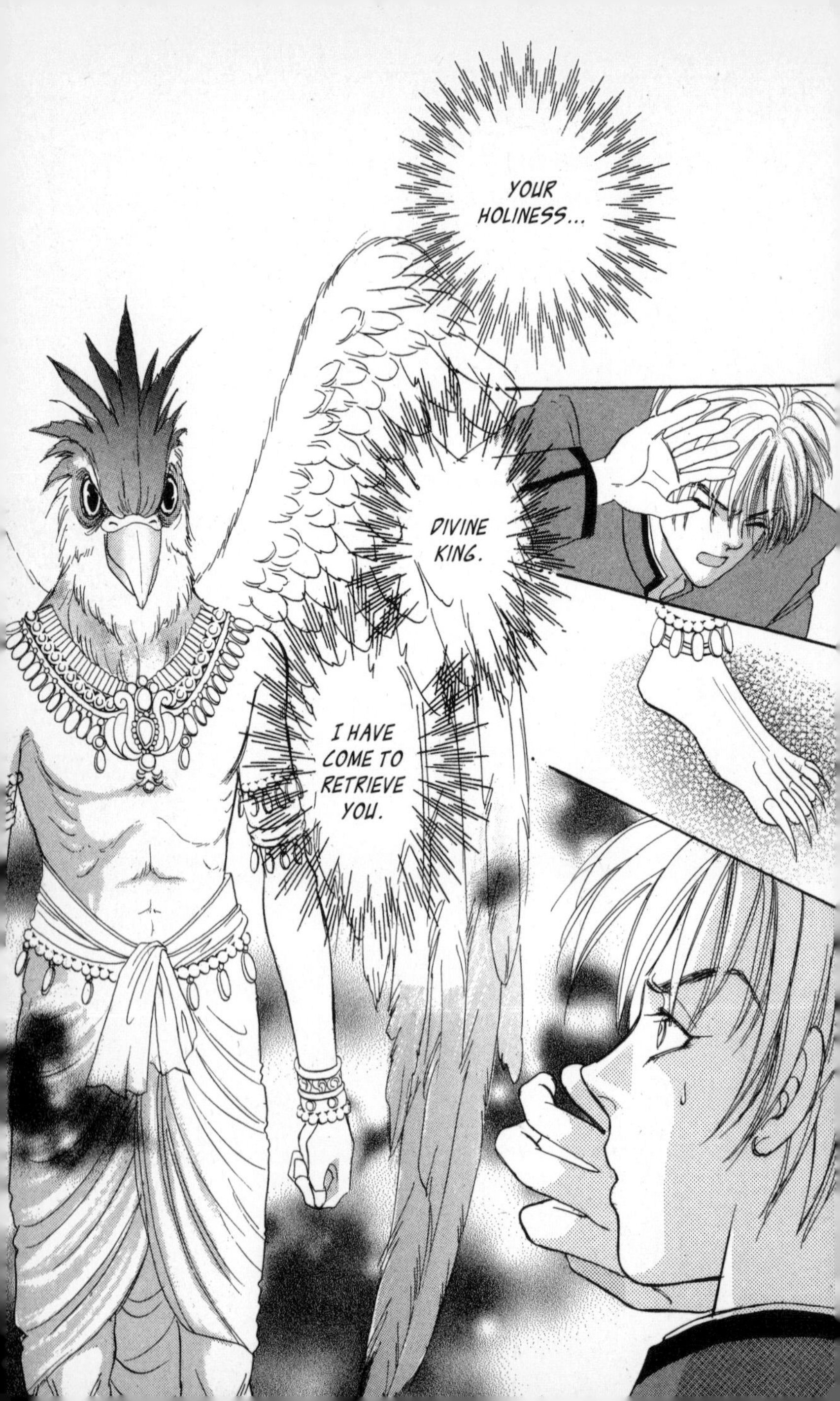
YOUR HOLINESS...
DIVINE KING.
I HAVE COME TO RETRIEVE YOU.

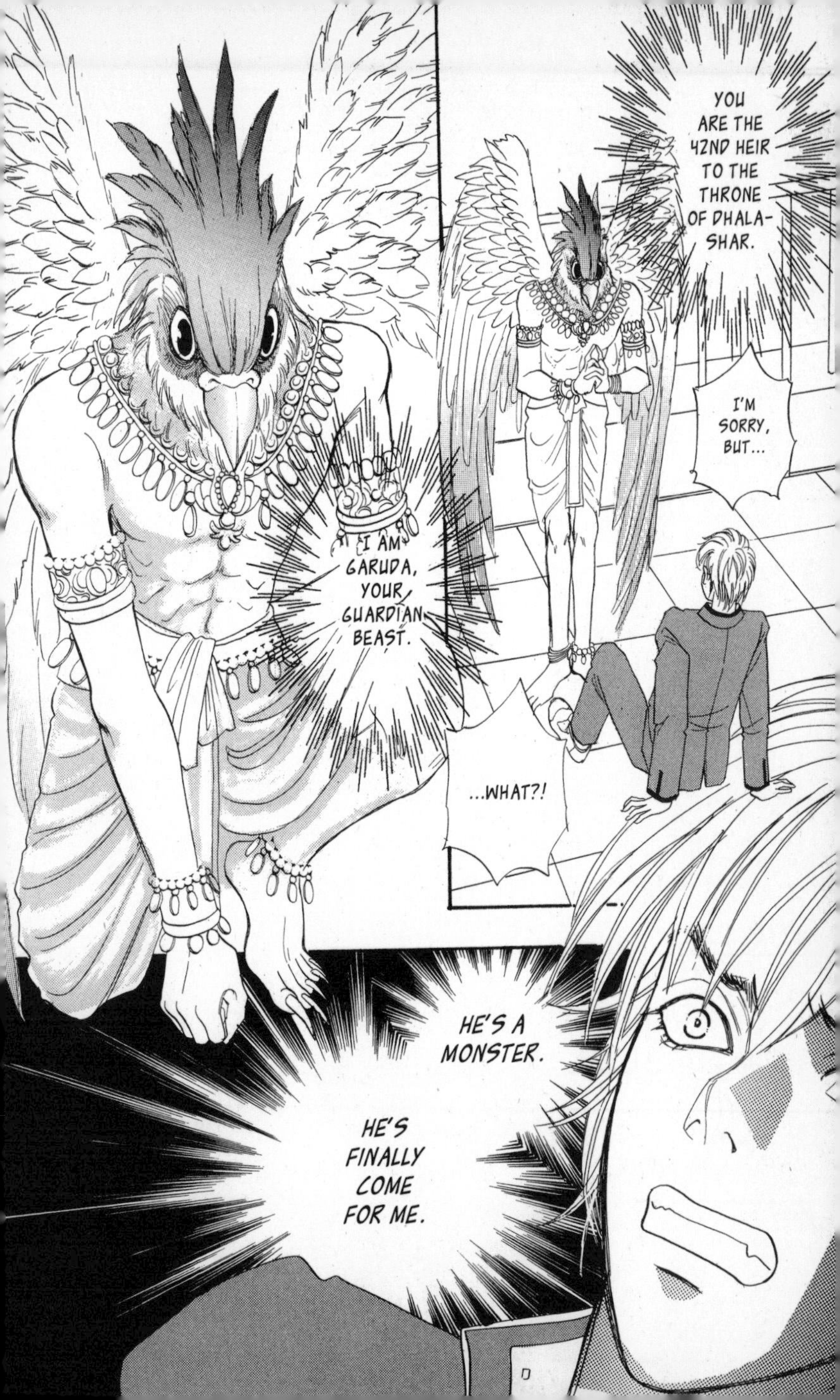
YOU ARE THE 42ND HEIR TO THE THRONE OF DHALA-SHAR.
I'M SORRY, BUT...
...WHAT?!
I AM GARUDA, YOUR GUARDIAN BEAST.
HE'S A MONSTER.
HE'S FINALLY COME FOR ME.

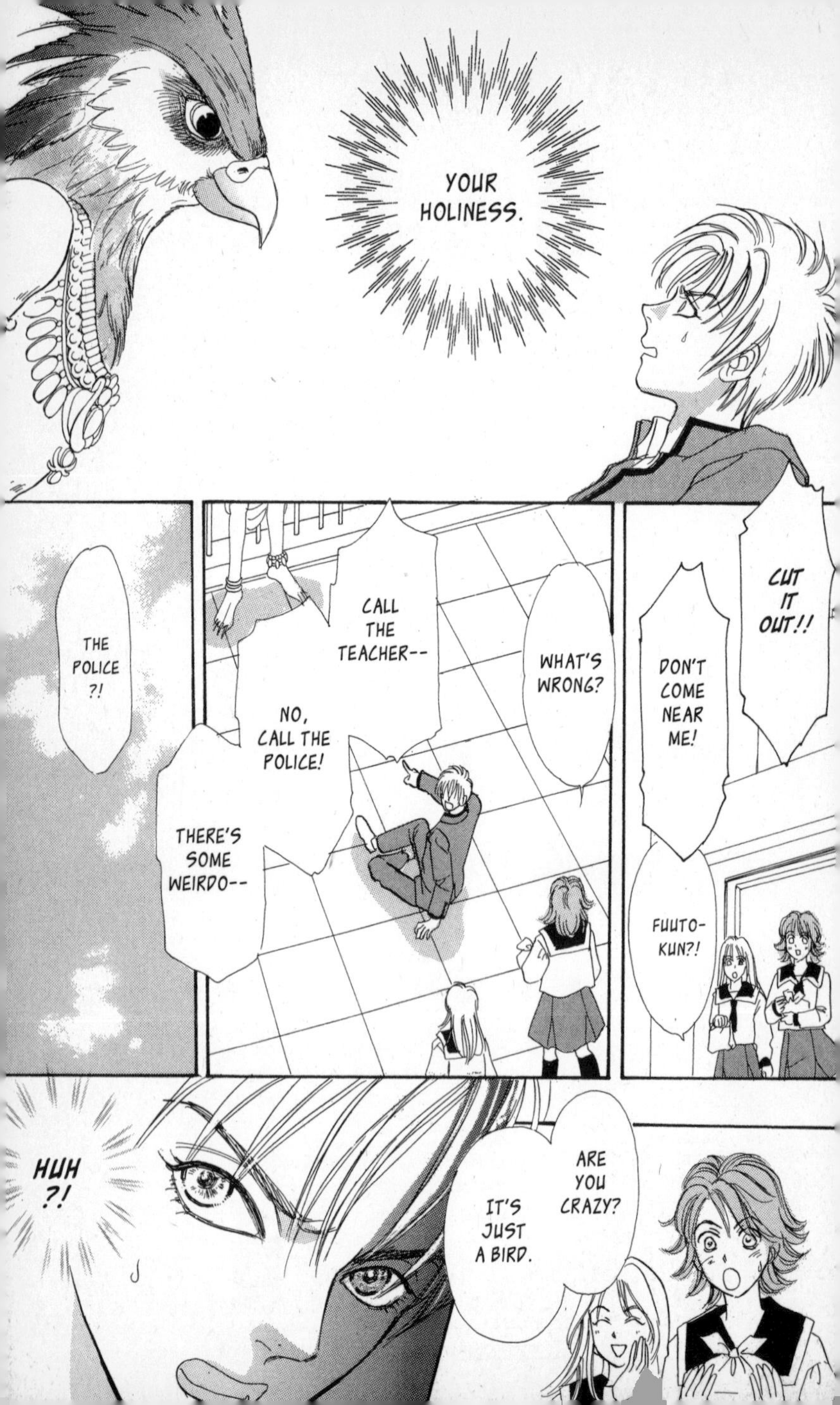
YOUR HOLINESS.
CUT IT OUT!!
DON'T COME NEAR ME!
FUUTO-KUN?!
WHAT'S WRONG?
CALL THE TEACHER--
NO, CALL THE POLICE!
THERE'S SOME WEIRDO--
THE POLICE?!
ARE YOU CRAZY?
IT'S JUST A BIRD.
HUH?!

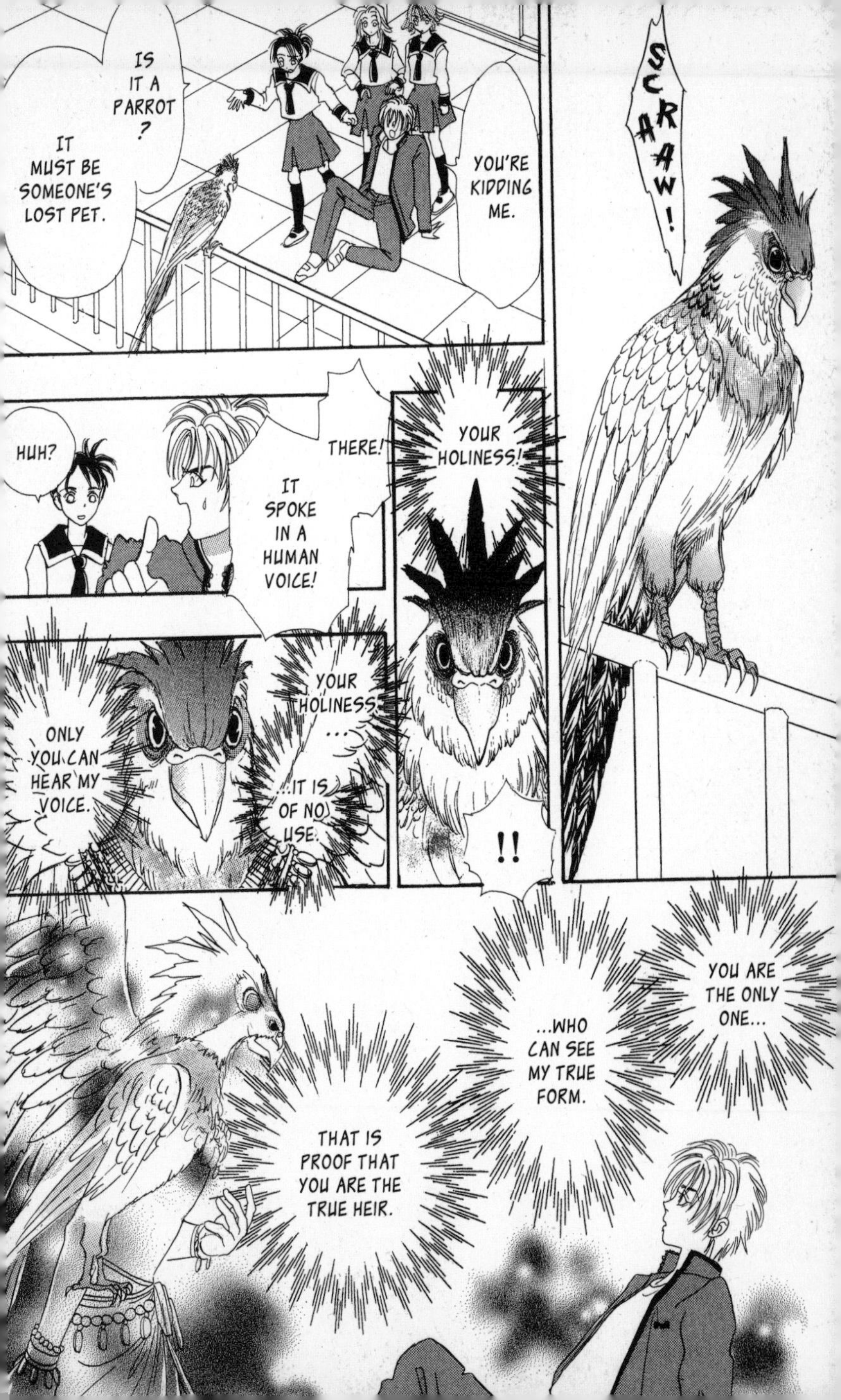

SCRAW!
YOU'RE KIDDING ME.
IS IT A PARROT?
IT MUST BE SOMEONE'S LOST PET.
YOUR HOLINESS!
!!
THERE!
IT SPOKE IN A HUMAN VOICE!
HUH?
YOUR HOLINESS...
...IT IS OF NO USE.
ONLY YOU CAN HEAR MY VOICE.
YOU ARE THE ONLY ONE...
...WHO CAN SEE MY TRUE FORM.
THAT IS PROOF THAT YOU ARE THE TRUE HEIR.

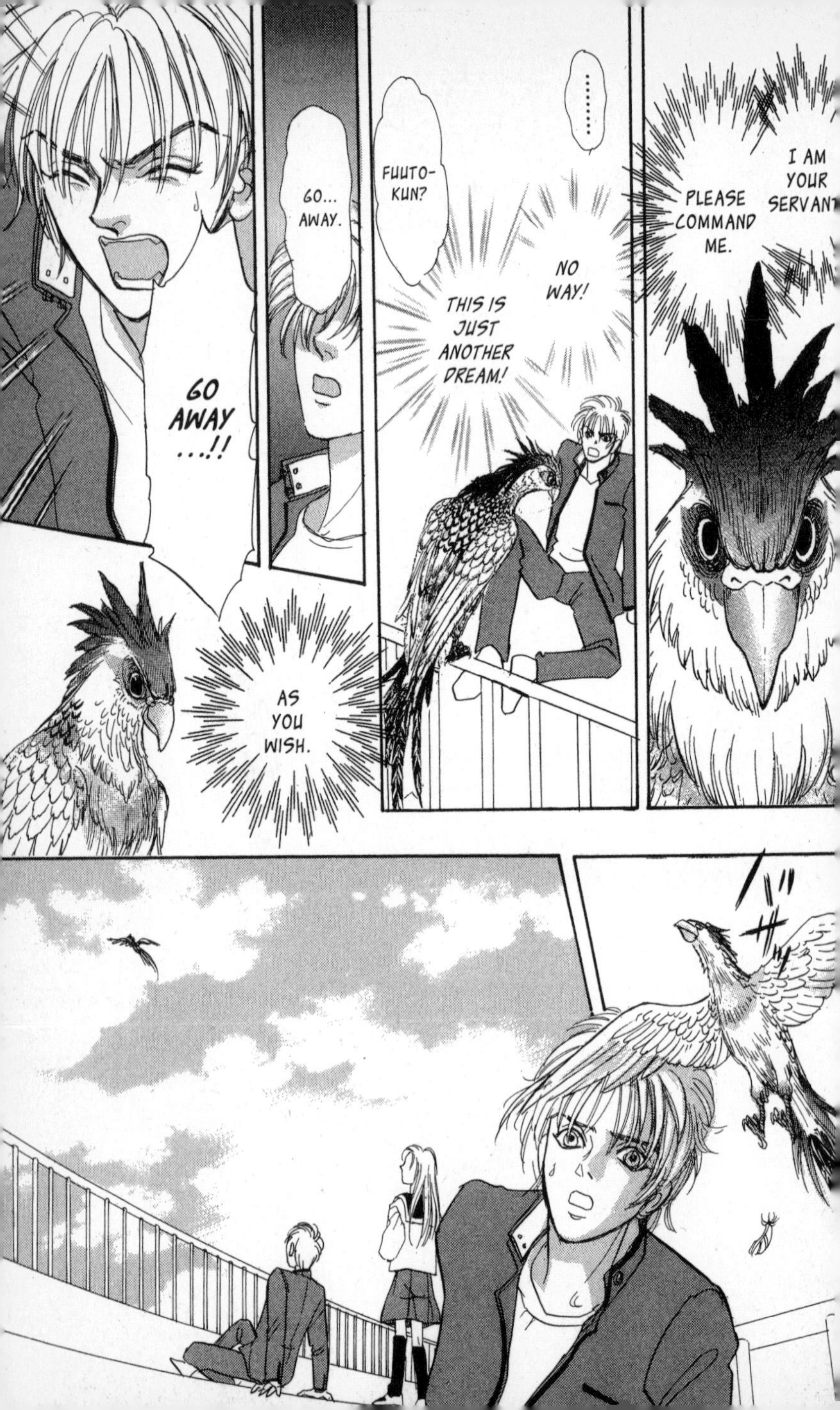
I AM YOUR SERVANT.
PLEASE COMMAND ME.
......
FUUTO-KUN?
NO WAY!
THIS IS JUST ANOTHER DREAM!
GO... AWAY.
GO AWAY...!!
AS YOU WISH.

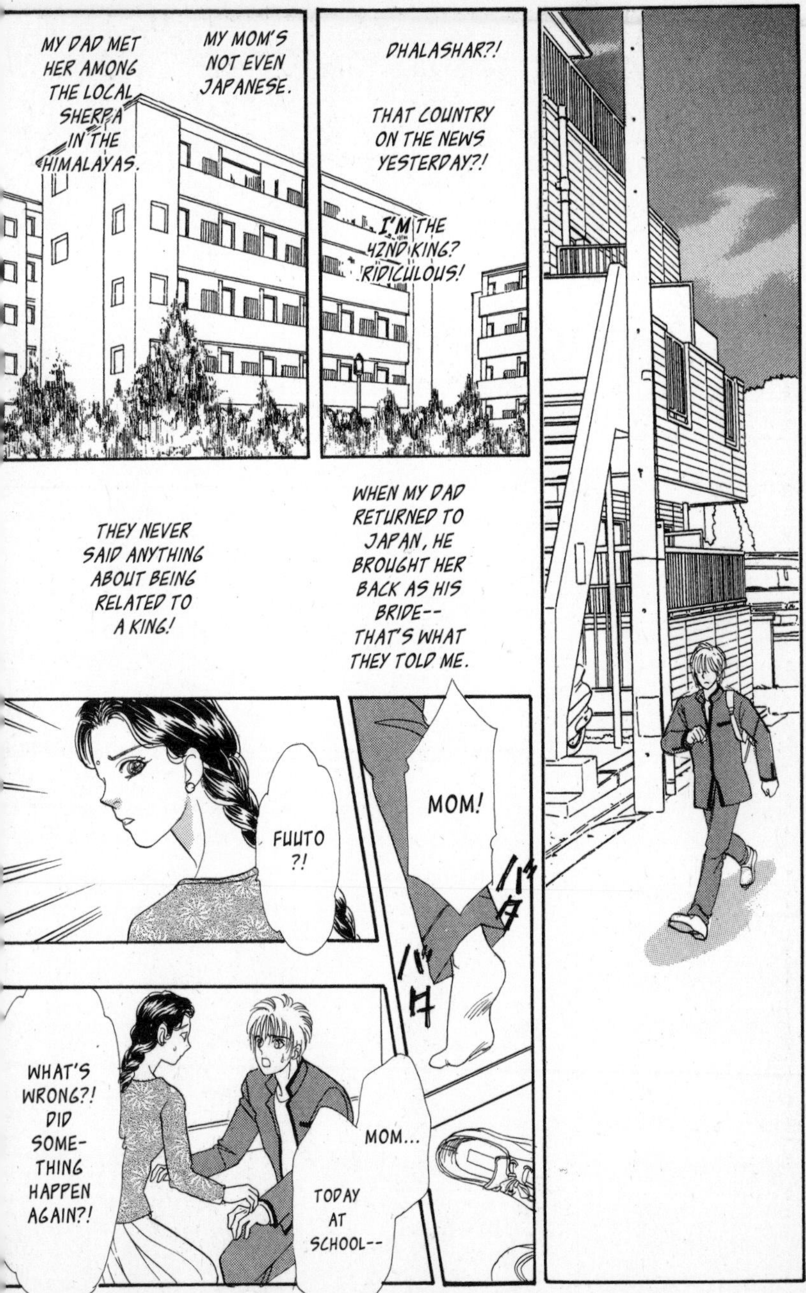

DHALASHAR?!
THAT COUNTRY ON THE NEWS YESTERDAY?!
I'M THE 42ND KING? RIDICULOUS!
MY MOM'S NOT EVEN JAPANESE.
MY DAD MET HER AMONG THE LOCAL SHERPA IN THE HIMALAYAS.
WHEN MY DAD RETURNED TO JAPAN, HE BROUGHT HER BACK AS HIS BRIDE-- THAT'S WHAT THEY TOLD ME.
THEY NEVER SAID ANYTHING ABOUT BEING RELATED TO A KING!
MOM!
バタ
バタ
FUUTO ?!
MOM...
TODAY AT SCHOOL--
WHAT'S WRONG?! DID SOME-THING HAPPEN AGAIN?!

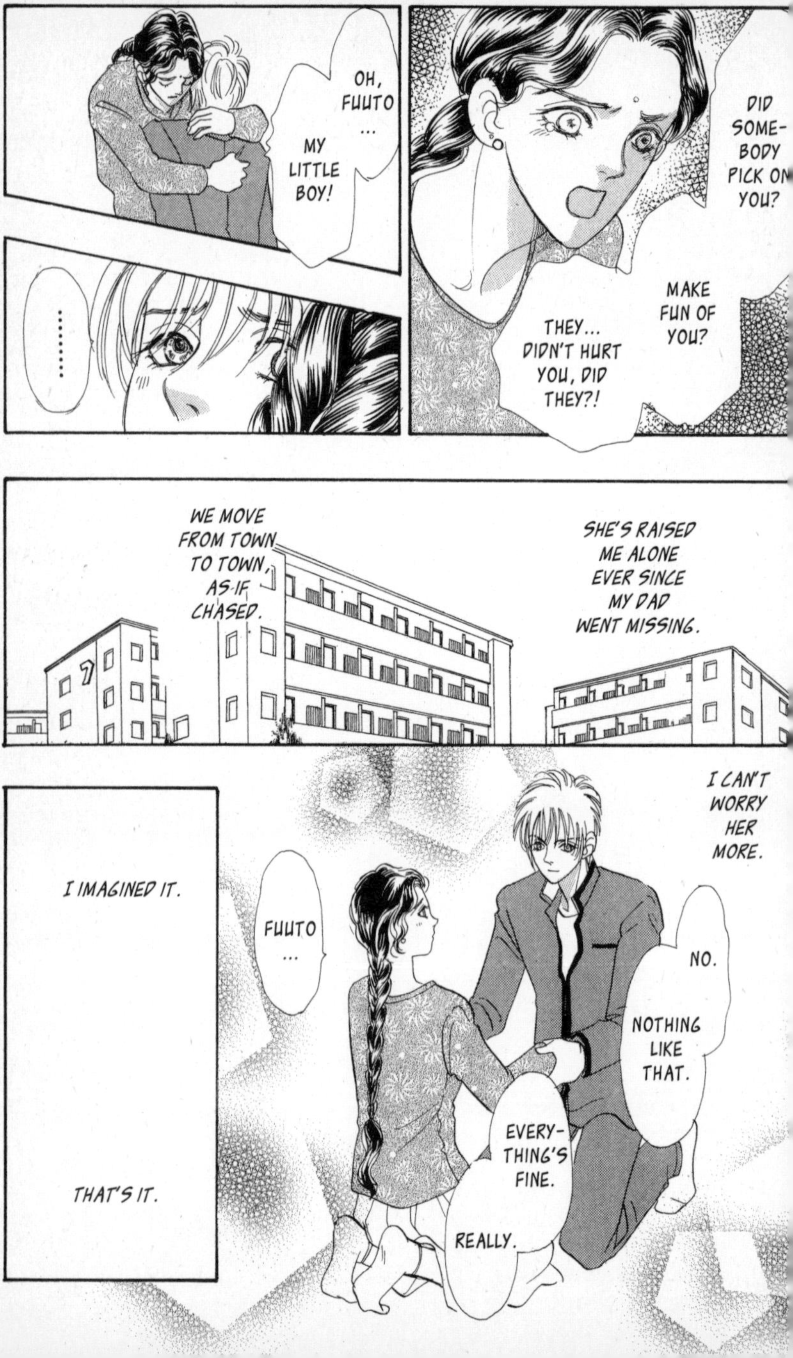

DID SOMEBODY PICK ON YOU?
MAKE FUN OF YOU?
THEY... DIDN'T HURT YOU, DID THEY?!
OH, FUUTO ...
MY LITTLE BOY!
......
SHE'S RAISED ME ALONE EVER SINCE MY DAD WENT MISSING.
WE MOVE FROM TOWN TO TOWN, AS IF CHASED.
I CAN'T WORRY HER MORE.
NO.
NOTHING LIKE THAT.
EVERYTHING'S FINE.
REALLY.
FUUTO ...
I IMAGINED IT.
THAT'S IT.

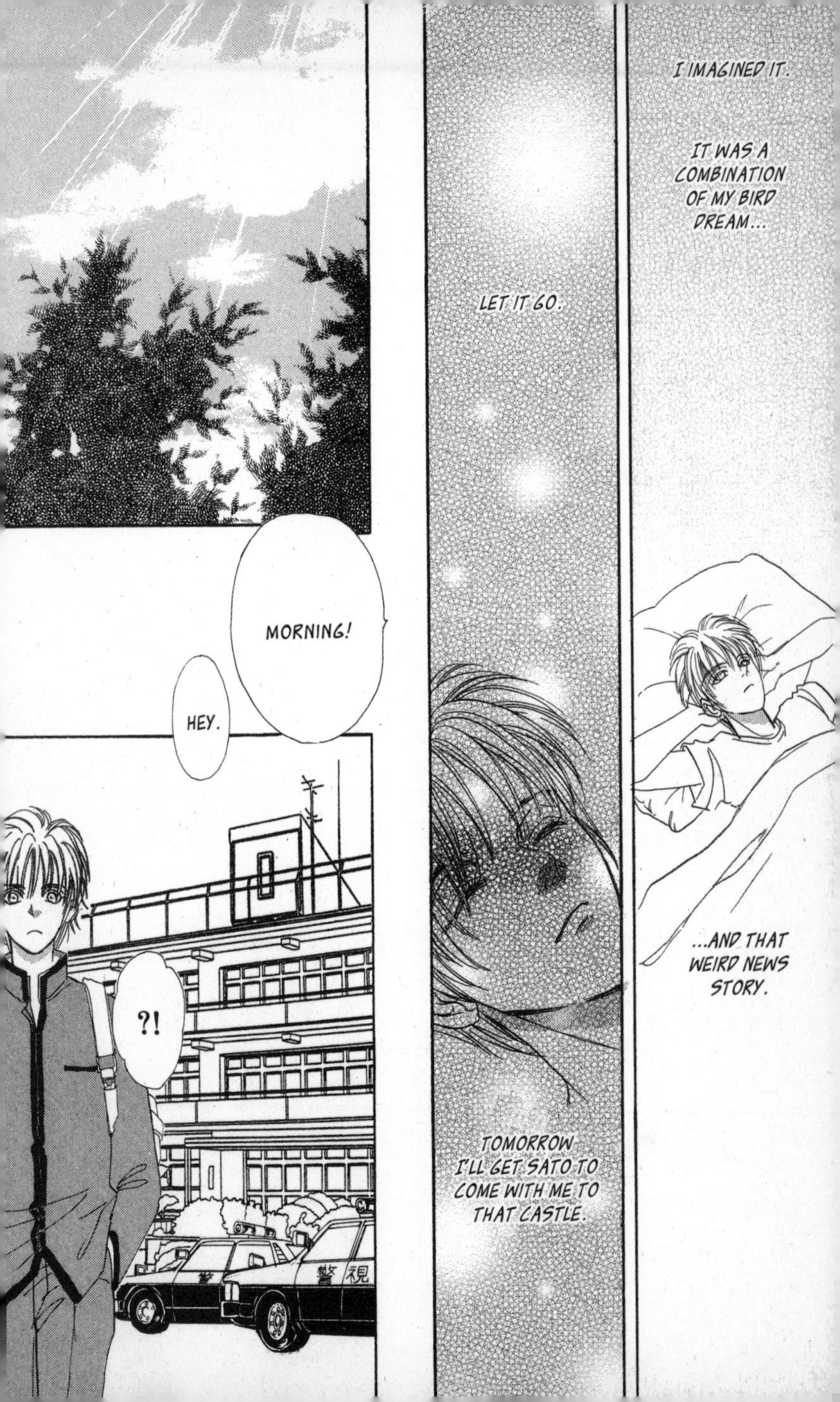
I IMAGINED IT.
IT WAS A COMBINATION OF MY BIRD DREAM...
...AND THAT WEIRD NEWS STORY.
LET IT GO.
TOMORROW I'LL GET SATO TO COME WITH ME TO THAT CASTLE.
MORNING!
HEY.
?!

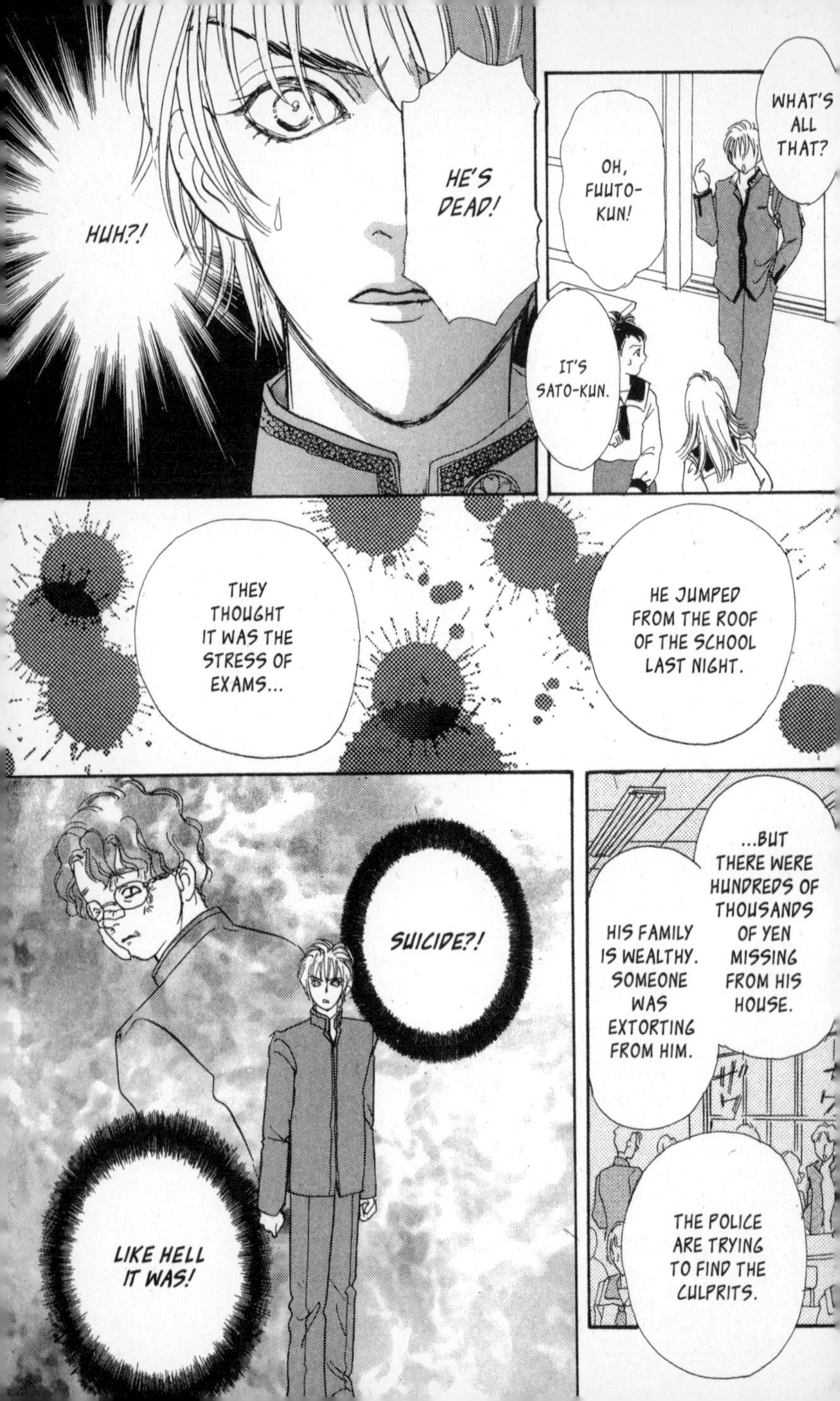
WHAT'S ALL THAT?
OH, FUUTO-KUN!
IT'S SATO-KUN.
HE'S DEAD!
HUH?!
HE JUMPED FROM THE ROOF OF THE SCHOOL LAST NIGHT.
THEY THOUGHT IT WAS THE STRESS OF EXAMS...
...BUT THERE WERE HUNDREDS OF THOUSANDS OF YEN MISSING FROM HIS HOUSE.
HIS FAMILY IS WEALTHY. SOMEONE WAS EXTORTING FROM HIM.
THE POLICE ARE TRYING TO FIND THE CULPRITS.
SUICIDE?!
LIKE HELL IT WAS!

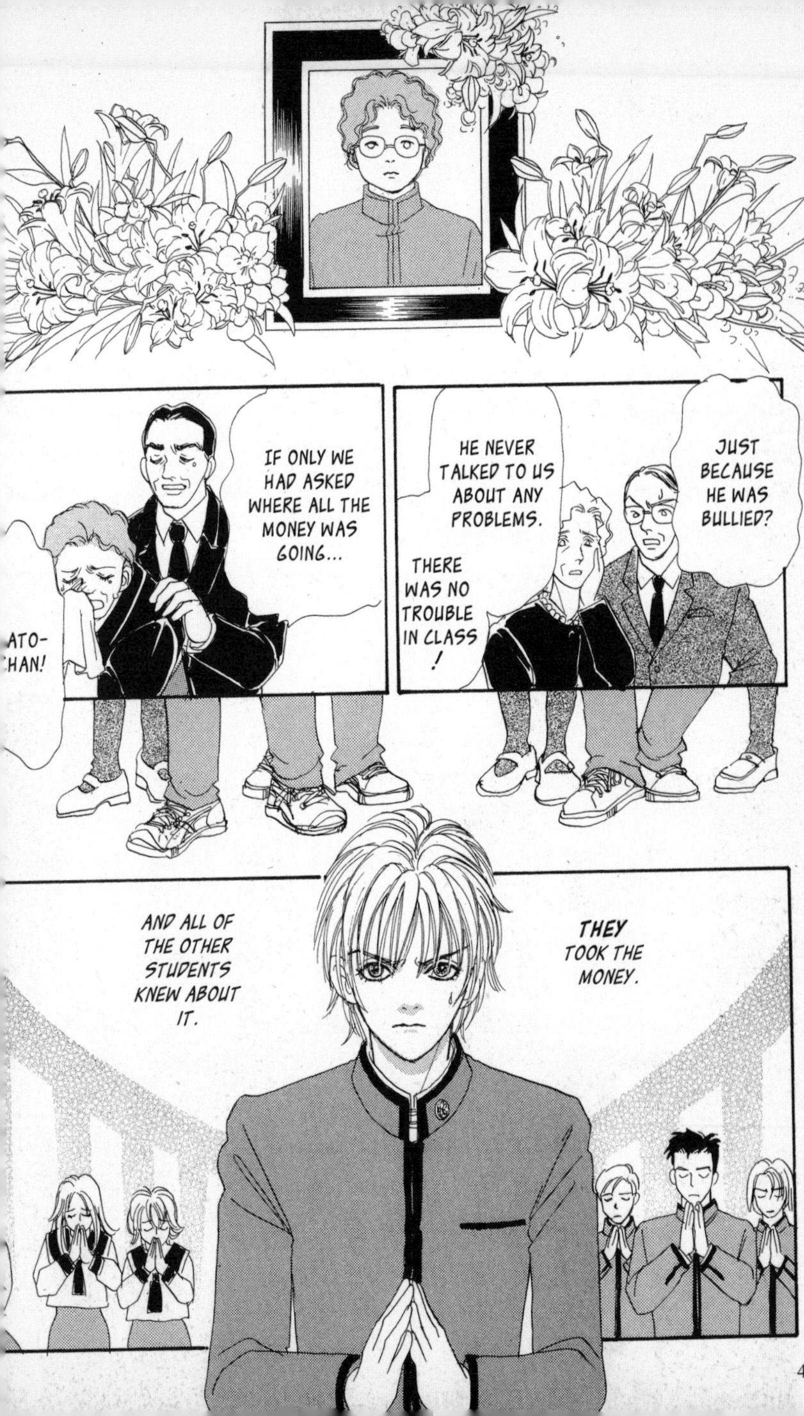
JUST BECAUSE HE WAS BULLIED?
HE NEVER TALKED TO US ABOUT ANY PROBLEMS.
THERE WAS NO TROUBLE IN CLASS!
IF ONLY WE HAD ASKED WHERE ALL THE MONEY WAS GOING...
ATO- HAN!
THEY TOOK THE MONEY.
AND ALL OF THE OTHER STUDENTS KNEW ABOUT IT.

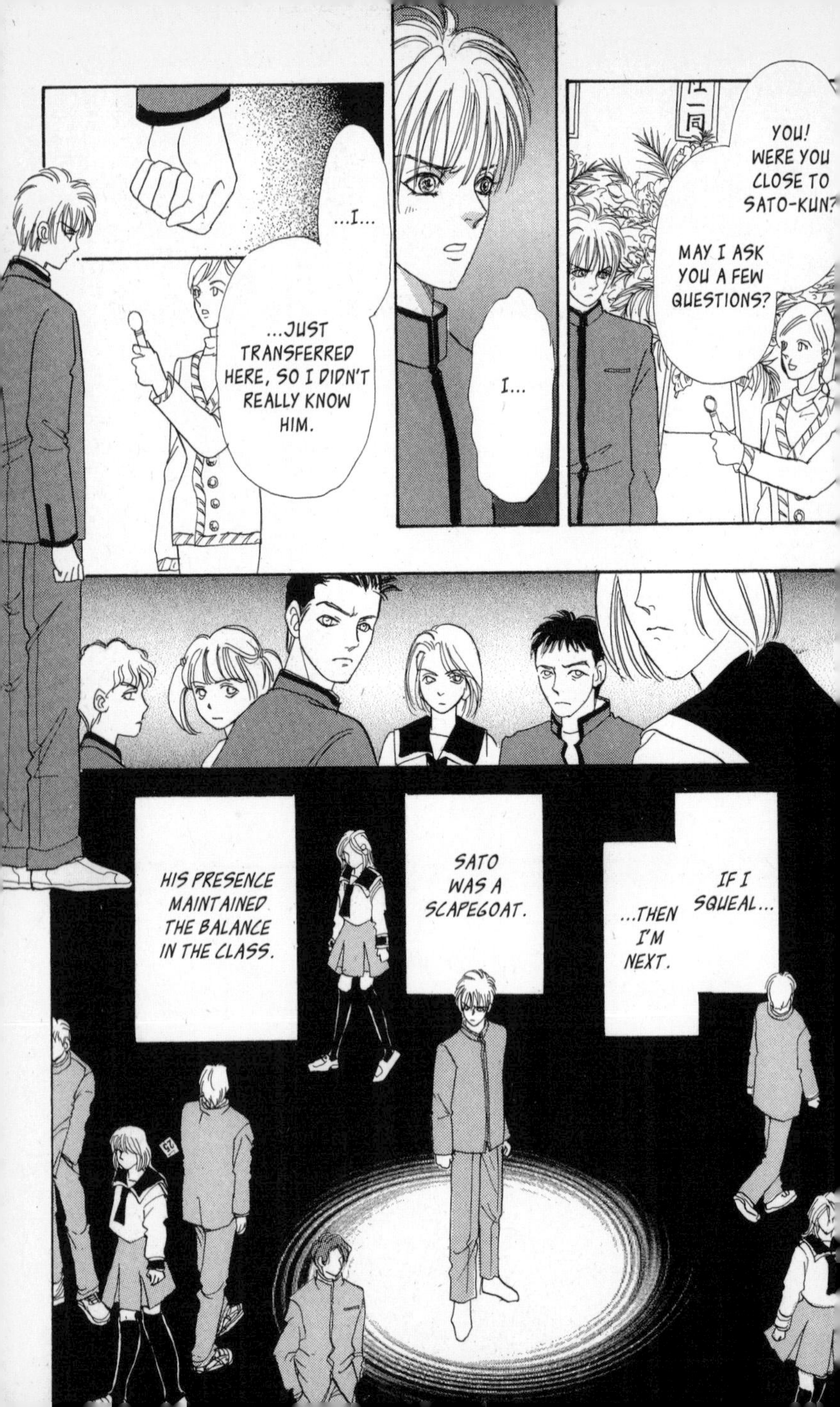
YOU! WERE YOU CLOSE TO SATO-KUN?
MAY I ASK YOU A FEW QUESTIONS?
I...
...I...
...JUST TRANSFERRED HERE, SO I DIDN'T REALLY KNOW HIM.
IF I SQUEAL...
...THEN I'M NEXT.
SATO WAS A SCAPEGOAT.
HIS PRESENCE MAINTAINED THE BALANCE IN THE CLASS.

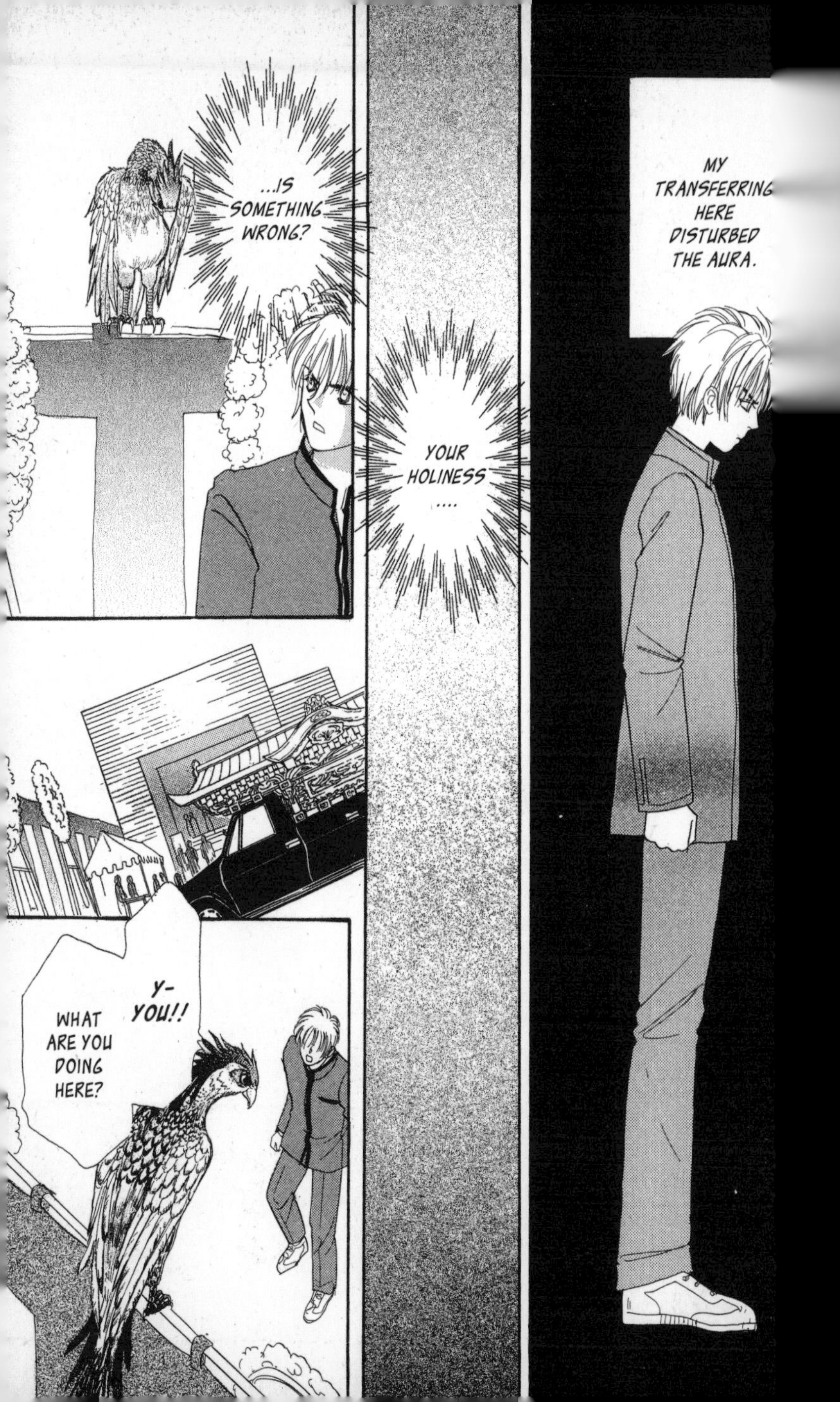
MY TRANSFERRING HERE DISTURBED THE AURA.
YOUR HOLINESS ....
...IS SOMETHING WRONG?
Y- YOU!!
WHAT ARE YOU DOING HERE?

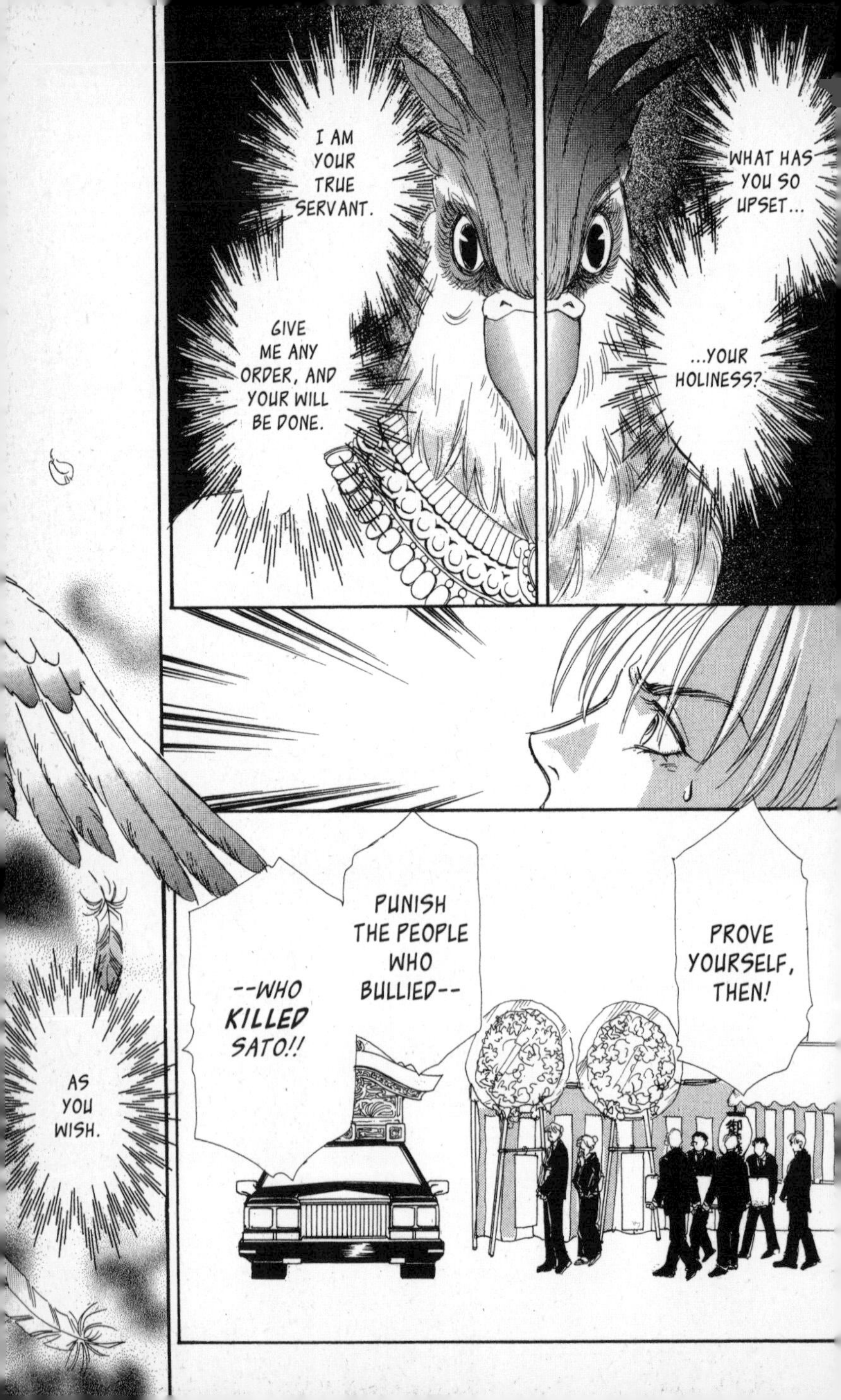

WHAT HAS YOU SO UPSET...
...YOUR HOLINESS?
I AM YOUR TRUE SERVANT.
GIVE ME ANY ORDER, AND YOUR WILL BE DONE.
PROVE YOURSELF, THEN!
PUNISH THE PEOPLE WHO BULLIED--
--WHO **KILLED** SATO!!
AS YOU WISH.

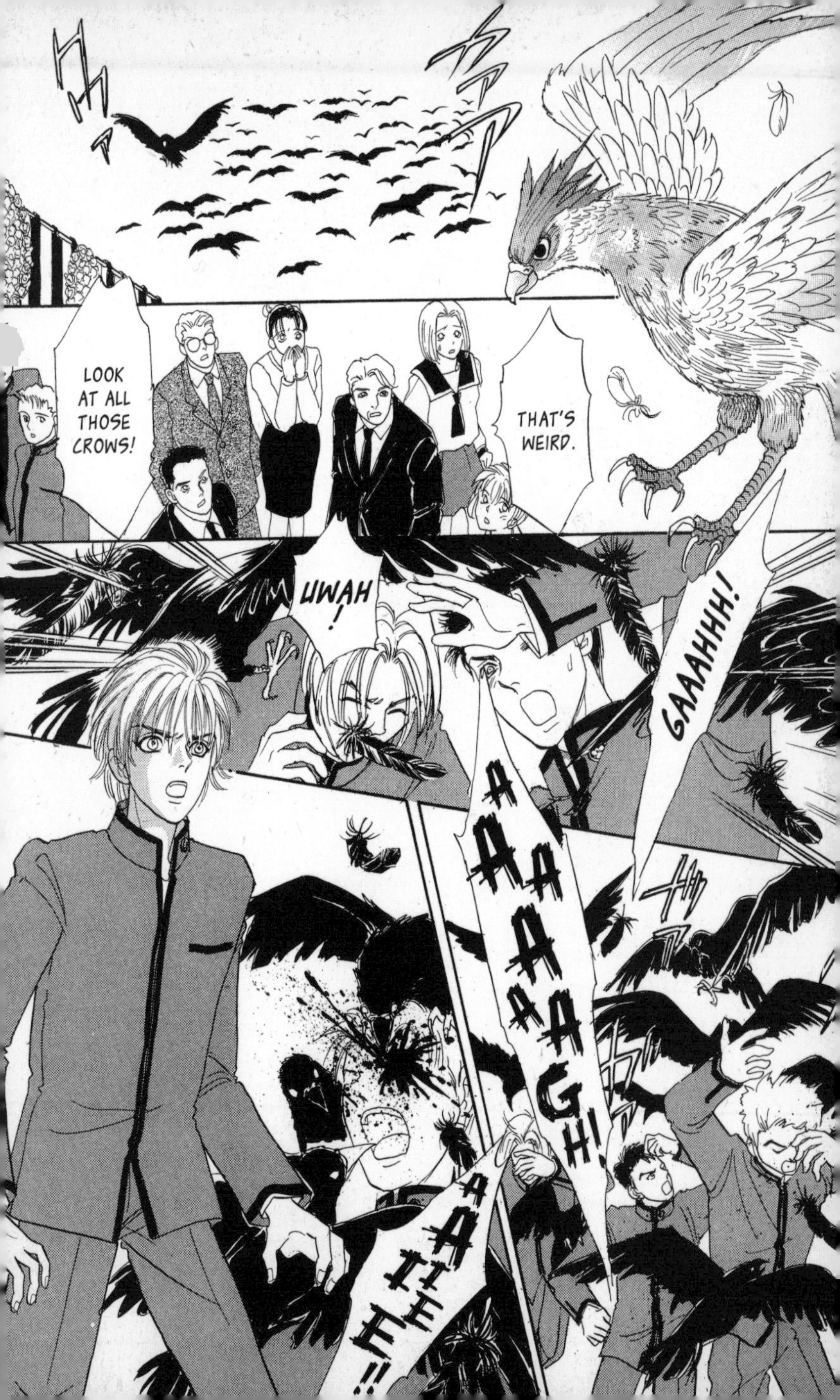
THAT'S WEIRD.
LOOK AT ALL THOSE CROWS!
GAAAHHH!
UWAH!
AAAAAAGH!
AAIIEE!!

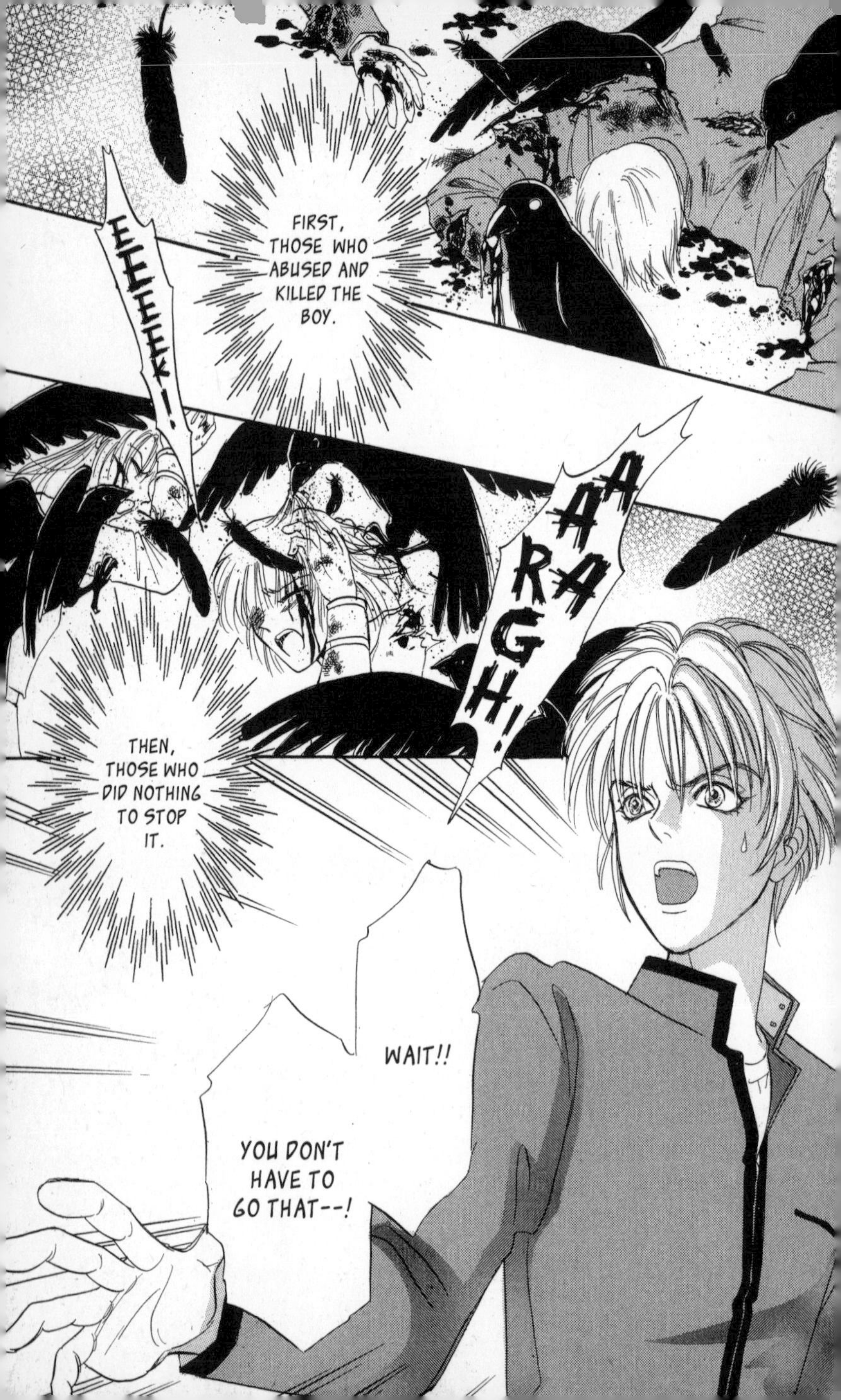
FIRST, THOSE WHO ABUSED AND KILLED THE BOY.
EEEEEEK!
AARAGH!
THEN, THOSE WHO DID NOTHING TO STOP IT.
WAIT!!
YOU DON'T HAVE TO GO THAT--!

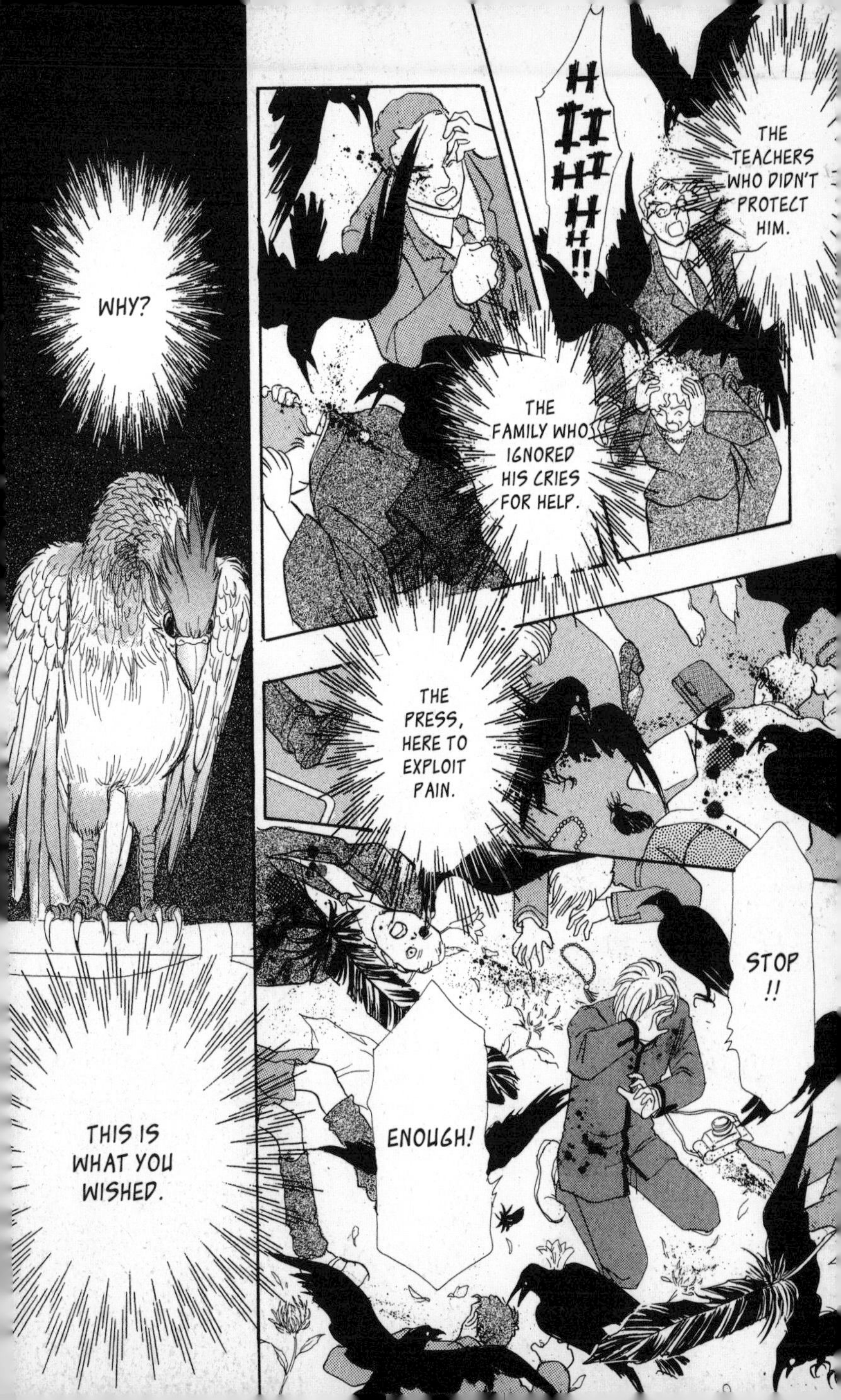

HIIHIHH!!
THE TEACHERS WHO DIDN'T PROTECT HIM.
THE FAMILY WHO IGNORED HIS CRIES FOR HELP.
THE PRESS, HERE TO EXPLOIT PAIN.
STOP !!
ENOUGH!
WHY?
THIS IS WHAT YOU WISHED.

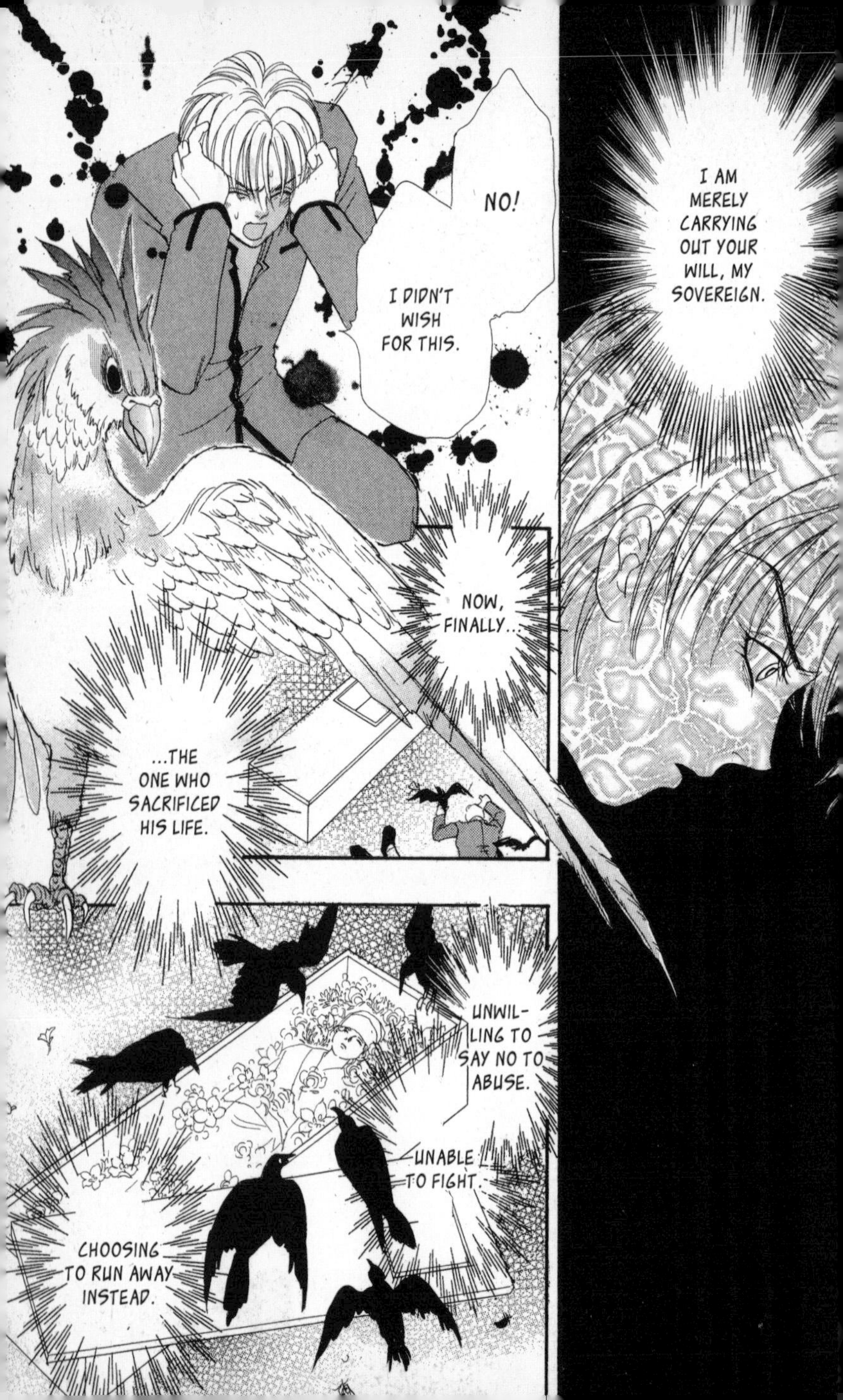
I AM MERELY CARRYING OUT YOUR WILL, MY SOVEREIGN.
NO!
I DIDN'T WISH FOR THIS.
NOW, FINALLY...
...THE ONE WHO SACRIFICED HIS LIFE.
UNWIL-LING TO SAY NO TO ABUSE.
UNABLE TO FIGHT.
CHOOSING TO RUN AWAY INSTEAD.

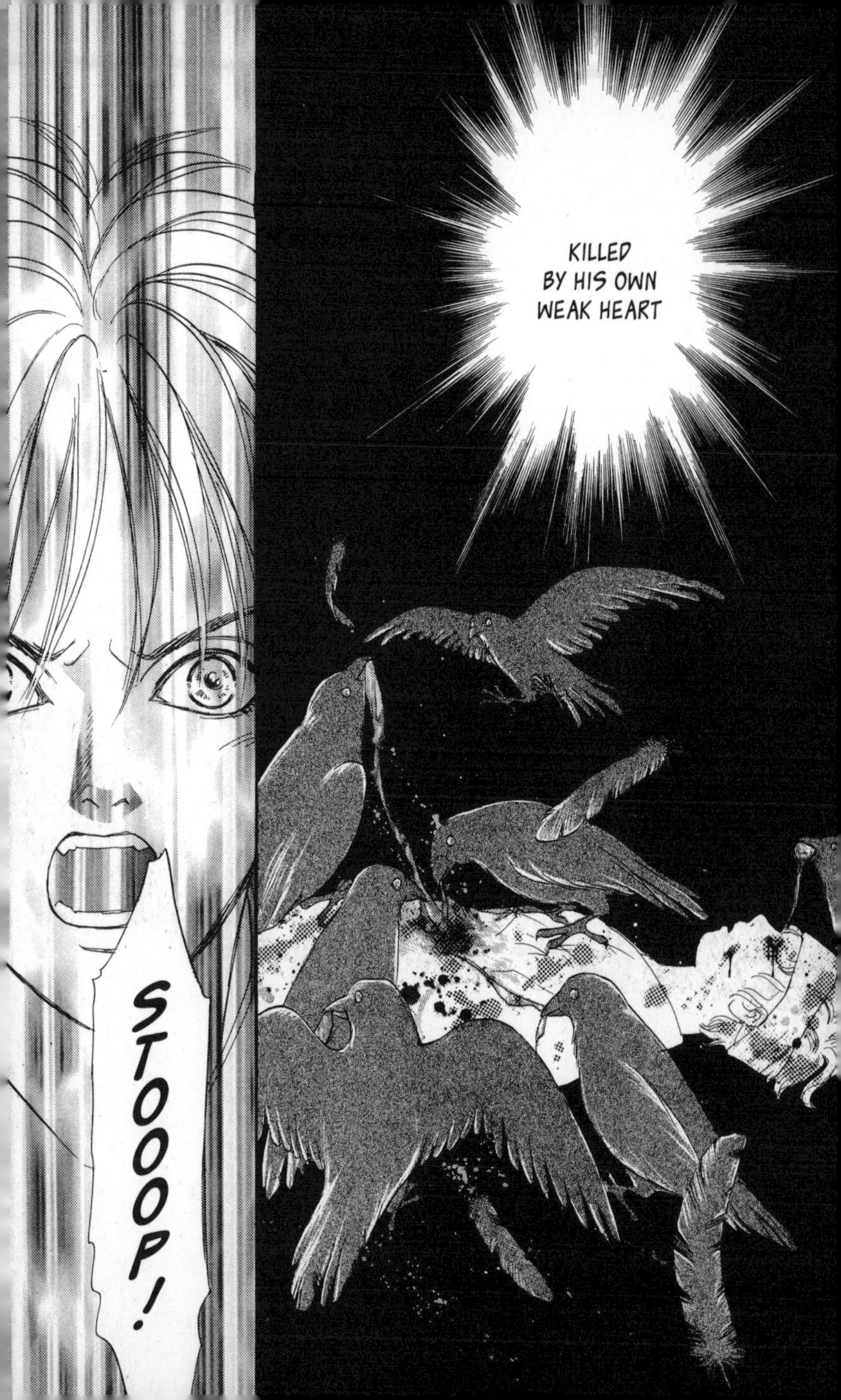
KILLED
BY HIS OWN
WEAK HEART
STOOOOP!

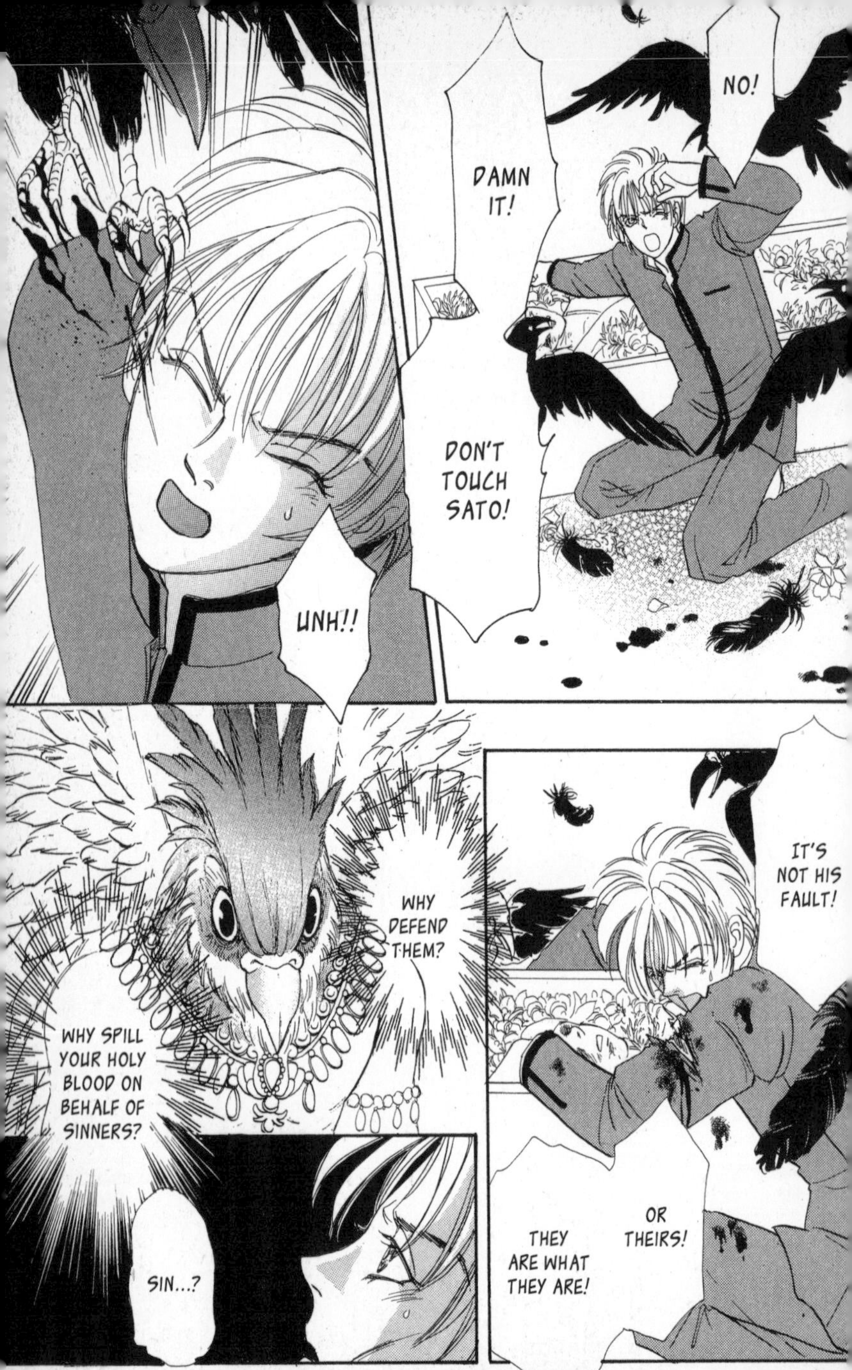
NO!
DAMN IT!
DON'T TOUCH SATO!
UNH!!
IT'S NOT HIS FAULT!
OR THEIRS!
THEY ARE WHAT THEY ARE!
WHY DEFEND THEM?
WHY SPILL YOUR HOLY BLOOD ON BEHALF OF SINNERS?
SIN...?

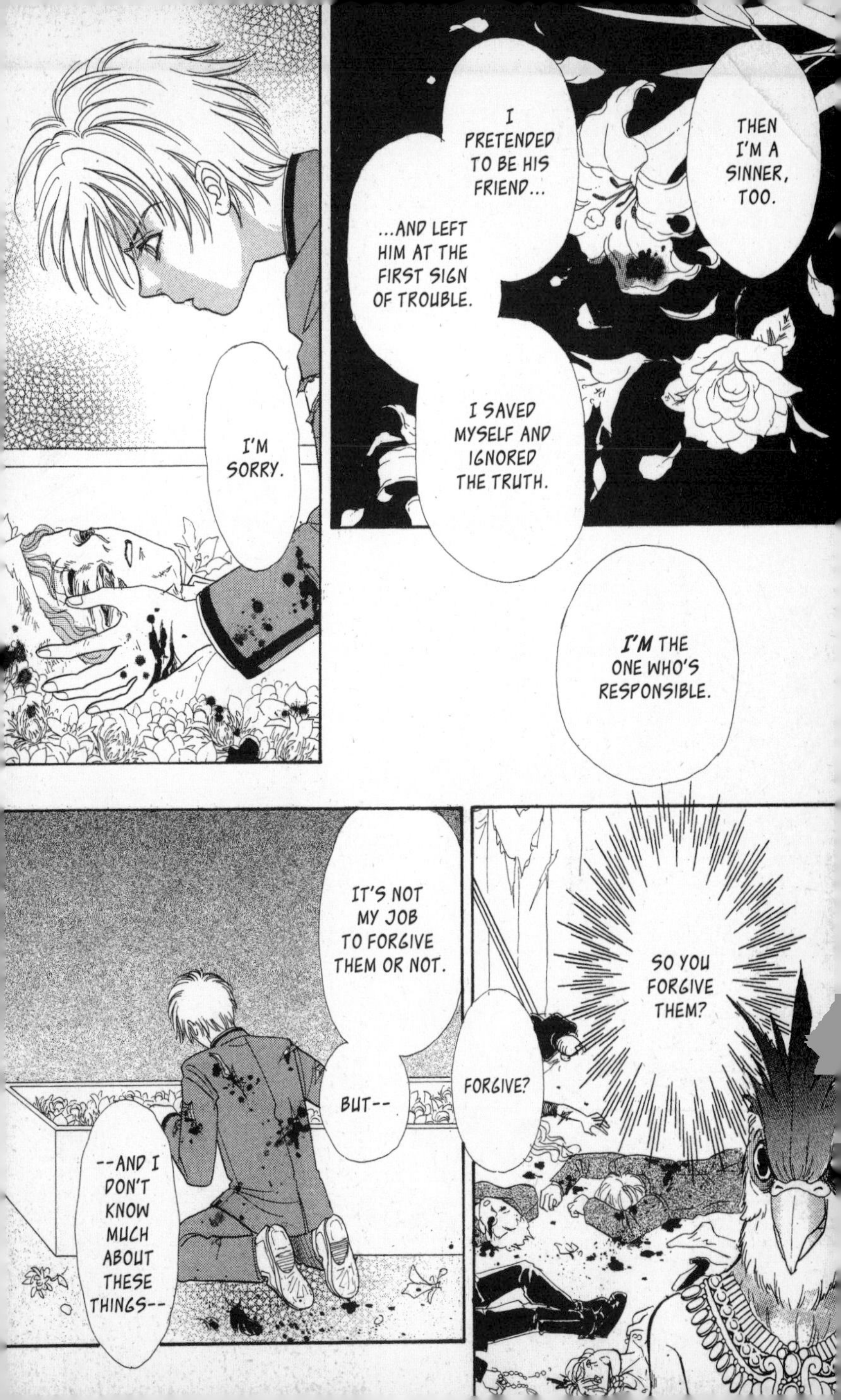

THEN I'M A SINNER, TOO.
I PRETENDED TO BE HIS FRIEND...
...AND LEFT HIM AT THE FIRST SIGN OF TROUBLE.
I SAVED MYSELF AND IGNORED THE TRUTH.
I'M THE ONE WHO'S RESPONSIBLE.
I'M SORRY.
SO YOU FORGIVE THEM?
FORGIVE?
IT'S NOT MY JOB TO FORGIVE THEM OR NOT.
BUT--
--AND I DON'T KNOW MUCH ABOUT THESE THINGS--

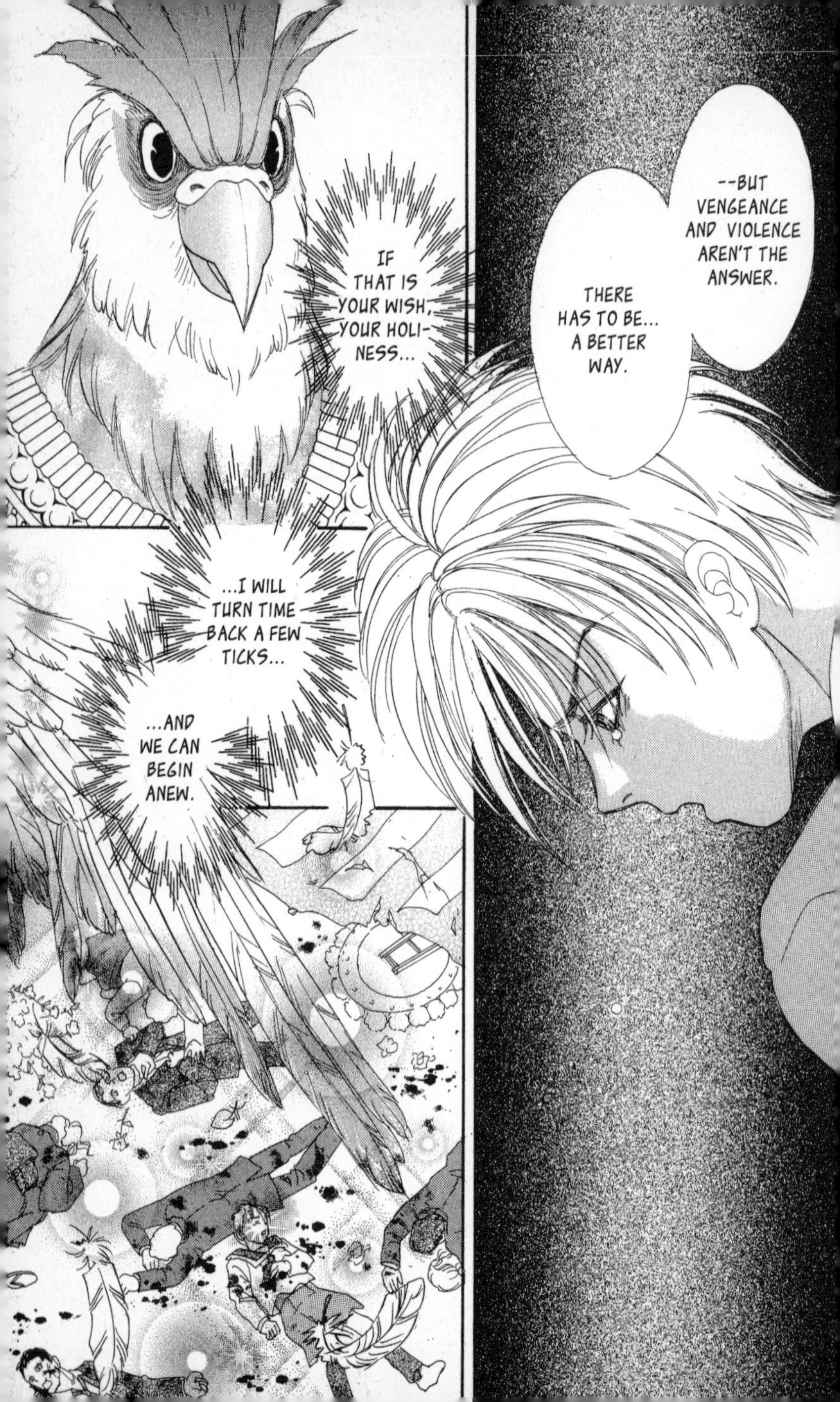
--BUT VENGEANCE AND VIOLENCE AREN'T THE ANSWER.
THERE HAS TO BE... A BETTER WAY.
IF THAT IS YOUR WISH, YOUR HOLINESS...
...I WILL TURN TIME BACK A FEW TICKS...
...AND WE CAN BEGIN ANEW.

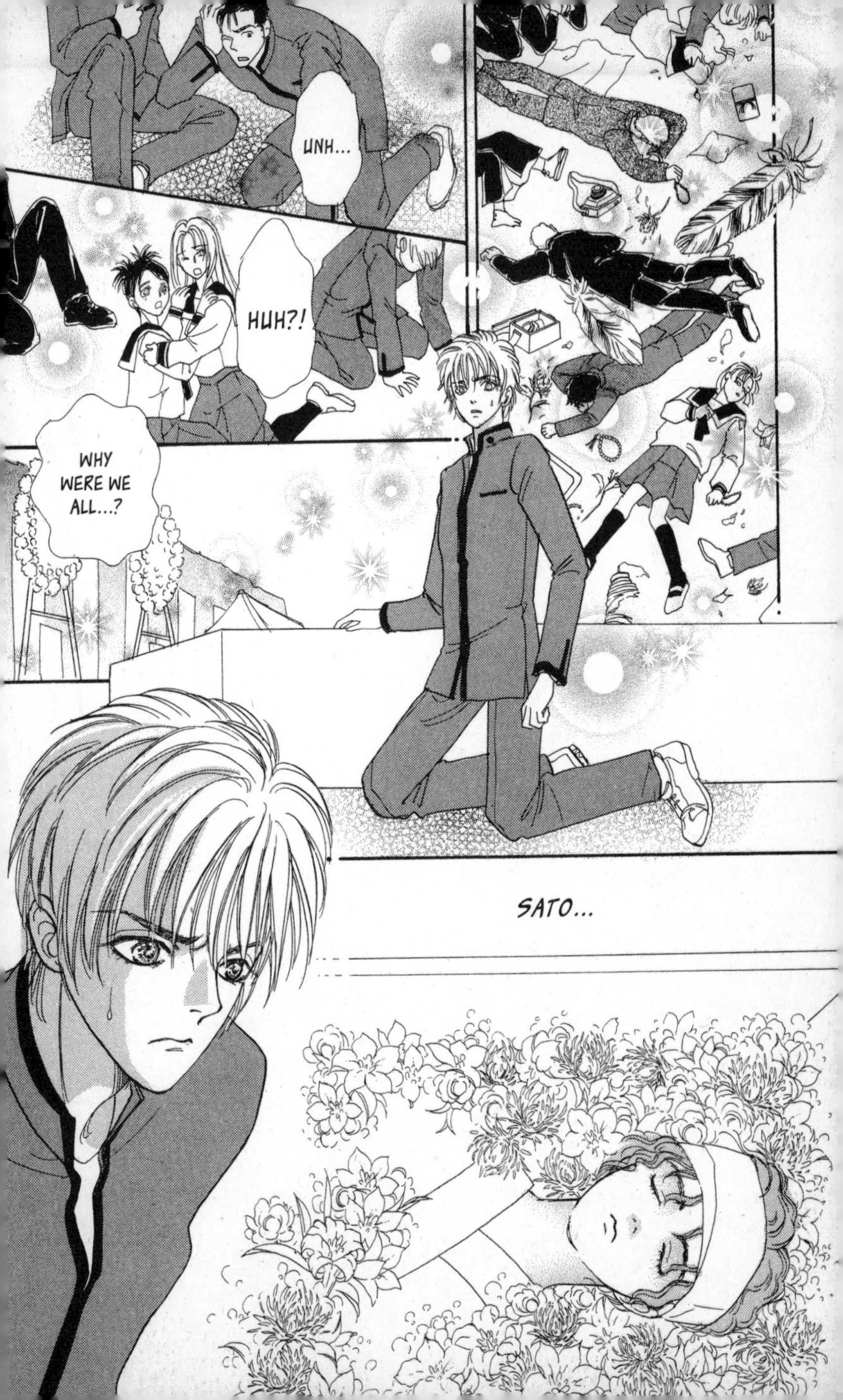
UNH...
HUH?!
WHY WERE WE ALL...?
SATO...

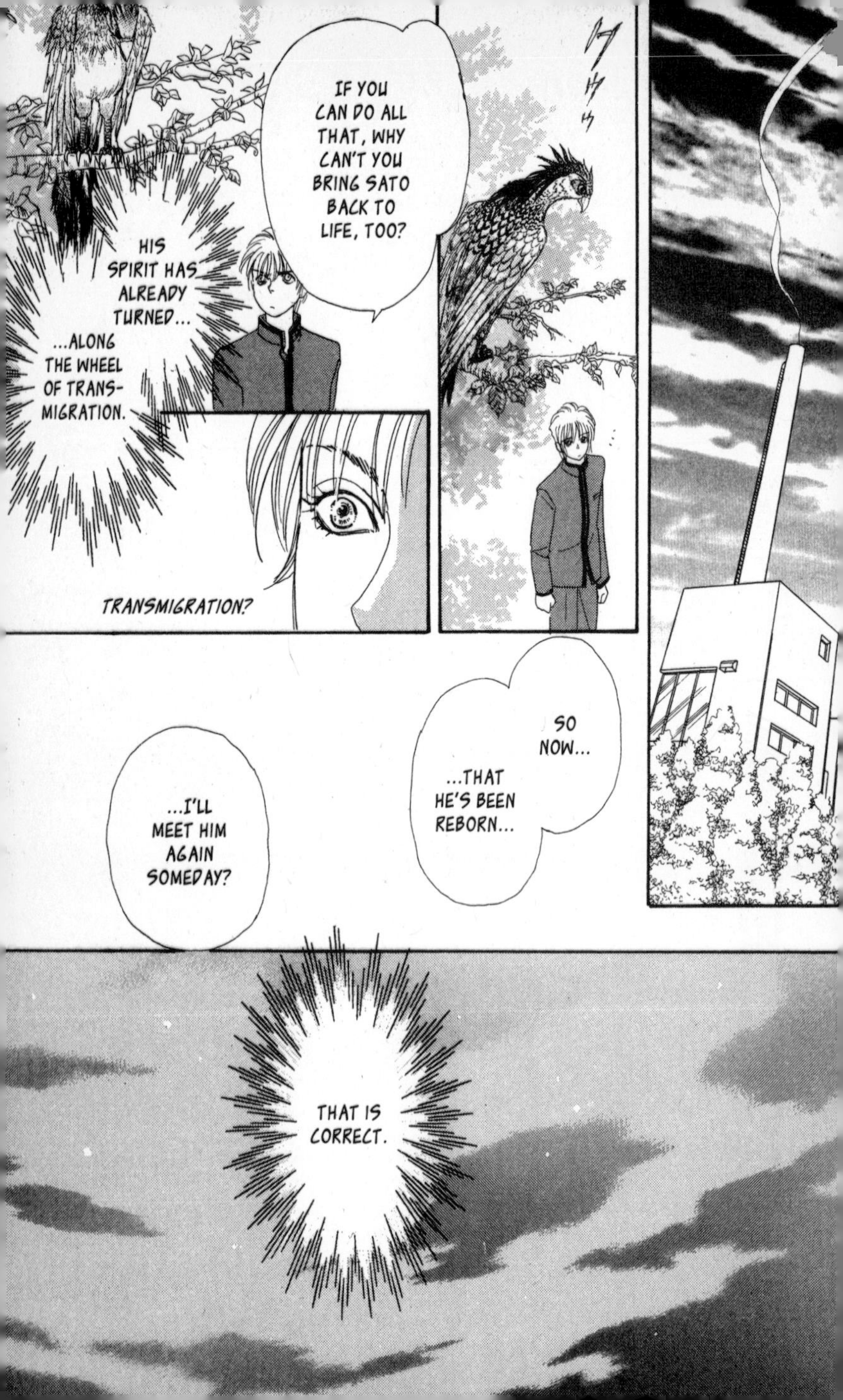
IF YOU CAN DO ALL THAT, WHY CAN'T YOU BRING SATO BACK TO LIFE, TOO?
HIS SPIRIT HAS ALREADY TURNED...
...ALONG THE WHEEL OF TRANS-MIGRATION.
TRANSMIGRATION?
SO NOW...
...THAT HE'S BEEN REBORN...
...I'LL MEET HIM AGAIN SOMEDAY?
THAT IS CORRECT.

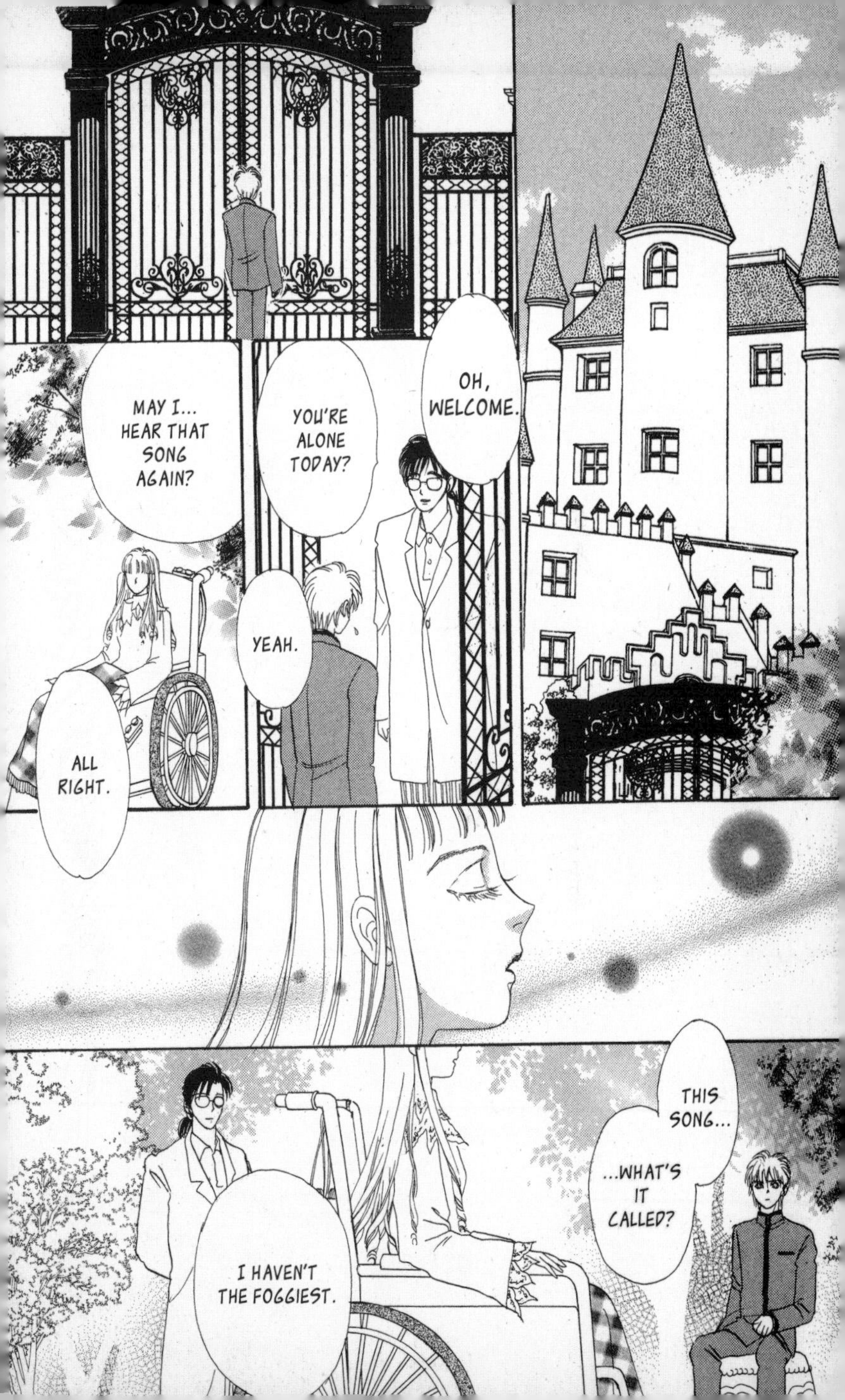
OH, WELCOME.
YOU'RE ALONE TODAY?
YEAH.
MAY I... HEAR THAT SONG AGAIN?
ALL RIGHT.
THIS SONG...
...WHAT'S IT CALLED?
I HAVEN'T THE FOGGIEST.

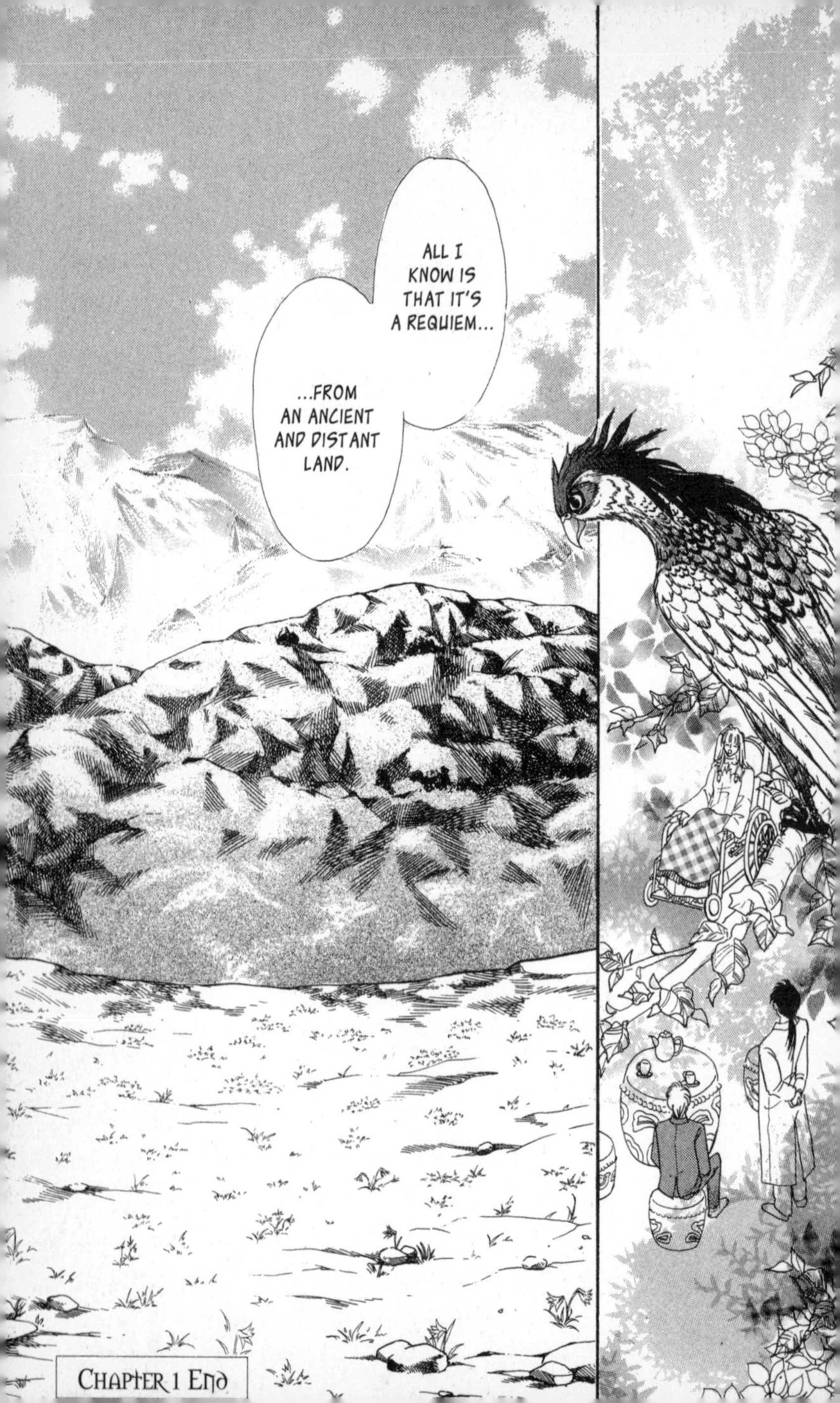
ALL I KNOW IS THAT IT'S A REQUIEM...
...FROM AN ANCIENT AND DISTANT LAND.
CHAPTER 1 END

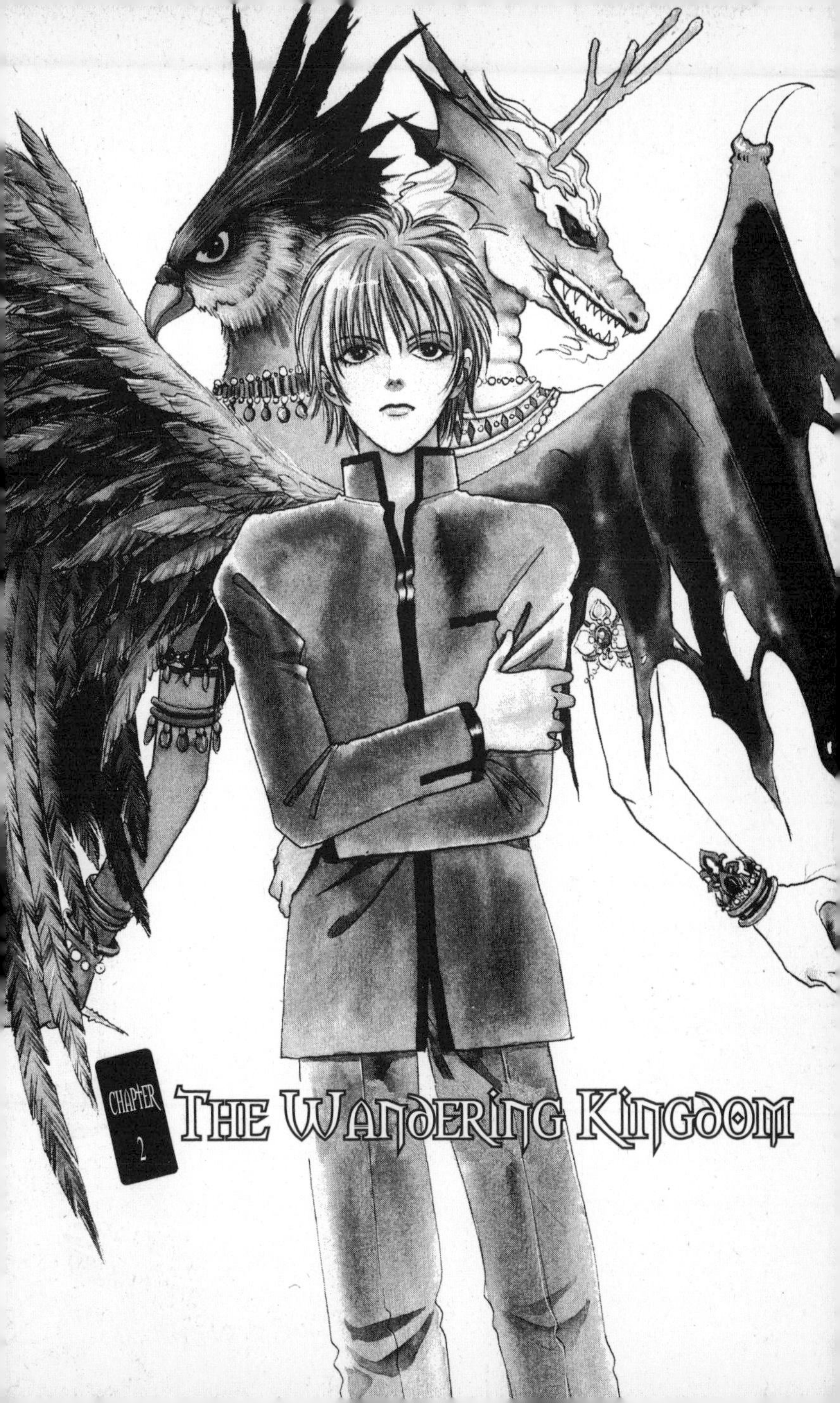
CHAPTER 2
THE WANDERING KINGDOM

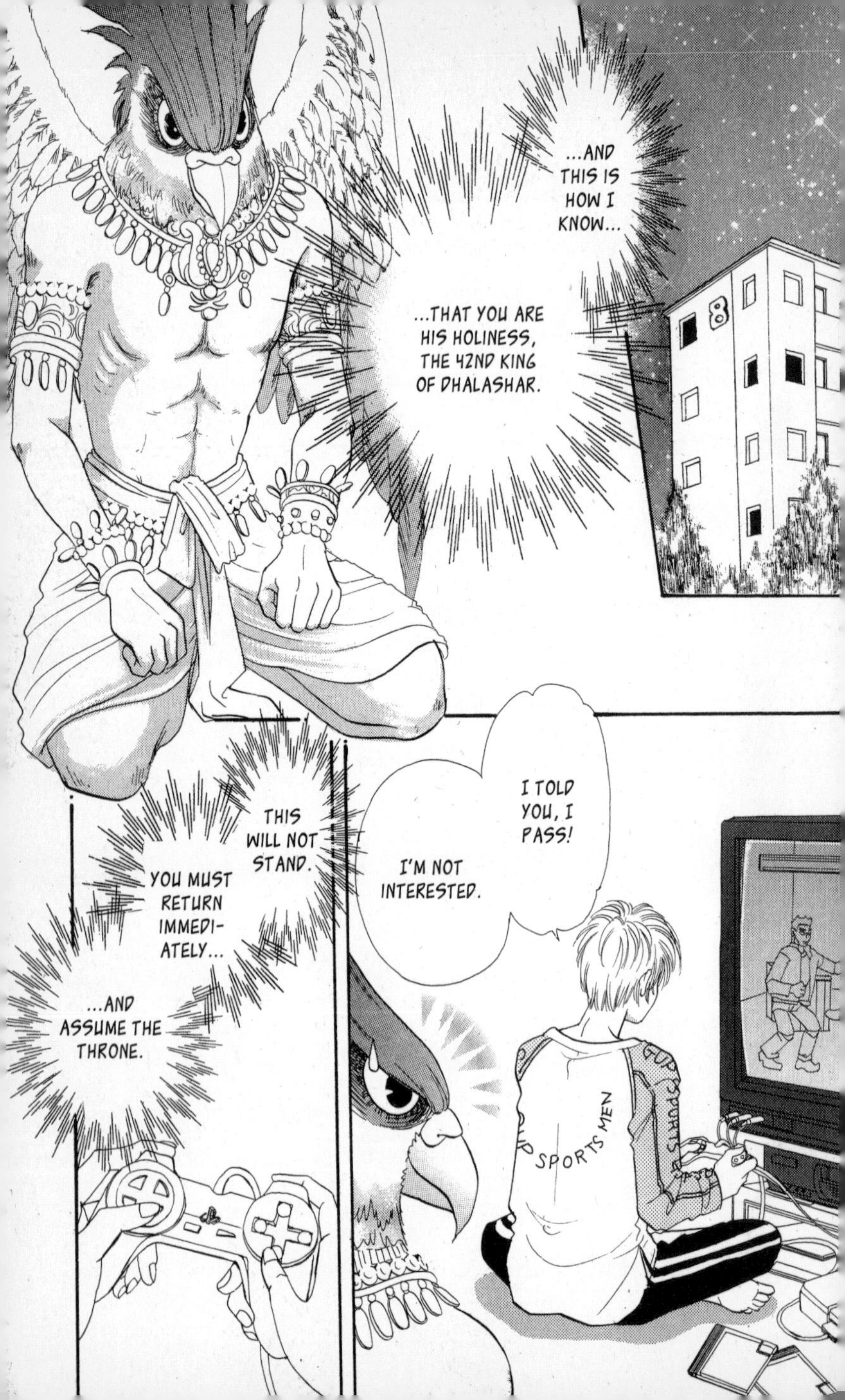
...AND THIS IS HOW I KNOW...
...THAT YOU ARE HIS HOLINESS, THE 42ND KING OF DHALASHAR.
I TOLD YOU, I PASS!
I'M NOT INTERESTED.
THIS WILL NOT STAND.
YOU MUST RETURN IMMEDI-ATELY...
...AND ASSUME THE THRONE.

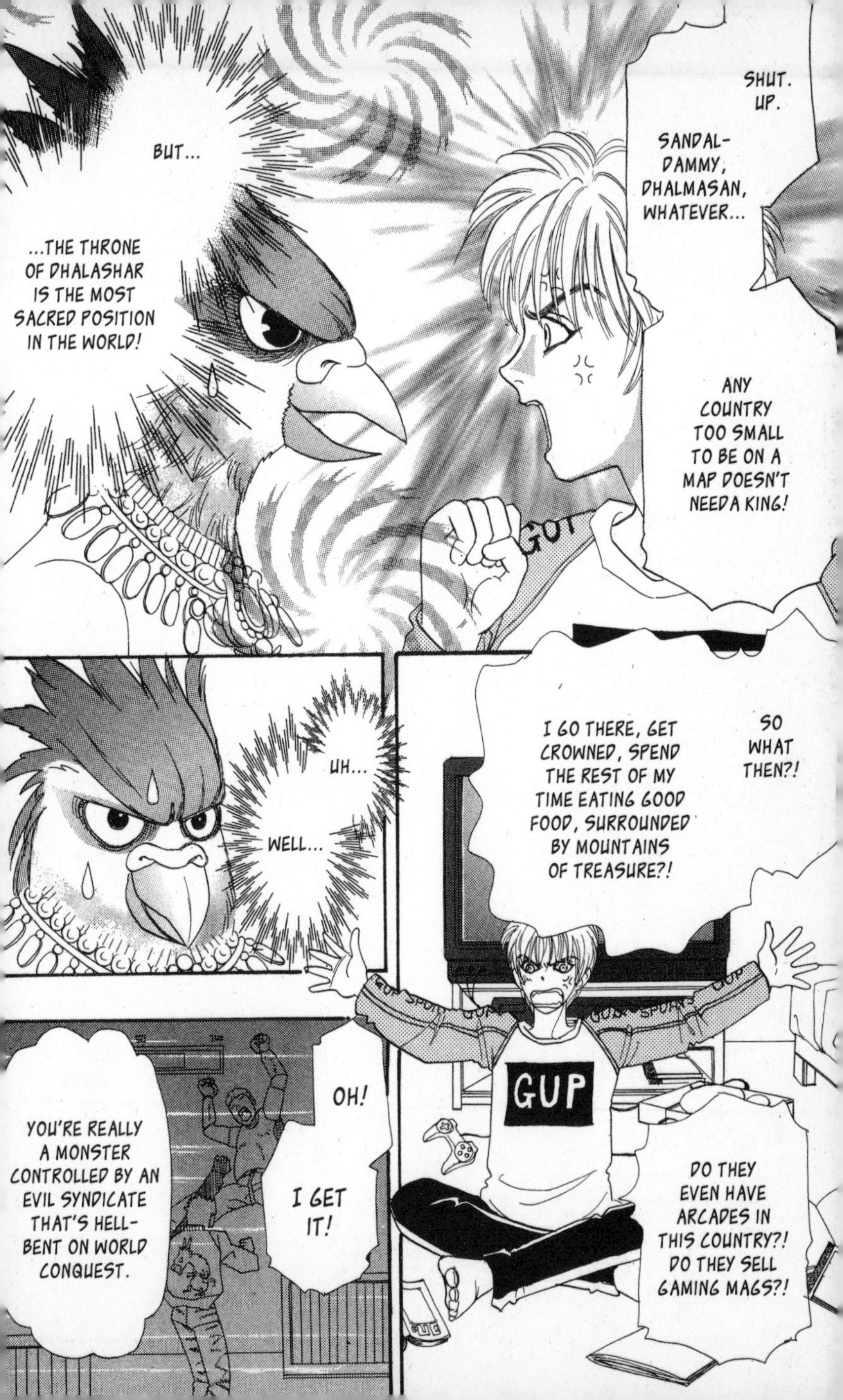
SHUT. UP.
SANDAL-DAMMY, DHALMASAN, WHATEVER...
ANY COUNTRY TOO SMALL TO BE ON A MAP DOESN'T NEEDA KING!
BUT...
...THE THRONE OF DHALASHAR IS THE MOST SACRED POSITION IN THE WORLD!
SO WHAT THEN?!
I GO THERE, GET CROWNED, SPEND THE REST OF MY TIME EATING GOOD FOOD, SURROUNDED BY MOUNTAINS OF TREASURE?!
DO THEY EVEN HAVE ARCADES IN THIS COUNTRY?! DO THEY SELL GAMING MAGS?!
UH...
WELL...
OH!
I GET IT!
YOU'RE REALLY A MONSTER CONTROLLED BY AN EVIL SYNDICATE THAT'S HELL-BENT ON WORLD CONQUEST.

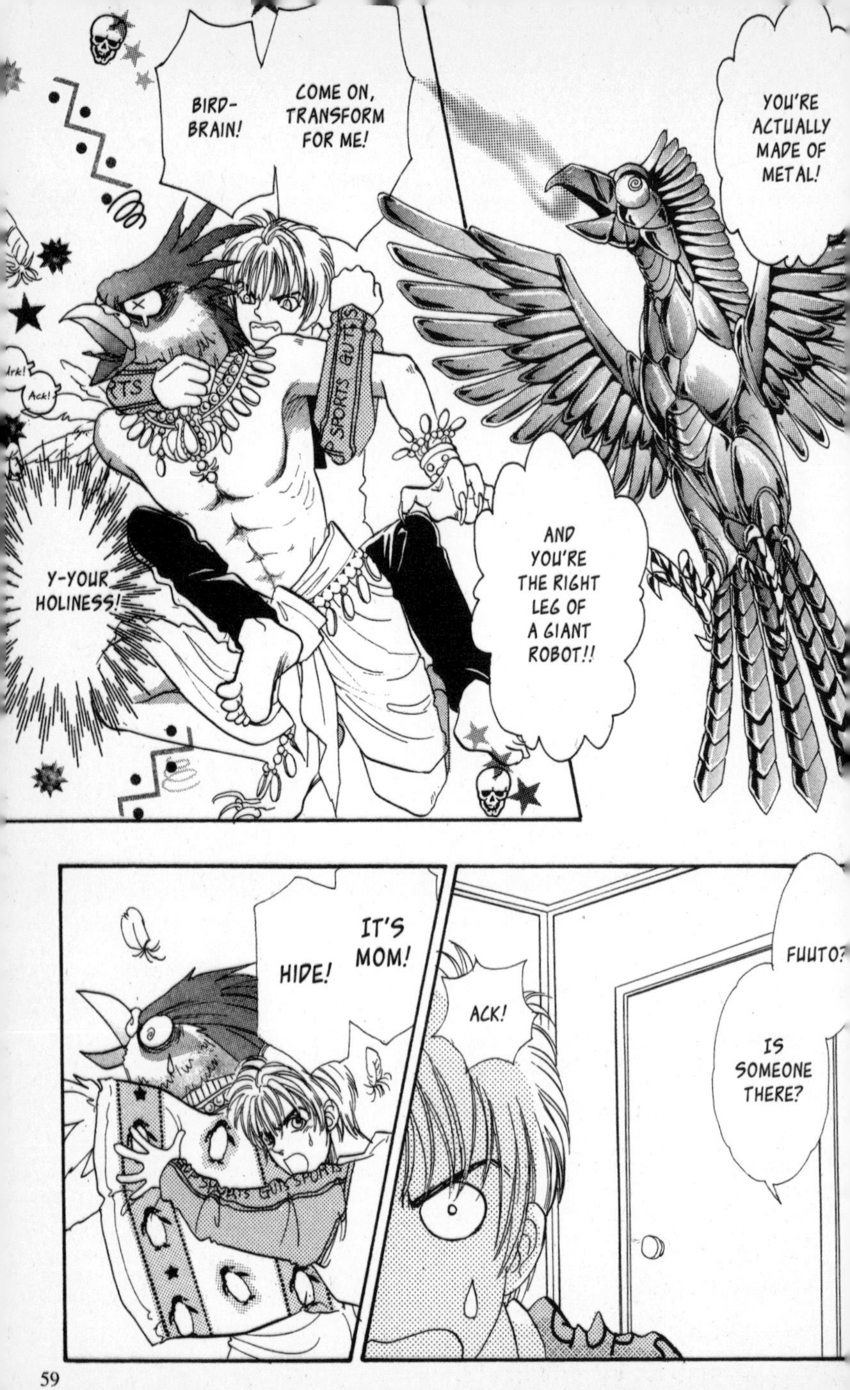
YOU'RE ACTUALLY MADE OF METAL!
BIRD-BRAIN! COME ON, TRANSFORM FOR ME!
AND YOU'RE THE RIGHT LEG OF A GIANT ROBOT!!
Y-YOUR HOLINESS!
Ark!
Ack!
FUUTO?
IS SOMEONE THERE?
ACK!
IT'S MOM!
HIDE!

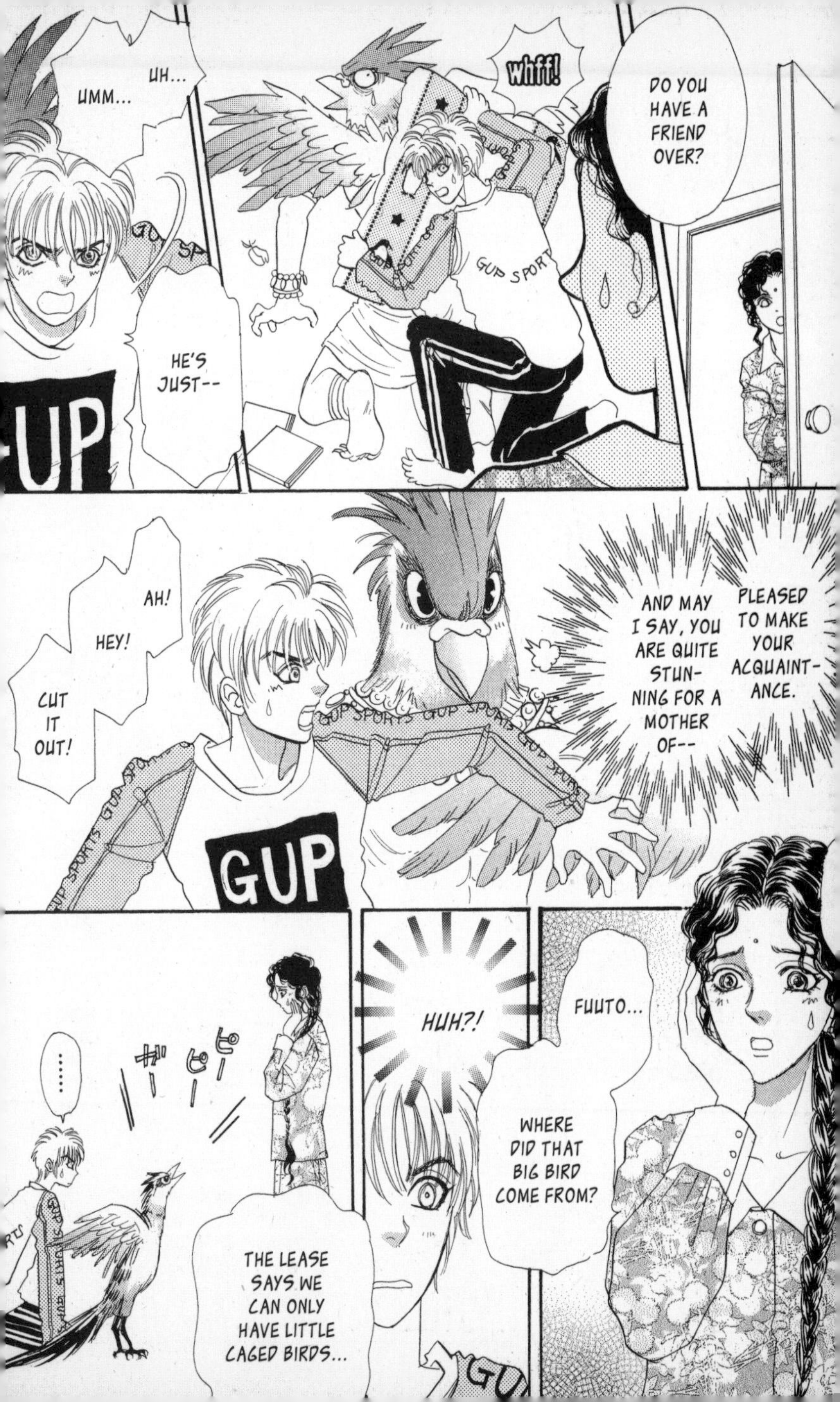

DO YOU HAVE A FRIEND OVER?
whff!
UH...
UMM...
HE'S JUST--
PLEASED TO MAKE YOUR ACQUAINT-ANCE.
AND MAY I SAY, YOU ARE QUITE STUN-NING FOR A MOTHER OF--
AH!
HEY!
CUT IT OUT!
FUUTO...
WHERE DID THAT BIG BIRD COME FROM?
HUH?!
ピー
ガー
......
THE LEASE SAYS WE CAN ONLY HAVE LITTLE CAGED BIRDS...

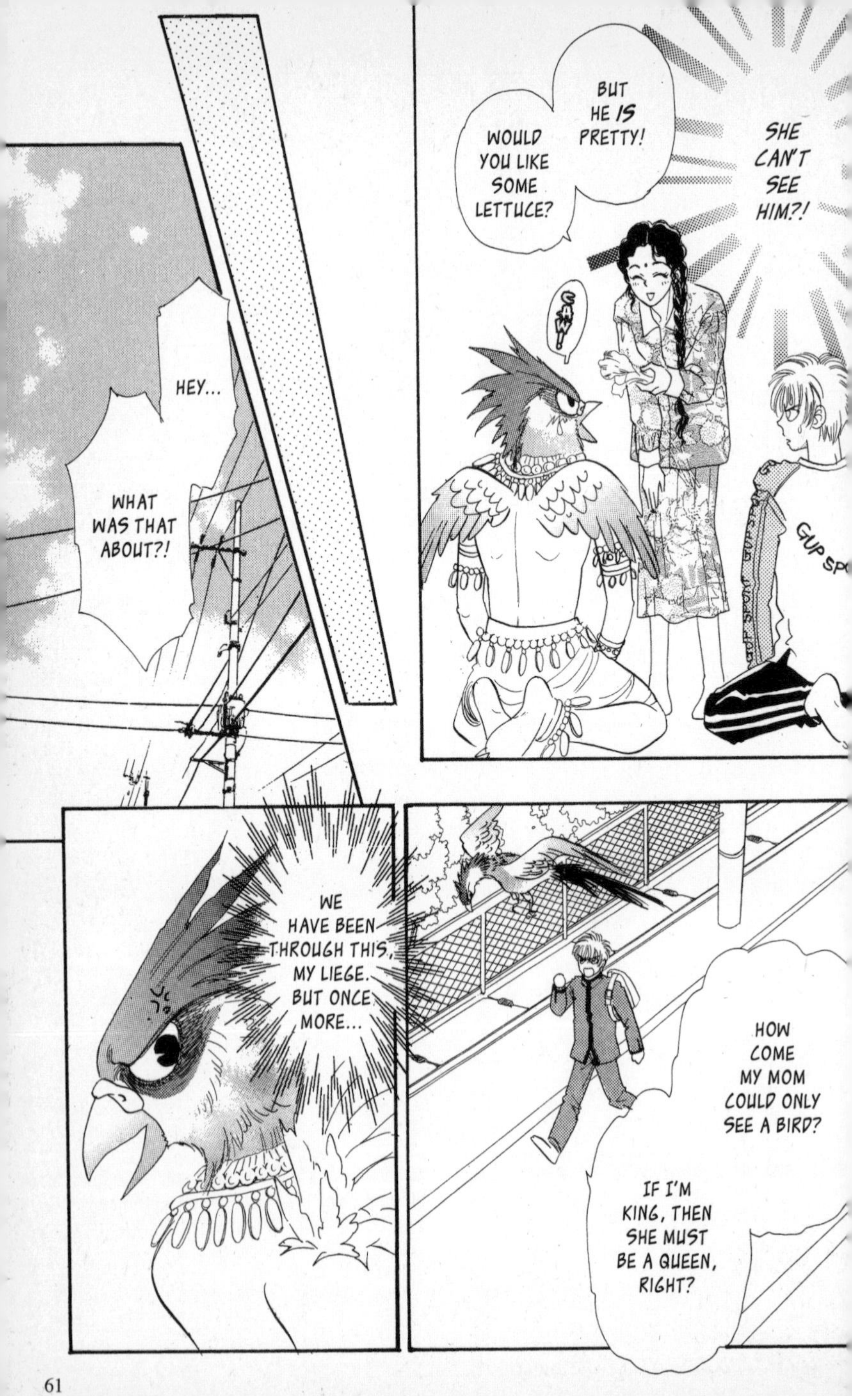
BUT HE *IS* PRETTY!
WOULD YOU LIKE SOME LETTUCE?
SHE CAN'T SEE HIM?!
GAW!
GUP SPORT
HEY...
WHAT WAS THAT ABOUT?!
HOW COME MY MOM COULD ONLY SEE A BIRD?
IF I'M KING, THEN SHE MUST BE A QUEEN, RIGHT?
WE HAVE BEEN THROUGH THIS, MY LIEGE. BUT ONCE MORE...

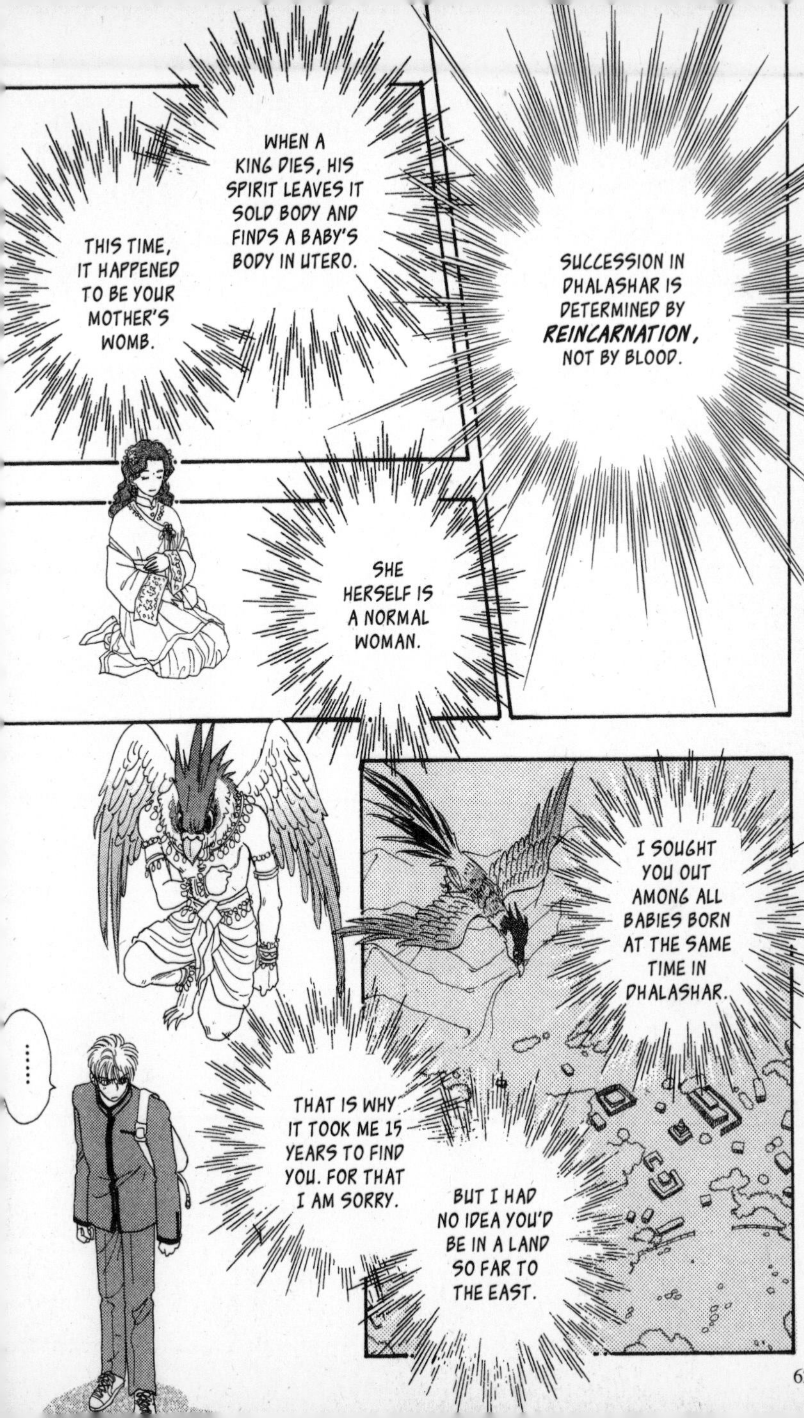
SUCCESSION IN DHALASHAR IS DETERMINED BY *REINCARNATION*, NOT BY BLOOD.
WHEN A KING DIES, HIS SPIRIT LEAVES IT SOLD BODY AND FINDS A BABY'S BODY IN UTERO.
THIS TIME, IT HAPPENED TO BE YOUR MOTHER'S WOMB.
SHE HERSELF IS A NORMAL WOMAN.
I SOUGHT YOU OUT AMONG ALL BABIES BORN AT THE SAME TIME IN DHALASHAR.
THAT IS WHY IT TOOK ME 15 YEARS TO FIND YOU. FOR THAT I AM SORRY.
BUT I HAD NO IDEA YOU'D BE IN A LAND SO FAR TO THE EAST.
......

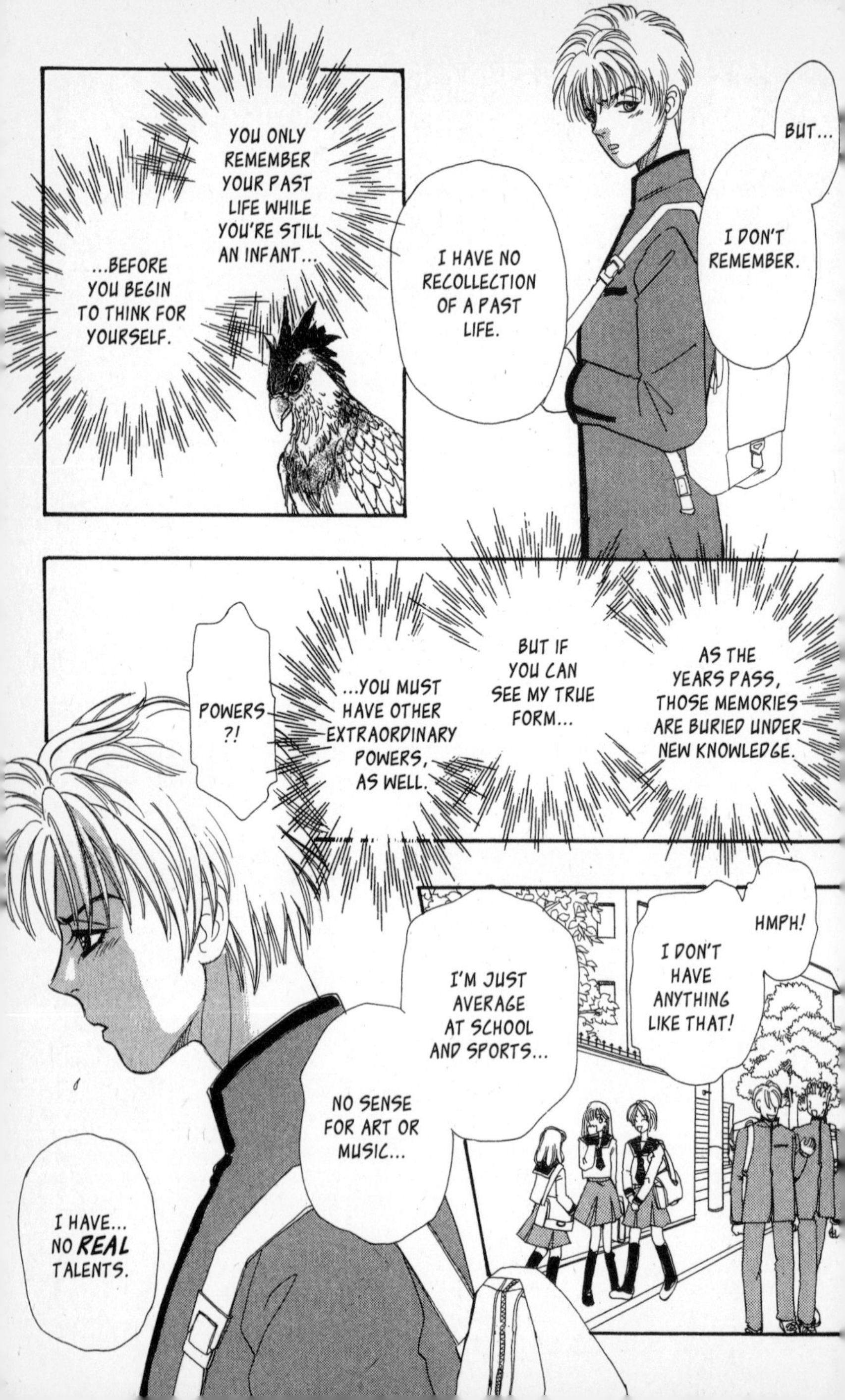
BUT...
I DON'T REMEMBER.
I HAVE NO RECOLLECTION OF A PAST LIFE.
YOU ONLY REMEMBER YOUR PAST LIFE WHILE YOU'RE STILL AN INFANT...
...BEFORE YOU BEGIN TO THINK FOR YOURSELF.
AS THE YEARS PASS, THOSE MEMORIES ARE BURIED UNDER NEW KNOWLEDGE.
BUT IF YOU CAN SEE MY TRUE FORM...
...YOU MUST HAVE OTHER EXTRAORDINARY POWERS, AS WELL.
POWERS ?!
HMPH!
I DON'T HAVE ANYTHING LIKE THAT!
I'M JUST AVERAGE AT SCHOOL AND SPORTS...
NO SENSE FOR ART OR MUSIC...
I HAVE... NO ***REAL*** TALENTS.

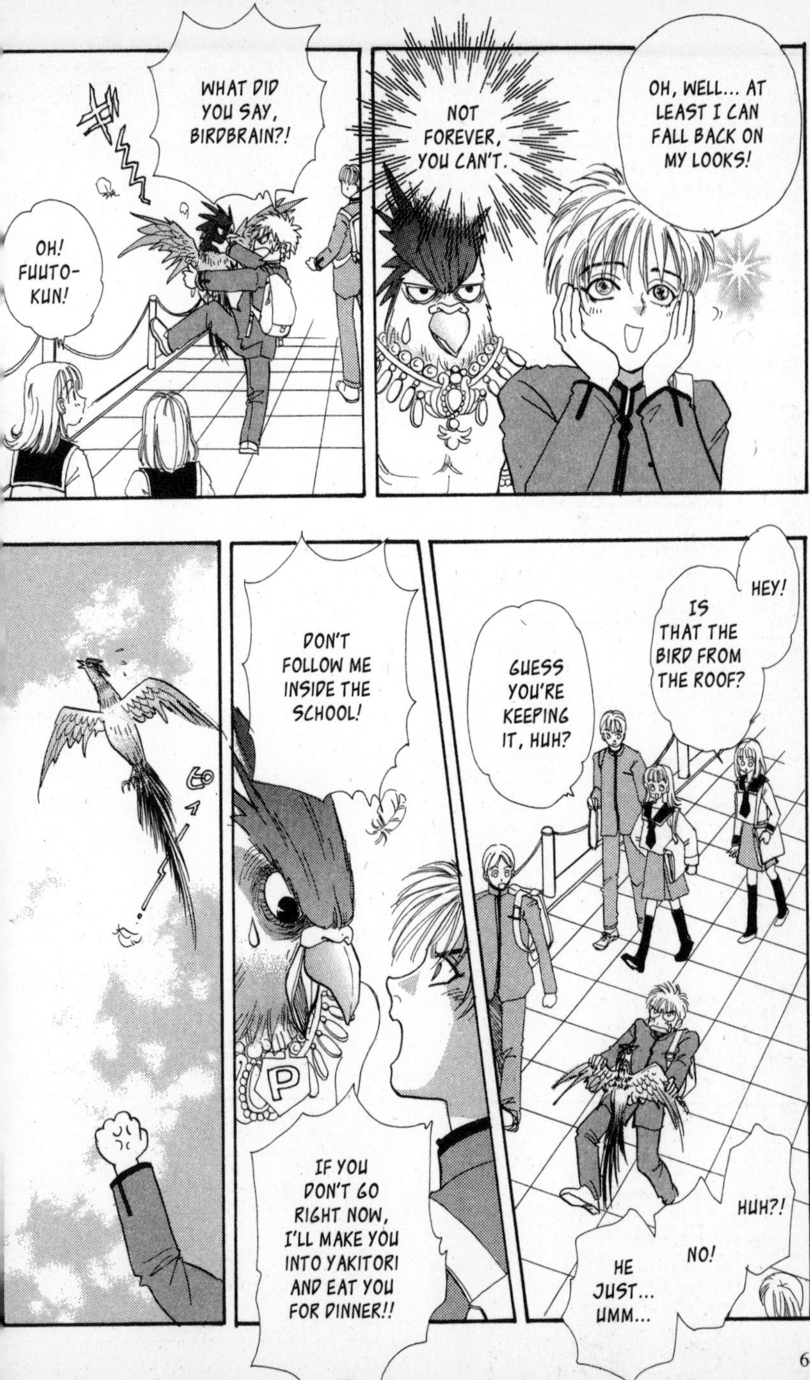

OH, WELL... AT LEAST I CAN FALL BACK ON MY LOOKS!
NOT FOREVER, YOU CAN'T.
WHAT DID YOU SAY, BIRDBRAIN?!
OH! FUUTO-KUN!
HEY!
IS THAT THE BIRD FROM THE ROOF?
GUESS YOU'RE KEEPING IT, HUH?
HUH?!
NO!
HE JUST... UMM...
DON'T FOLLOW ME INSIDE THE SCHOOL!
IF YOU DON'T GO RIGHT NOW, I'LL MAKE YOU INTO YAKITORI AND EAT YOU FOR DINNER!!

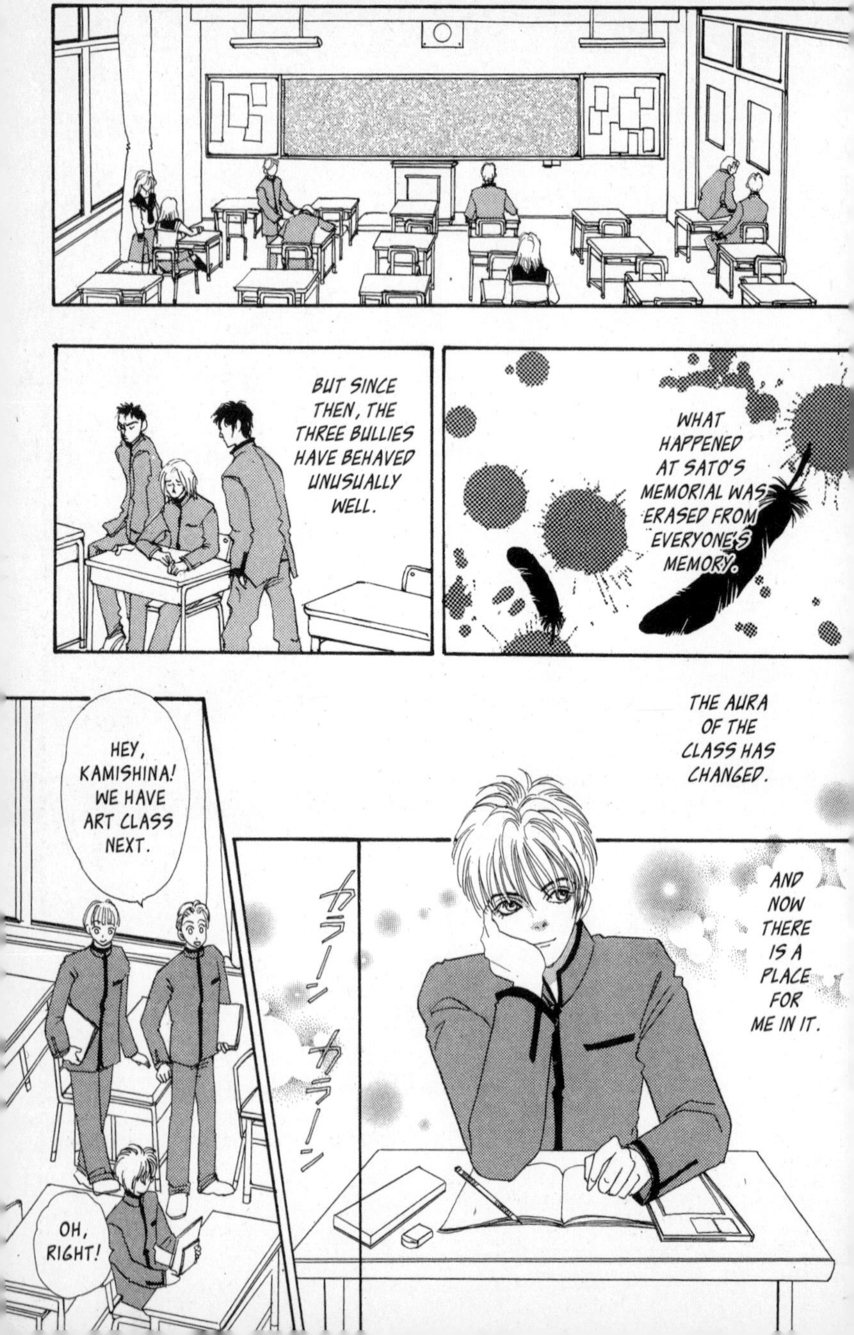
WHAT HAPPENED AT SATO'S MEMORIAL WAS ERASED FROM EVERYONE'S MEMORY.
BUT SINCE THEN, THE THREE BULLIES HAVE BEHAVED UNUSUALLY WELL.
THE AURA OF THE CLASS HAS CHANGED.
AND NOW THERE IS A PLACE FOR ME IN IT.
カラーン
カラーン
HEY, KAMISHINA! WE HAVE ART CLASS NEXT.
OH, RIGHT!

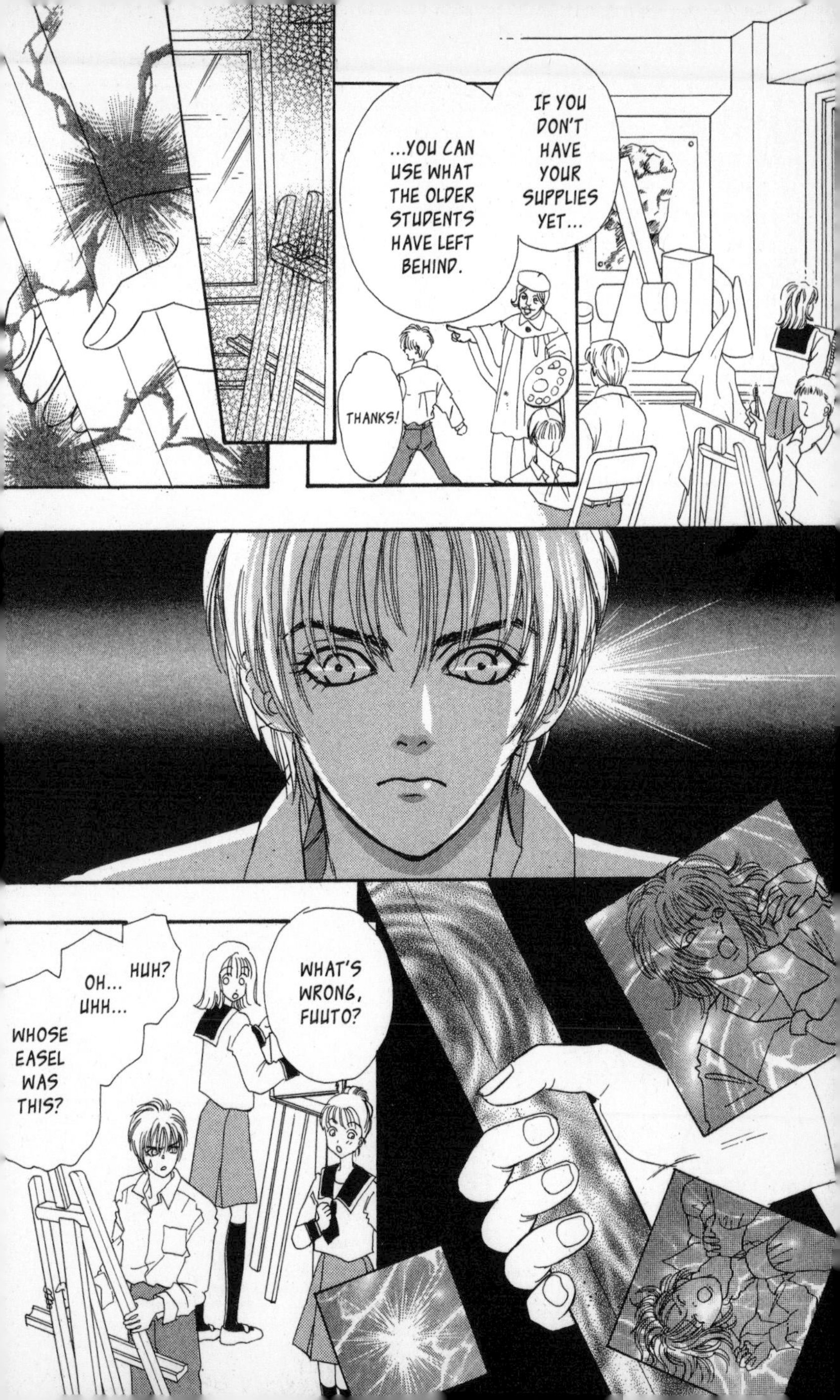
IF YOU DON'T HAVE YOUR SUPPLIES YET...
...YOU CAN USE WHAT THE OLDER STUDENTS HAVE LEFT BEHIND.
THANKS!
WHAT'S WRONG, FUUTO?
HUH?
OH... UHH...
WHOSE EASEL WAS THIS?

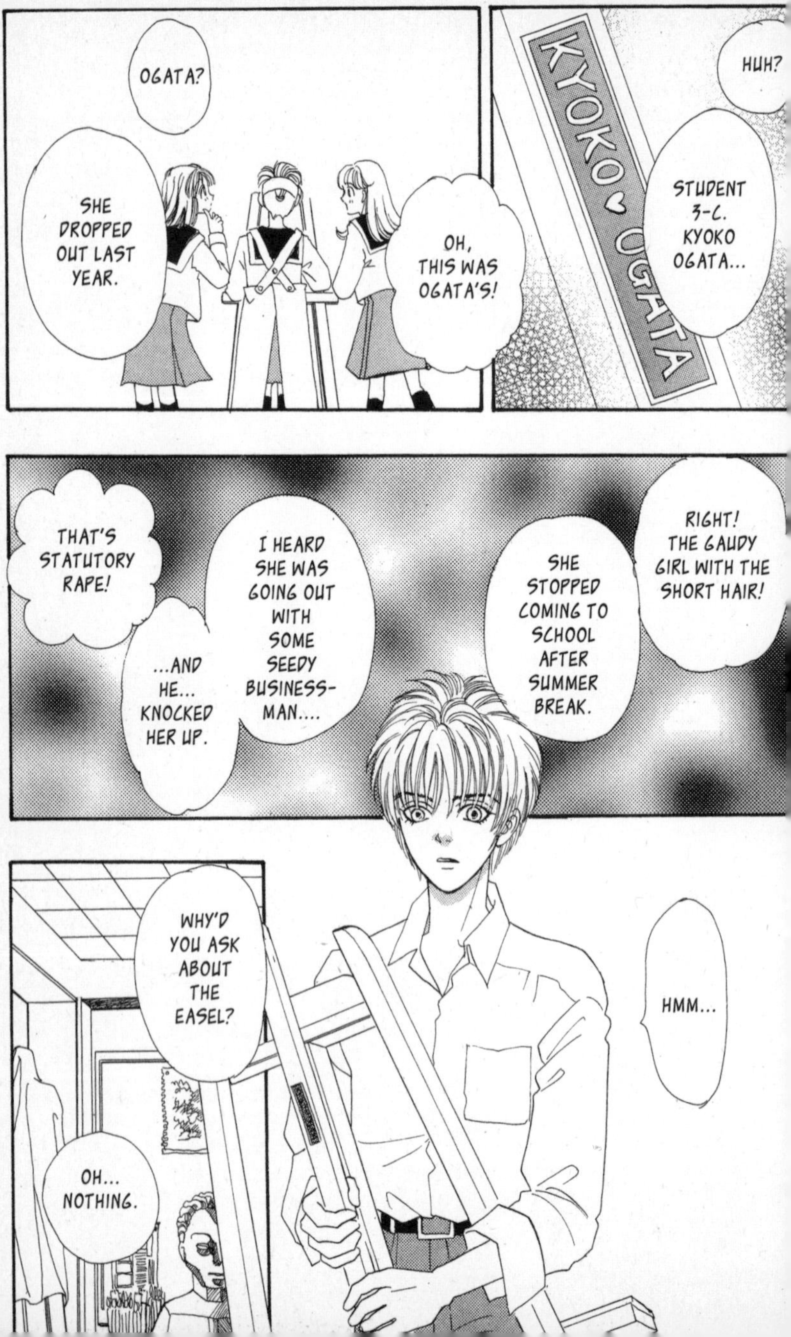
KYOKO ♥ OGATA
HUH?
STUDENT 3-C. KYOKO OGATA...
OH, THIS WAS OGATA'S!
OGATA?
SHE DROPPED OUT LAST YEAR.
RIGHT! THE GAUDY GIRL WITH THE SHORT HAIR!
SHE STOPPED COMING TO SCHOOL AFTER SUMMER BREAK.
I HEARD SHE WAS GOING OUT WITH SOME SEEDY BUSINESS-MAN....
...AND HE... KNOCKED HER UP.
THAT'S STATUTORY RAPE!
HMM...
WHY'D YOU ASK ABOUT THE EASEL?
OH... NOTHING.

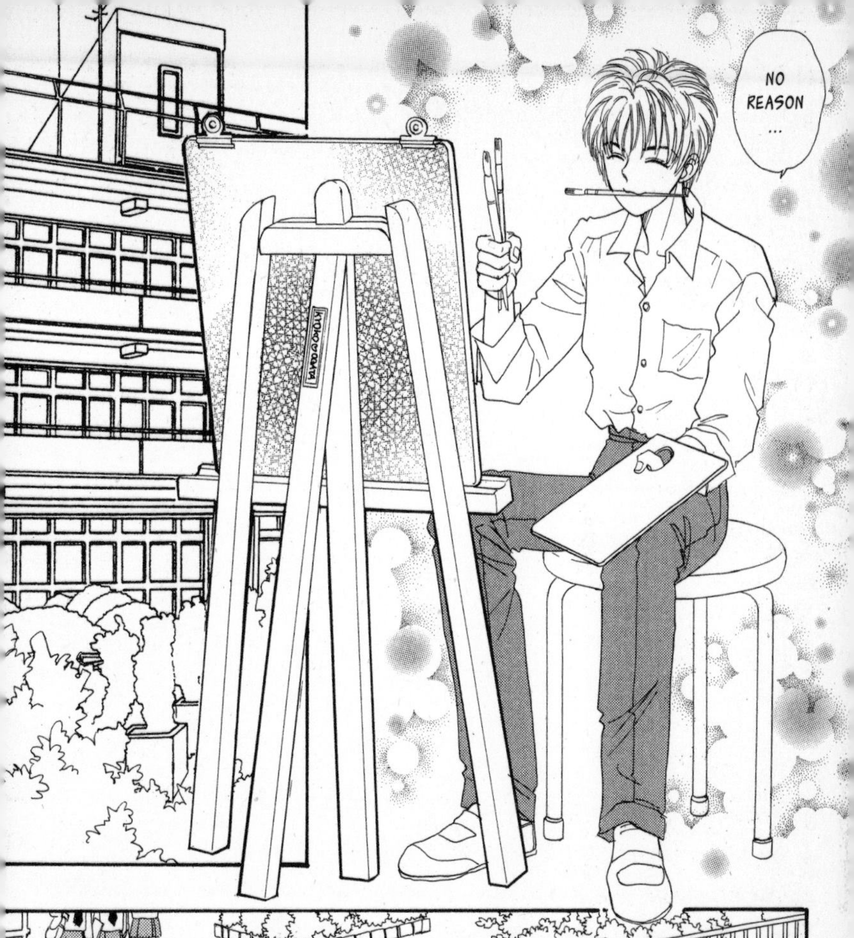
NO REASON ...

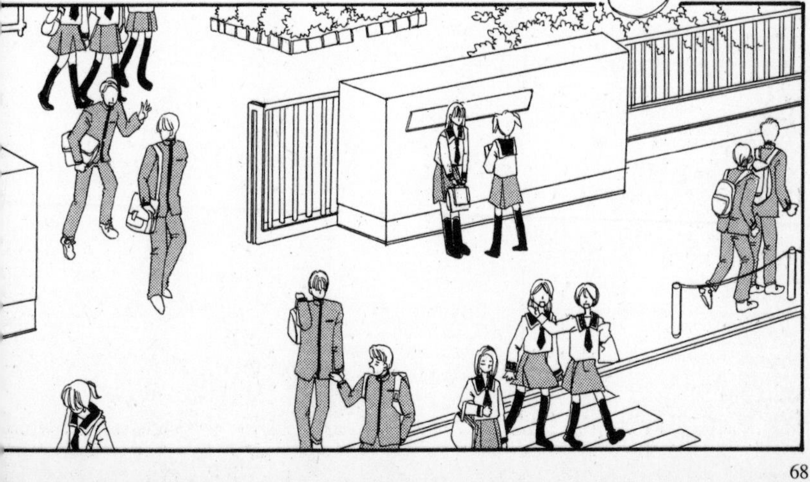

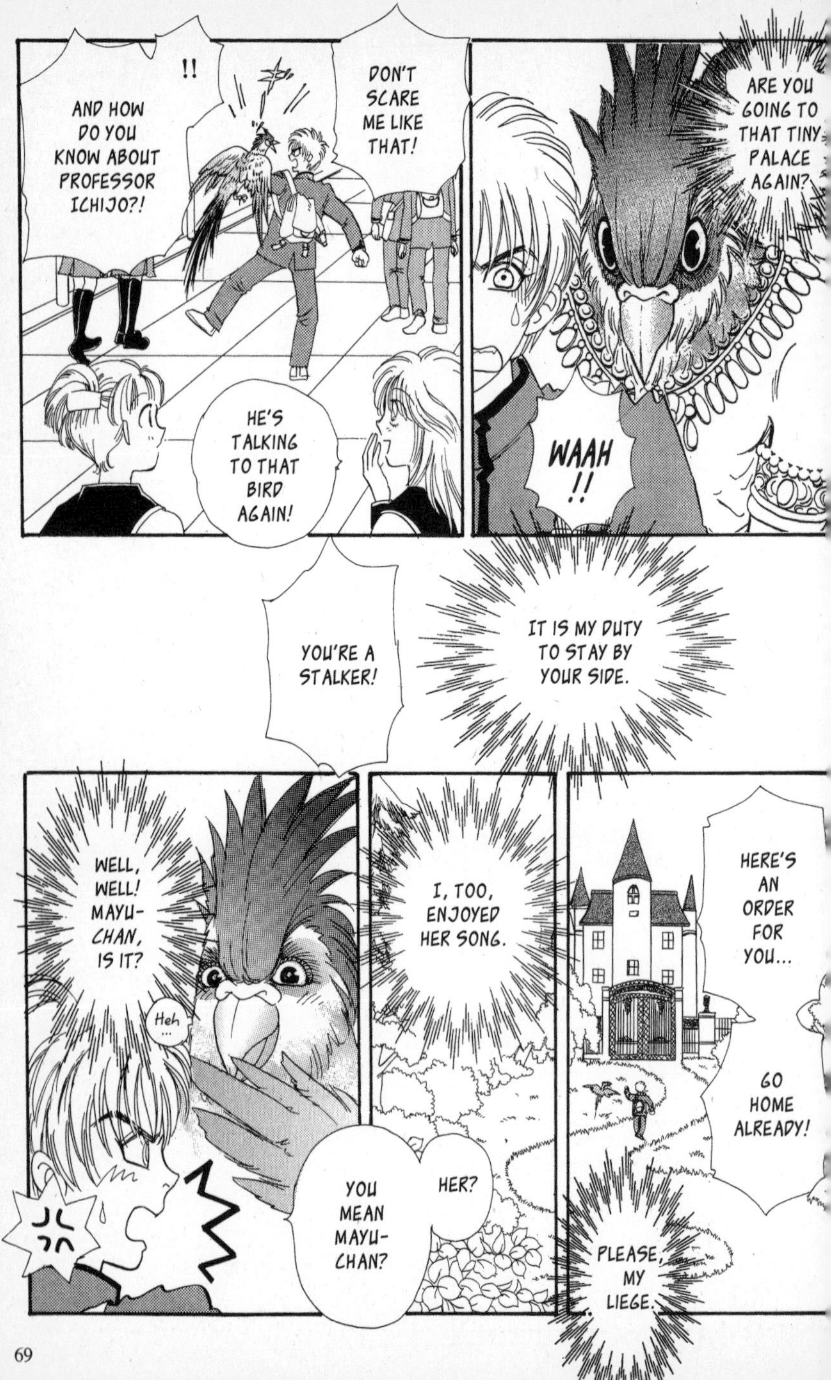
ARE YOU GOING TO THAT TINY PALACE AGAIN?
WAAH !!
DON'T SCARE ME LIKE THAT!
!!
AND HOW DO YOU KNOW ABOUT PROFESSOR ICHIJO?!
HE'S TALKING TO THAT BIRD AGAIN!
IT IS MY DUTY TO STAY BY YOUR SIDE.
YOU'RE A STALKER!
HERE'S AN ORDER FOR YOU...
GO HOME ALREADY!
PLEASE, MY LIEGE.
I, TOO, ENJOYED HER SONG.
HER?
YOU MEAN MAYU-CHAN?
WELL, WELL! MAYU-CHAN, IS IT?
Heh...

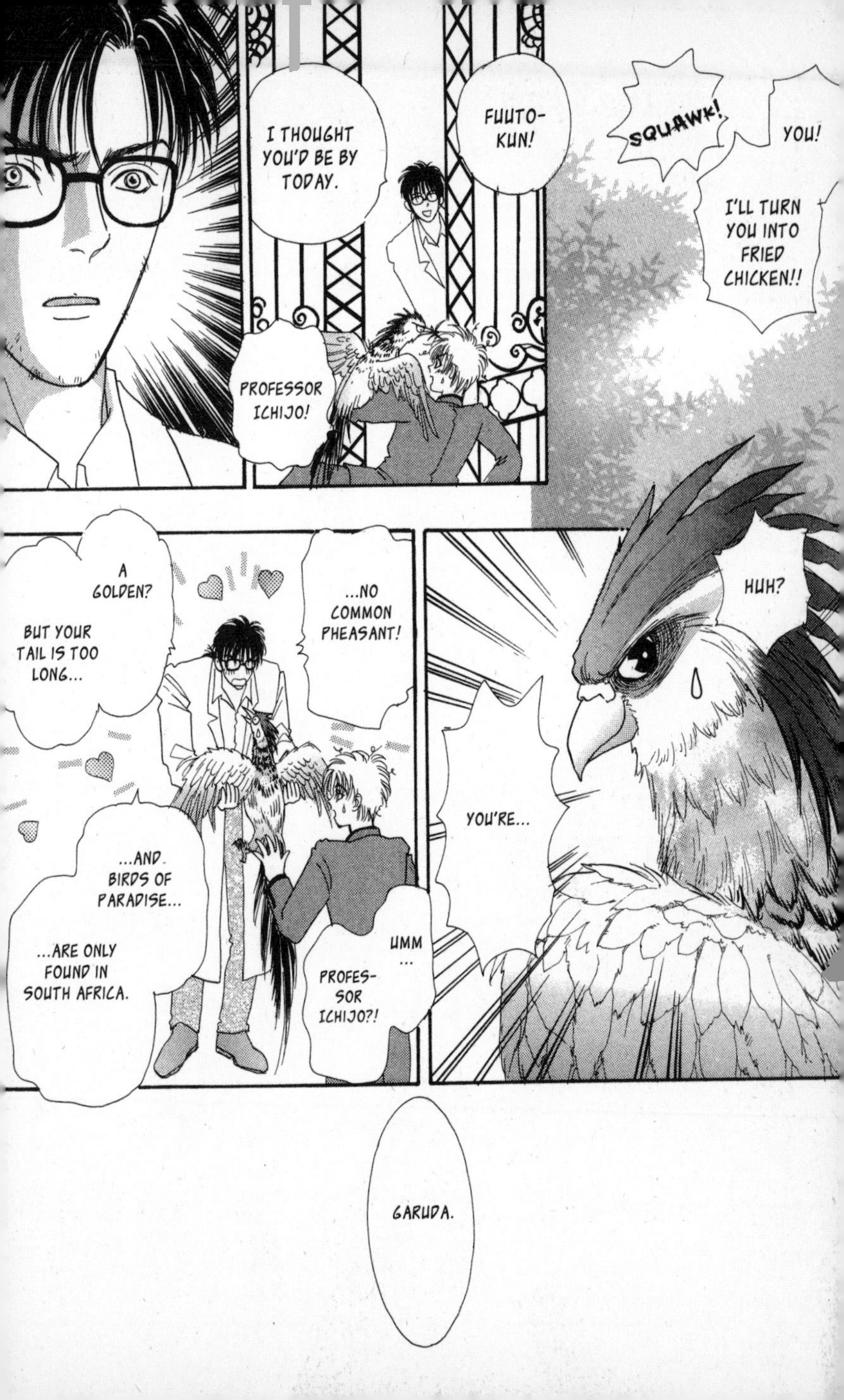
SQUAWK!
YOU!
I'LL TURN YOU INTO FRIED CHICKEN!!
FUUTO-KUN!
I THOUGHT YOU'D BE BY TODAY.
PROFESSOR ICHIJO!
HUH?
YOU'RE...
...NO COMMON PHEASANT!
A GOLDEN?
BUT YOUR TAIL IS TOO LONG...
...AND BIRDS OF PARADISE...
...ARE ONLY FOUND IN SOUTH AFRICA.
UMM ...
PROFES-SOR ICHIJO?!
GARUDA.

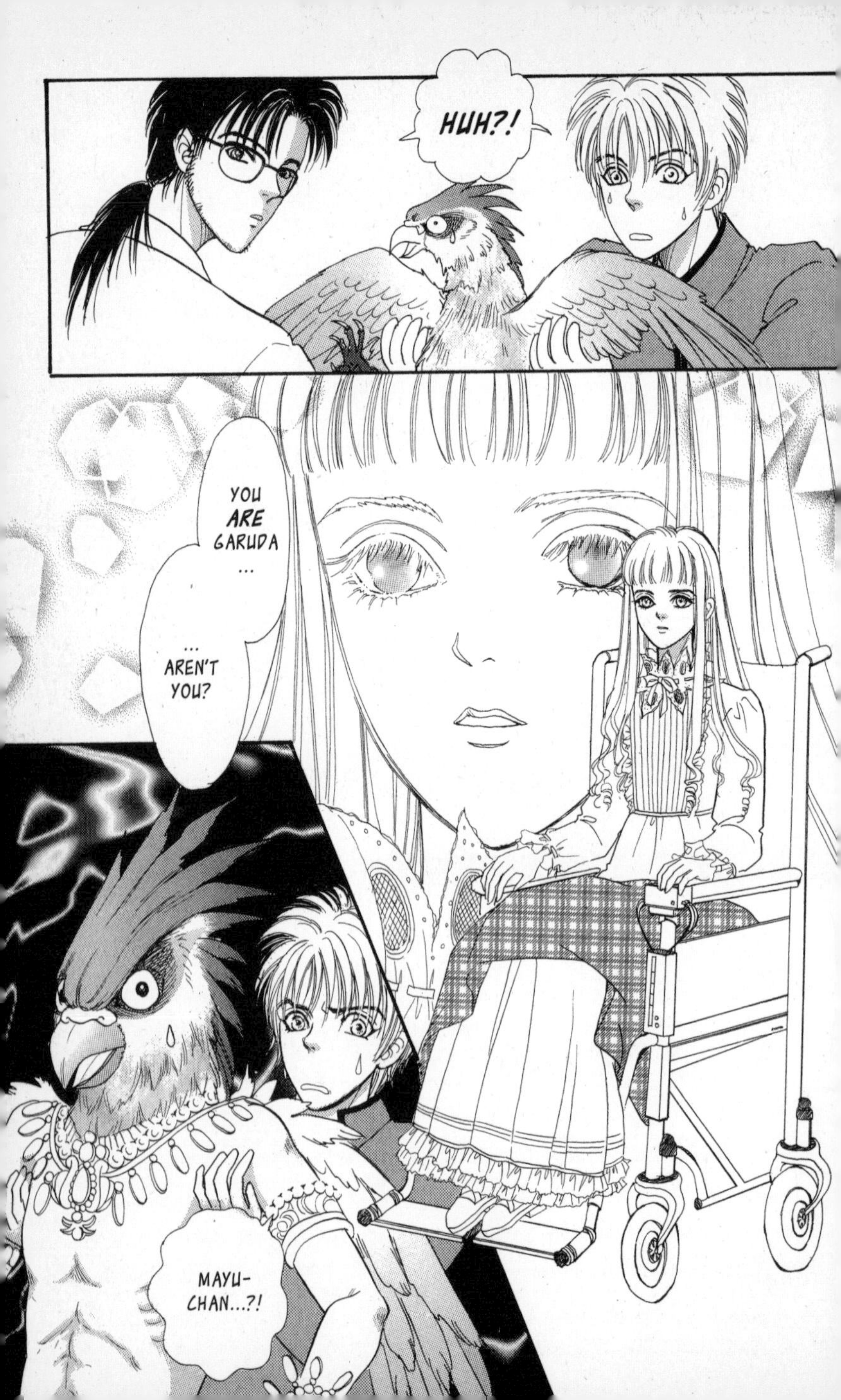
HUH?!
YOU ARE GARUDA ...
... AREN'T YOU?
MAYU-CHAN...?!

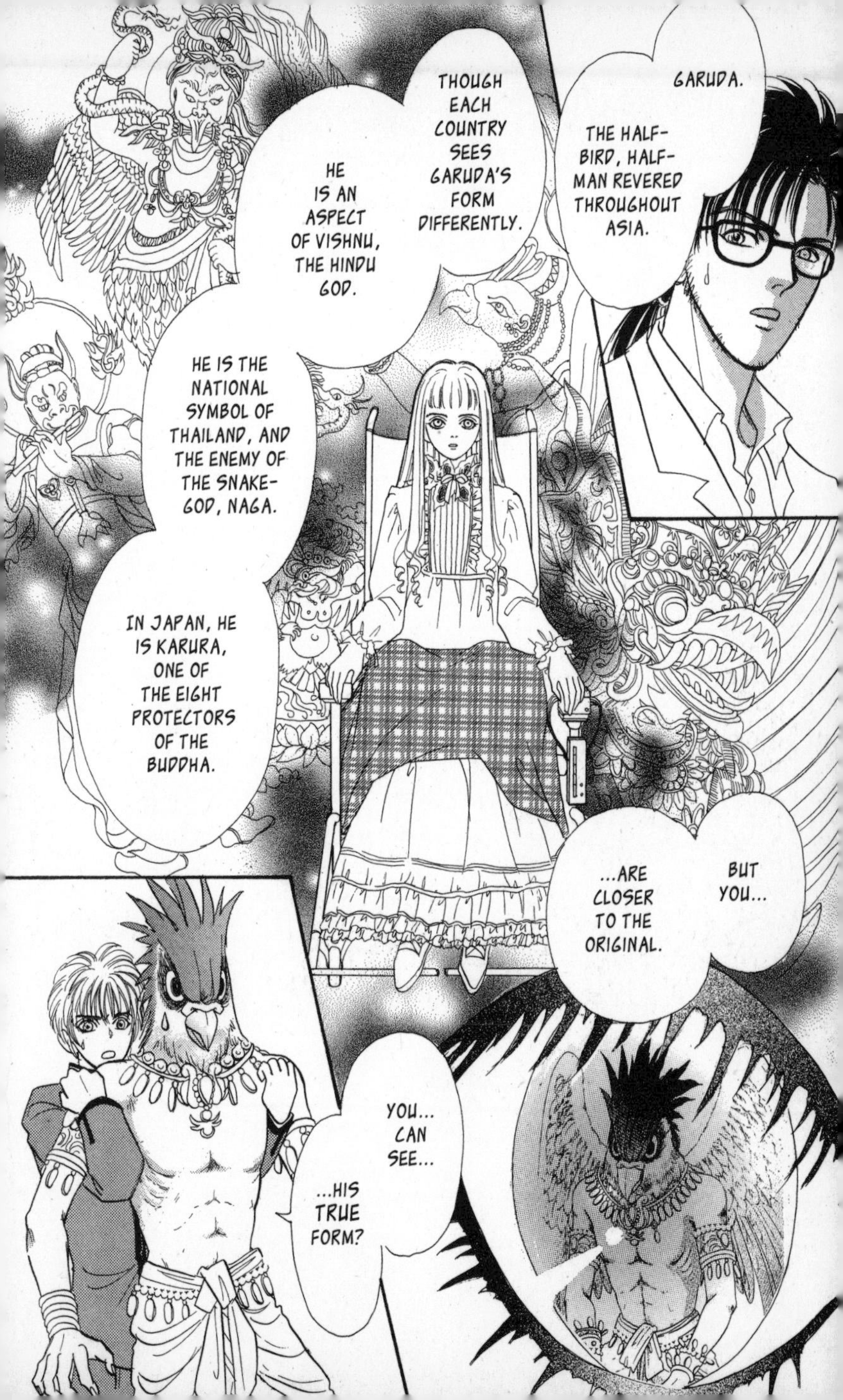
GARUDA.
THE HALF-BIRD, HALF-MAN REVERED THROUGHOUT ASIA.
THOUGH EACH COUNTRY SEES GARUDA'S FORM DIFFERENTLY.
HE IS AN ASPECT OF VISHNU, THE HINDU GOD.
HE IS THE NATIONAL SYMBOL OF THAILAND, AND THE ENEMY OF THE SNAKE-GOD, NAGA.
IN JAPAN, HE IS KARURA, ONE OF THE EIGHT PROTECTORS OF THE BUDDHA.
BUT YOU...
...ARE CLOSER TO THE ORIGINAL.
YOU... CAN SEE...
...HIS TRUE FORM?

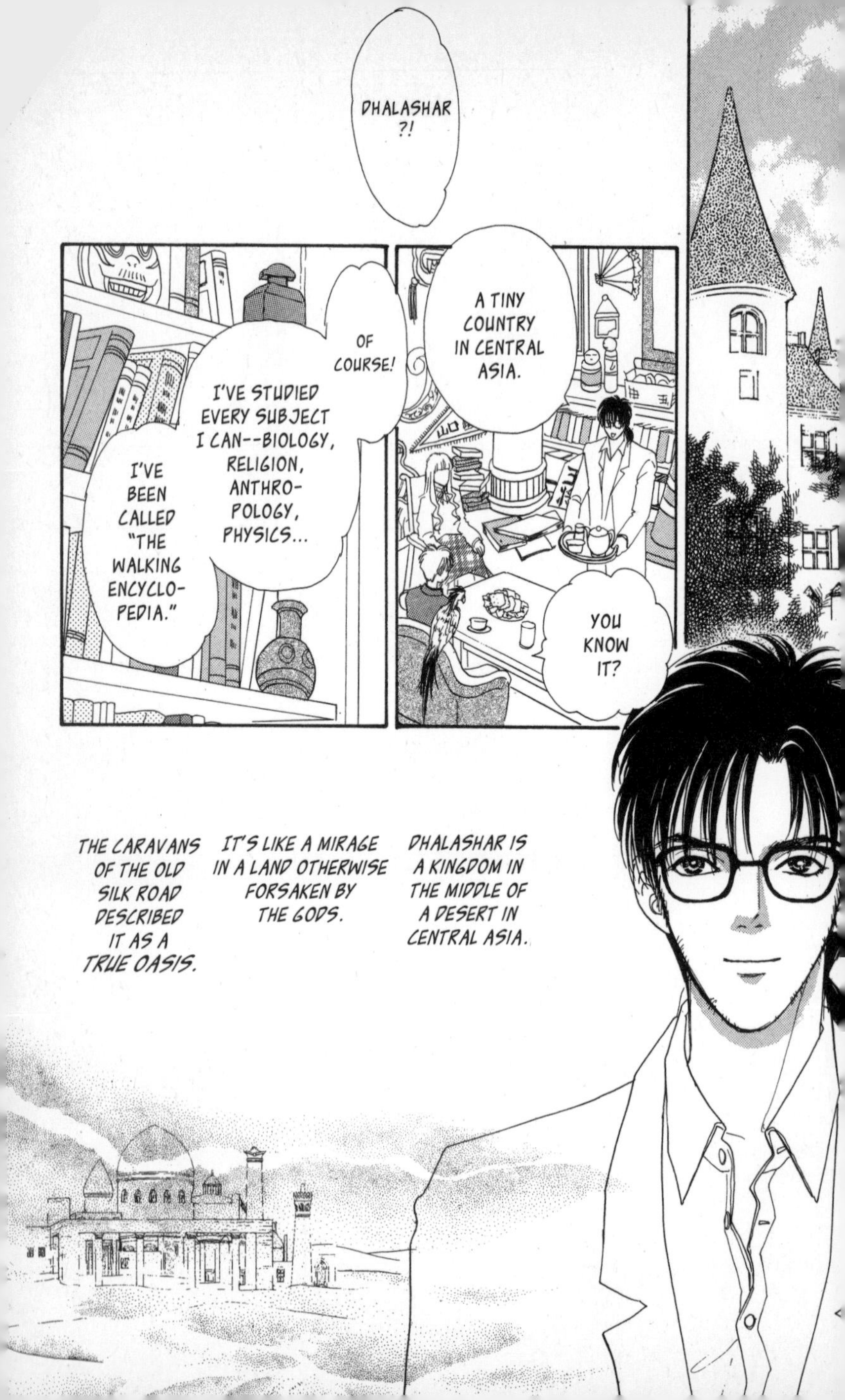
DHALASHAR ?!
A TINY COUNTRY IN CENTRAL ASIA.
YOU KNOW IT?
OF COURSE!
I'VE STUDIED EVERY SUBJECT I CAN--BIOLOGY, RELIGION, ANTHROPOLOGY, PHYSICS...
I'VE BEEN CALLED "THE WALKING ENCYCLOPEDIA."
DHALASHAR IS A KINGDOM IN THE MIDDLE OF A DESERT IN CENTRAL ASIA.
IT'S LIKE A MIRAGE IN A LAND OTHERWISE FORSAKEN BY THE GODS.
THE CARAVANS OF THE OLD SILK ROAD DESCRIBED IT AS A TRUE OASIS.

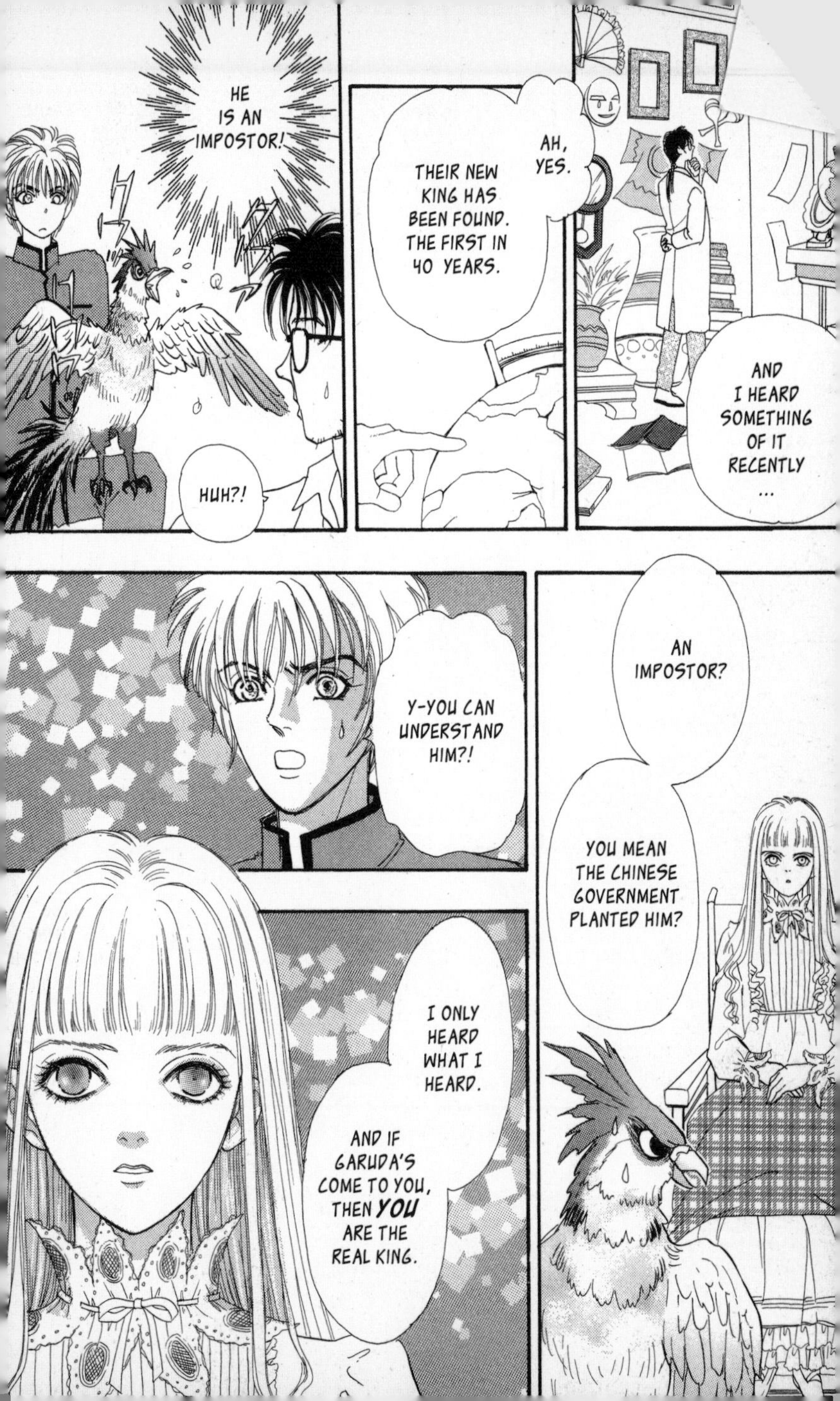
AND I HEARD SOMETHING OF IT RECENTLY ...
AH, YES.
THEIR NEW KING HAS BEEN FOUND. THE FIRST IN 40 YEARS.
HE IS AN IMPOSTOR!
HUH?!
AN IMPOSTOR?
YOU MEAN THE CHINESE GOVERNMENT PLANTED HIM?
Y-YOU CAN UNDERSTAND HIM?!
I ONLY HEARD WHAT I HEARD.
AND IF GARUDA'S COME TO YOU, THEN ***YOU*** ARE THE REAL KING.

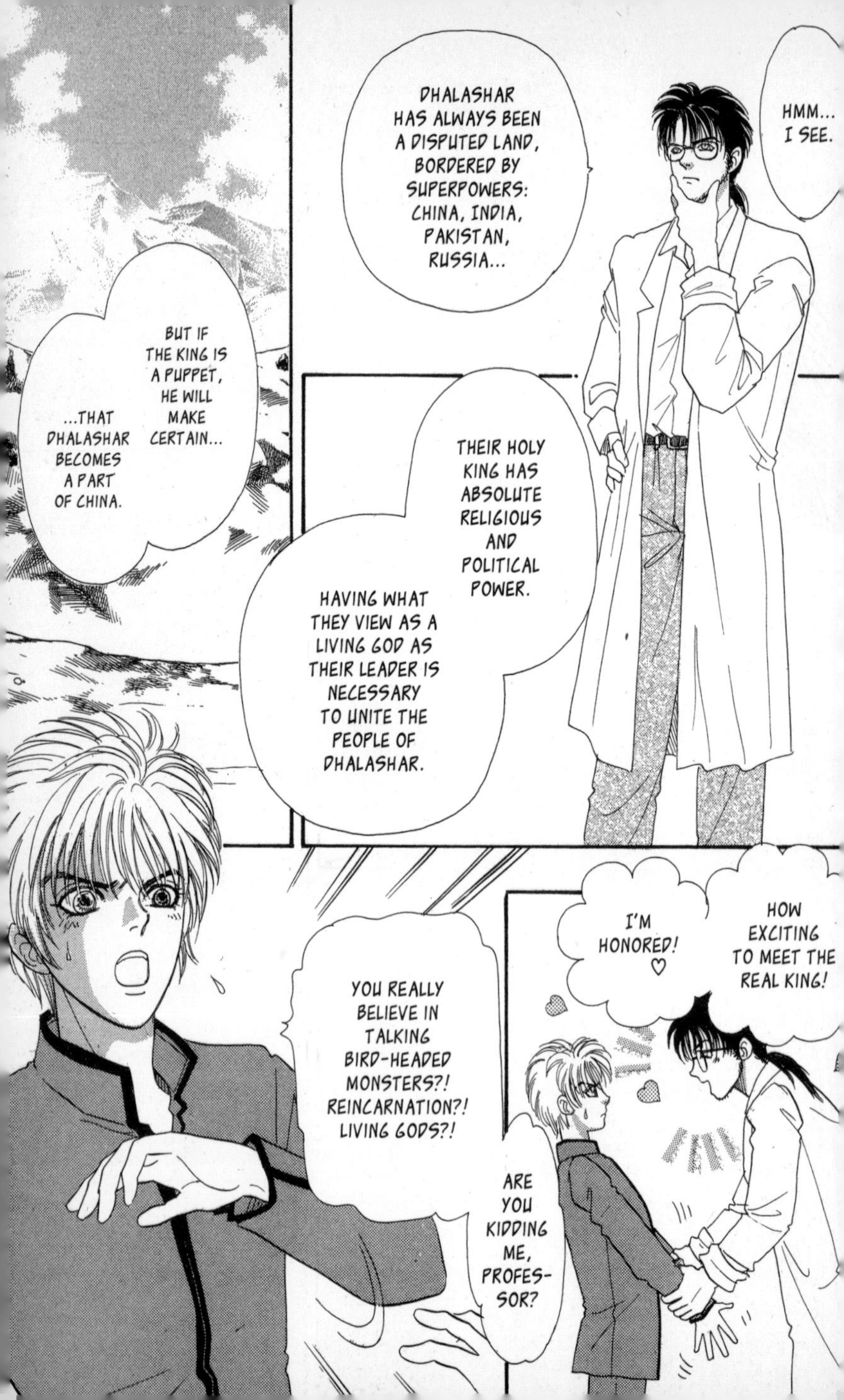
HMM... I SEE.
DHALASHAR HAS ALWAYS BEEN A DISPUTED LAND, BORDERED BY SUPERPOWERS: CHINA, INDIA, PAKISTAN, RUSSIA...
THEIR HOLY KING HAS ABSOLUTE RELIGIOUS AND POLITICAL POWER.
HAVING WHAT THEY VIEW AS A LIVING GOD AS THEIR LEADER IS NECESSARY TO UNITE THE PEOPLE OF DHALASHAR.
BUT IF THE KING IS A PUPPET, HE WILL MAKE CERTAIN...
...THAT DHALASHAR BECOMES A PART OF CHINA.
HOW EXCITING TO MEET THE REAL KING!
I'M HONORED! ♡
ARE YOU KIDDING ME, PROFES-SOR?
YOU REALLY BELIEVE IN TALKING BIRD-HEADED MONSTERS?! REINCARNATION?! LIVING GODS?!

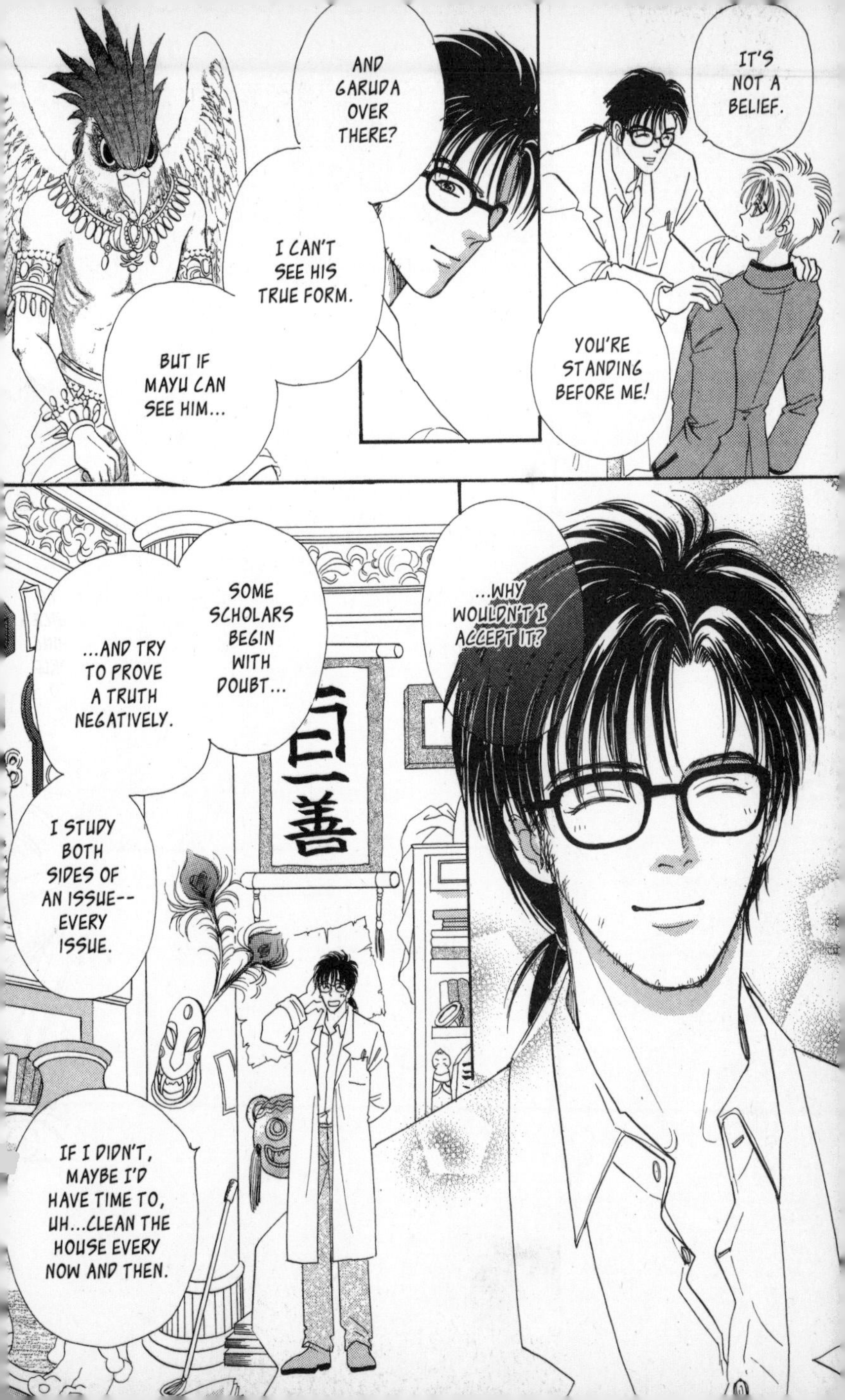
IT'S NOT A BELIEF.
YOU'RE STANDING BEFORE ME!
AND GARUDA OVER THERE?
I CAN'T SEE HIS TRUE FORM.
BUT IF MAYU CAN SEE HIM...
...WHY WOULDN'T I ACCEPT IT?
SOME SCHOLARS BEGIN WITH DOUBT...
...AND TRY TO PROVE A TRUTH NEGATIVELY.
I STUDY BOTH SIDES OF AN ISSUE--EVERY ISSUE.
IF I DIDN'T, MAYBE I'D HAVE TIME TO, UH...CLEAN THE HOUSE EVERY NOW AND THEN.

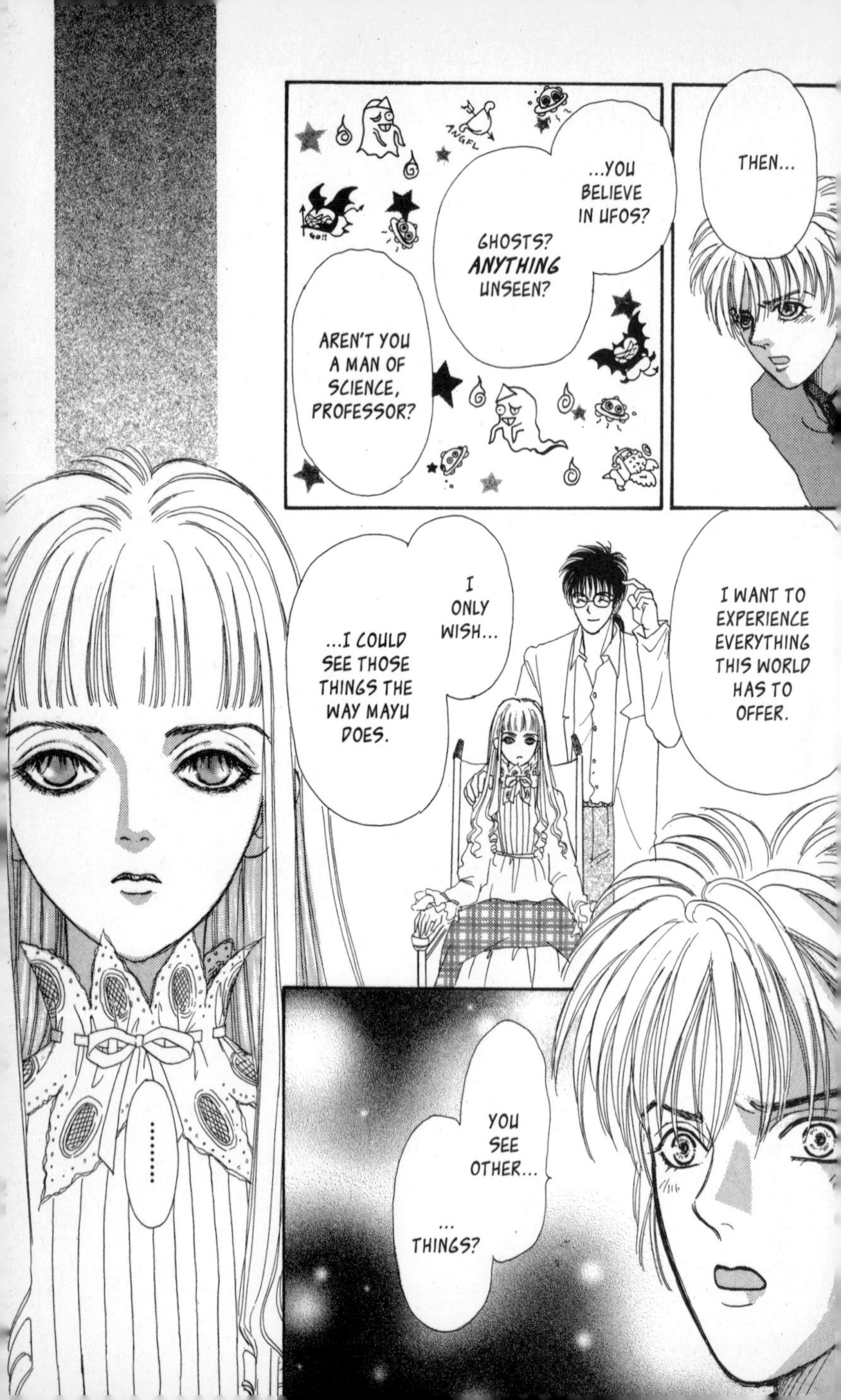
THEN...
...YOU BELIEVE IN UFOS?
GHOSTS? **ANYTHING** UNSEEN?
AREN'T YOU A MAN OF SCIENCE, PROFESSOR?
I WANT TO EXPERIENCE EVERYTHING THIS WORLD HAS TO OFFER.
I ONLY WISH...
...I COULD SEE THOSE THINGS THE WAY MAYU DOES.
YOU SEE OTHER...
...THINGS?
....

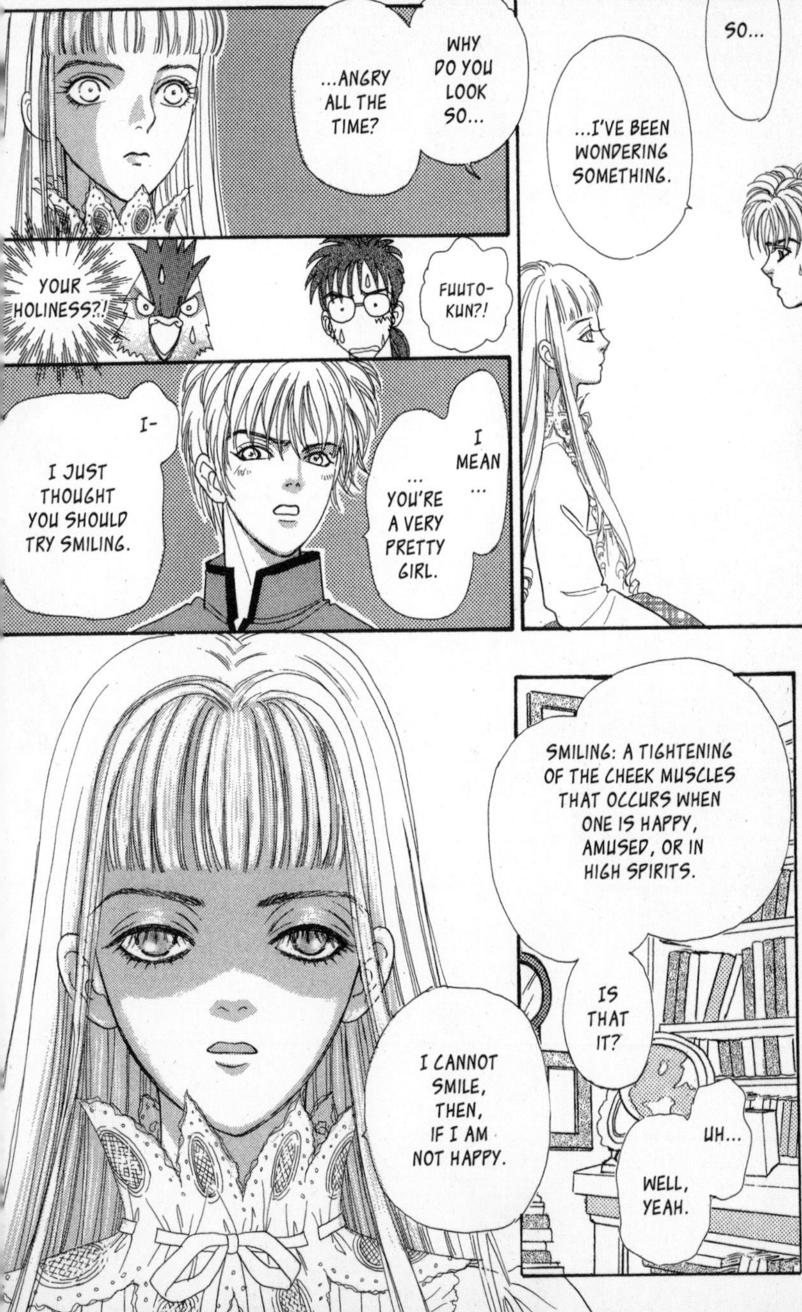
SO...
...I'VE BEEN WONDERING SOMETHING.
WHY DO YOU LOOK SO...
...ANGRY ALL THE TIME?
FUUTO-KUN?!
YOUR HOLINESS?!
I MEAN ...
... YOU'RE A VERY PRETTY GIRL.
I-
I JUST THOUGHT YOU SHOULD TRY SMILING.
SMILING: A TIGHTENING OF THE CHEEK MUSCLES THAT OCCURS WHEN ONE IS HAPPY, AMUSED, OR IN HIGH SPIRITS.
IS THAT IT?
UH...
WELL, YEAH.
I CANNOT SMILE, THEN, IF I AM NOT HAPPY.

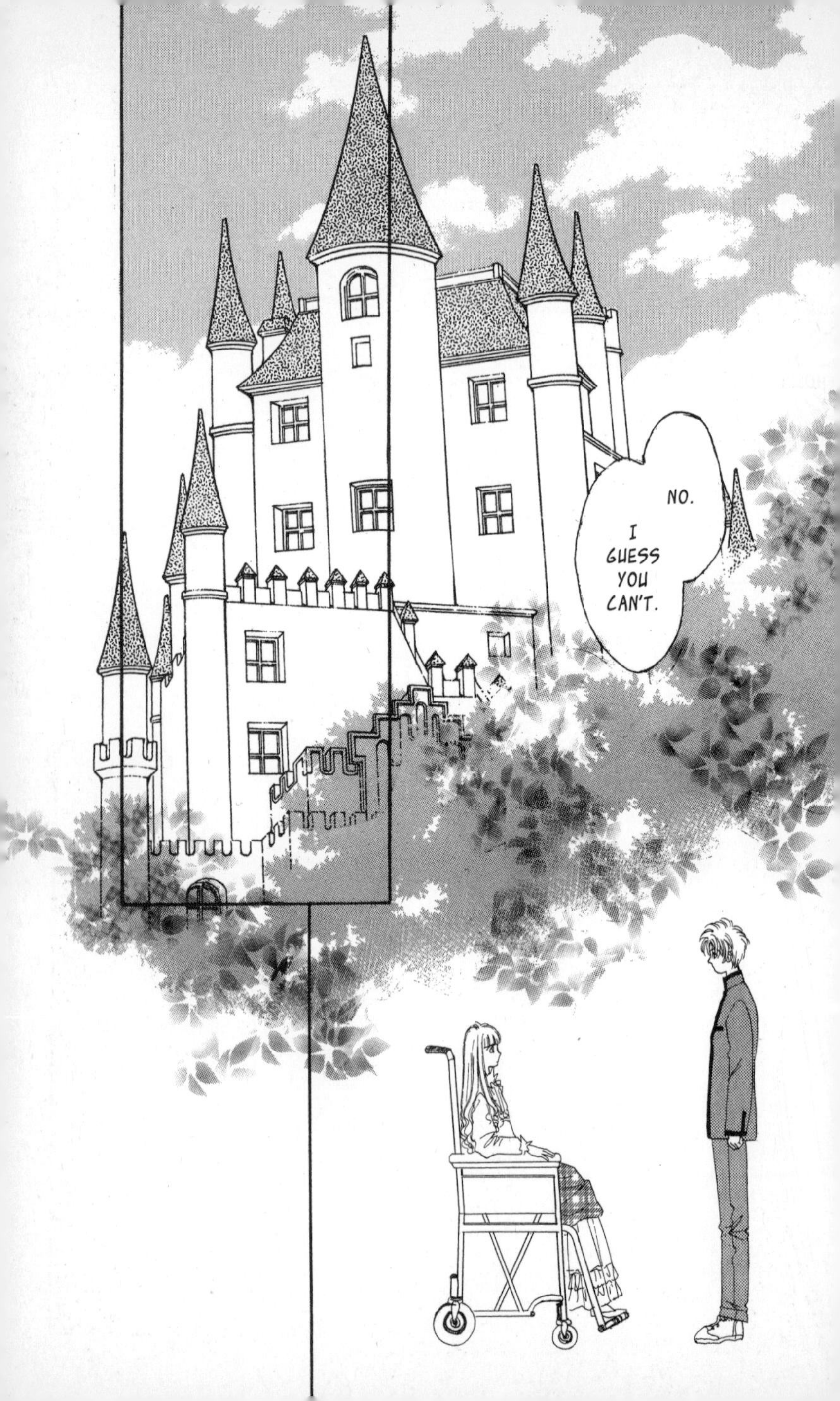
NO.
I GUESS YOU CAN'T.

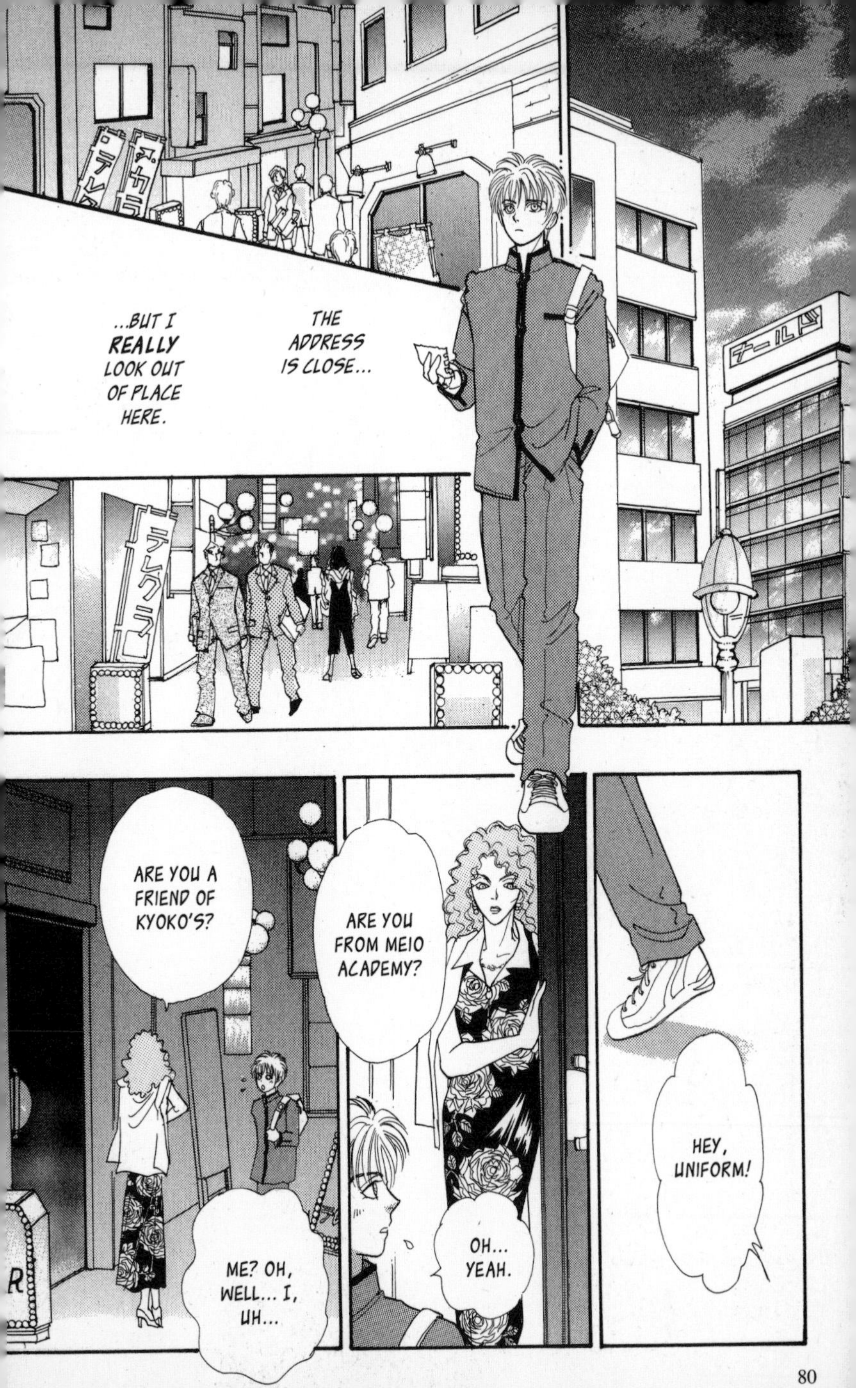
THE ADDRESS IS CLOSE...
...BUT I **REALLY** LOOK OUT OF PLACE HERE.
テレクラ
HEY, UNIFORM!
ARE YOU FROM MEIO ACADEMY?
OH... YEAH.
ARE YOU A FRIEND OF KYOKO'S?
ME? OH, WELL... I, UH...

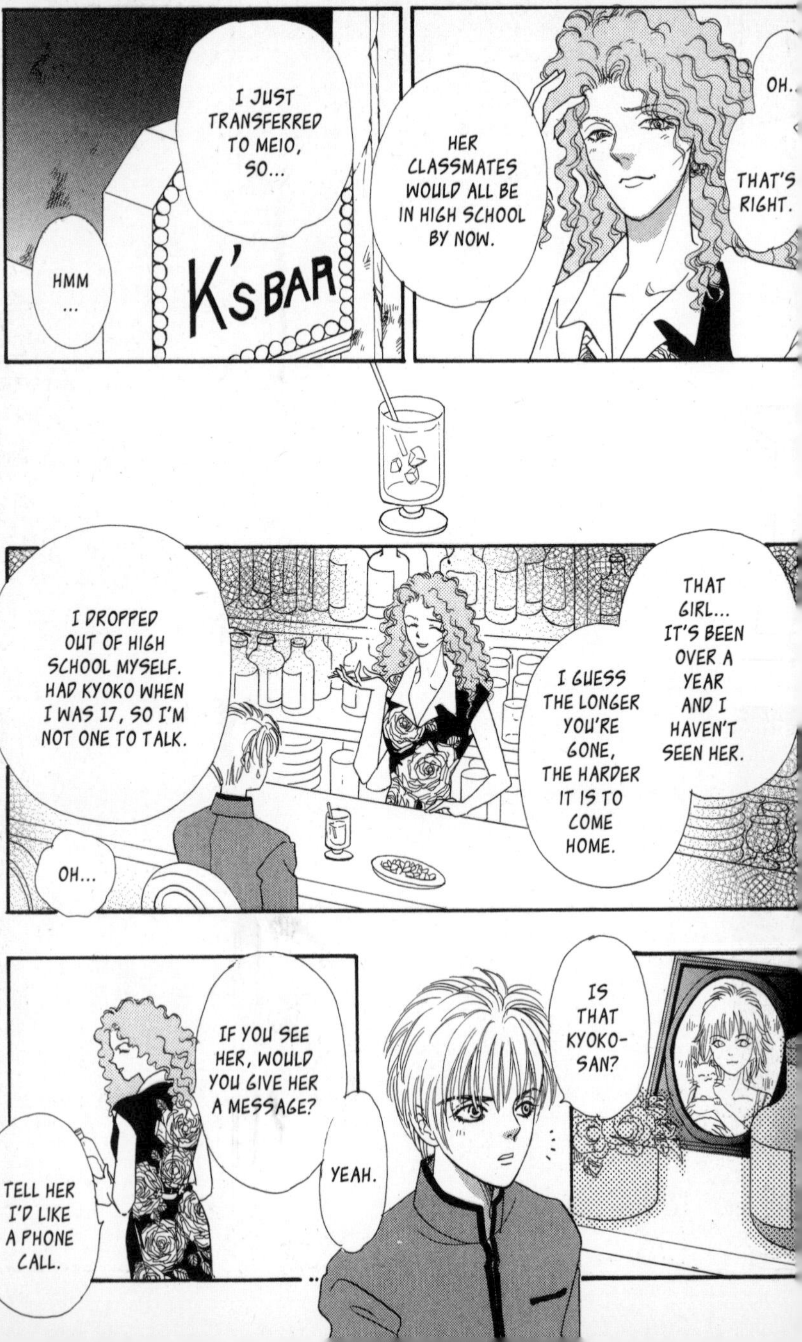
OH...
THAT'S RIGHT.
HER CLASSMATES WOULD ALL BE IN HIGH SCHOOL BY NOW.
I JUST TRANSFERRED TO MEIO, SO...
K'S BAR
HMM...
THAT GIRL... IT'S BEEN OVER A YEAR AND I HAVEN'T SEEN HER.
I GUESS THE LONGER YOU'RE GONE, THE HARDER IT IS TO COME HOME.
I DROPPED OUT OF HIGH SCHOOL MYSELF. HAD KYOKO WHEN I WAS 17, SO I'M NOT ONE TO TALK.
OH...
IS THAT KYOKO-SAN?
IF YOU SEE HER, WOULD YOU GIVE HER A MESSAGE?
YEAH.
TELL HER I'D LIKE A PHONE CALL.

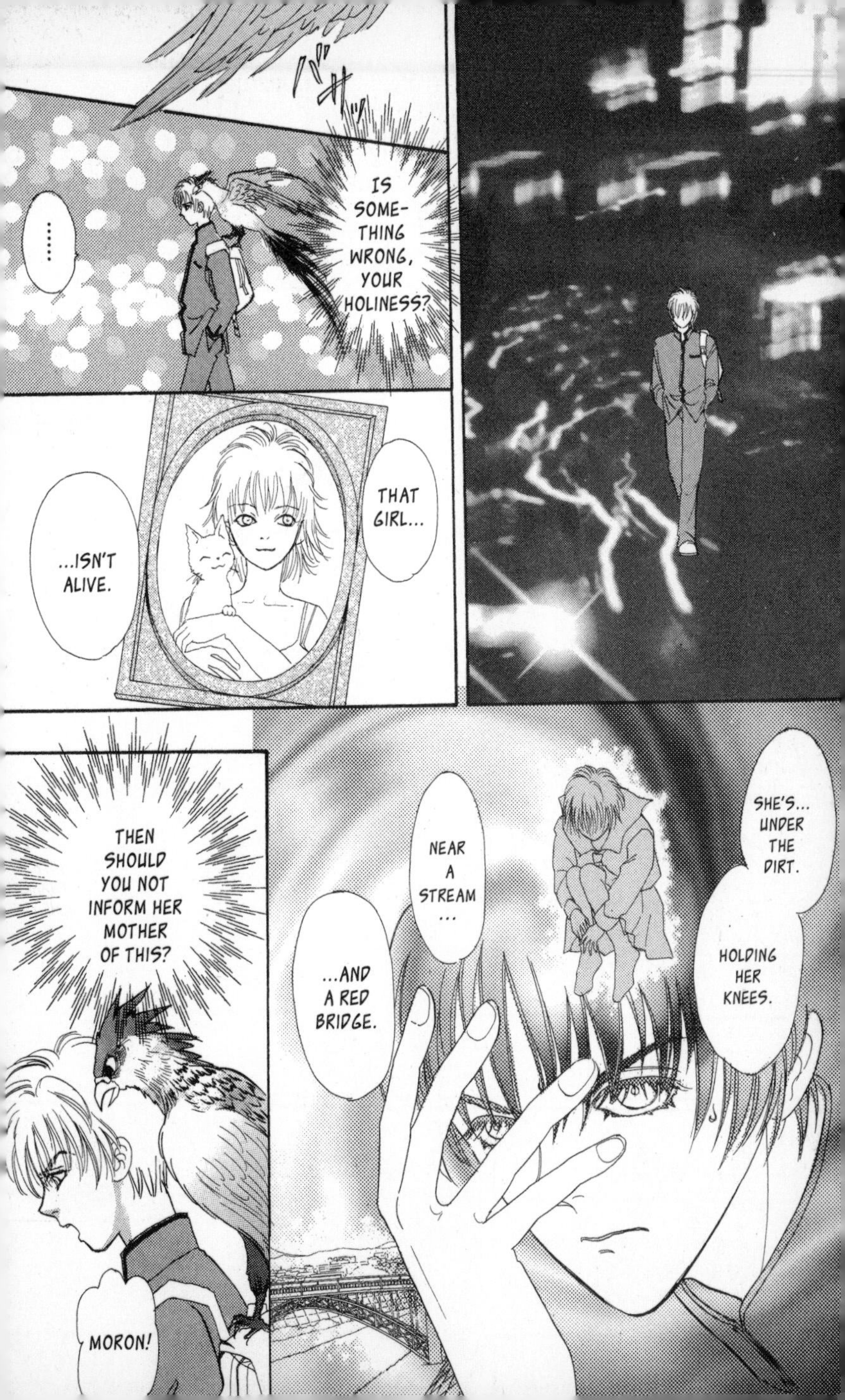
IS SOME-THING WRONG, YOUR HOLINESS?
......
THAT GIRL...
...ISN'T ALIVE.
SHE'S... UNDER THE DIRT.
HOLDING HER KNEES.
NEAR A STREAM...
...AND A RED BRIDGE.
THEN SHOULD YOU NOT INFORM HER MOTHER OF THIS?
MORON!

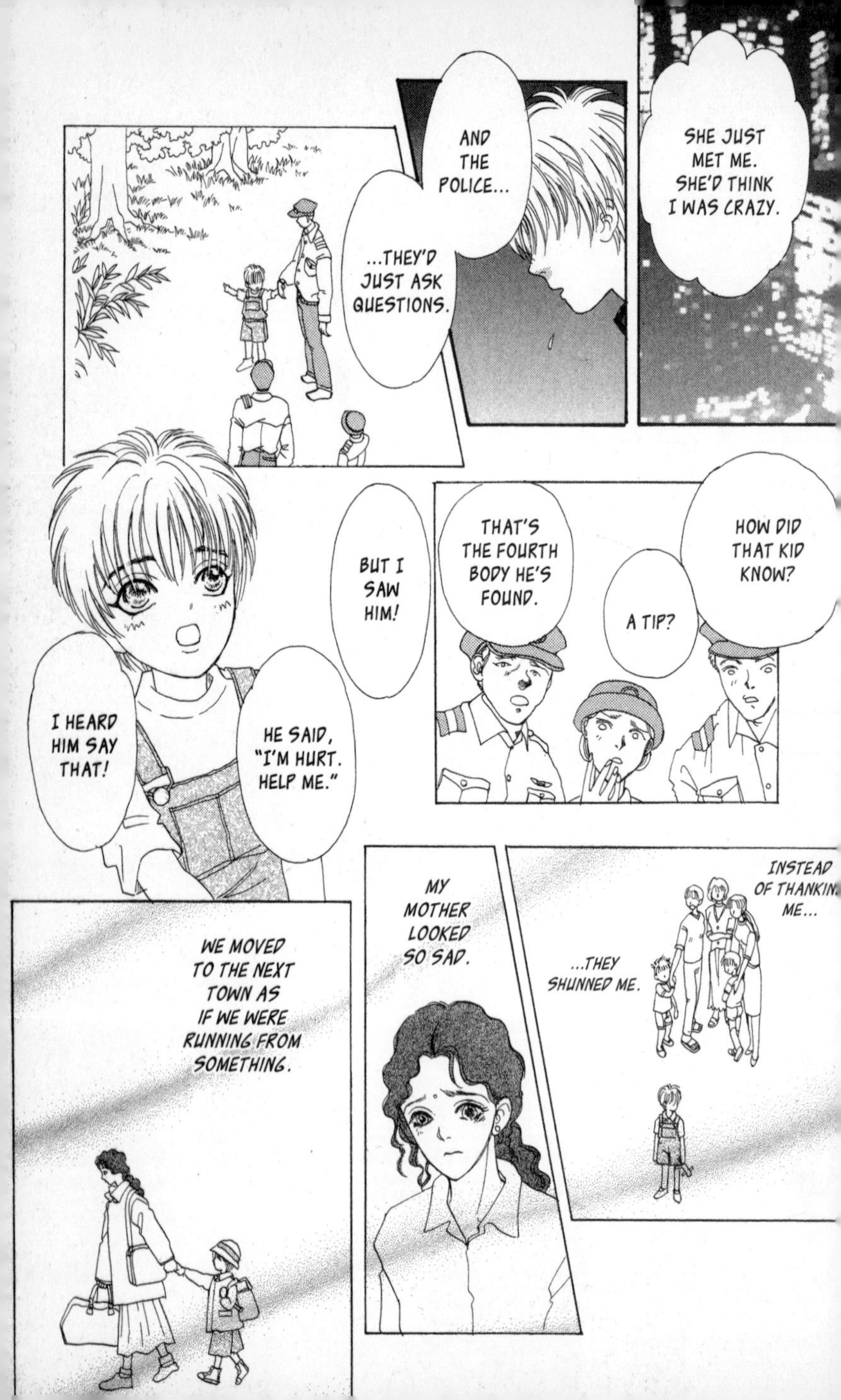
SHE JUST MET ME. SHE'D THINK I WAS CRAZY.
AND THE POLICE...
...THEY'D JUST ASK QUESTIONS.
HOW DID THAT KID KNOW?
A TIP?
THAT'S THE FOURTH BODY HE'S FOUND.
BUT I SAW HIM!
HE SAID, "I'M HURT. HELP ME."
I HEARD HIM SAY THAT!
INSTEAD OF THANKIN ME...
...THEY SHUNNED ME.
MY MOTHER LOOKED SO SAD.
WE MOVED TO THE NEXT TOWN AS IF WE WERE RUNNING FROM SOMETHING.

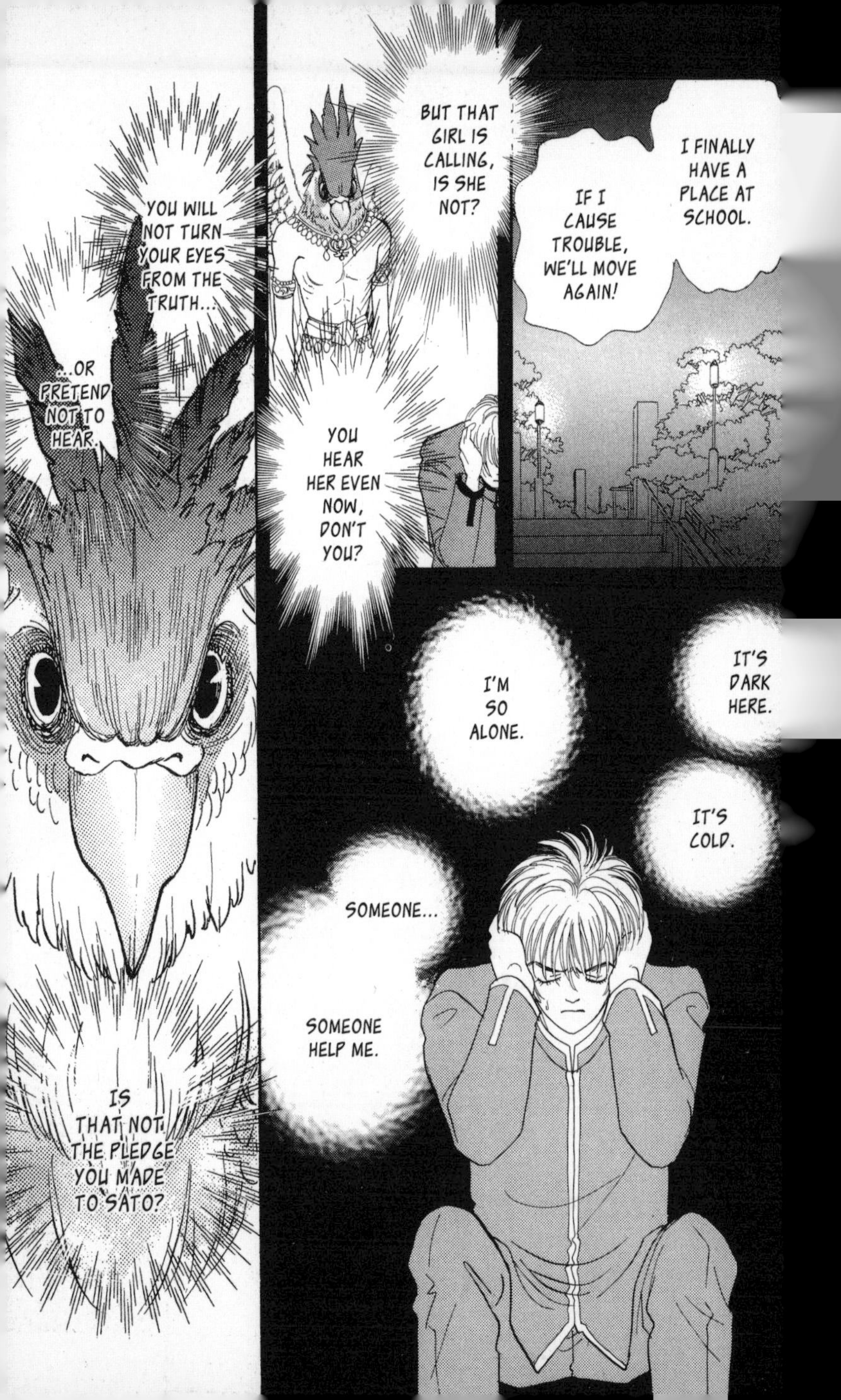
I FINALLY HAVE A PLACE AT SCHOOL.
IF I CAUSE TROUBLE, WE'LL MOVE AGAIN!
BUT THAT GIRL IS CALLING, IS SHE NOT?
YOU HEAR HER EVEN NOW, DON'T YOU?
IT'S DARK HERE.
I'M SO ALONE.
IT'S COLD.
SOMEONE...
SOMEONE HELP ME.
YOU WILL NOT TURN YOUR EYES FROM THE TRUTH...
...OR PRETEND NOT TO HEAR.
IS THAT NOT THE PLEDGE YOU MADE TO SATO?

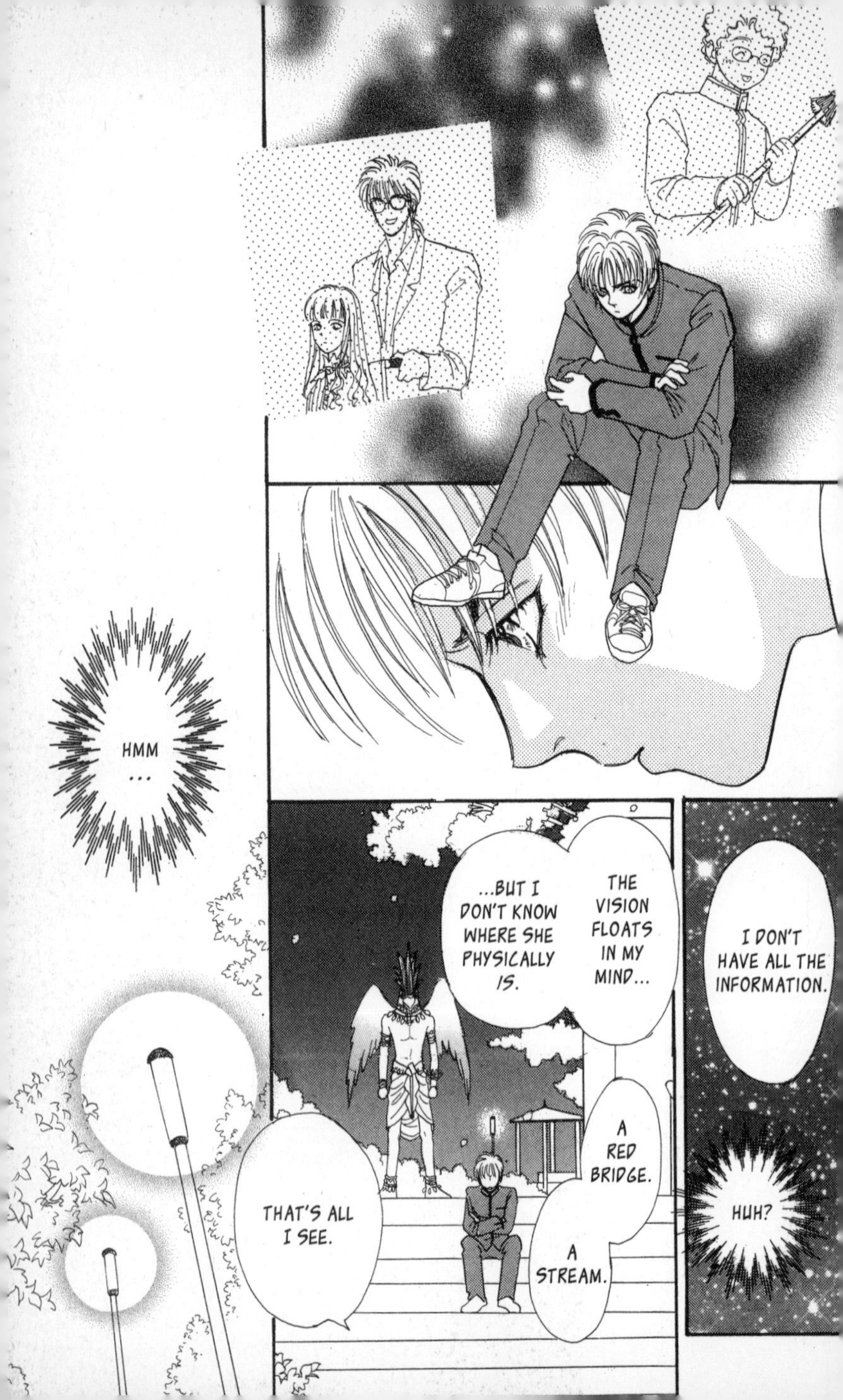
I DON'T HAVE ALL THE INFORMATION.
HUH?
THE VISION FLOATS IN MY MIND...
...BUT I DON'T KNOW WHERE SHE PHYSICALLY IS.
A RED BRIDGE.
A STREAM.
THAT'S ALL I SEE.
HMM ...

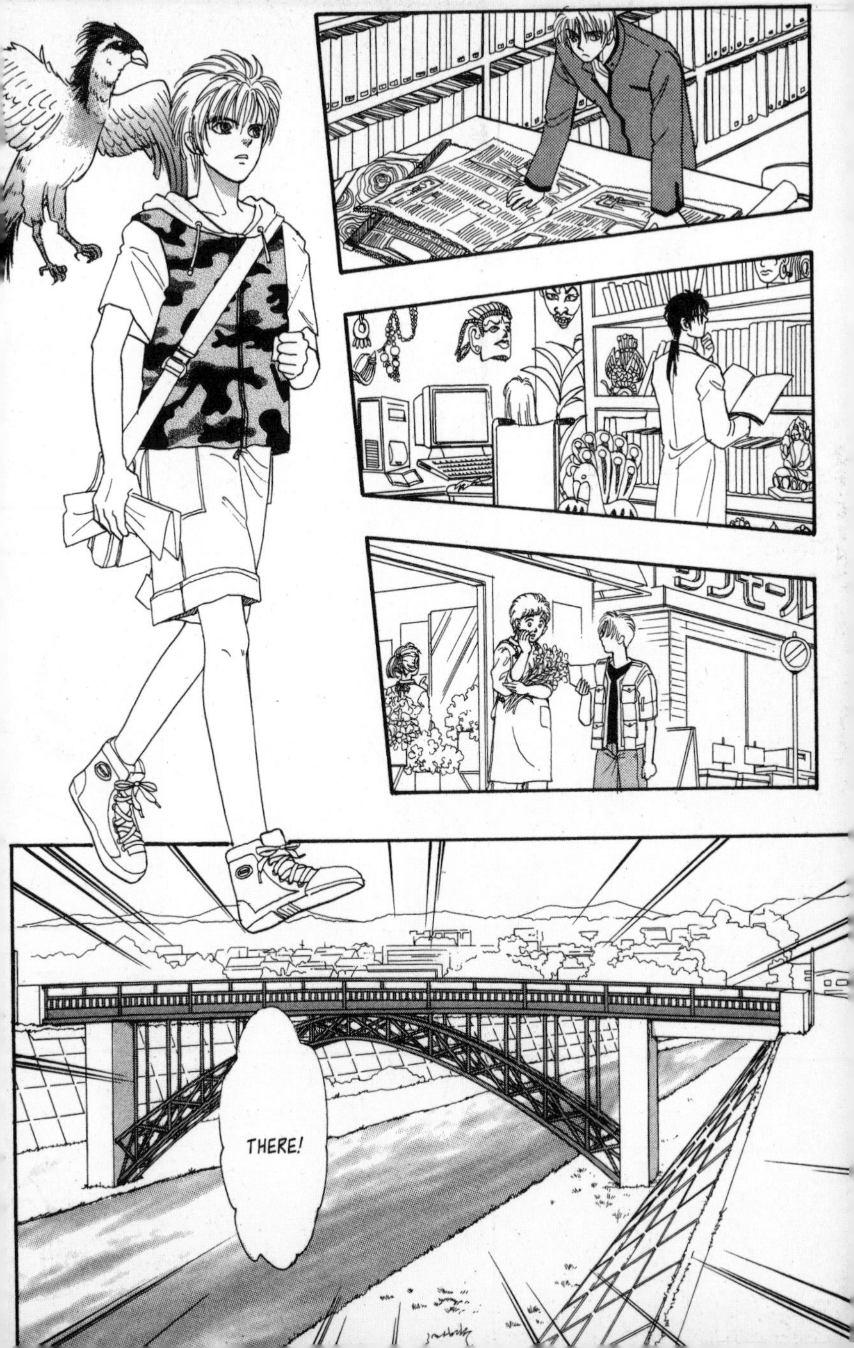
THERE!

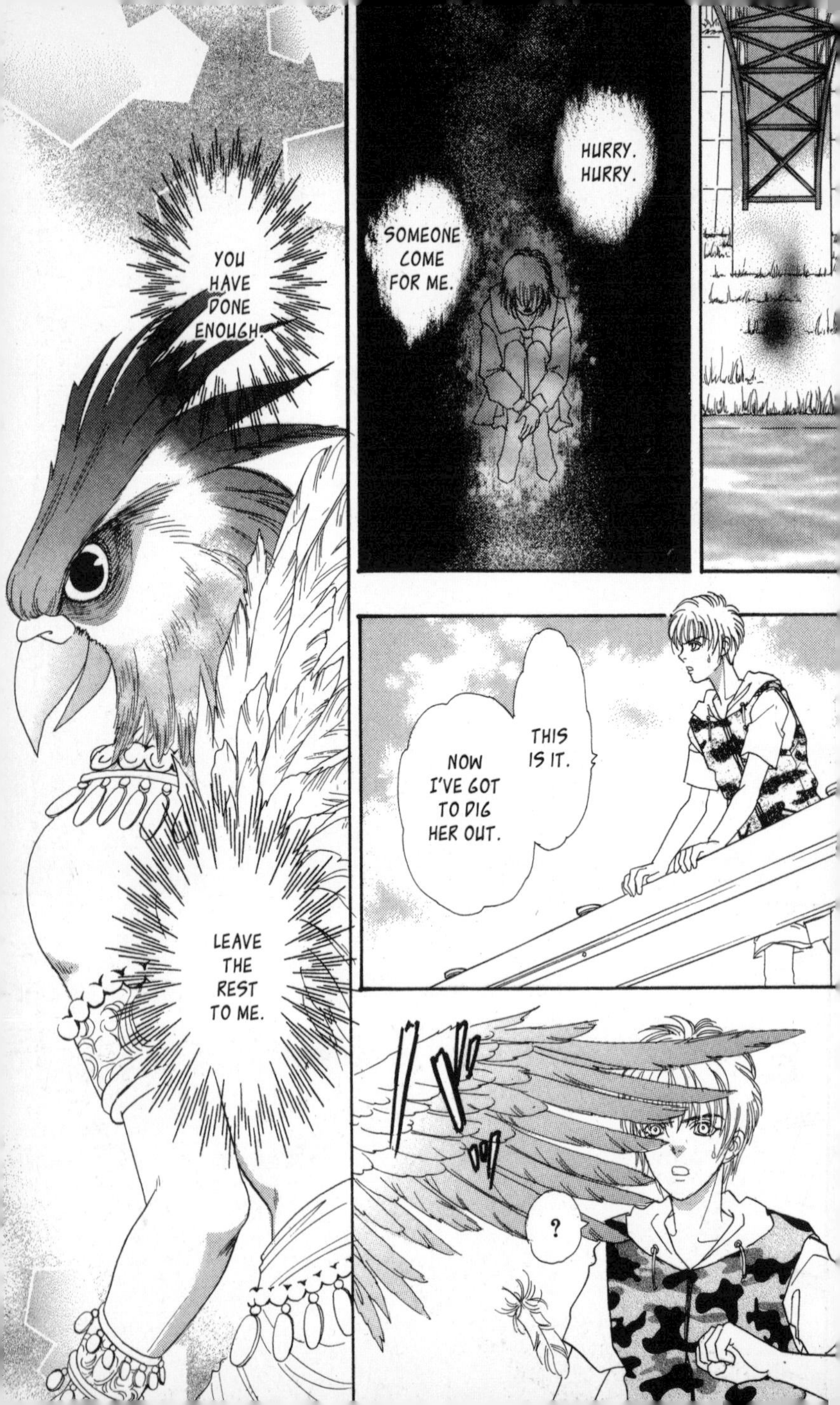
HURRY. HURRY.
SOMEONE COME FOR ME.
THIS IS IT.
NOW I'VE GOT TO DIG HER OUT.
?
YOU HAVE DONE ENOUGH.
LEAVE THE REST TO ME.

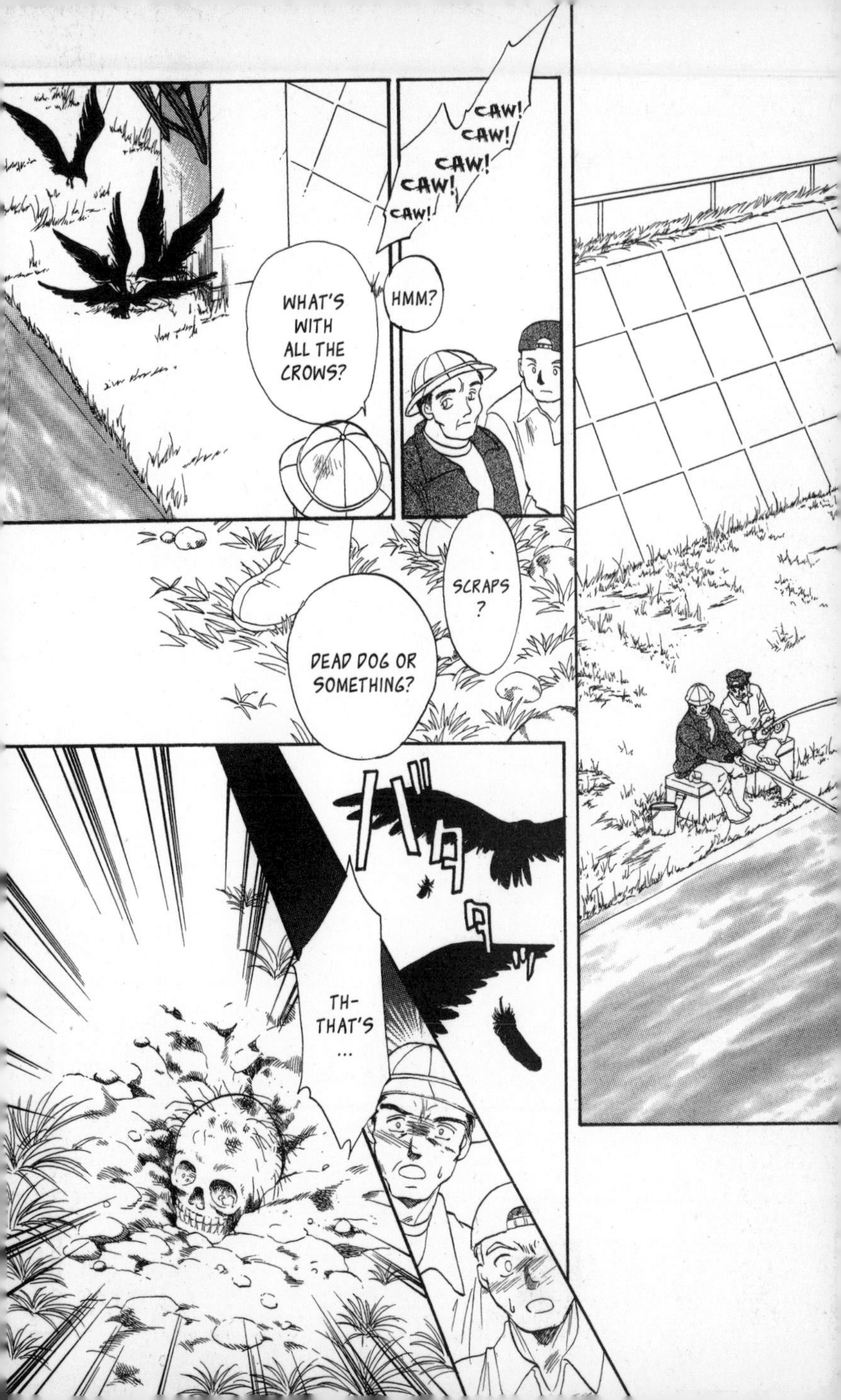
CAW! CAW! CAW! CAW! CAW!
HMM?
WHAT'S WITH ALL THE CROWS?
SCRAPS?
DEAD DOG OR SOMETHING?
バタタッ
TH- THAT'S ...

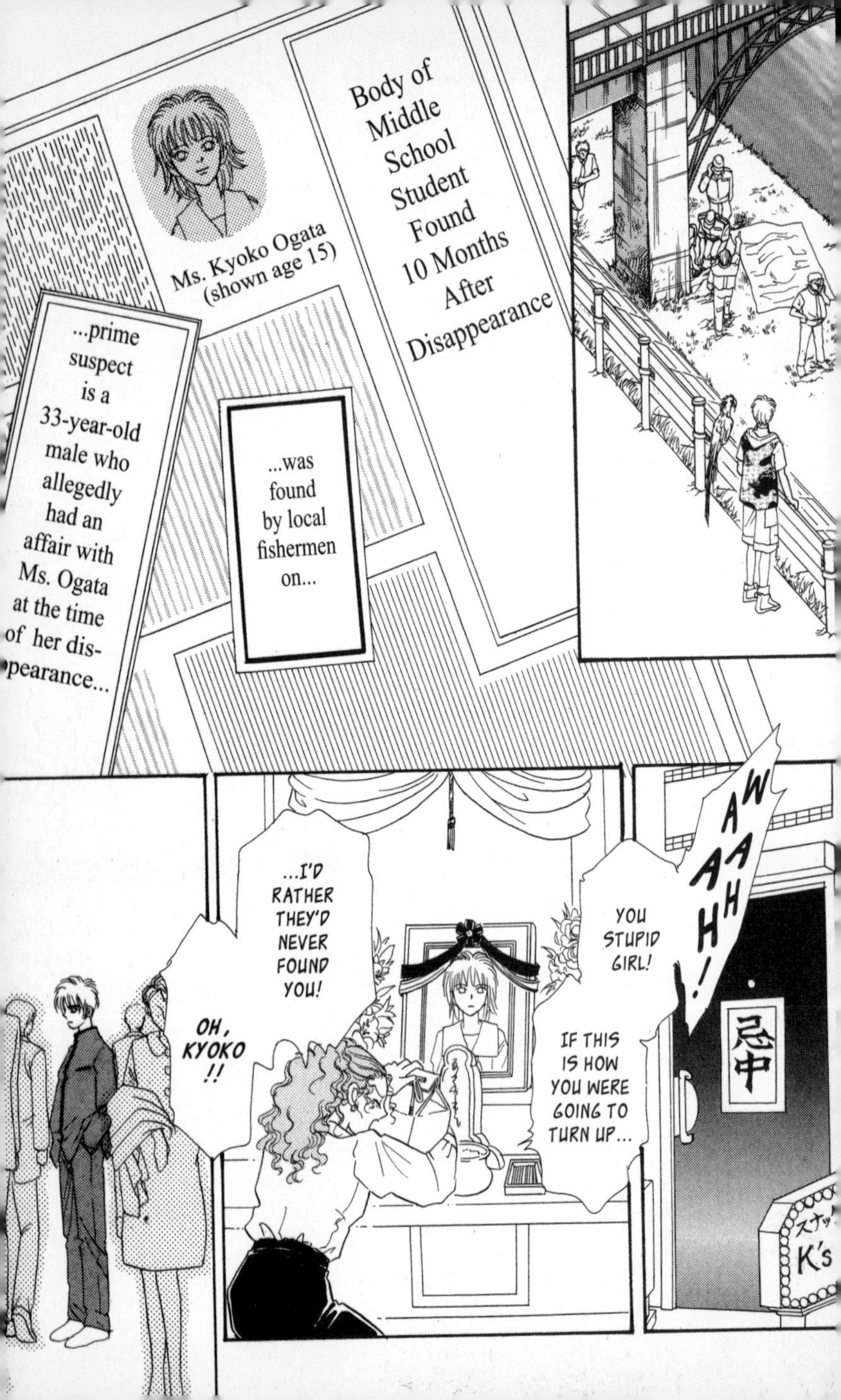
Body of Middle School Student Found 10 Months After Disappearance
Ms. Kyoko Ogata (shown age 15)
...was found by local fishermen on...
...prime suspect is a 33-year-old male who allegedly had an affair with Ms. Ogata at the time of her disappearance...
WAAAHH!
忌中
K's
YOU STUPID GIRL!
IF THIS IS HOW YOU WERE GOING TO TURN UP...
...I'D RATHER THEY'D NEVER FOUND YOU!
OH, KYOKO!!

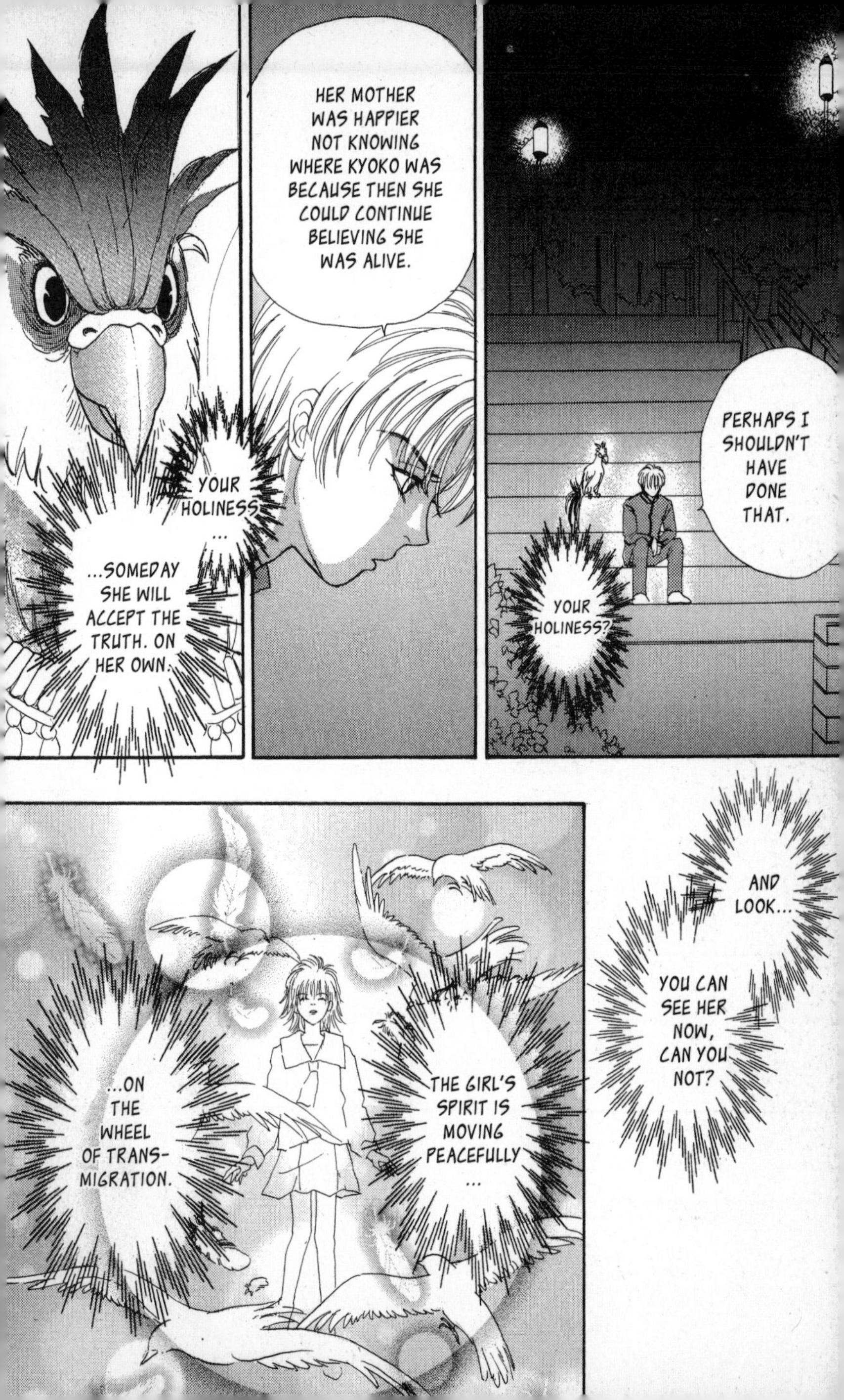
PERHAPS I SHOULDN'T HAVE DONE THAT.
YOUR HOLINESS?
HER MOTHER WAS HAPPIER NOT KNOWING WHERE KYOKO WAS BECAUSE THEN SHE COULD CONTINUE BELIEVING SHE WAS ALIVE.
YOUR HOLINESS...
...SOMEDAY SHE WILL ACCEPT THE TRUTH. ON HER OWN.
AND LOOK...
YOU CAN SEE HER NOW, CAN YOU NOT?
THE GIRL'S SPIRIT IS MOVING PEACEFULLY...
...ON THE WHEEL OF TRANS-MIGRATION.

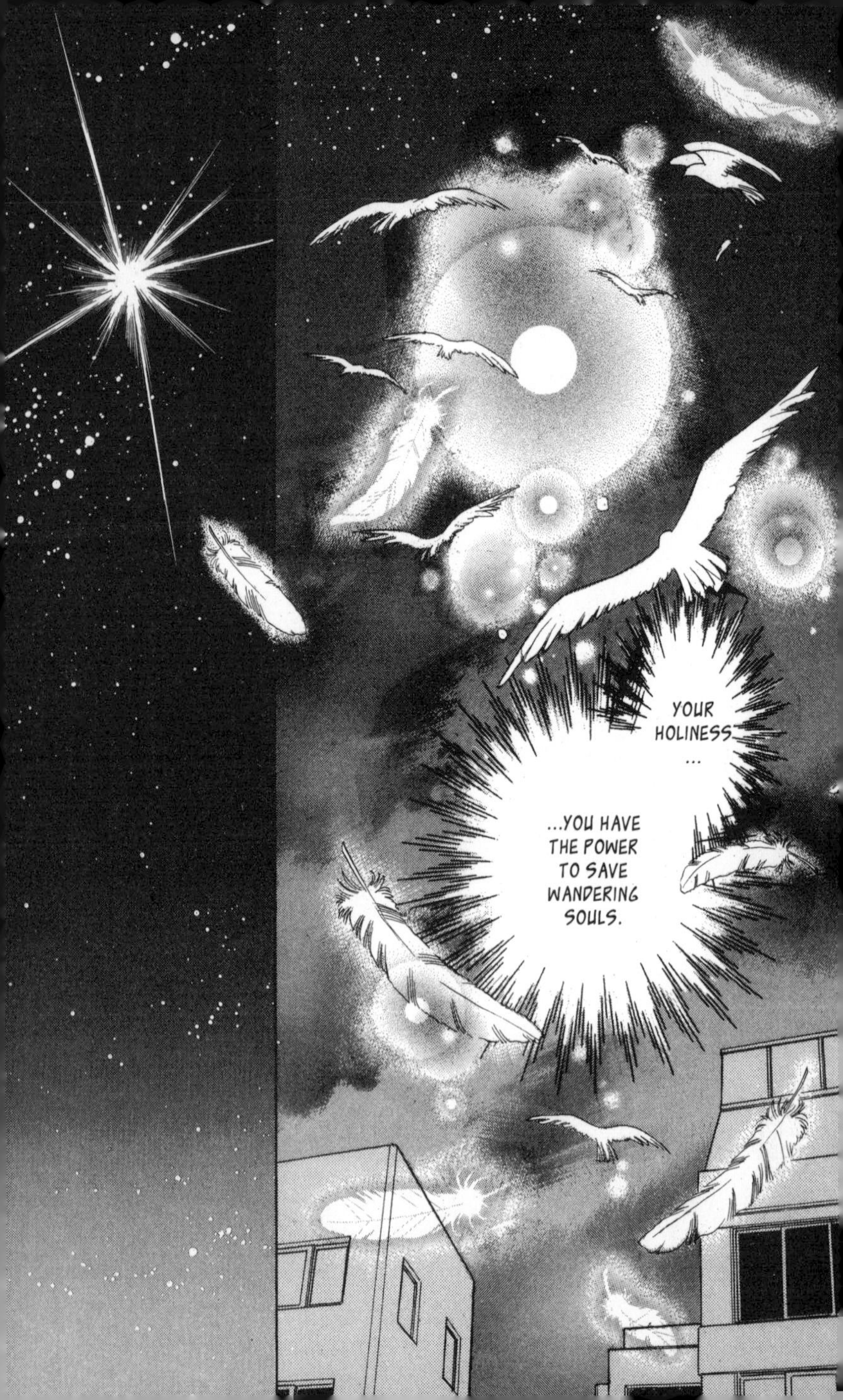
YOUR HOLINESS ...
...YOU HAVE THE POWER TO SAVE WANDERING SOULS.

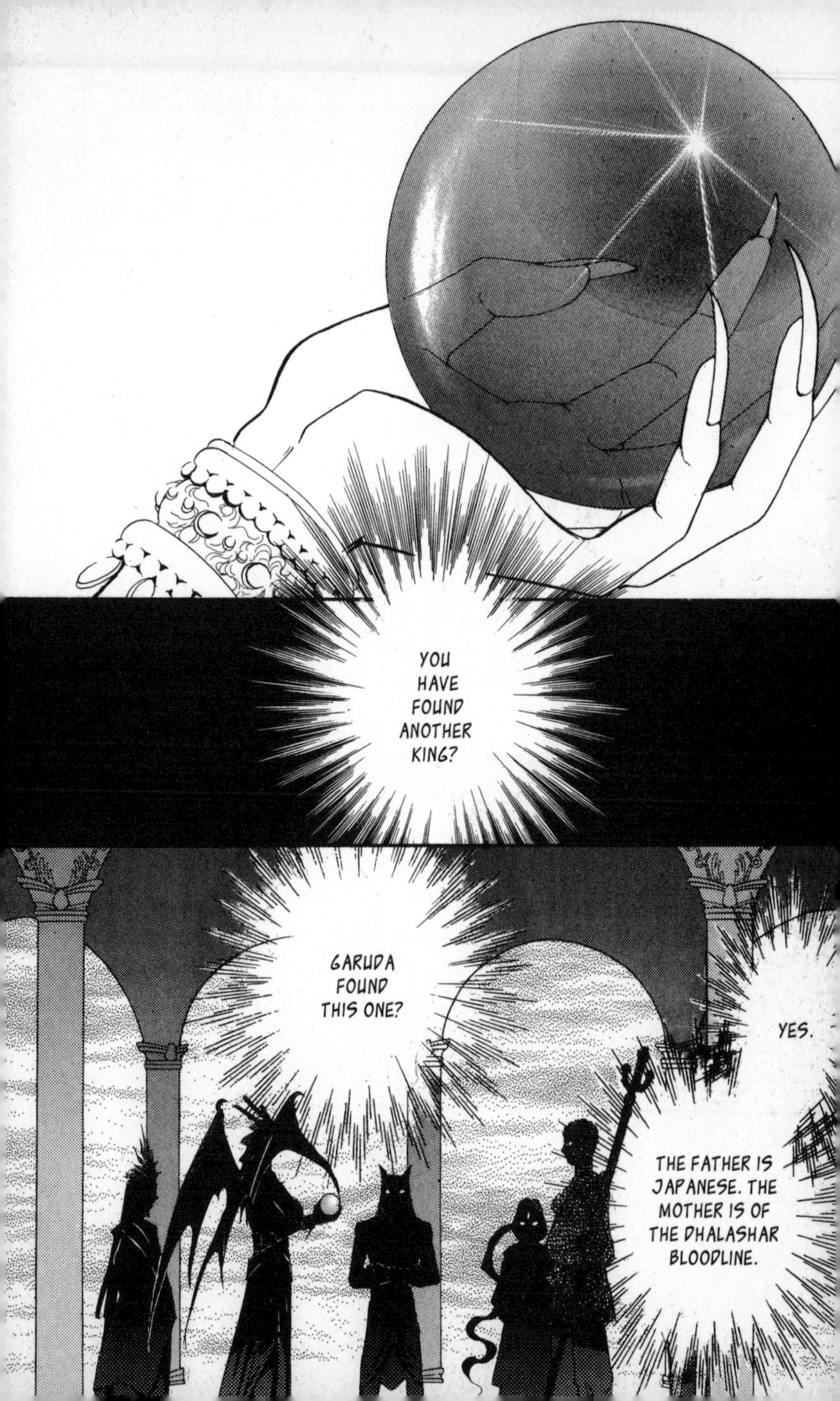
YOU HAVE FOUND ANOTHER KING?
YES.
GARUDA FOUND THIS ONE?
THE FATHER IS JAPANESE. THE MOTHER IS OF THE DHALASHAR BLOODLINE.

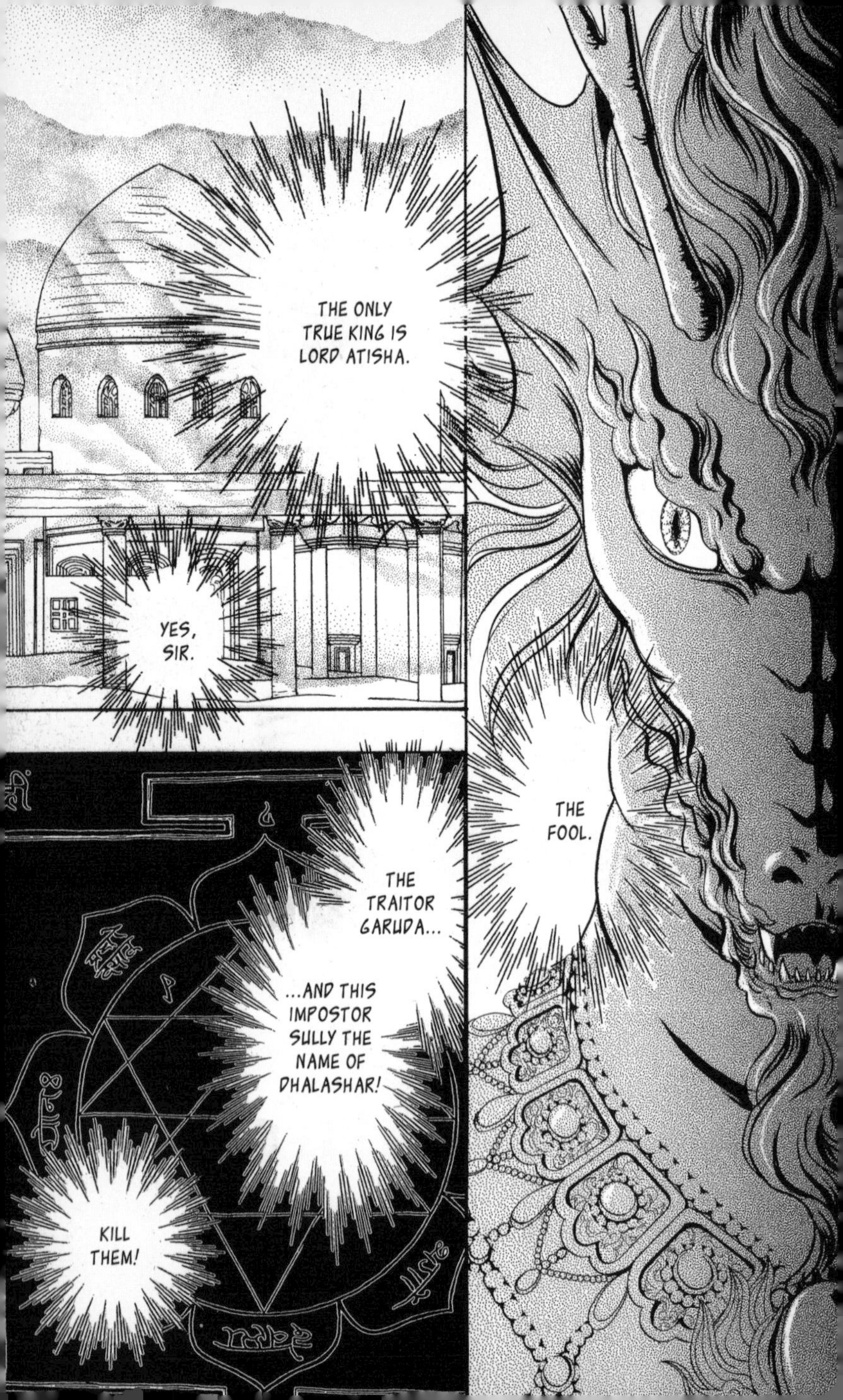
THE FOOL.
THE ONLY TRUE KING IS LORD ATISHA.
YES, SIR.
THE TRAITOR GARUDA...
...AND THIS IMPOSTOR SULLY THE NAME OF DHALASHAR!
KILL THEM!

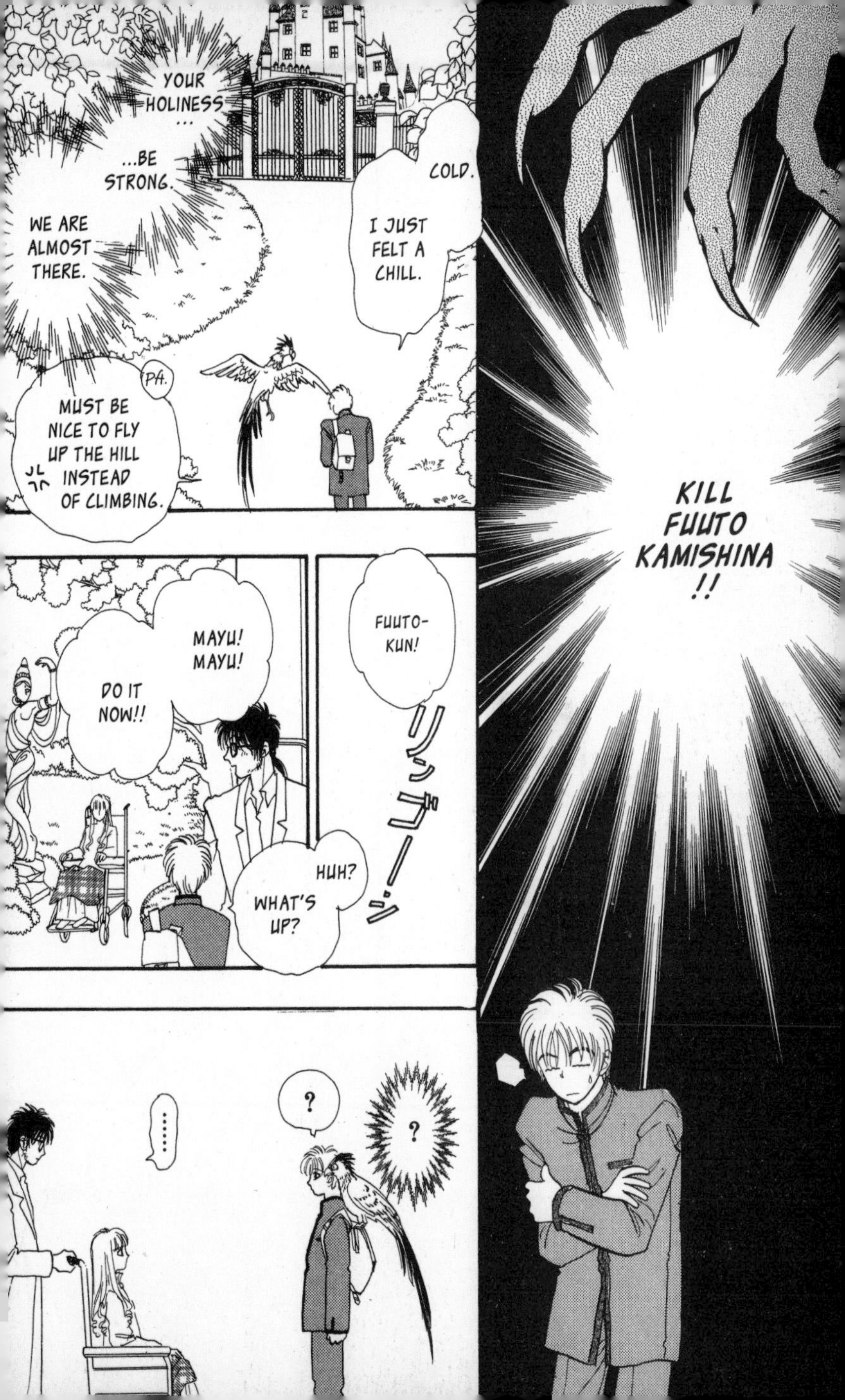
KILL FUUTO KAMISHINA!!
COLD.
I JUST FELT A CHILL.
YOUR HOLINESS...
...BE STRONG.
WE ARE ALMOST THERE.
PA.
MUST BE NICE TO FLY UP THE HILL INSTEAD OF CLIMBING.
FUUTO-KUN!
リンゴーン
MAYU! MAYU!
DO IT NOW!!
HUH?
WHAT'S UP?
?
?
......

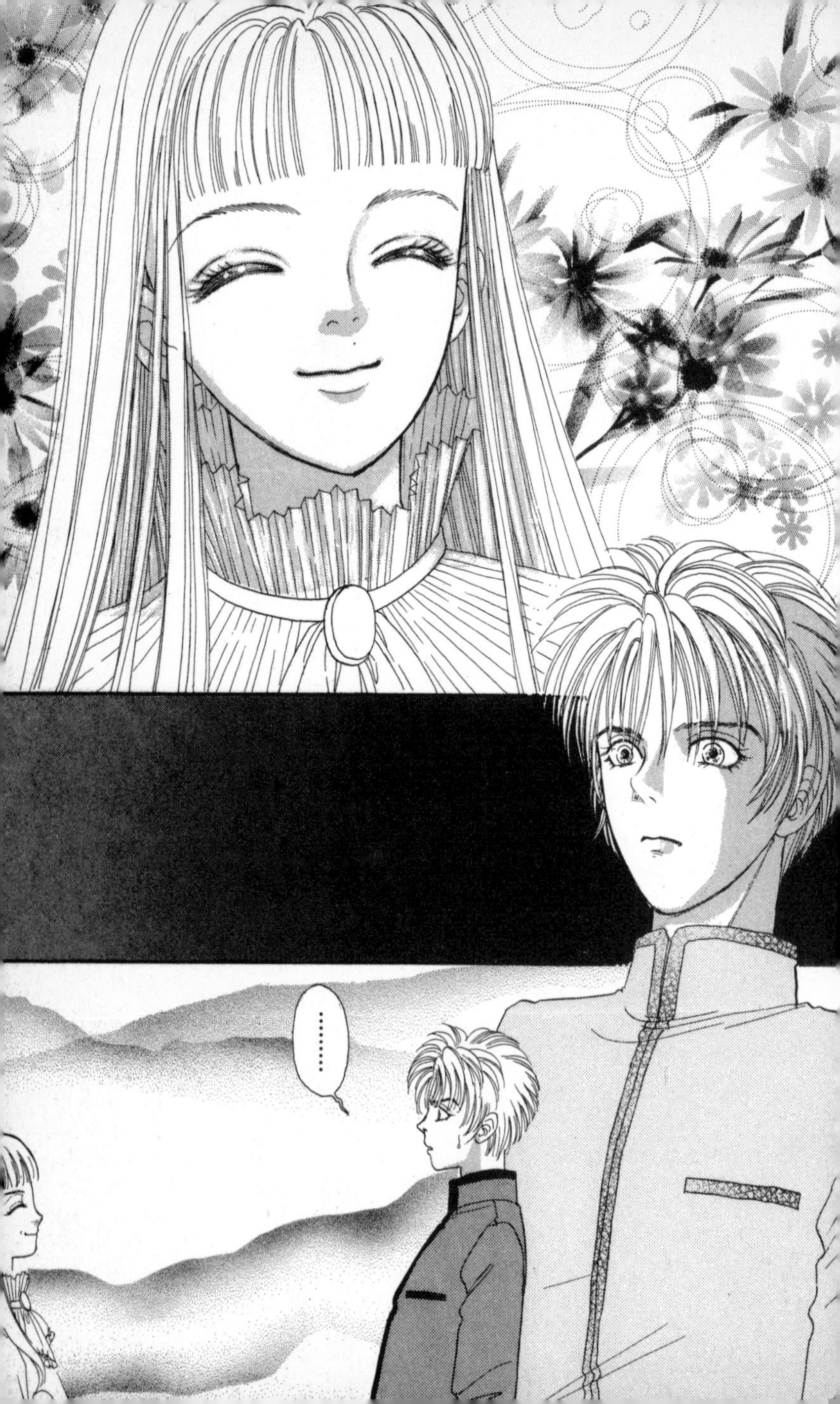
……

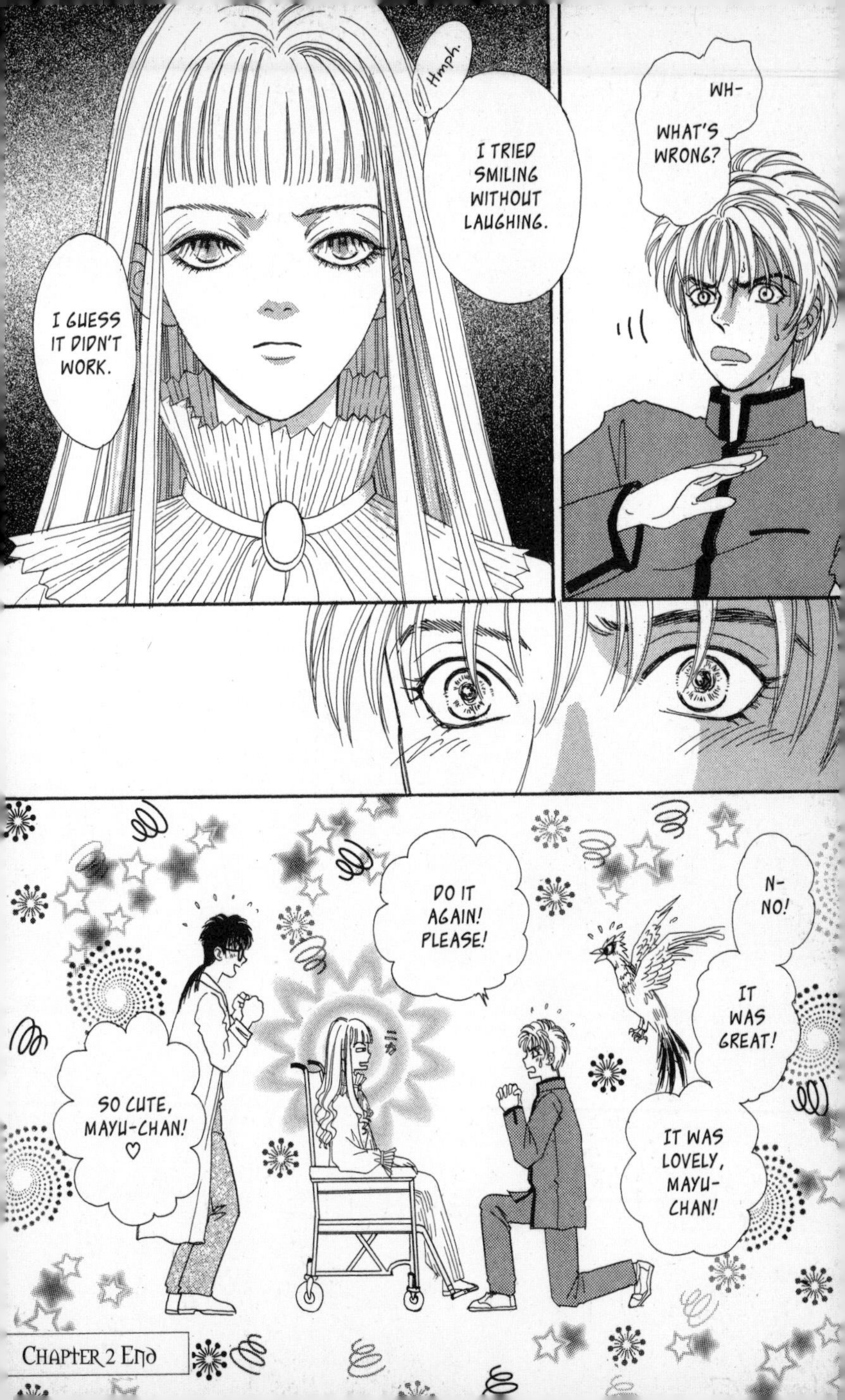
WH- WHAT'S WRONG?
Hmph.
I TRIED SMILING WITHOUT LAUGHING.
I GUESS IT DIDN'T WORK.
N- NO!
IT WAS GREAT!
IT WAS LOVELY, MAYU-CHAN!
DO IT AGAIN! PLEASE!
SO CUTE, MAYU-CHAN! ♡

Chapter 2 End

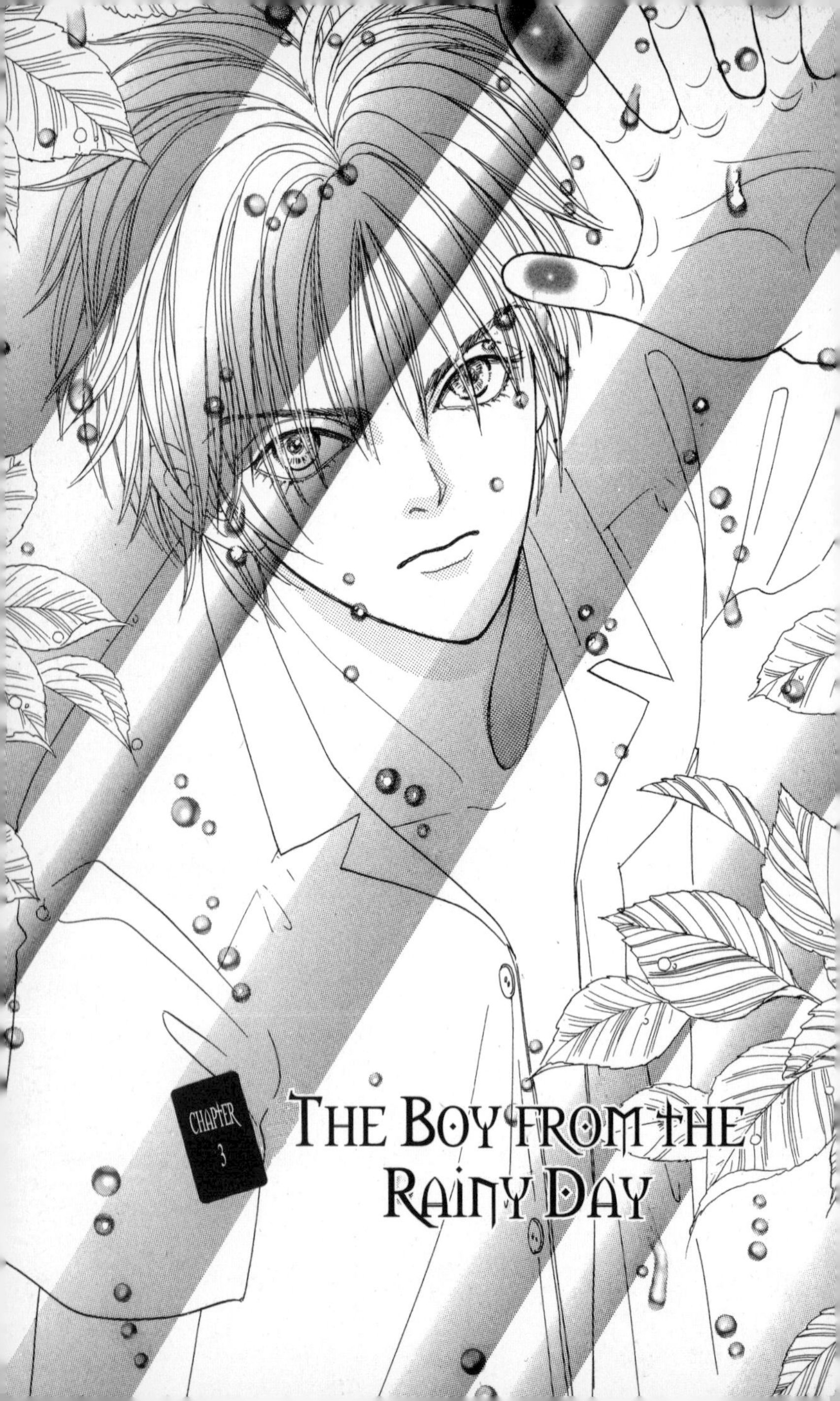
CHAPTER 3
THE BOY FROM THE RAINY DAY

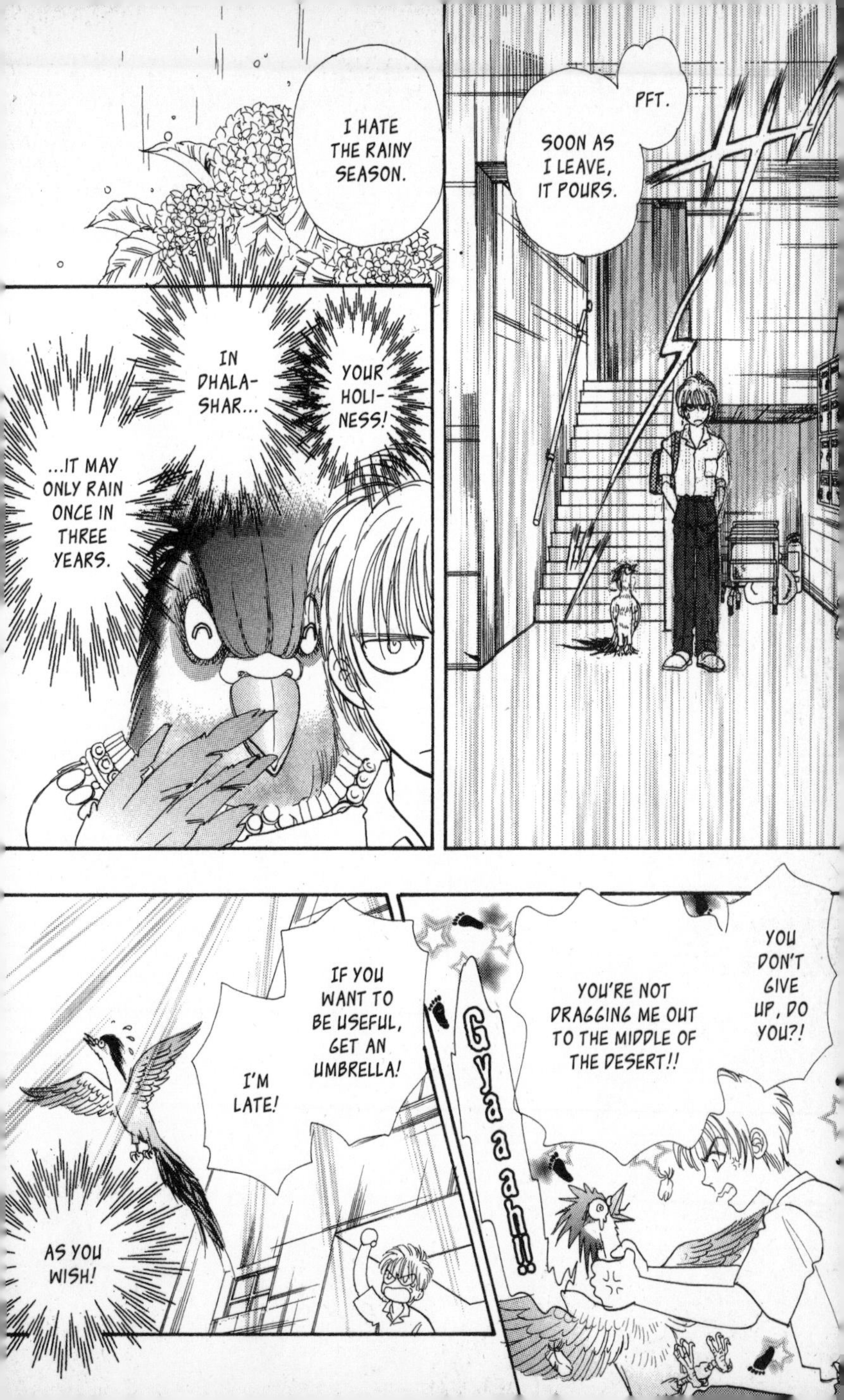
PFT.
SOON AS I LEAVE, IT POURS.
I HATE THE RAINY SEASON.
YOUR HOLINESS!
IN DHALASHAR...
...IT MAY ONLY RAIN ONCE IN THREE YEARS.
YOU DON'T GIVE UP, DO YOU?!
YOU'RE NOT DRAGGING ME OUT TO THE MIDDLE OF THE DESERT!!
Gyaaah!!
IF YOU WANT TO BE USEFUL, GET AN UMBRELLA!
I'M LATE!
AS YOU WISH!

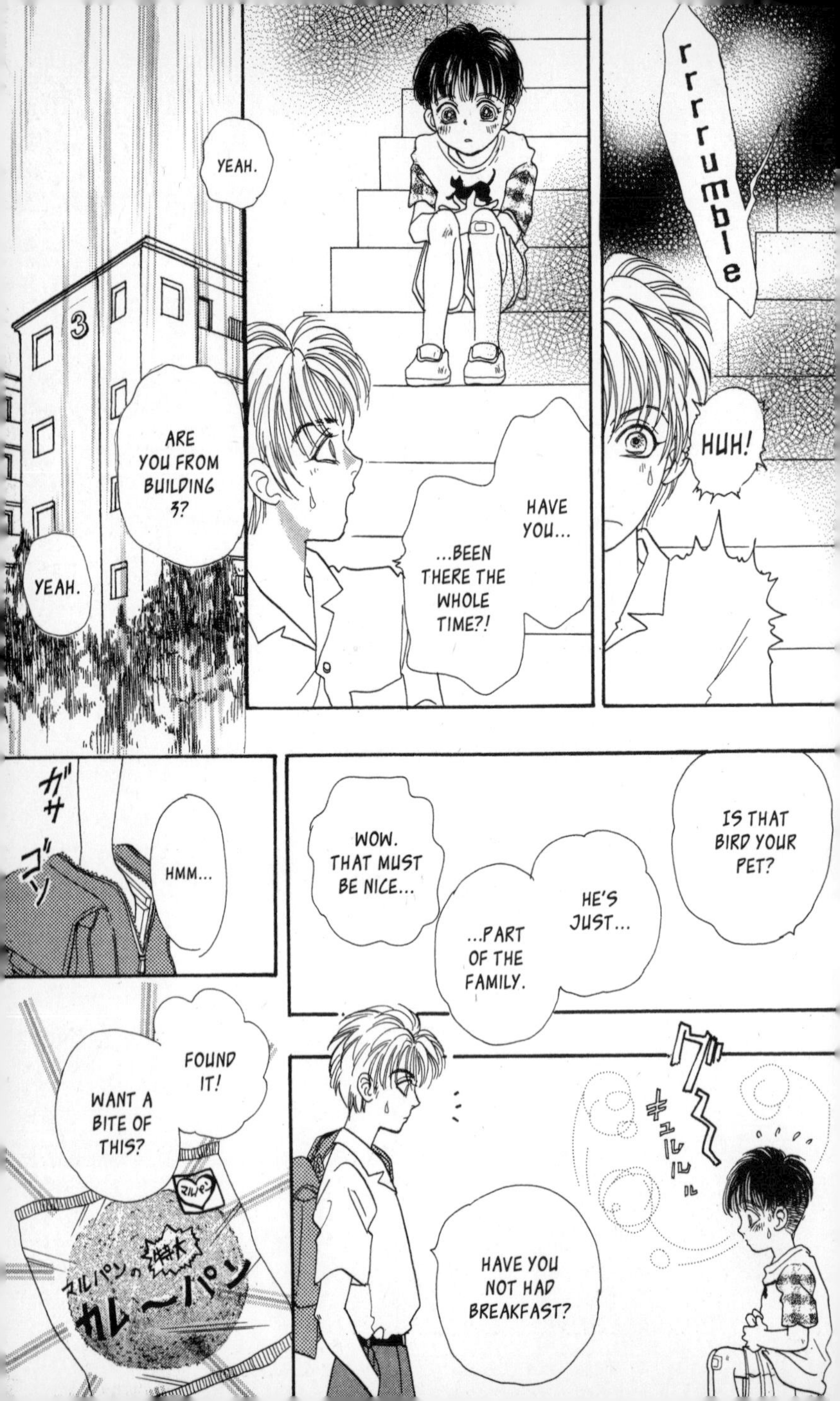
rrrumble
HUH!
HAVE YOU...
...BEEN THERE THE WHOLE TIME?!
YEAH.
ARE YOU FROM BUILDING 3?
YEAH.
IS THAT BIRD YOUR PET?
HE'S JUST...
...PART OF THE FAMILY.
WOW. THAT MUST BE NICE...
ガサ
ゴソ
HMM...
グ〜〜
キュルルル
HAVE YOU NOT HAD BREAKFAST?
FOUND IT!
WANT A BITE OF THIS?
マルパン
マルパンの
特大
カレ〜パン

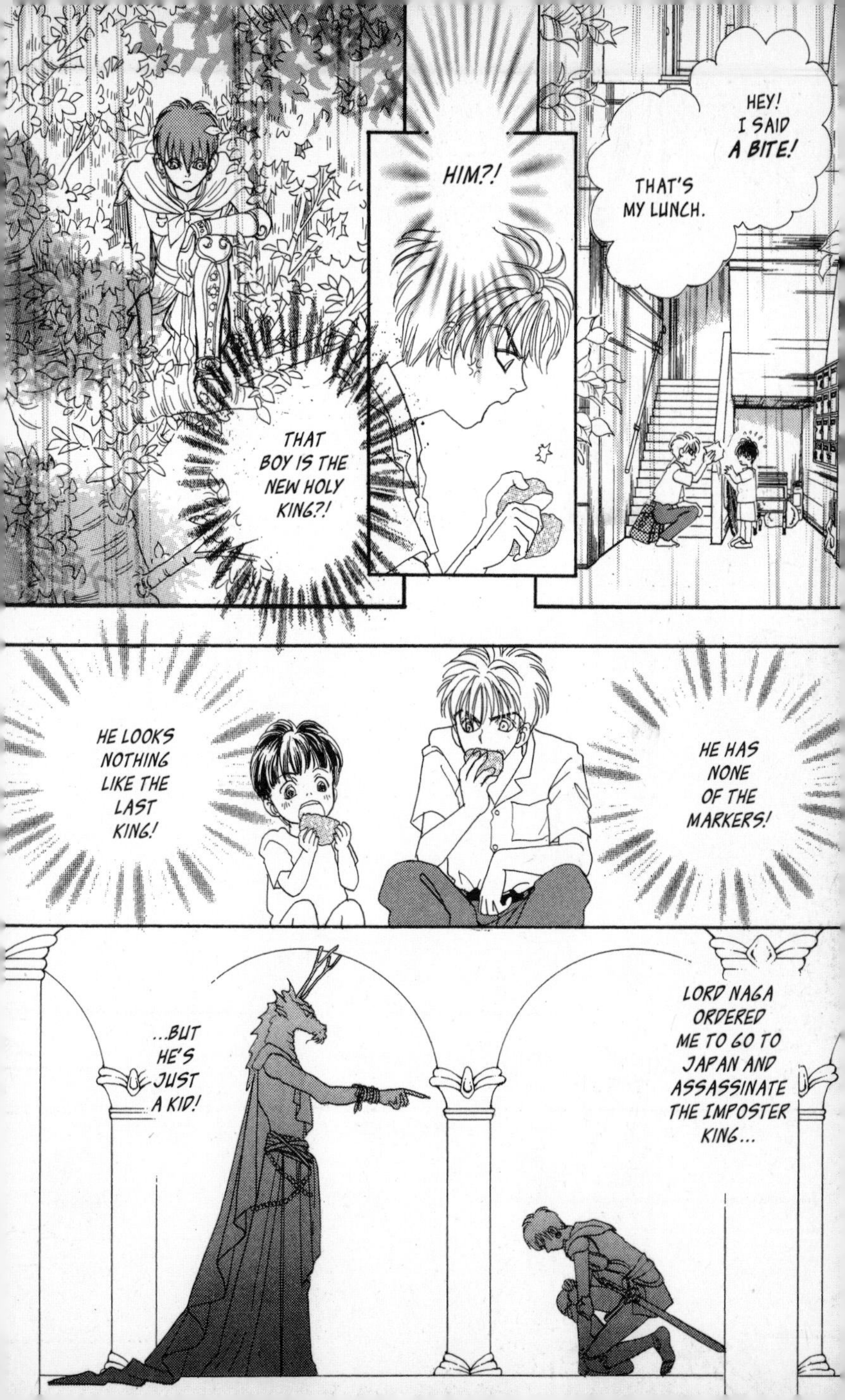
HEY! I SAID A BITE!
THAT'S MY LUNCH.
HIM?!
THAT BOY IS THE NEW HOLY KING?!
HE HAS NONE OF THE MARKERS!
HE LOOKS NOTHING LIKE THE LAST KING!
LORD NAGA ORDERED ME TO GO TO JAPAN AND ASSASSINATE THE IMPOSTER KING...
...BUT HE'S JUST A KID!

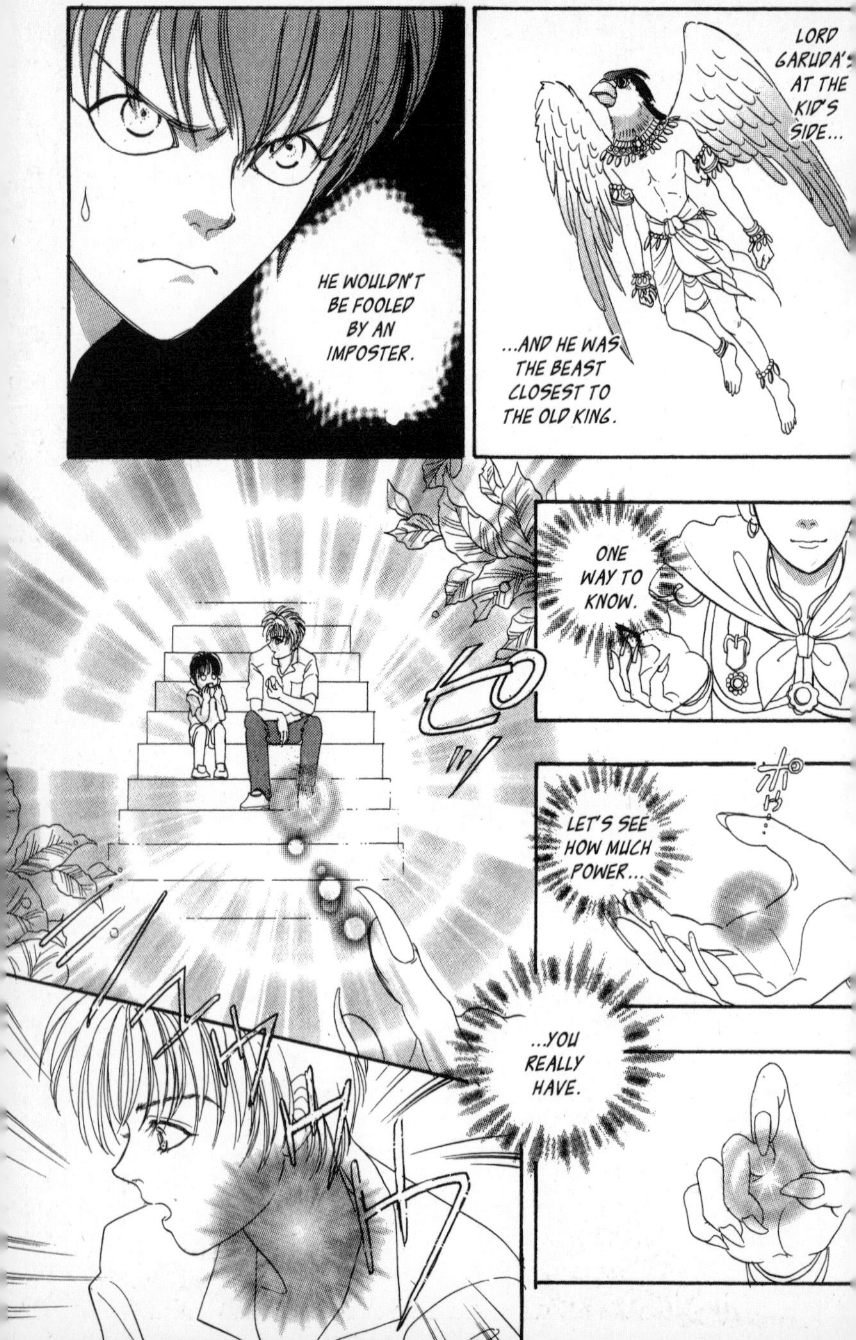
LORD GARUDA'S AT THE KID'S SIDE...
...AND HE WAS THE BEAST CLOSEST TO THE OLD KING.
HE WOULDN'T BE FOOLED BY AN IMPOSTER.
ONE WAY TO KNOW.
LET'S SEE HOW MUCH POWER...
...YOU REALLY HAVE.

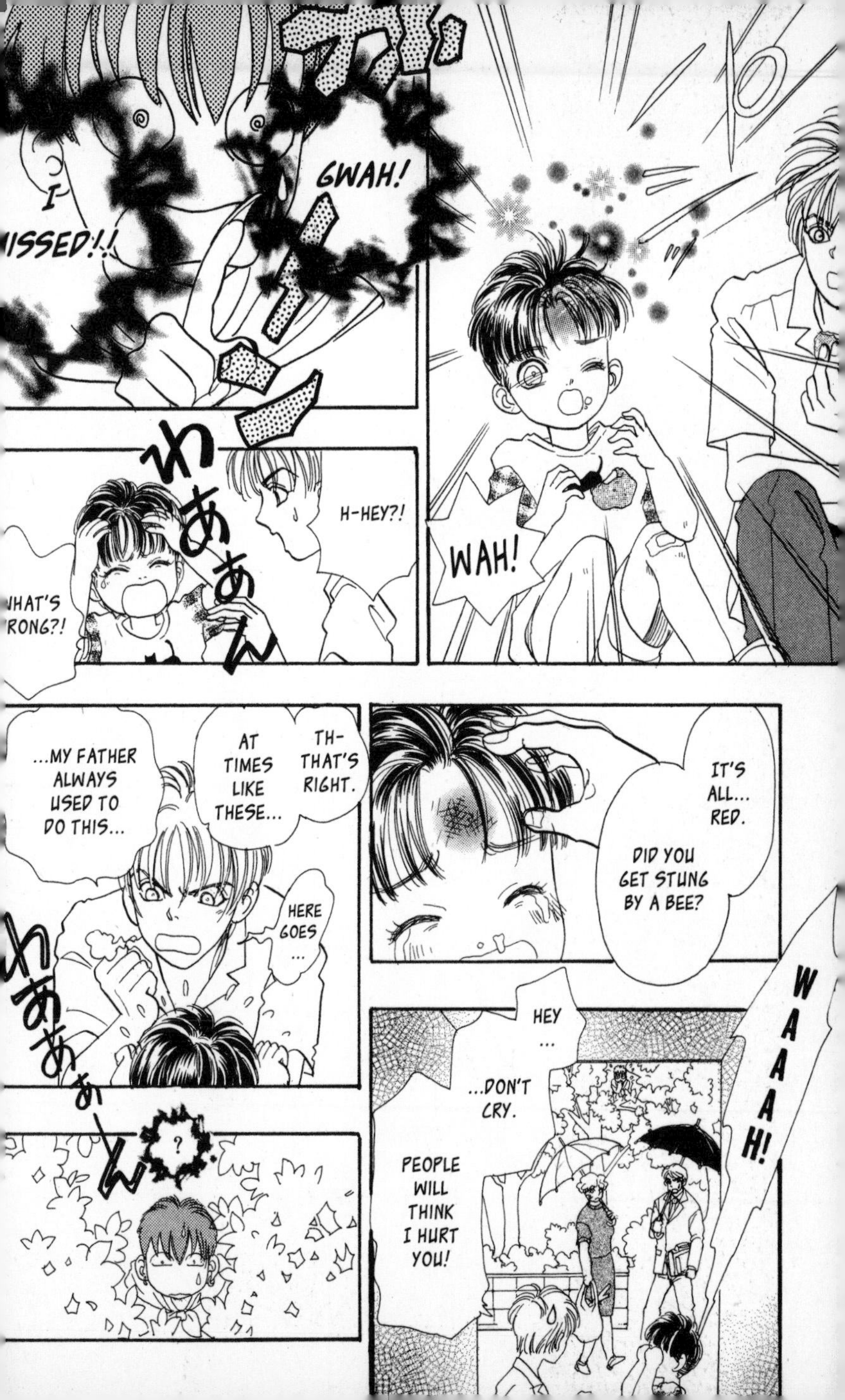
WAH!
GWAH!
I ISSED!!
わあぁん
H-HEY?!
HAT'S RONG?!
IT'S ALL... RED.
DID YOU GET STUNG BY A BEE?
TH- THAT'S RIGHT.
AT TIMES LIKE THESE...
...MY FATHER ALWAYS USED TO DO THIS...
HERE GOES...
わあぁぁん
WAAAAH!
HEY...
...DON'T CRY.
PEOPLE WILL THINK I HURT YOU!
?

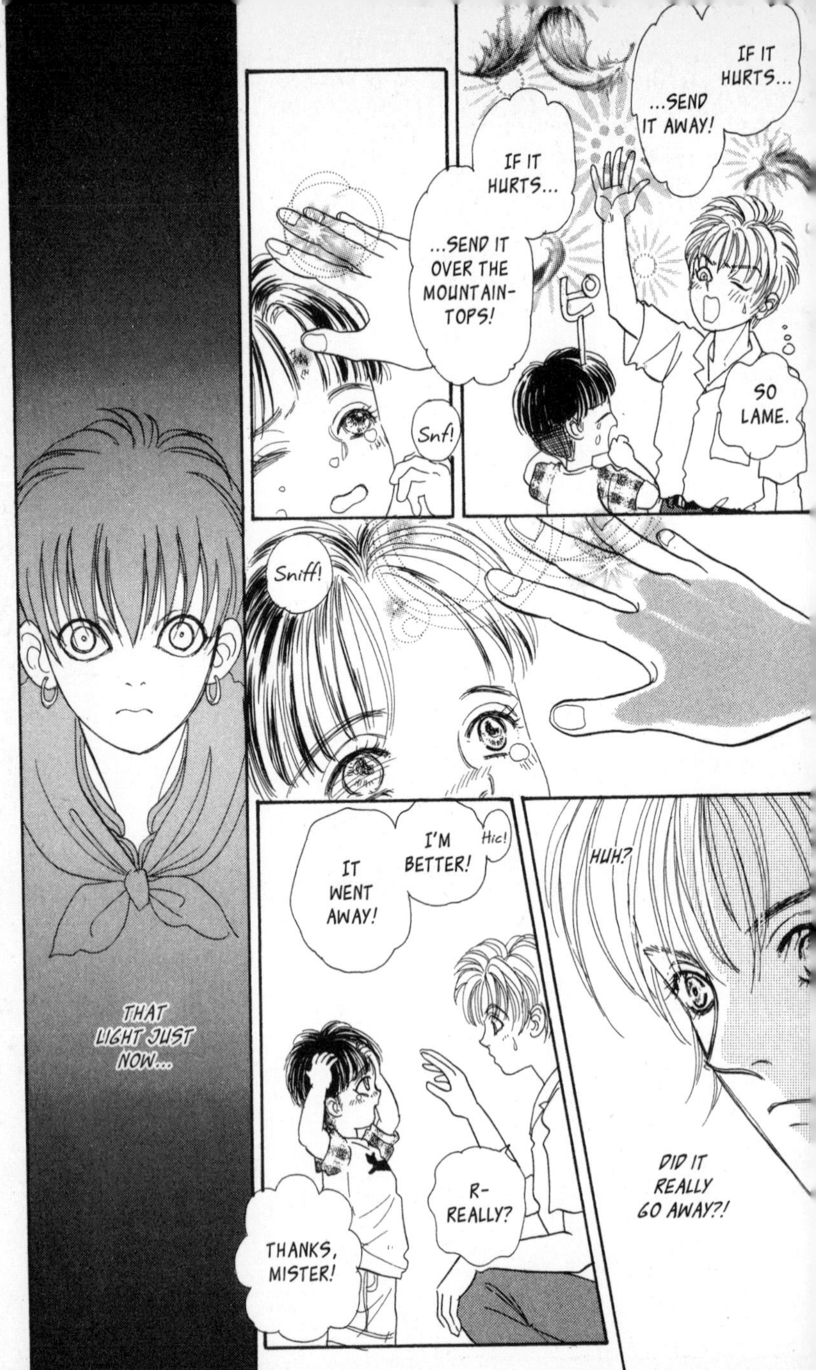
IF IT HURTS...
...SEND IT AWAY!
SO LAME.
IF IT HURTS...
...SEND IT OVER THE MOUNTAIN-TOPS!
Snf!
Sniff!
HUH?
DID IT REALLY GO AWAY?!
Hic!
I'M BETTER!
IT WENT AWAY!
R-REALLY?
THANKS, MISTER!
THAT LIGHT JUST NOW...

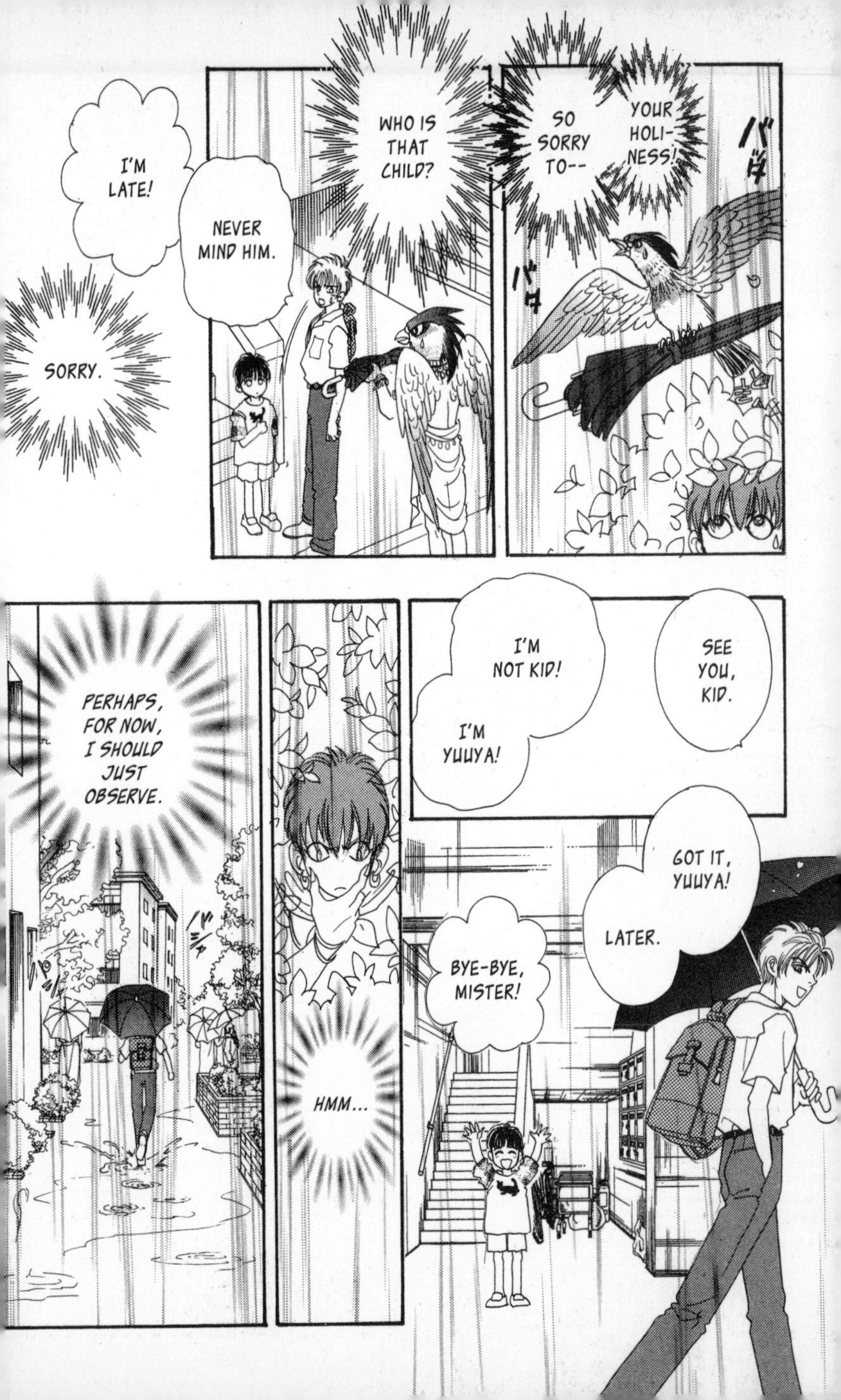
YOUR HOLI-NESS!
SO SORRY TO--
WHO IS THAT CHILD?
NEVER MIND HIM.
I'M LATE!
SORRY.
SEE YOU, KID.
I'M NOT KID! I'M YUUYA!
GOT IT, YUUYA!
LATER.
BYE-BYE, MISTER!
HMM...
PERHAPS, FOR NOW, I SHOULD JUST OBSERVE.

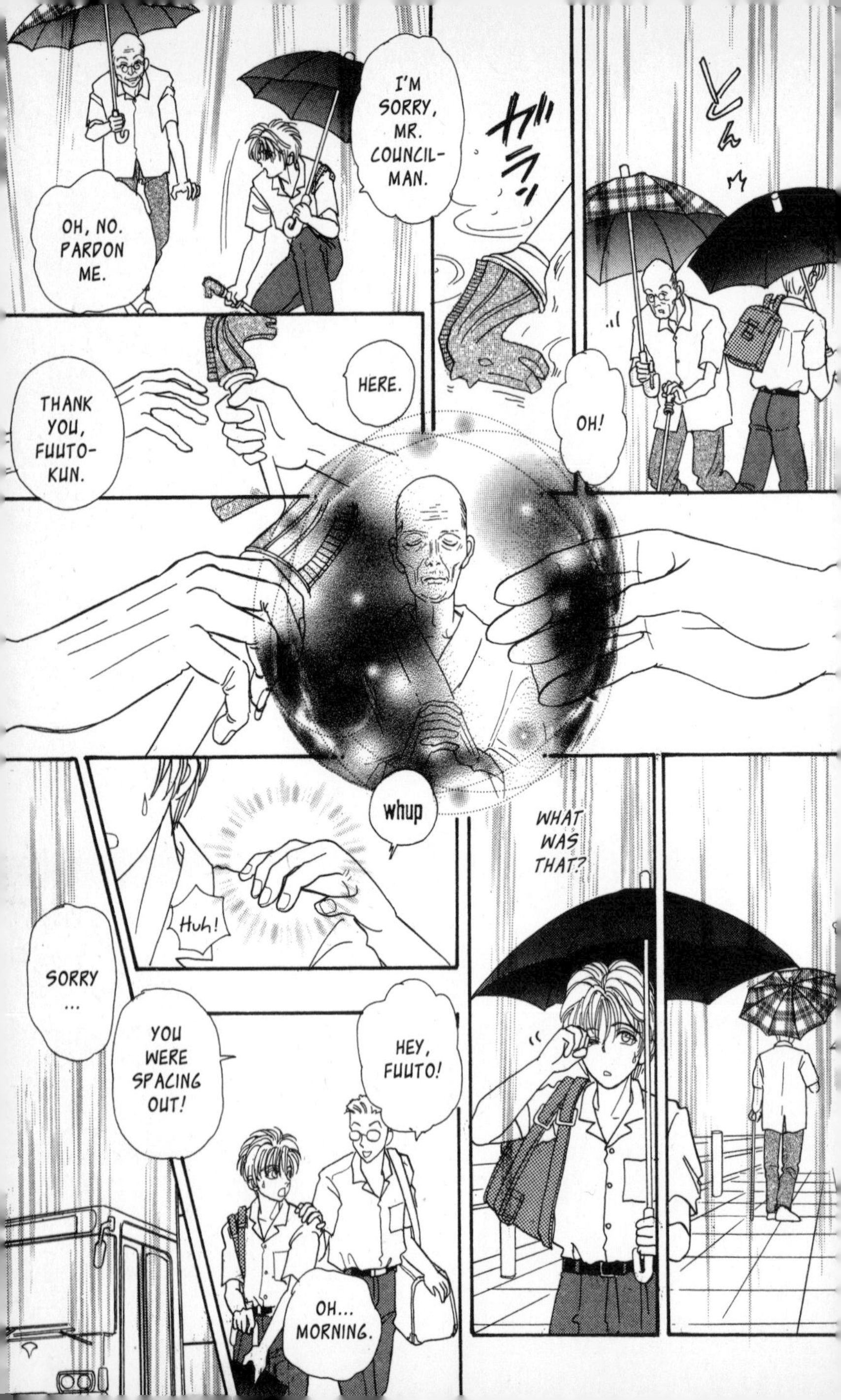

どん
OH!
ガラッ
I'M SORRY, MR. COUNCIL-MAN.
OH, NO. PARDON ME.
HERE.
THANK YOU, FUUTO-KUN.
WHAT WAS THAT?
whup
Huh!
HEY, FUUTO!
YOU WERE SPACING OUT!
SORRY ...
OH... MORNING.

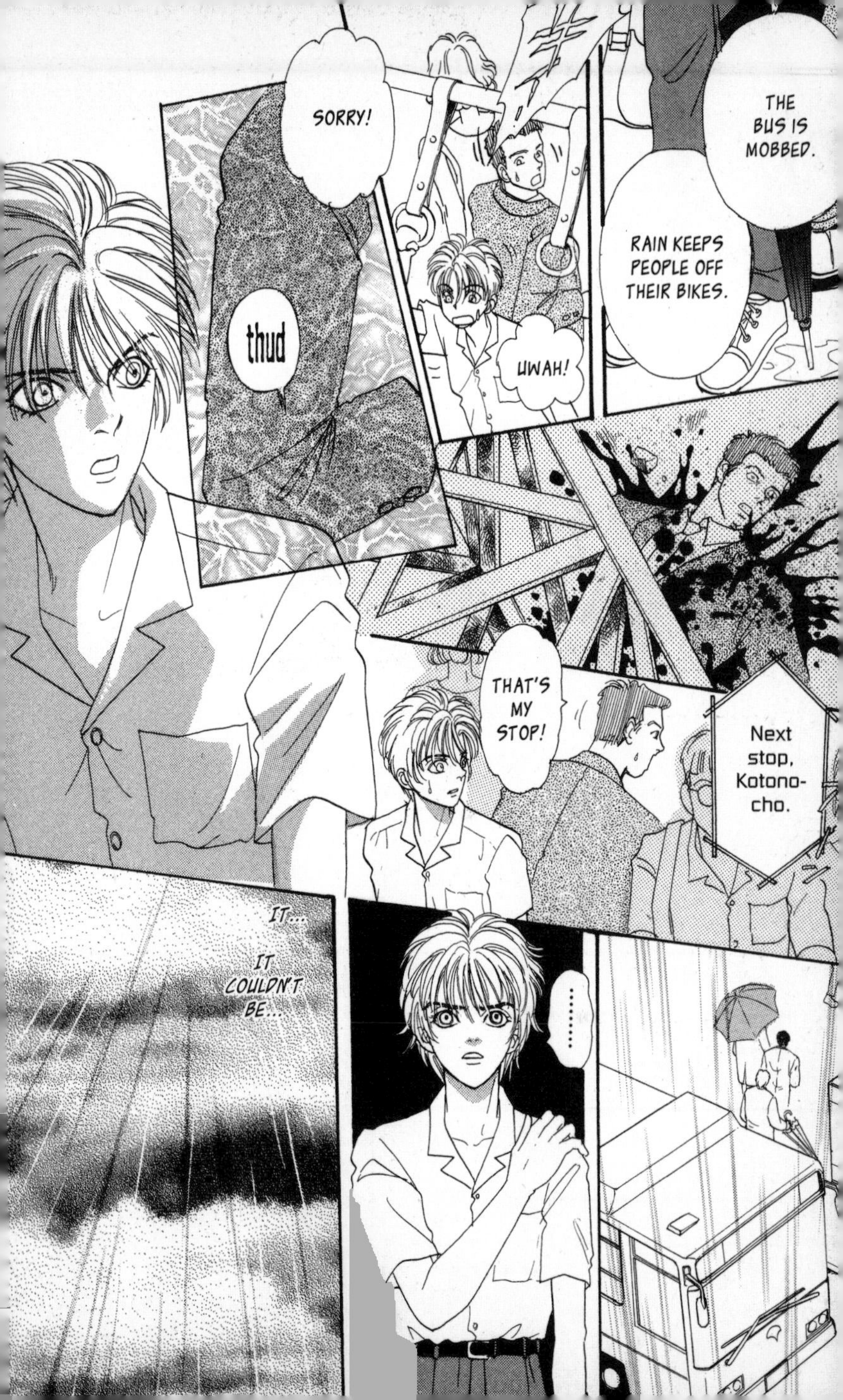
THE BUS IS MOBBED.
RAIN KEEPS PEOPLE OFF THEIR BIKES.
SORRY!
UWAH!
thud
Next stop, Kotono-cho.
THAT'S MY STOP!
......
IT...
IT COULDN'T BE...

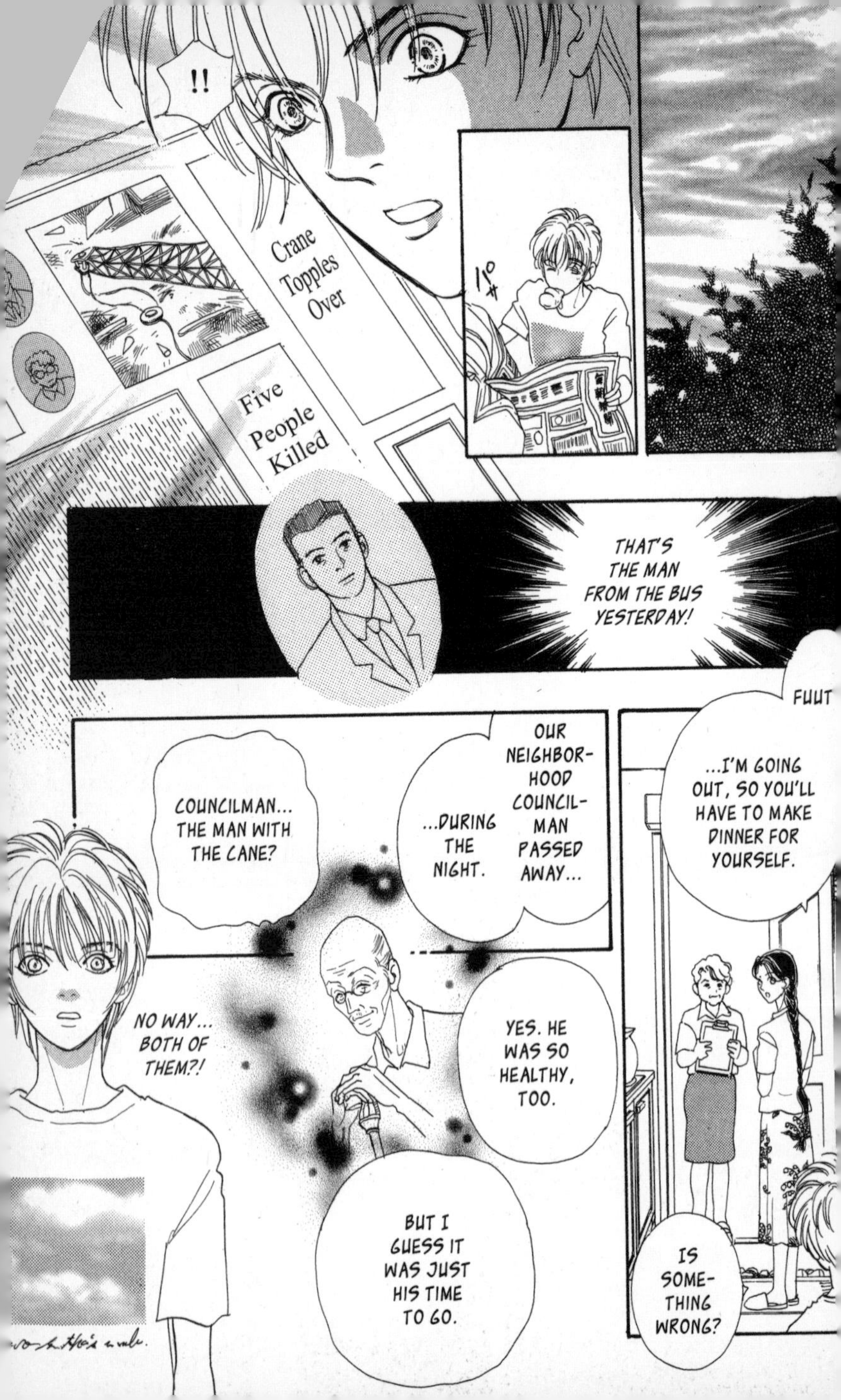
!!
Crane Topples Over
Five People Killed
THAT'S THE MAN FROM THE BUS YESTERDAY!
FUUT
...I'M GOING OUT, SO YOU'LL HAVE TO MAKE DINNER FOR YOURSELF.
IS SOME-THING WRONG?
OUR NEIGHBOR-HOOD COUNCIL-MAN PASSED AWAY...
...DURING THE NIGHT.
COUNCILMAN... THE MAN WITH THE CANE?
YES. HE WAS SO HEALTHY, TOO.
BUT I GUESS IT WAS JUST HIS TIME TO GO.
NO WAY... BOTH OF THEM?!

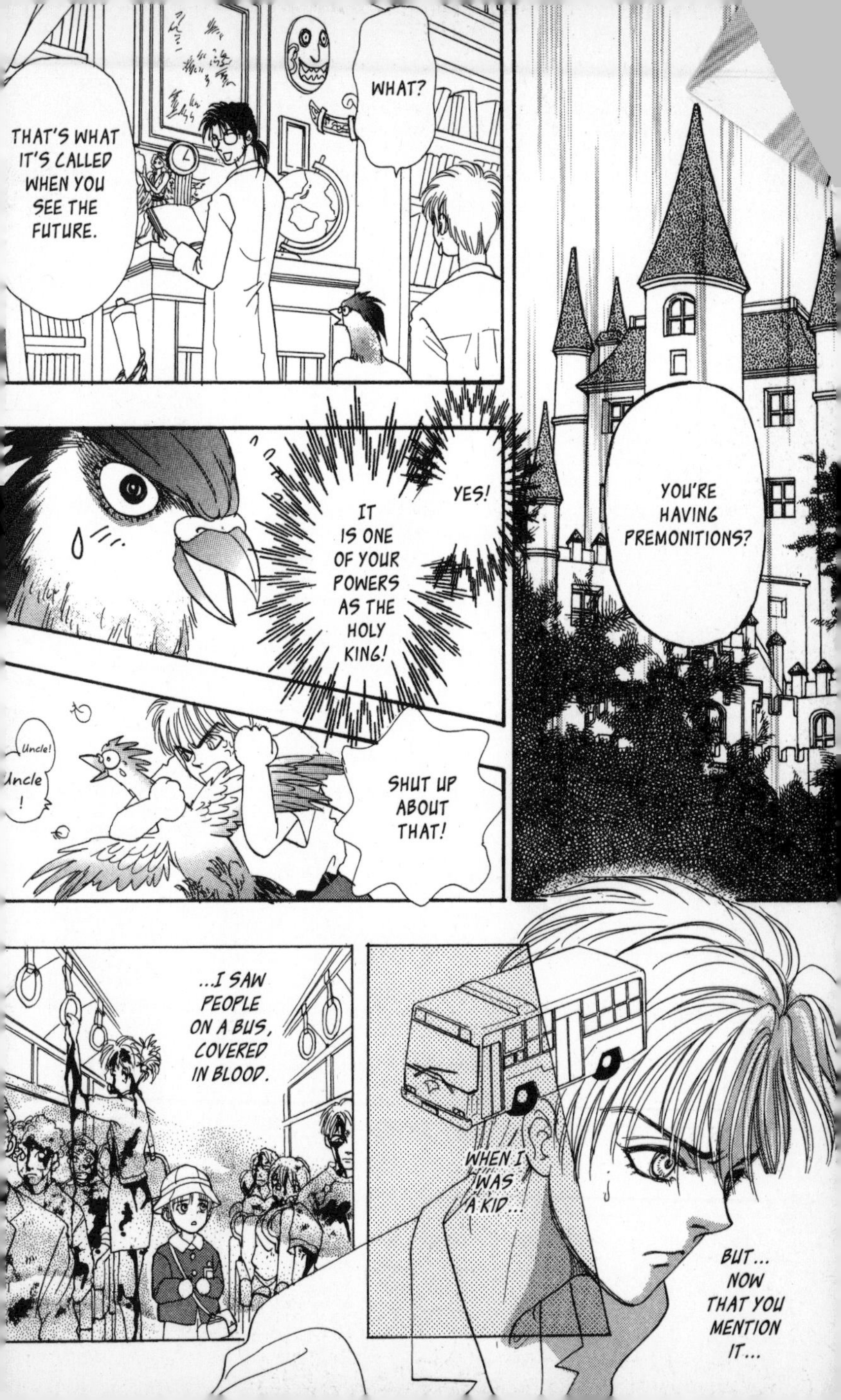
YOU'RE HAVING PREMONITIONS?
WHAT?
THAT'S WHAT IT'S CALLED WHEN YOU SEE THE FUTURE.
YES!
IT IS ONE OF YOUR POWERS AS THE HOLY KING!
SHUT UP ABOUT THAT!
Uncle!
Uncle!
BUT... NOW THAT YOU MENTION IT...
WHEN I WAS A KID...
...I SAW PEOPLE ON A BUS, COVERED IN BLOOD.

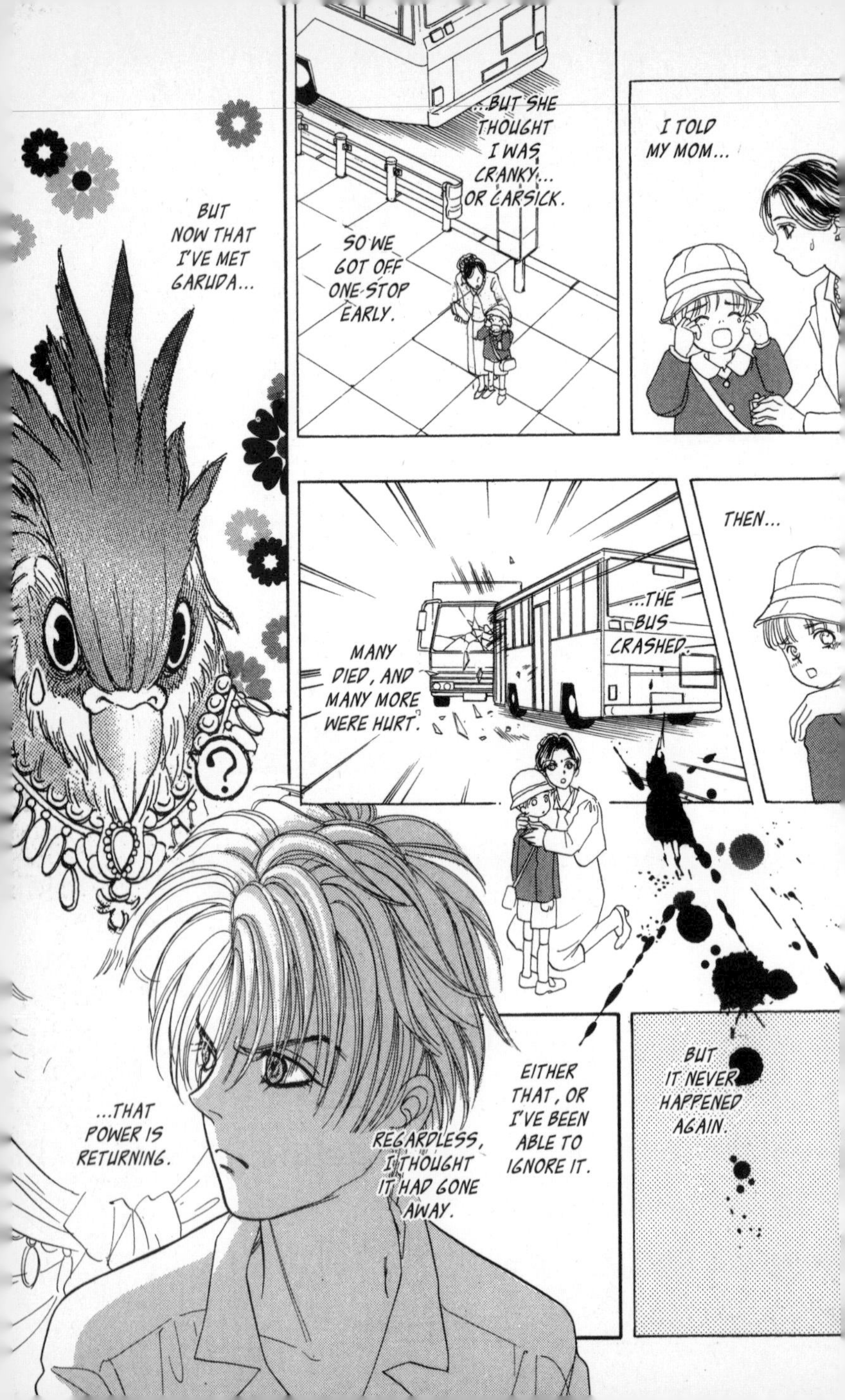
I TOLD MY MOM...
...BUT SHE THOUGHT I WAS CRANKY... OR CARSICK.
SO WE GOT OFF ONE STOP EARLY.
THEN...
...THE BUS CRASHED.
MANY DIED, AND MANY MORE WERE HURT.
BUT IT NEVER HAPPENED AGAIN.
EITHER THAT, OR I'VE BEEN ABLE TO IGNORE IT.
REGARDLESS, I THOUGHT IT HAD GONE AWAY.
BUT NOW THAT I'VE MET GARUDA...
...THAT POWER IS RETURNING.

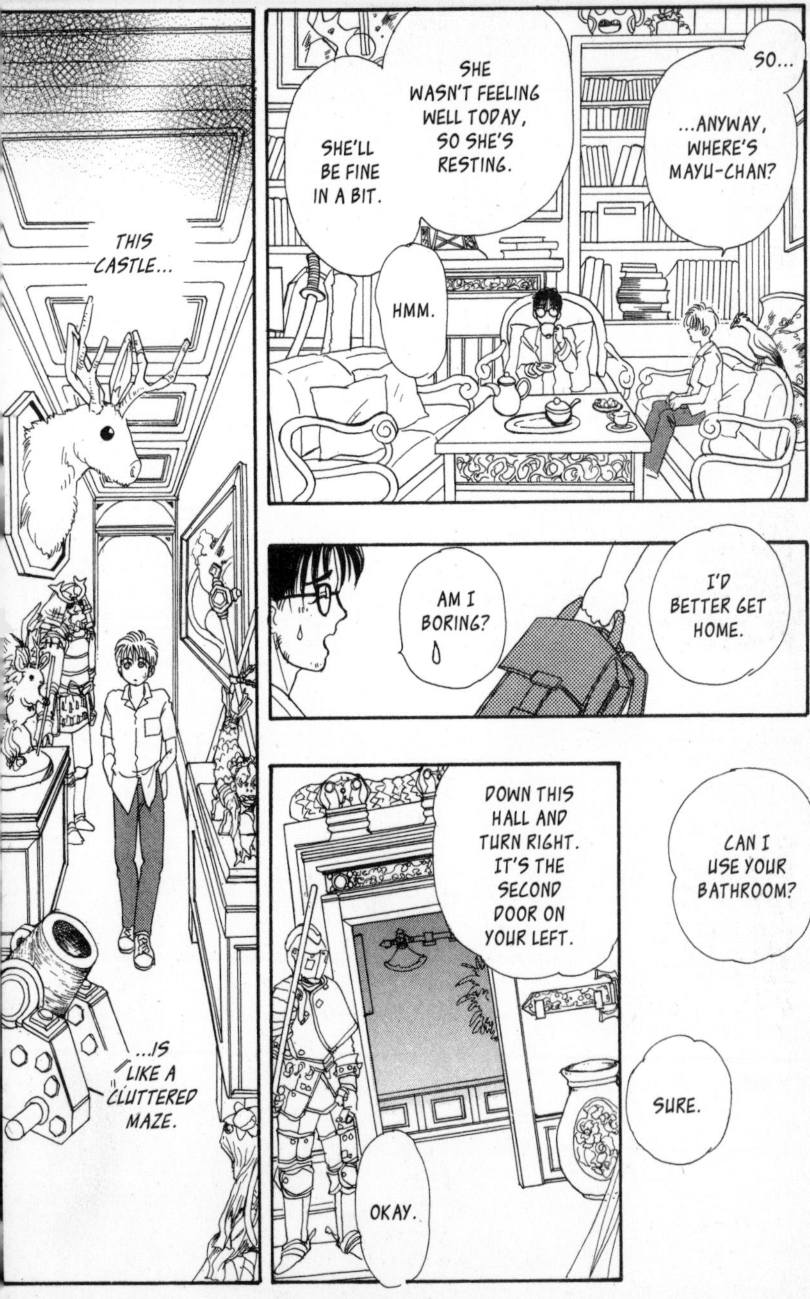
SO...
...ANYWAY, WHERE'S MAYU-CHAN?
SHE WASN'T FEELING WELL TODAY, SO SHE'S RESTING.
SHE'LL BE FINE IN A BIT.
HMM.
I'D BETTER GET HOME.
AM I BORING?
CAN I USE YOUR BATHROOM?
SURE.
DOWN THIS HALL AND TURN RIGHT. IT'S THE SECOND DOOR ON YOUR LEFT.
OKAY.
THIS CASTLE...
...IS LIKE A CLUTTERED MAZE.

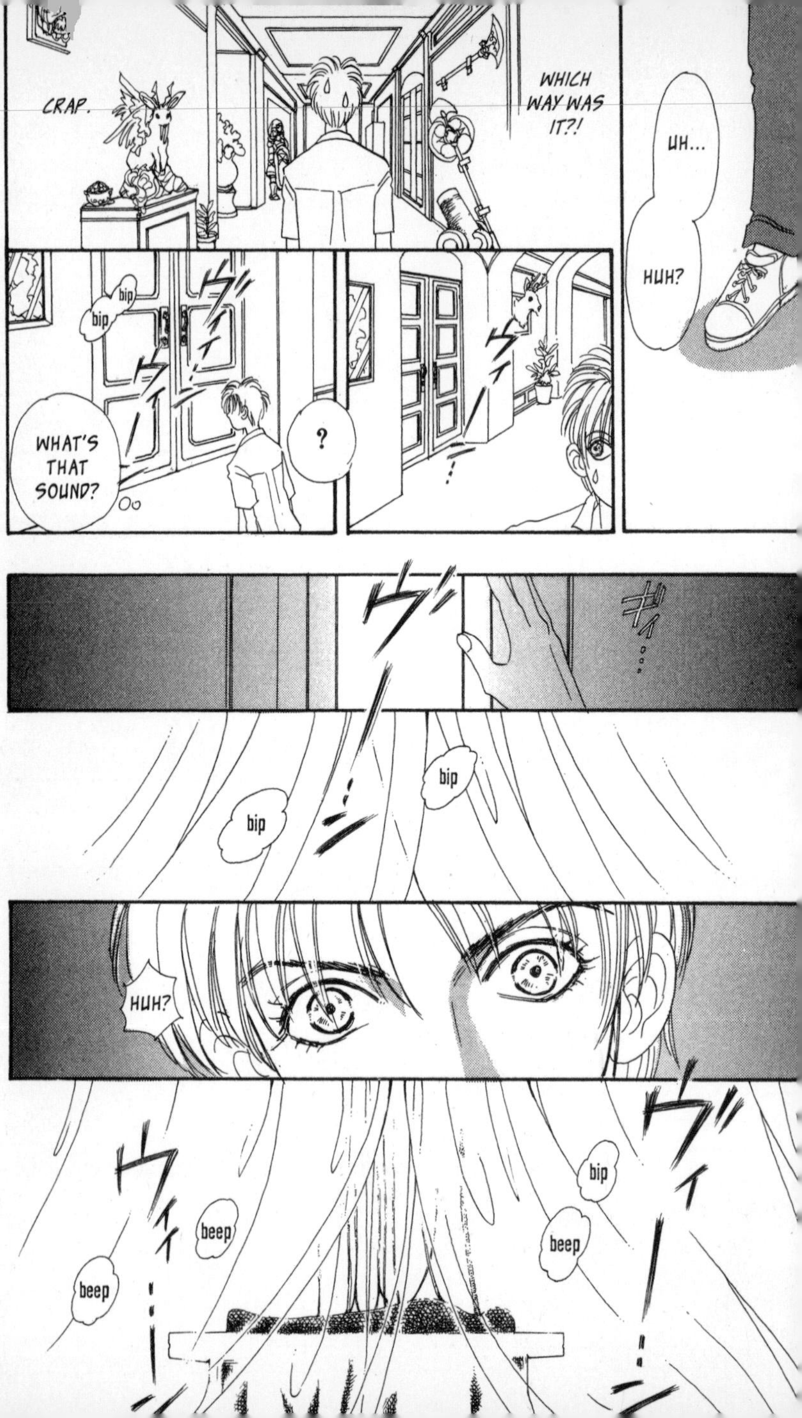
UH...
HUH?
WHICH WAY WAS IT?!
CRAP.
bip
bip
?
WHAT'S THAT SOUND?
bip
bip
HUH?
bip
beep
beep
beep

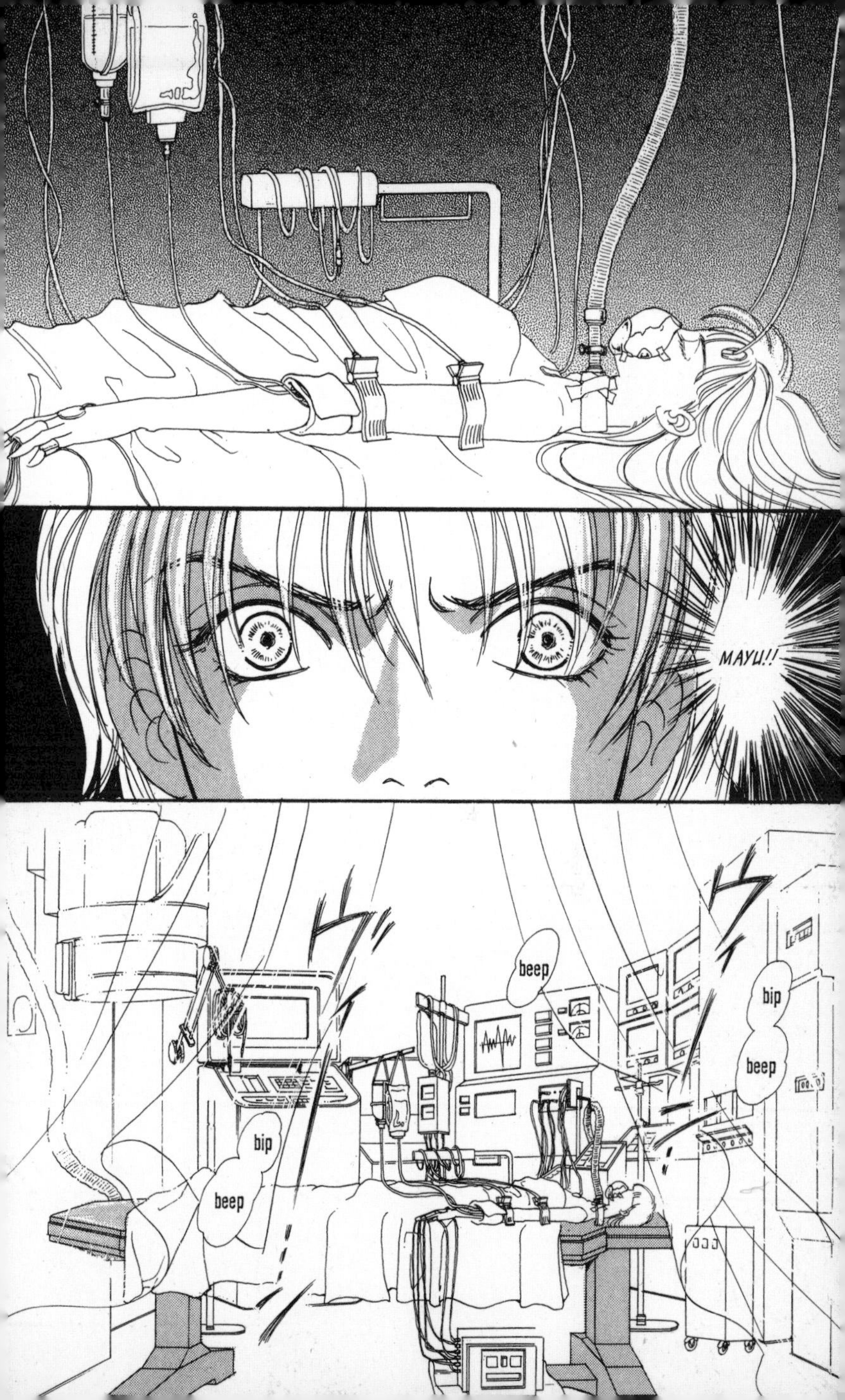
MAYU!!
bip
beep
beep
bip
beep

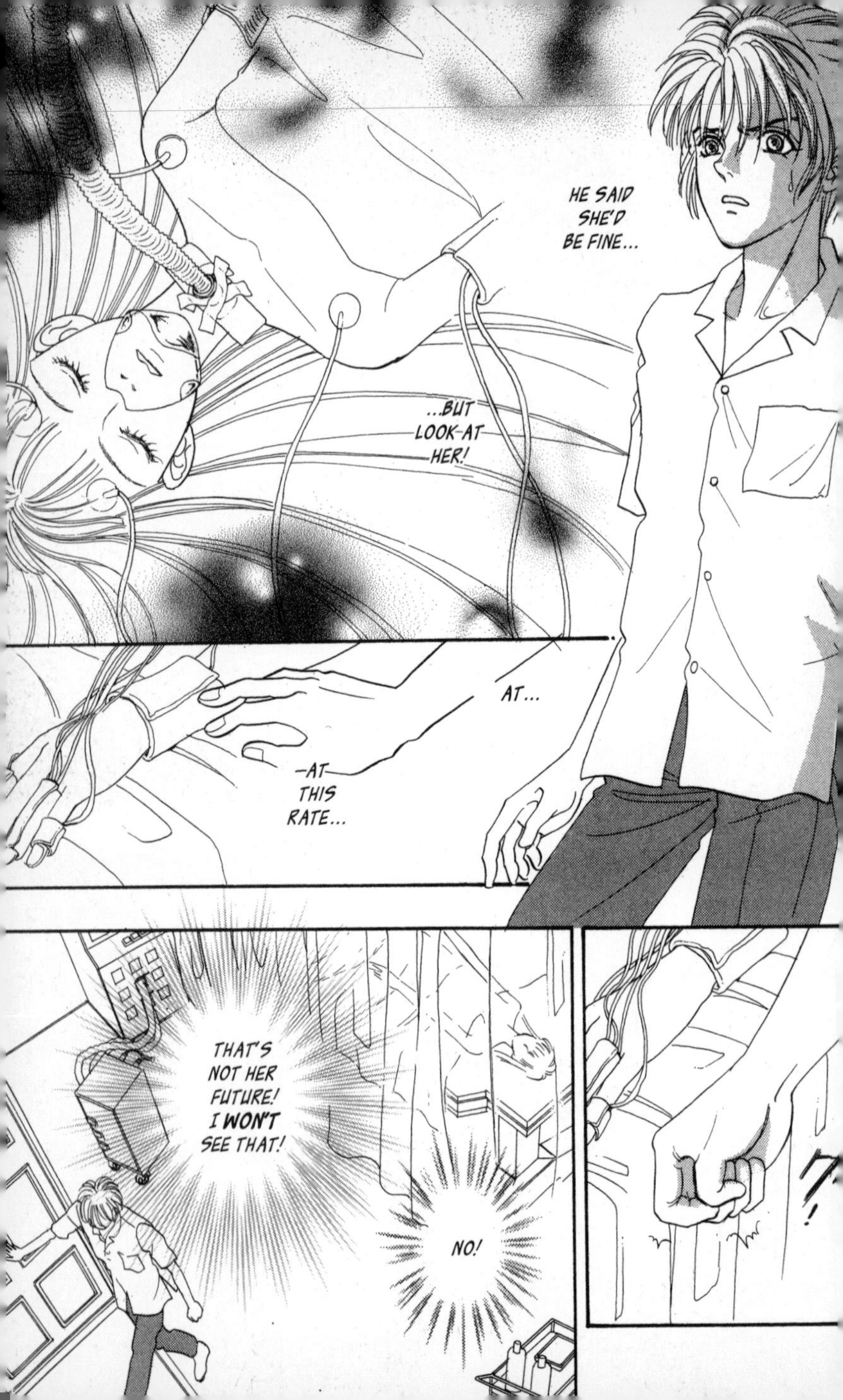
HE SAID SHE'D BE FINE...
...BUT LOOK AT HER!
AT...
—AT THIS RATE...
THAT'S NOT HER FUTURE! I WON'T SEE THAT!
NO!

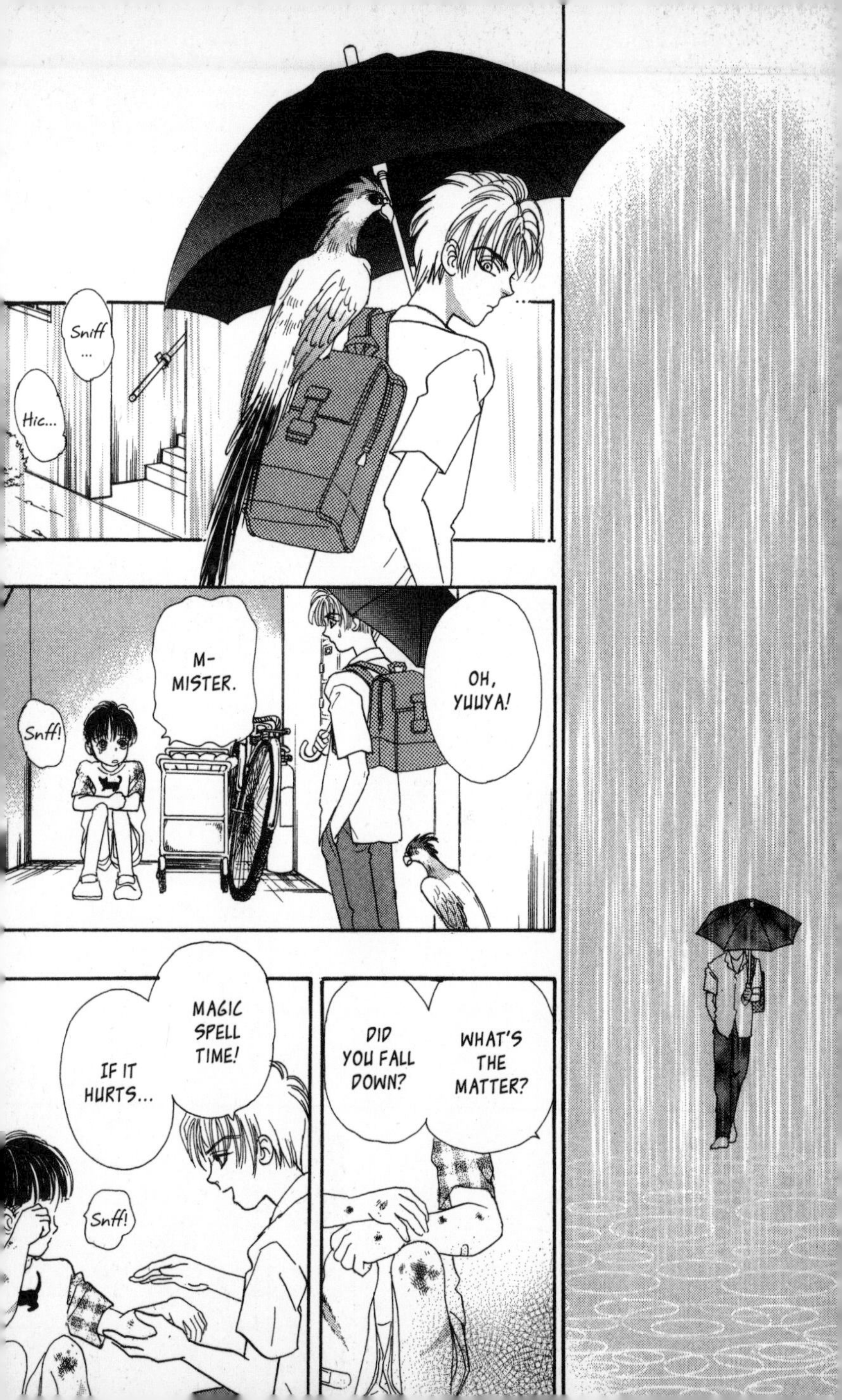
...
Sniff ...
Hic...
OH, YUUYA!
M-MISTER.
Snff!
WHAT'S THE MATTER?
DID YOU FALL DOWN?
MAGIC SPELL TIME!
IF IT HURTS...
Snff!

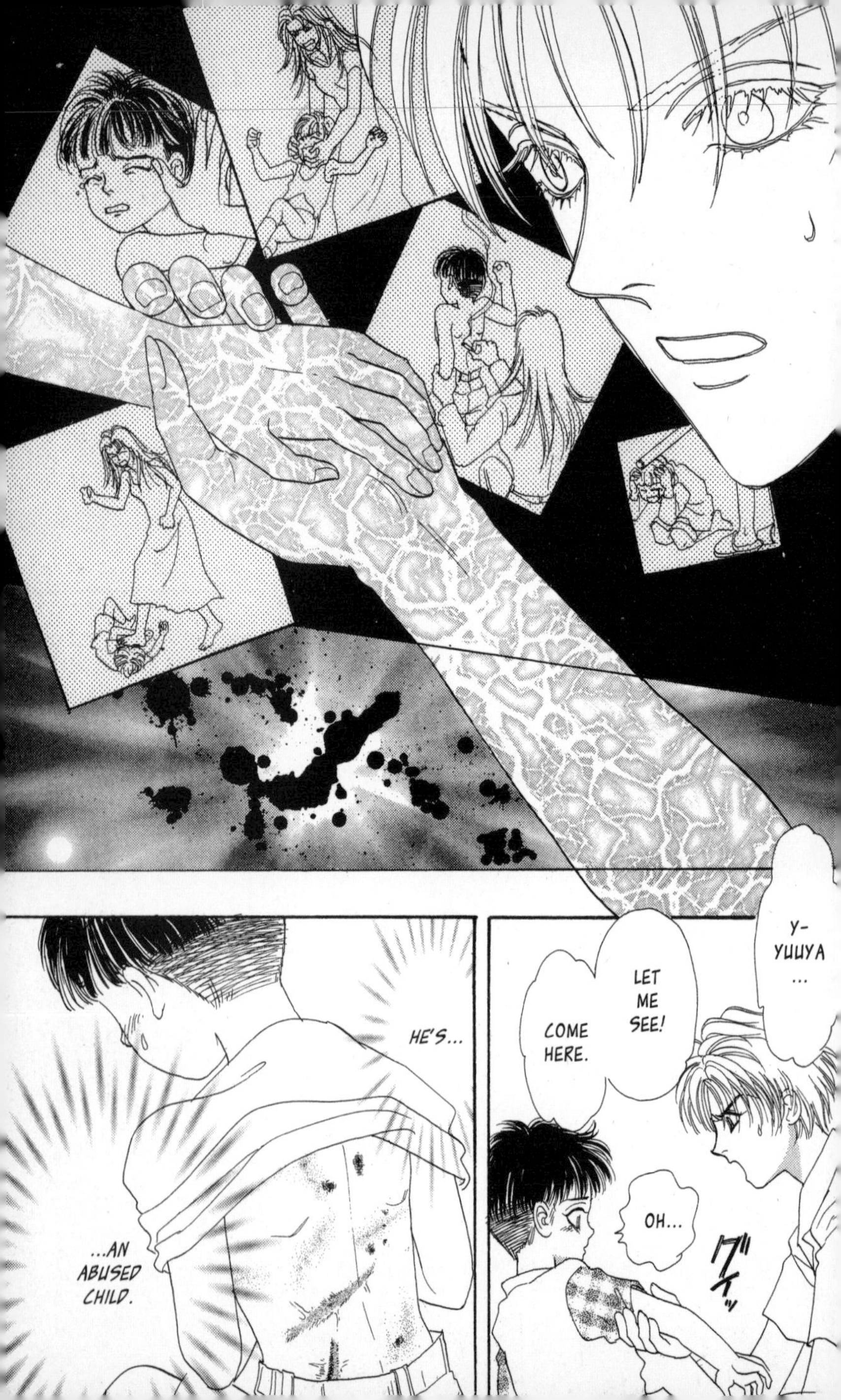
Y-YUUYA...
LET ME SEE!
COME HERE.
OH...
グイッ
HE'S...
...AN ABUSED CHILD.

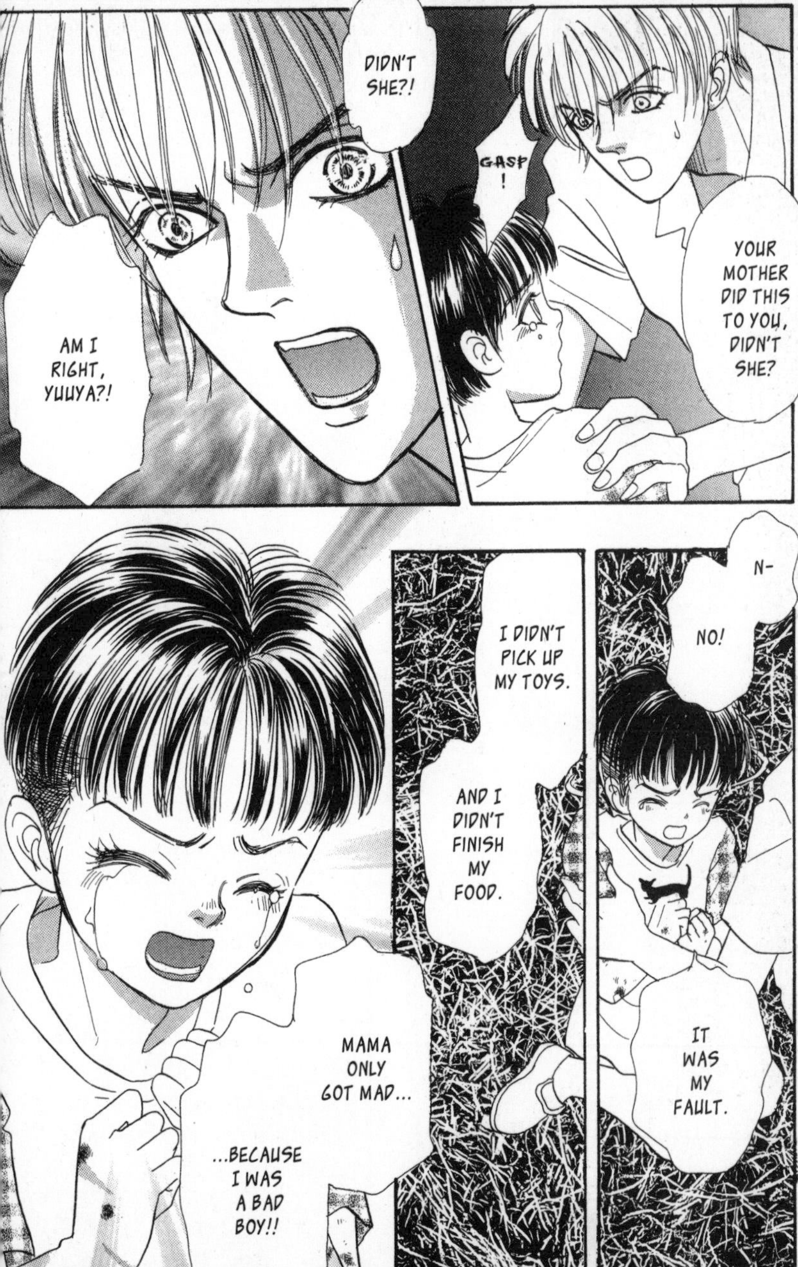
YOUR MOTHER DID THIS TO YOU, DIDN'T SHE?
GASP!
DIDN'T SHE?!
AM I RIGHT, YUUYA?!
N-
NO!
IT WAS MY FAULT.
I DIDN'T PICK UP MY TOYS.
AND I DIDN'T FINISH MY FOOD.
MAMA ONLY GOT MAD...
...BECAUSE I WAS A BAD BOY!!

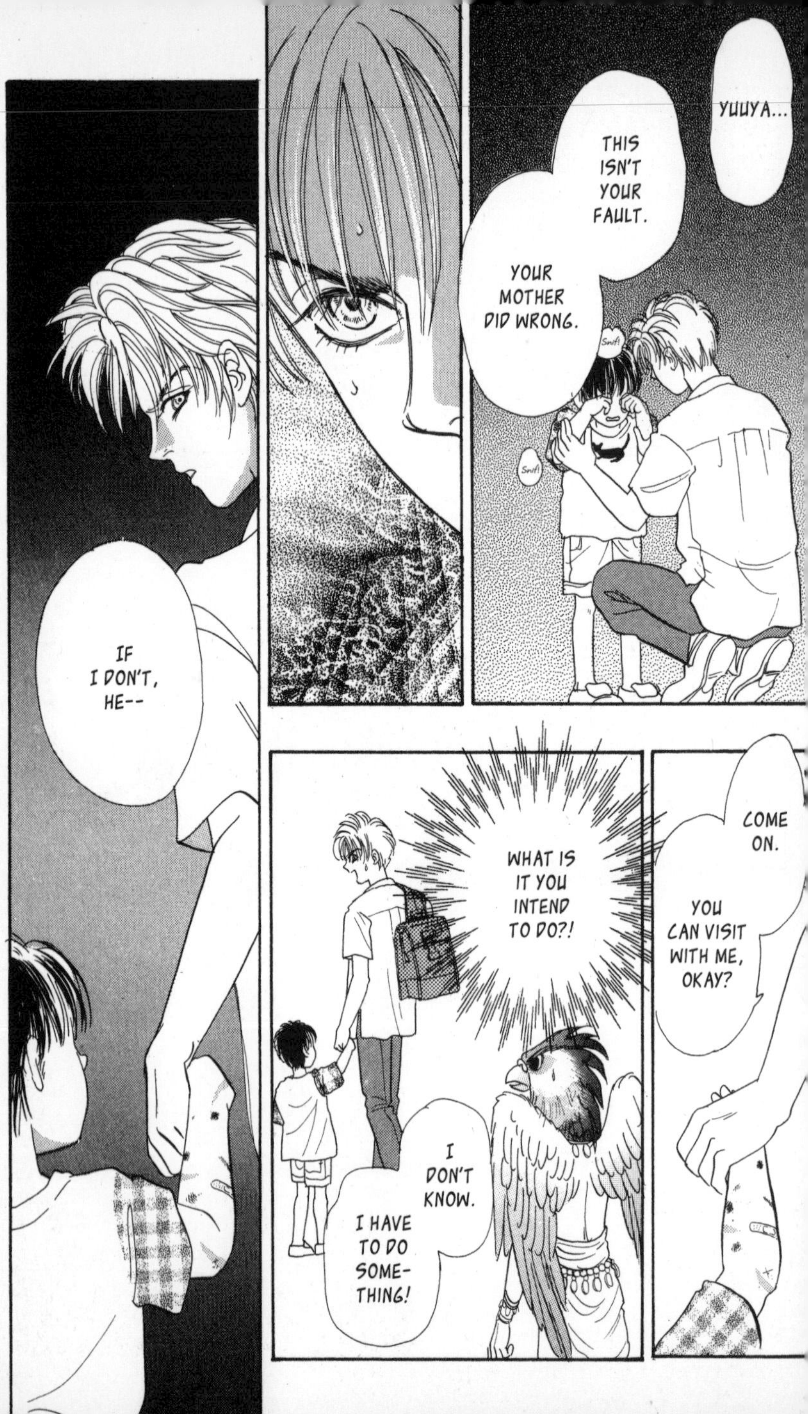
YUUYA...
THIS ISN'T YOUR FAULT.
YOUR MOTHER DID WRONG.
Snif!
Snif!
COME ON.
YOU CAN VISIT WITH ME, OKAY?
WHAT IS IT YOU INTEND TO DO?!
I DON'T KNOW.
I HAVE TO DO SOME-THING!
IF I DON'T, HE--

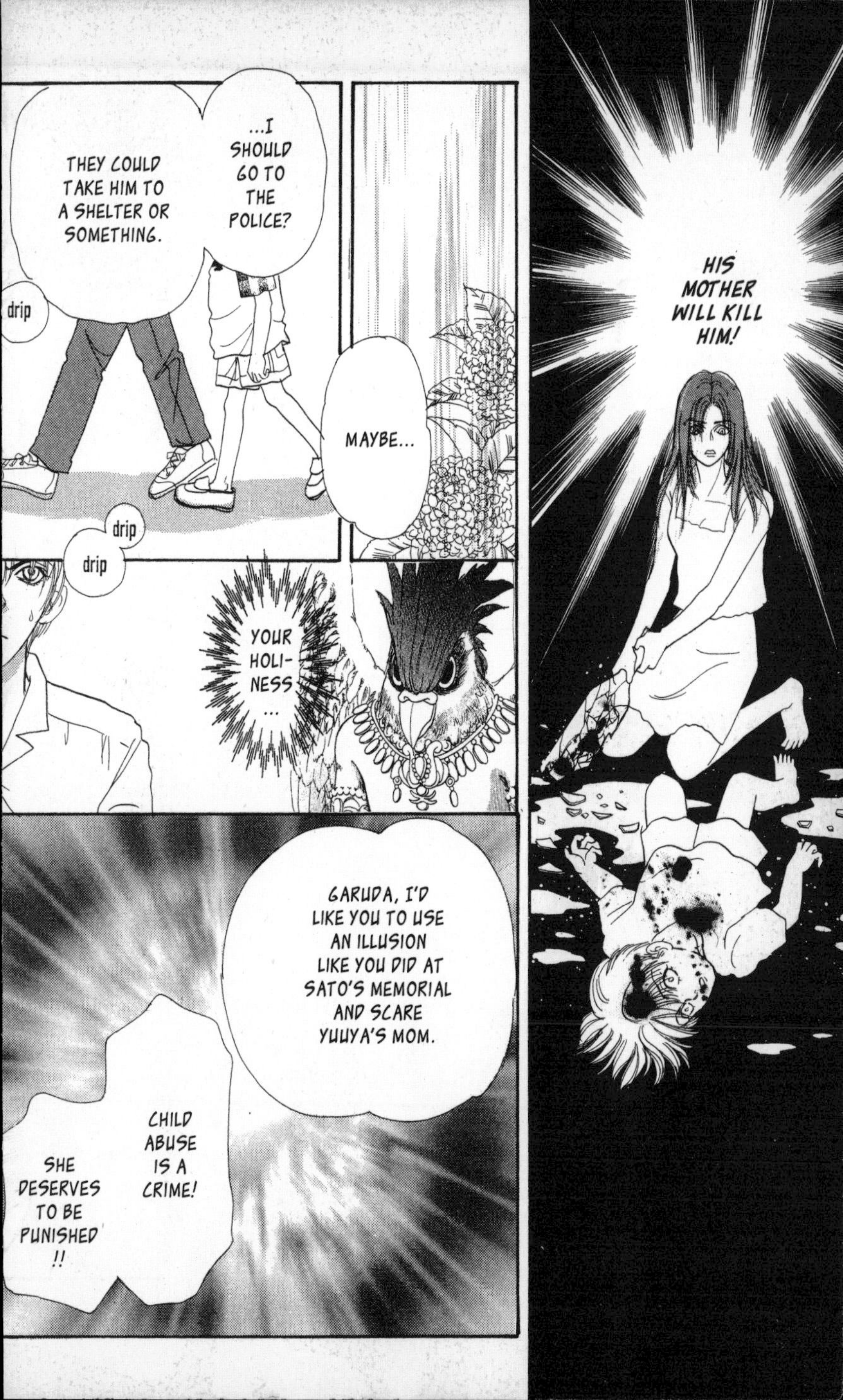
HIS MOTHER WILL KILL HIM!
MAYBE...
...I SHOULD GO TO THE POLICE?
THEY COULD TAKE HIM TO A SHELTER OR SOMETHING.
drip
drip
drip
YOUR HOLI-NESS...
GARUDA, I'D LIKE YOU TO USE AN ILLUSION LIKE YOU DID AT SATO'S MEMORIAL AND SCARE YUUYA'S MOM.
CHILD ABUSE IS A CRIME!
SHE DESERVES TO BE PUNISHED!!

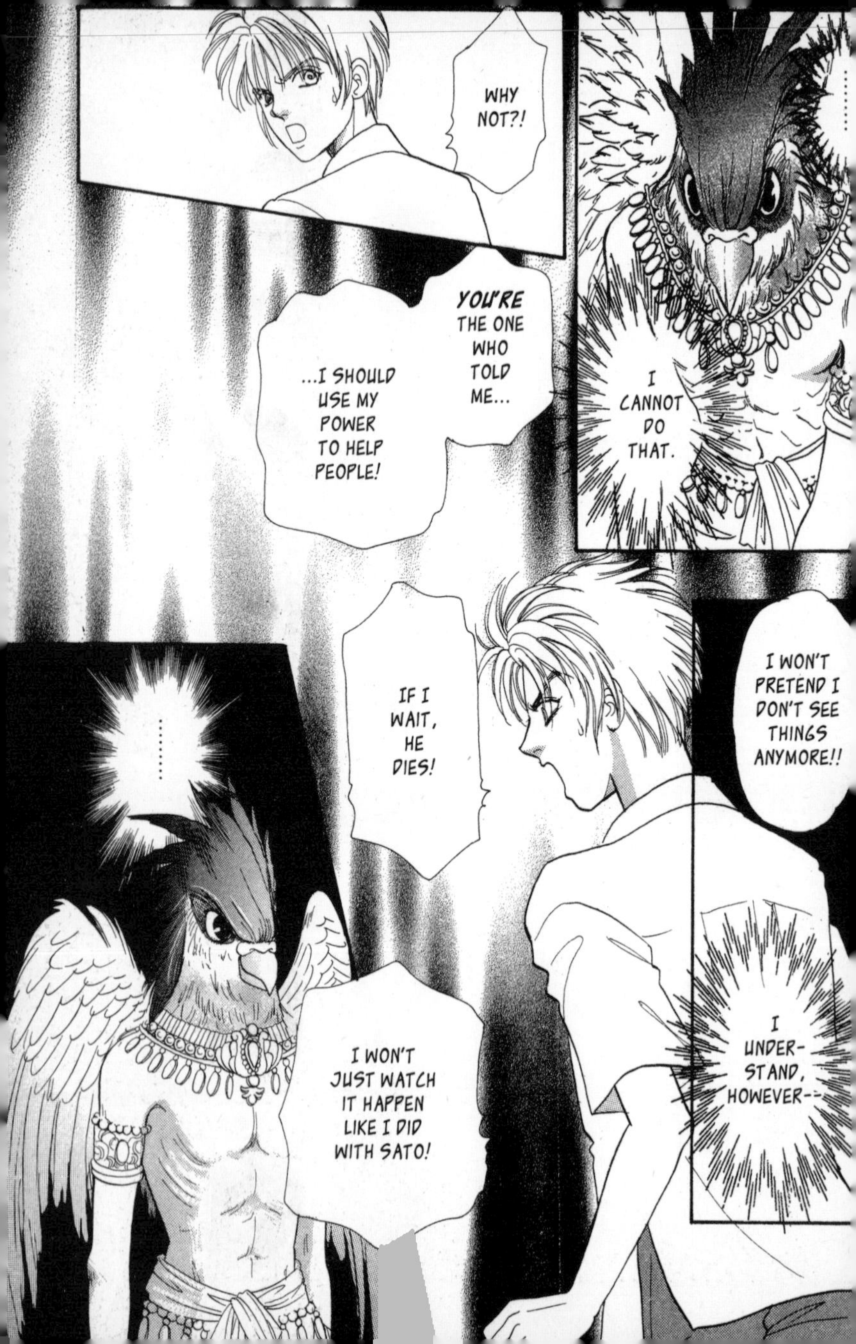
I CANNOT DO THAT.
WHY NOT?!
YOU'RE THE ONE WHO TOLD ME...
...I SHOULD USE MY POWER TO HELP PEOPLE!
I WON'T PRETEND I DON'T SEE THINGS ANYMORE!!
I UNDER-STAND, HOWEVER--
IF I WAIT, HE DIES!
......
I WON'T JUST WATCH IT HAPPEN LIKE I DID WITH SATO!

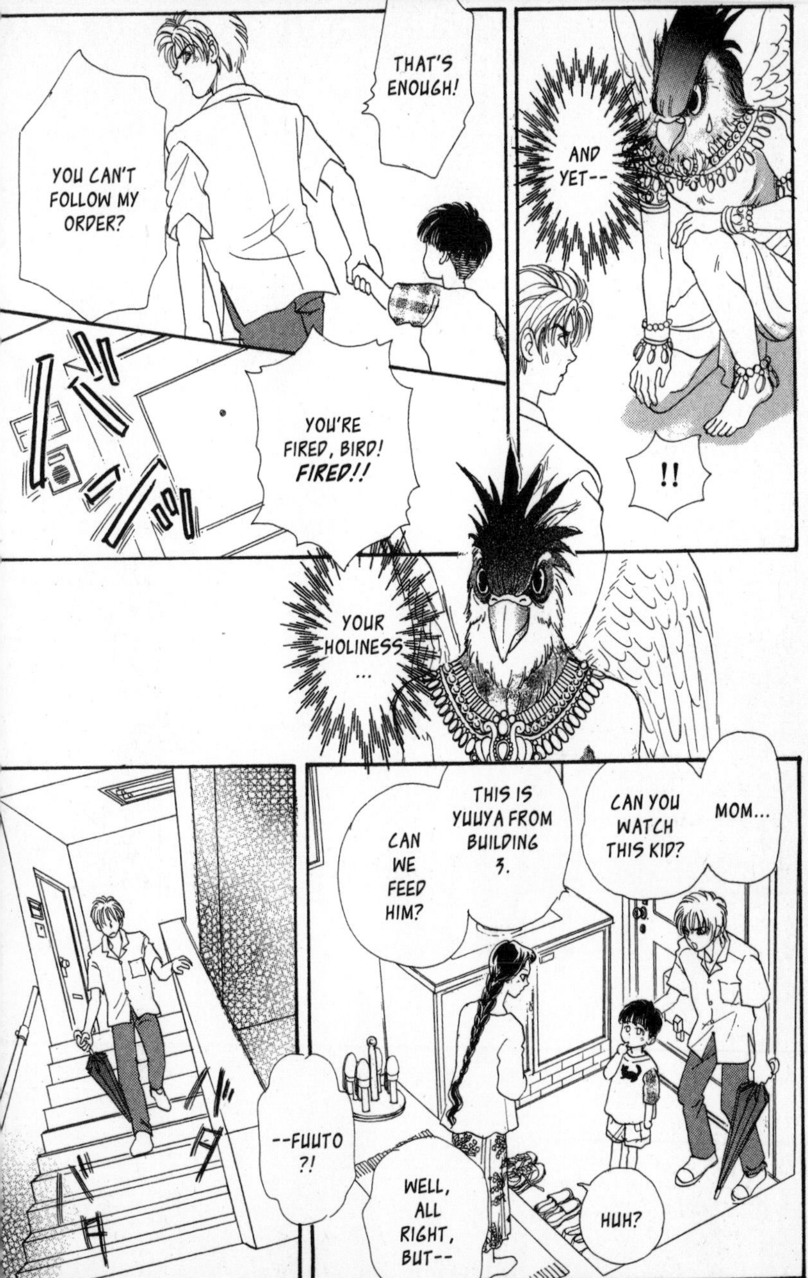
AND YET--
!!
THAT'S ENOUGH!
YOU CAN'T FOLLOW MY ORDER?
YOU'RE FIRED, BIRD! FIRED!!
YOUR HOLINESS...
MOM...
CAN YOU WATCH THIS KID?
THIS IS YUUYA FROM BUILDING 3.
CAN WE FEED HIM?
--FUUTO?!
HUH?
WELL, ALL RIGHT, BUT--

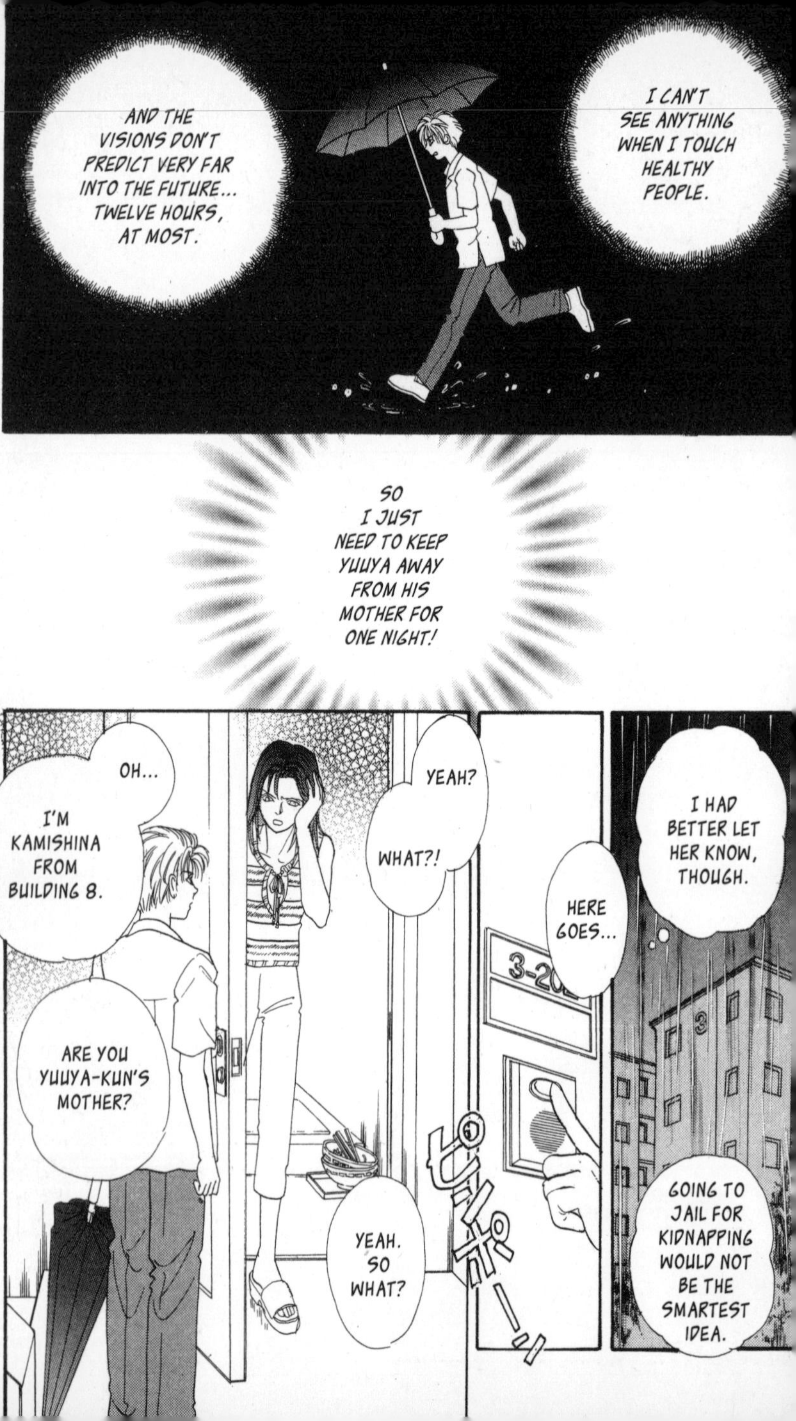
I CAN'T SEE ANYTHING WHEN I TOUCH HEALTHY PEOPLE.
AND THE VISIONS DON'T PREDICT VERY FAR INTO THE FUTURE... TWELVE HOURS, AT MOST.
SO I JUST NEED TO KEEP YUUYA AWAY FROM HIS MOTHER FOR ONE NIGHT!
I HAD BETTER LET HER KNOW, THOUGH.
GOING TO JAIL FOR KIDNAPPING WOULD NOT BE THE SMARTEST IDEA.
HERE GOES...
ピンポーン
YEAH?
OH...
I'M KAMISHINA FROM BUILDING 8.
WHAT?!
ARE YOU YUUYA-KUN'S MOTHER?
YEAH. SO WHAT?

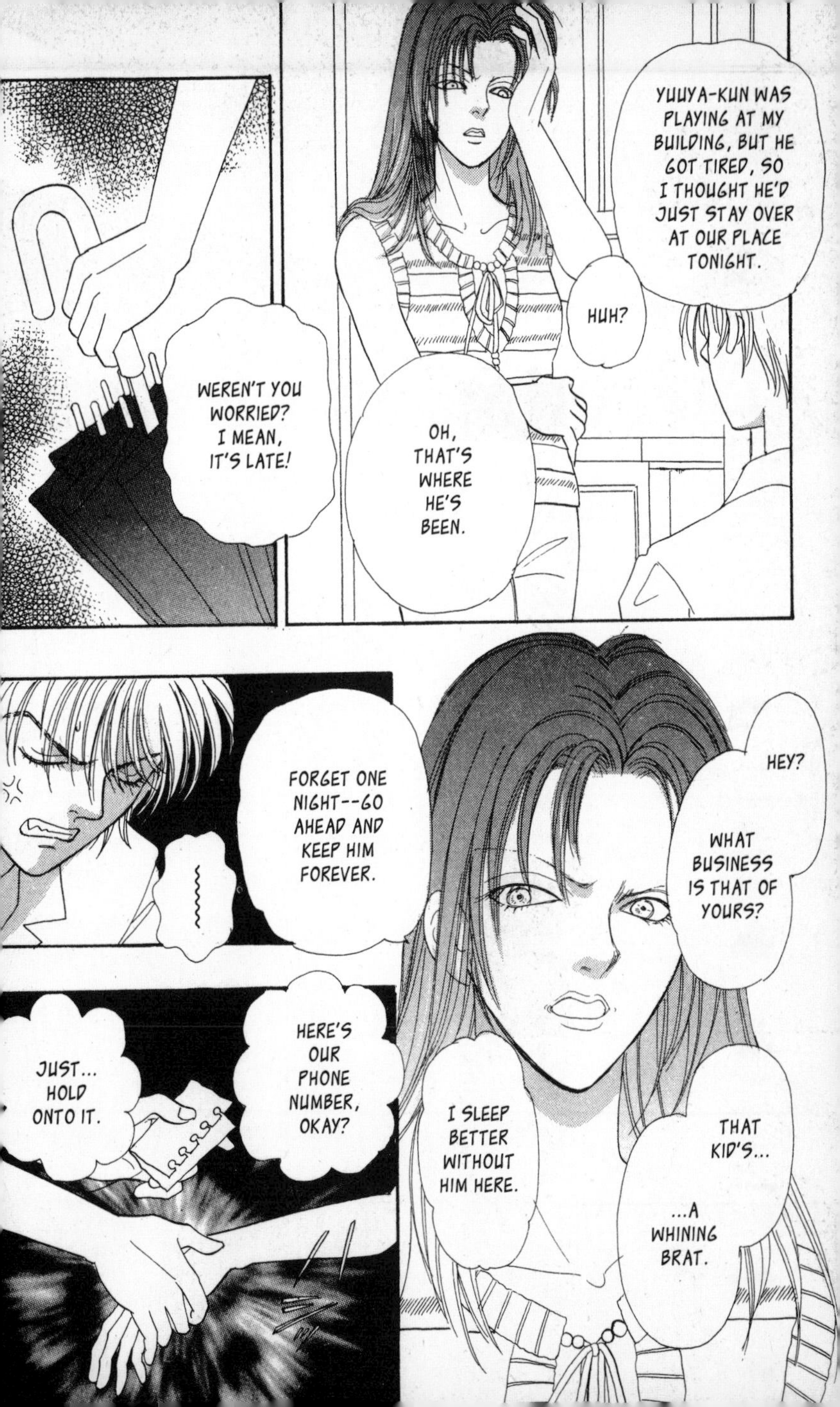
YUUYA-KUN WAS PLAYING AT MY BUILDING, BUT HE GOT TIRED, SO I THOUGHT HE'D JUST STAY OVER AT OUR PLACE TONIGHT.
HUH?
OH, THAT'S WHERE HE'S BEEN.
WEREN'T YOU WORRIED? I MEAN, IT'S LATE!
HEY?
WHAT BUSINESS IS THAT OF YOURS?
THAT KID'S...
...A WHINING BRAT.
I SLEEP BETTER WITHOUT HIM HERE.
FORGET ONE NIGHT--GO AHEAD AND KEEP HIM FOREVER.
HERE'S OUR PHONE NUMBER, OKAY?
JUST... HOLD ONTO IT.

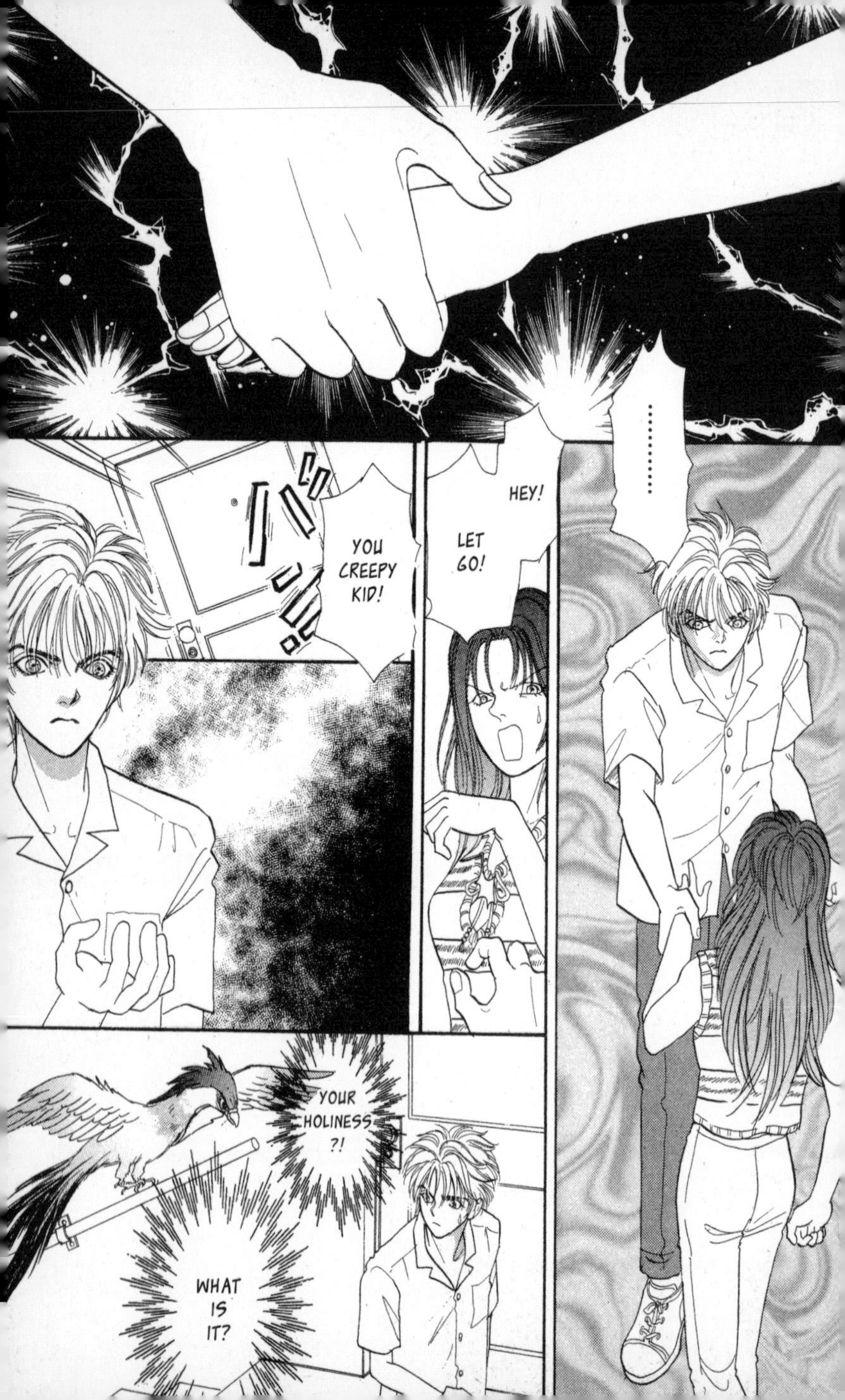

......
HEY!
LET GO!
YOU CREEPY KID!
YOUR HOLINESS?!
WHAT IS IT?

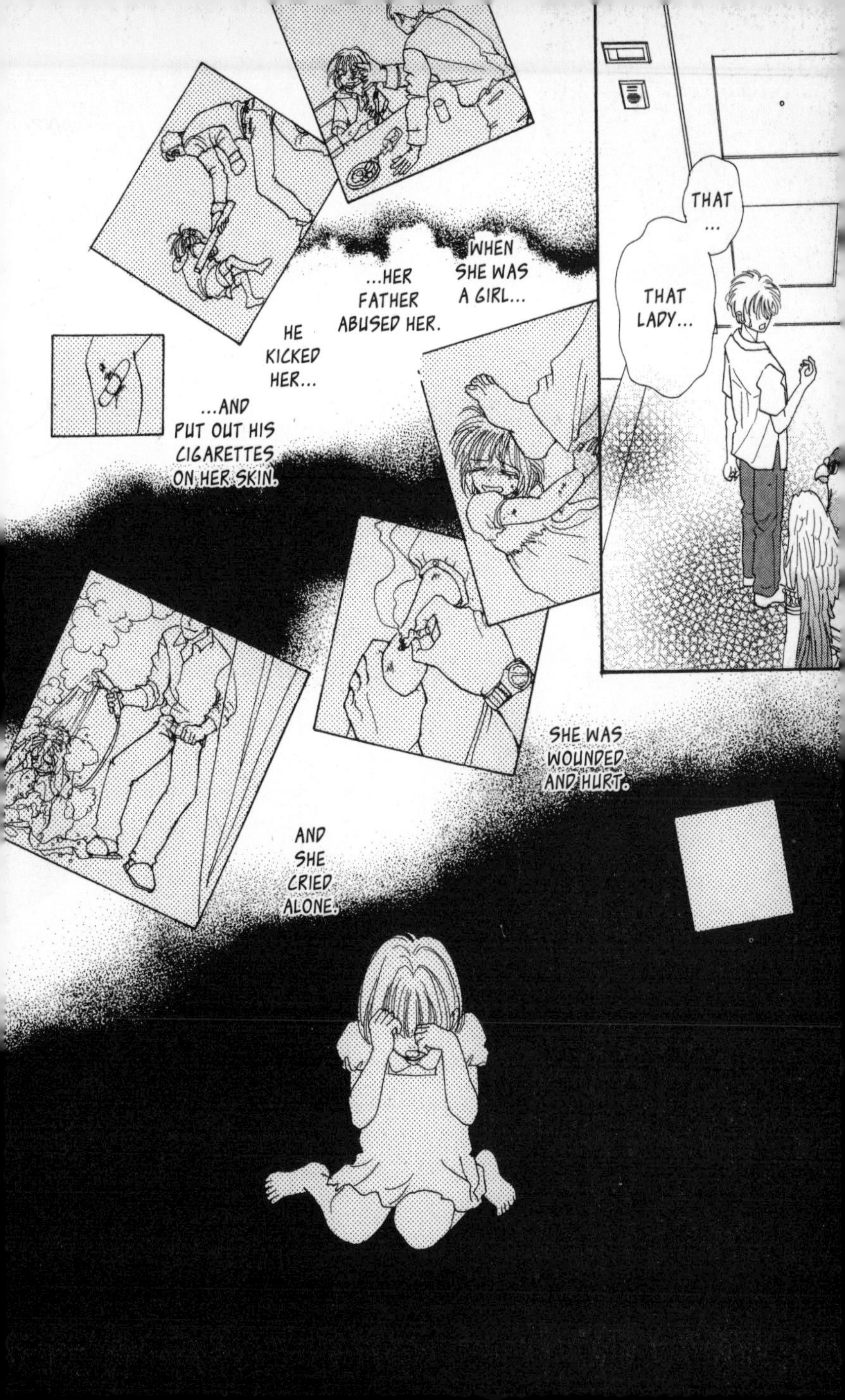
THAT...
THAT LADY...
WHEN SHE WAS A GIRL...
...HER FATHER ABUSED HER.
HE KICKED HER...
...AND PUT OUT HIS CIGARETTES ON HER SKIN.
SHE WAS WOUNDED AND HURT.
AND SHE CRIED ALONE.

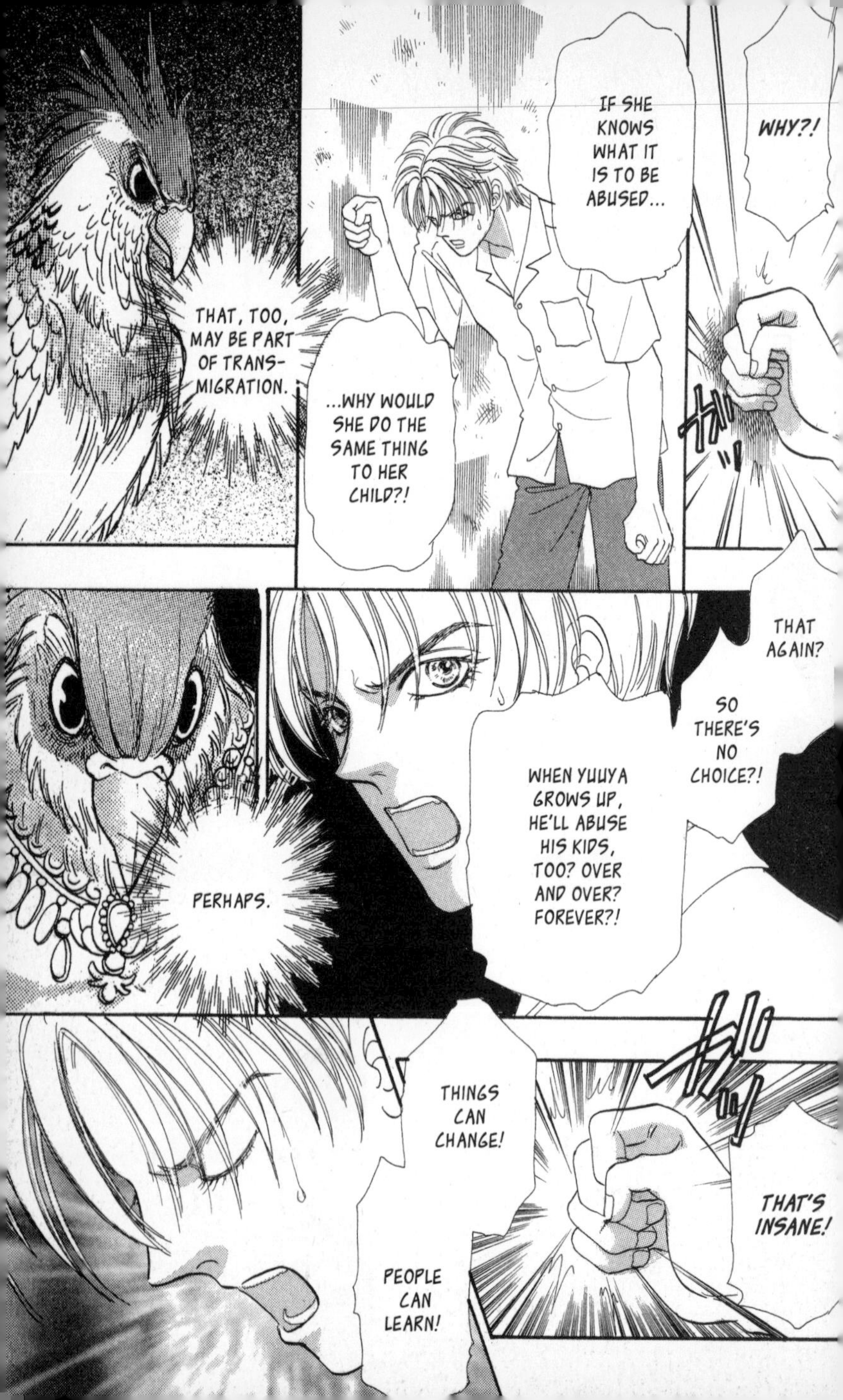
WHY?!
IF SHE KNOWS WHAT IT IS TO BE ABUSED...
...WHY WOULD SHE DO THE SAME THING TO HER CHILD?!
THAT, TOO, MAY BE PART OF TRANS-MIGRATION.
THAT AGAIN?
SO THERE'S NO CHOICE?!
WHEN YUUYA GROWS UP, HE'LL ABUSE HIS KIDS, TOO? OVER AND OVER? FOREVER?!
PERHAPS.
THAT'S INSANE!
THINGS CAN CHANGE!
PEOPLE CAN LEARN!

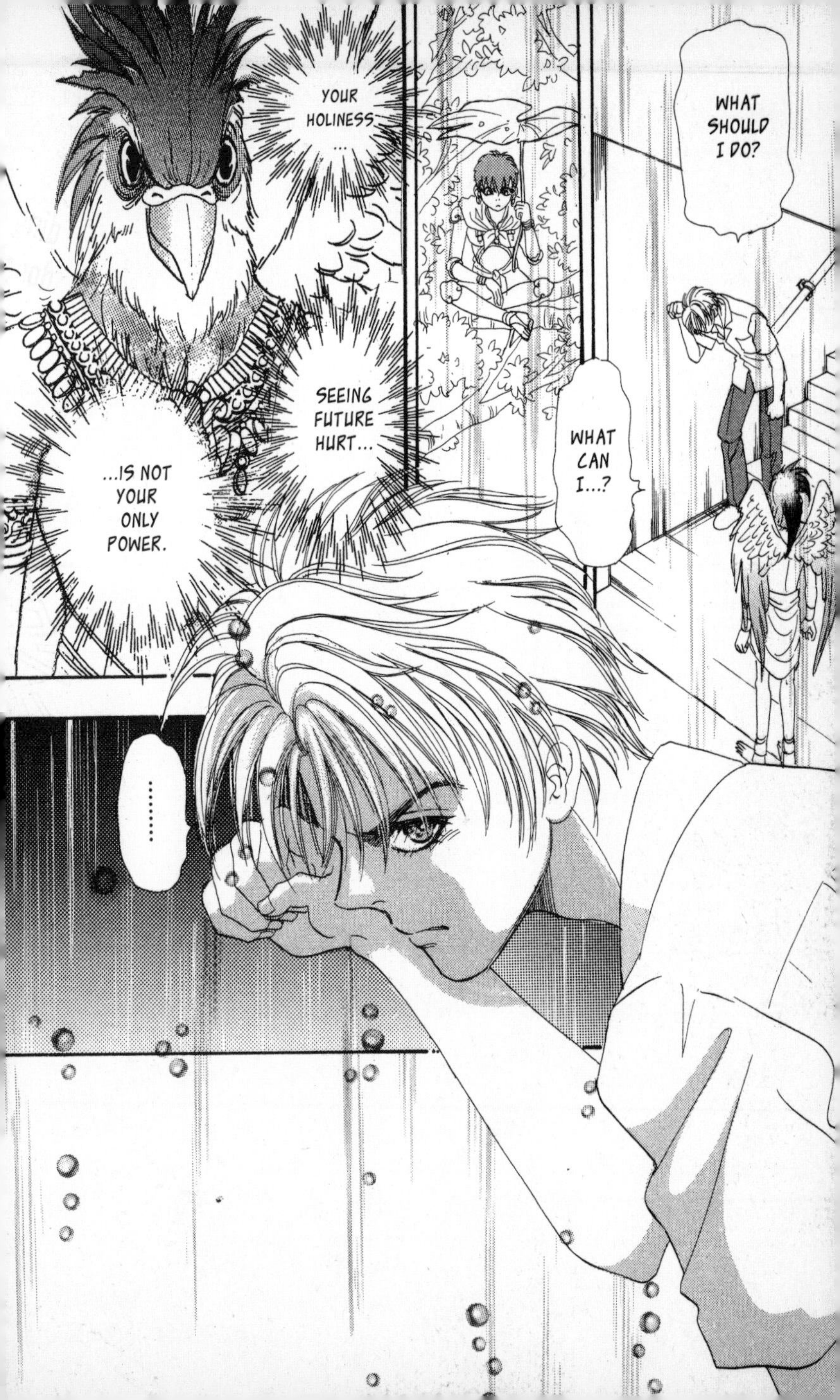
WHAT SHOULD I DO?
WHAT CAN I...?
YOUR HOLINESS...
SEEING FUTURE HURT...
...IS NOT YOUR ONLY POWER.
......

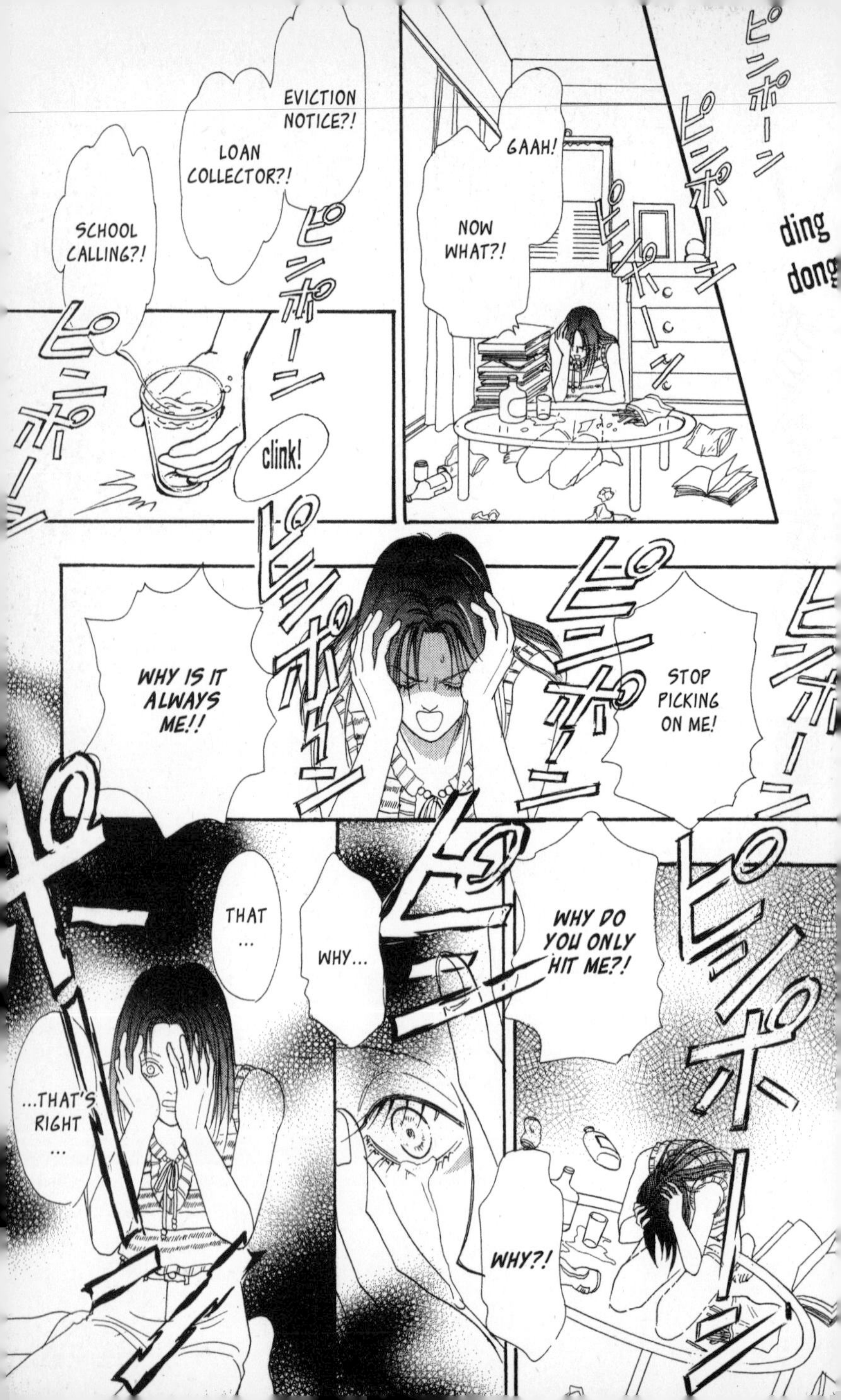

ピンポーン
ピンポーン
ding dong
GAAH!
NOW WHAT?!
EVICTION NOTICE?!
LOAN COLLECTOR?!
SCHOOL CALLING?!
ピンポーン
clink!
ピンポーン
STOP PICKING ON ME!
WHY IS IT ALWAYS ME!!
WHY DO YOU ONLY HIT ME?!
WHY?!
WHY...
THAT ...
...THAT'S RIGHT ...

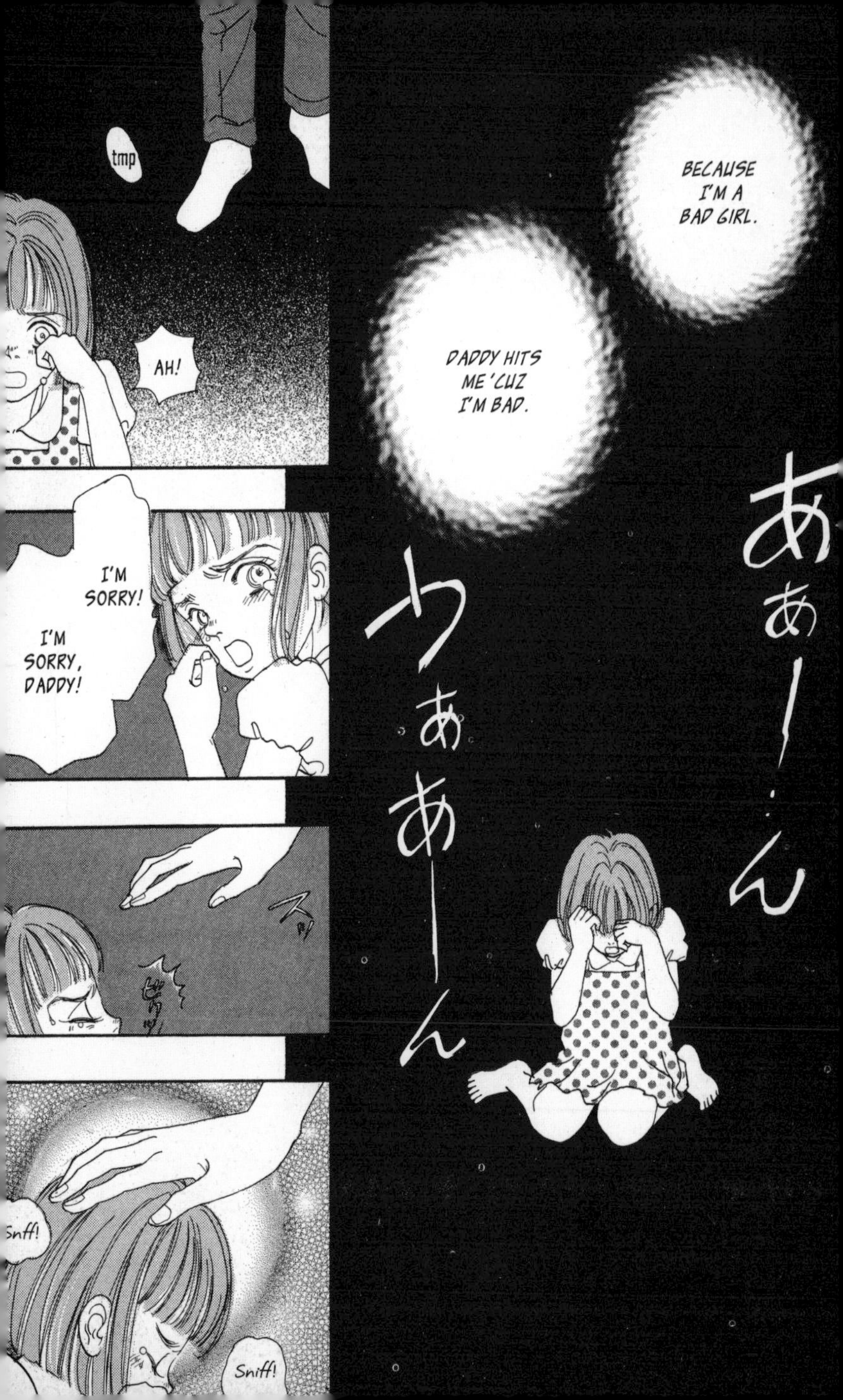
BECAUSE I'M A BAD GIRL.
DADDY HITS ME 'CUZ I'M BAD.
あぁー!ん
わああーん
tmp
AH!
I'M SORRY!
I'M SORRY, DADDY!
Sniff!
Sniff!

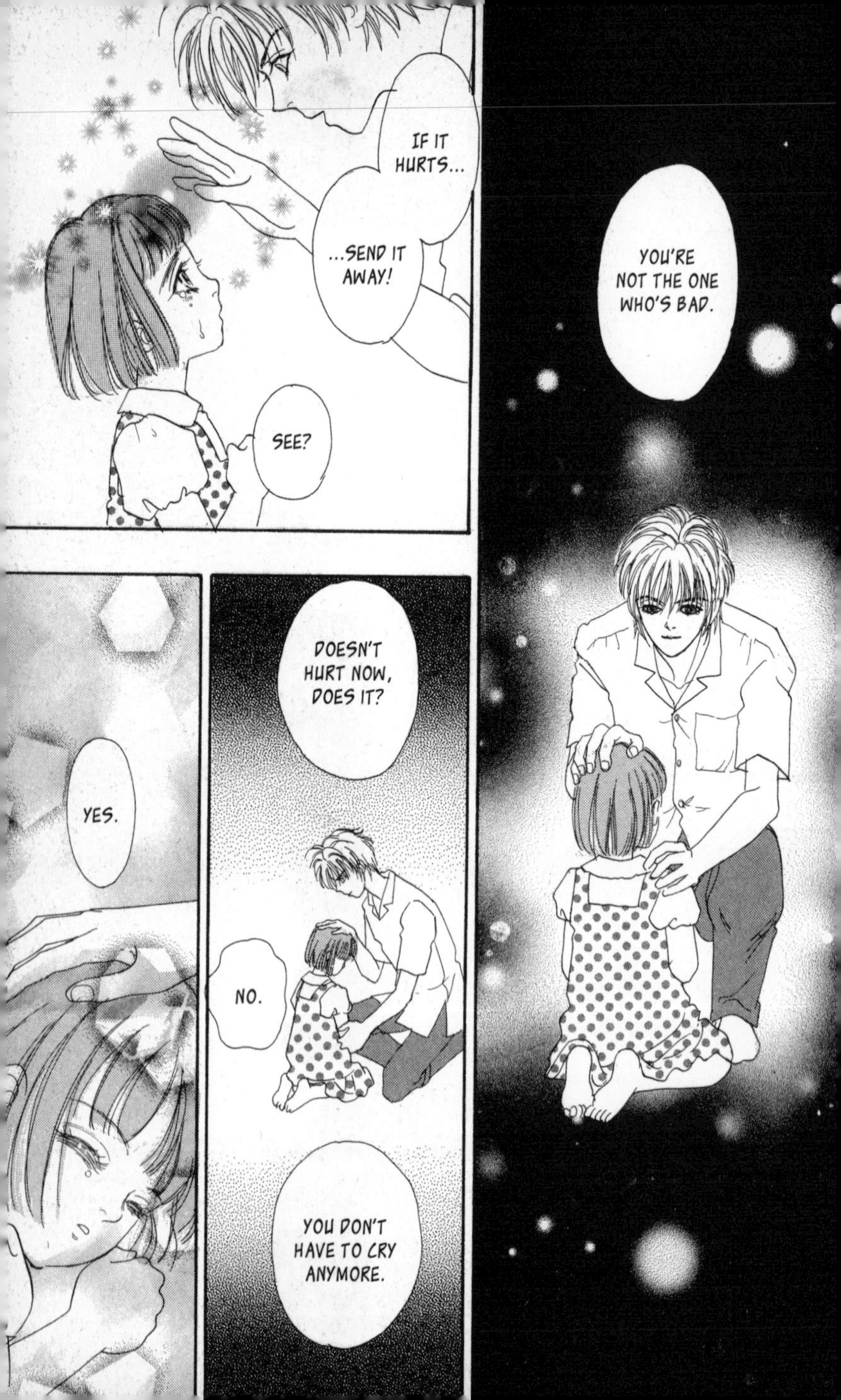
YOU'RE NOT THE ONE WHO'S BAD.
IF IT HURTS...
...SEND IT AWAY!
SEE?
DOESN'T HURT NOW, DOES IT?
NO.
YOU DON'T HAVE TO CRY ANYMORE.
YES.

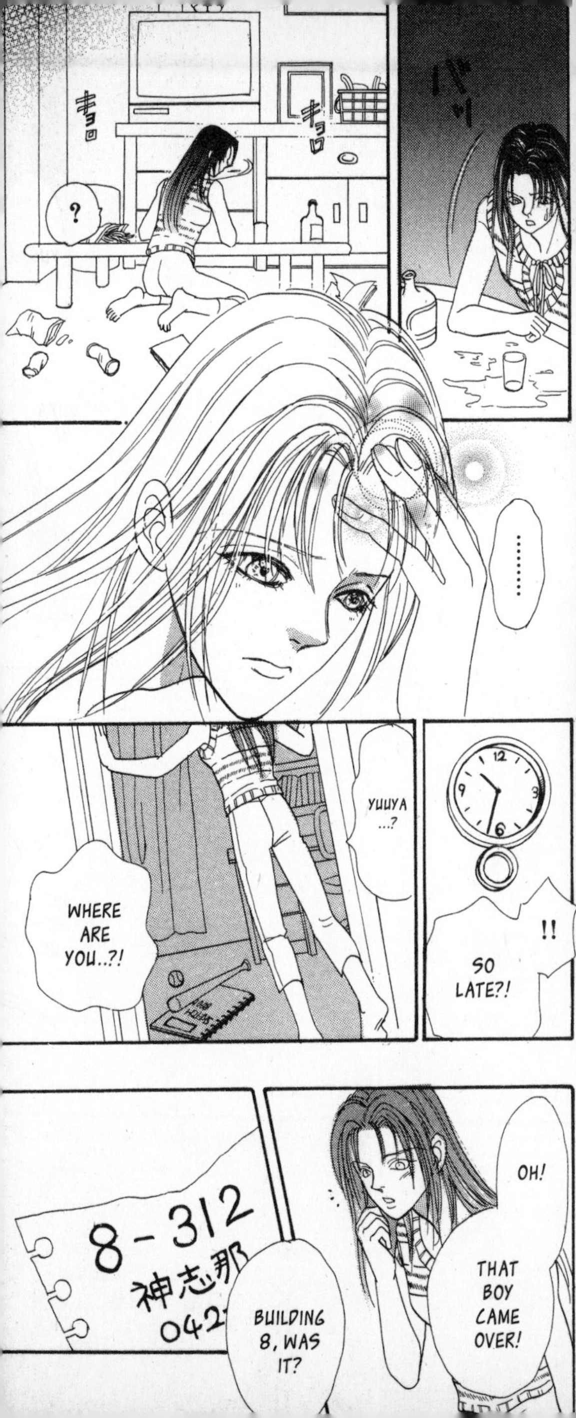

バッ
キョロ
キョロ
?
……
!!
SO LATE?!
YUUYA ...?
WHERE ARE YOU..?!
OH!
THAT BOY CAME OVER!
BUILDING 8, WAS IT?
8 - 312
神志那
042

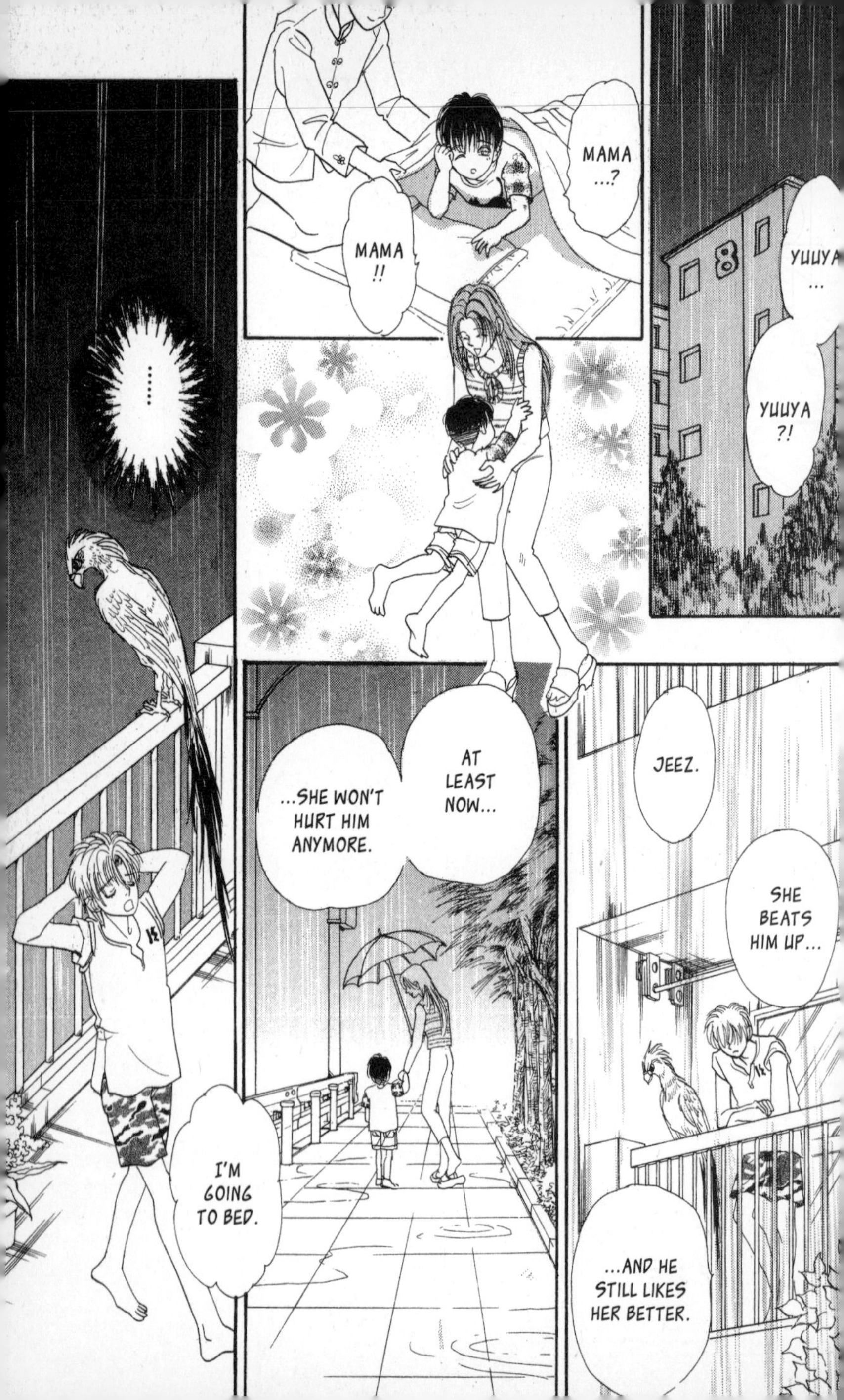
YUUYA
...
YUUYA
?!
MAMA
...?
MAMA
!!
JEEZ.
SHE BEATS HIM UP...
...AND HE STILL LIKES HER BETTER.
AT LEAST NOW...
...SHE WON'T HURT HIM ANYMORE.
......
I'M GOING TO BED.

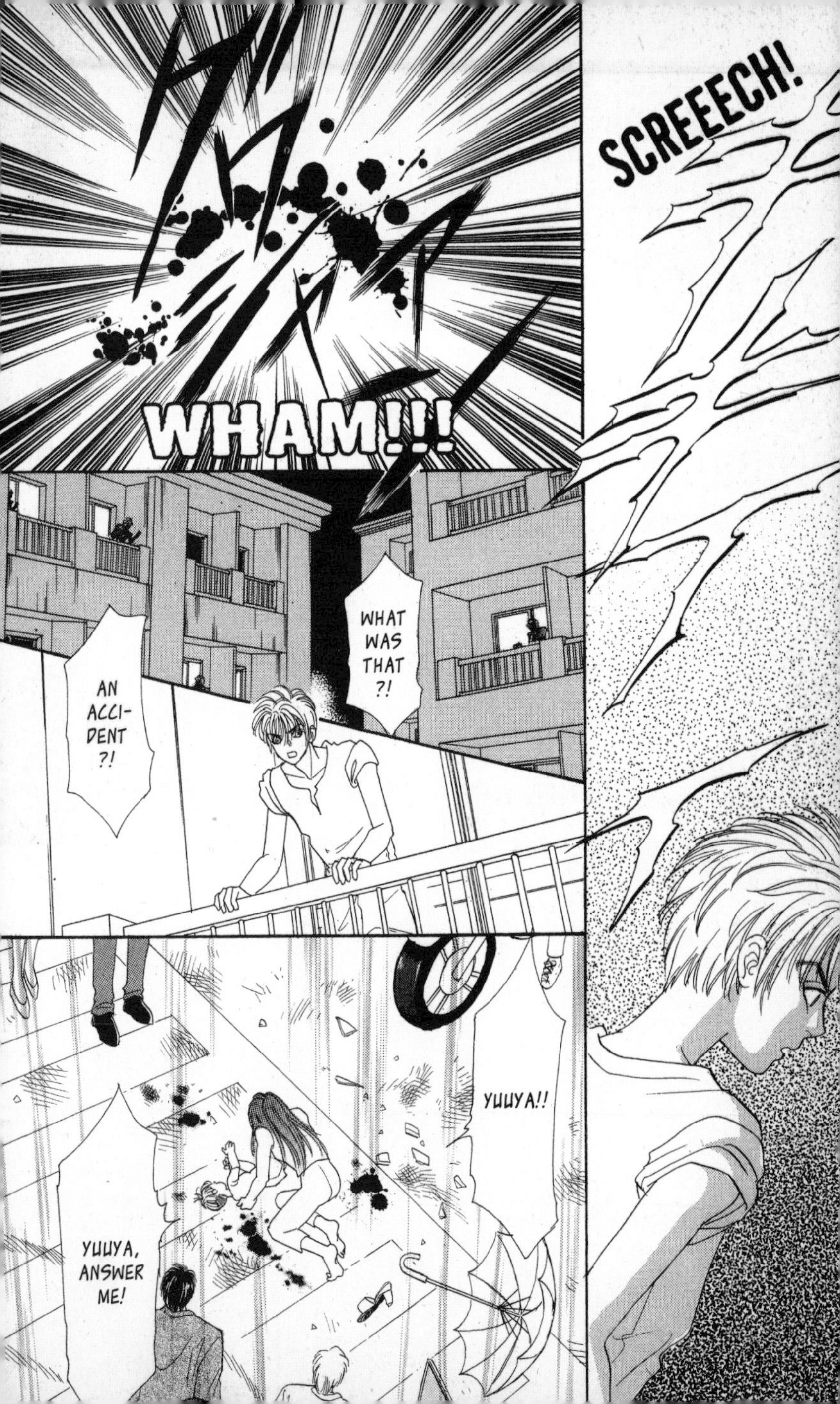

SCREEECH!
WHAM!!!
WHAT WAS THAT?!
AN ACCI-DENT?!
YUUYA!!
YUUYA, ANSWER ME!

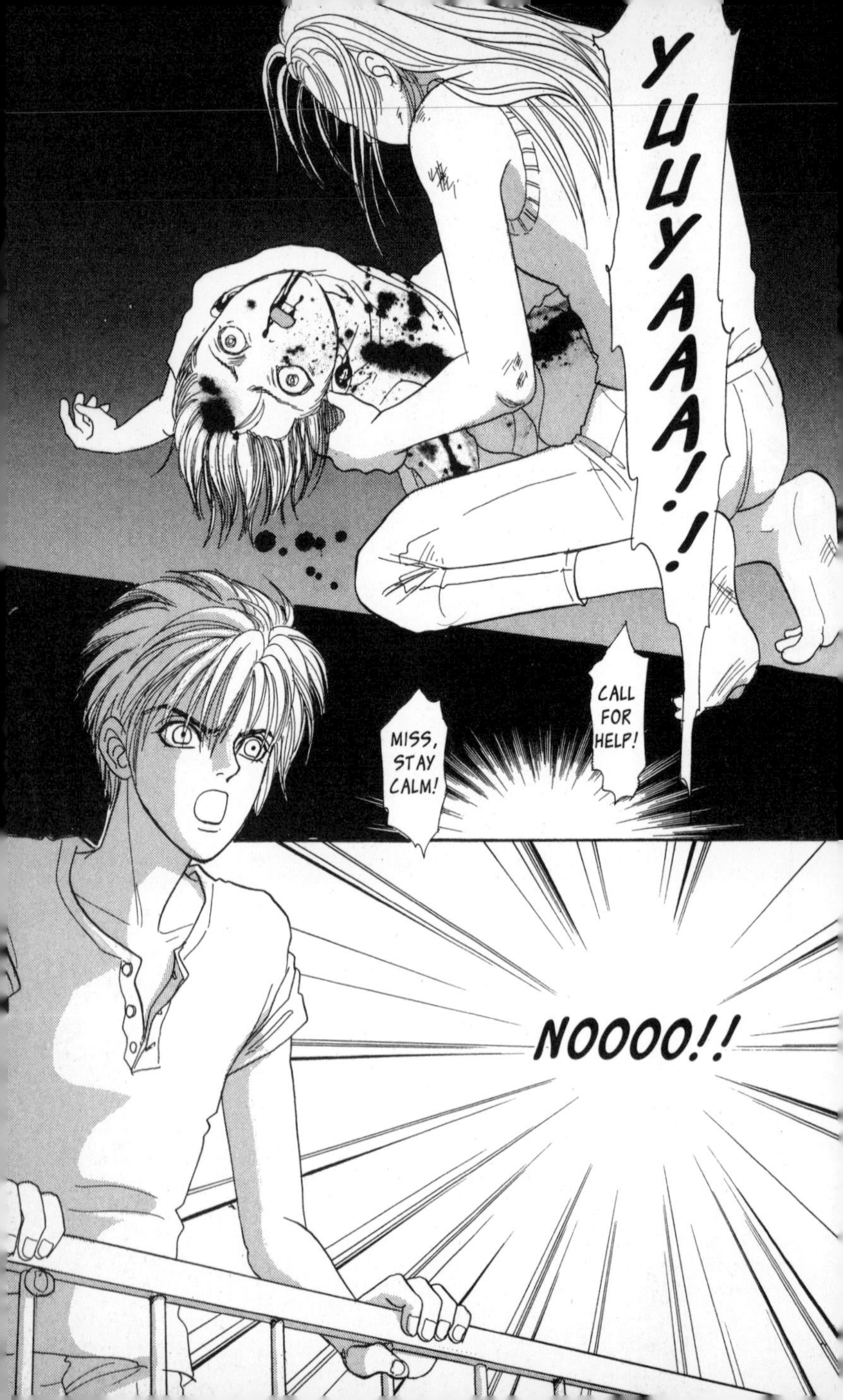

YUUYAAAA!!!
CALL FOR HELP!
MISS, STAY CALM!
NOOOO!!

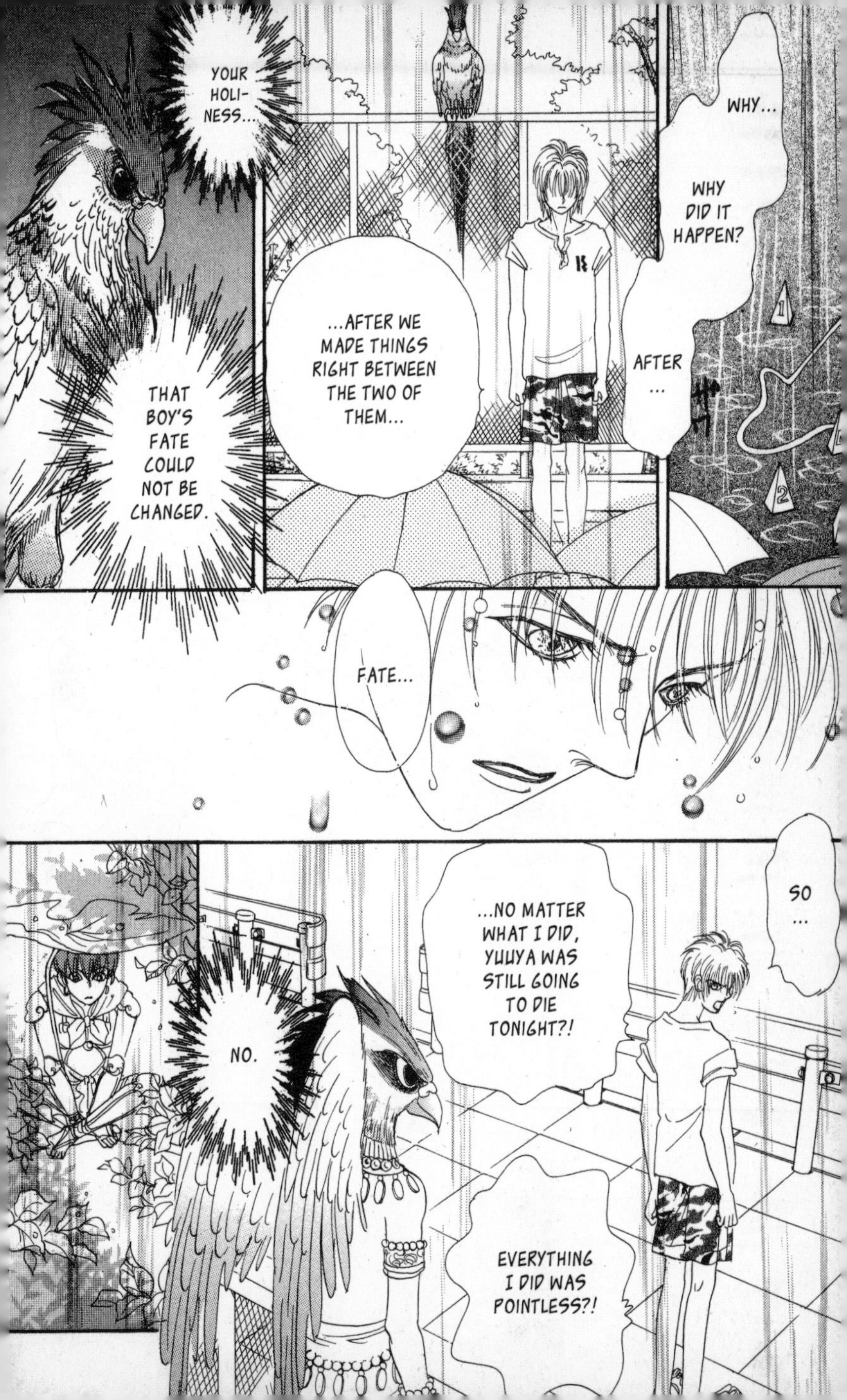
WHY...
WHY DID IT HAPPEN?
AFTER ...
...AFTER WE MADE THINGS RIGHT BETWEEN THE TWO OF THEM...
YOUR HOLINESS...
THAT BOY'S FATE COULD NOT BE CHANGED.
FATE...
SO ...
...NO MATTER WHAT I DID, YUUYA WAS STILL GOING TO DIE TONIGHT?!
EVERYTHING I DID WAS POINTLESS?!
NO.

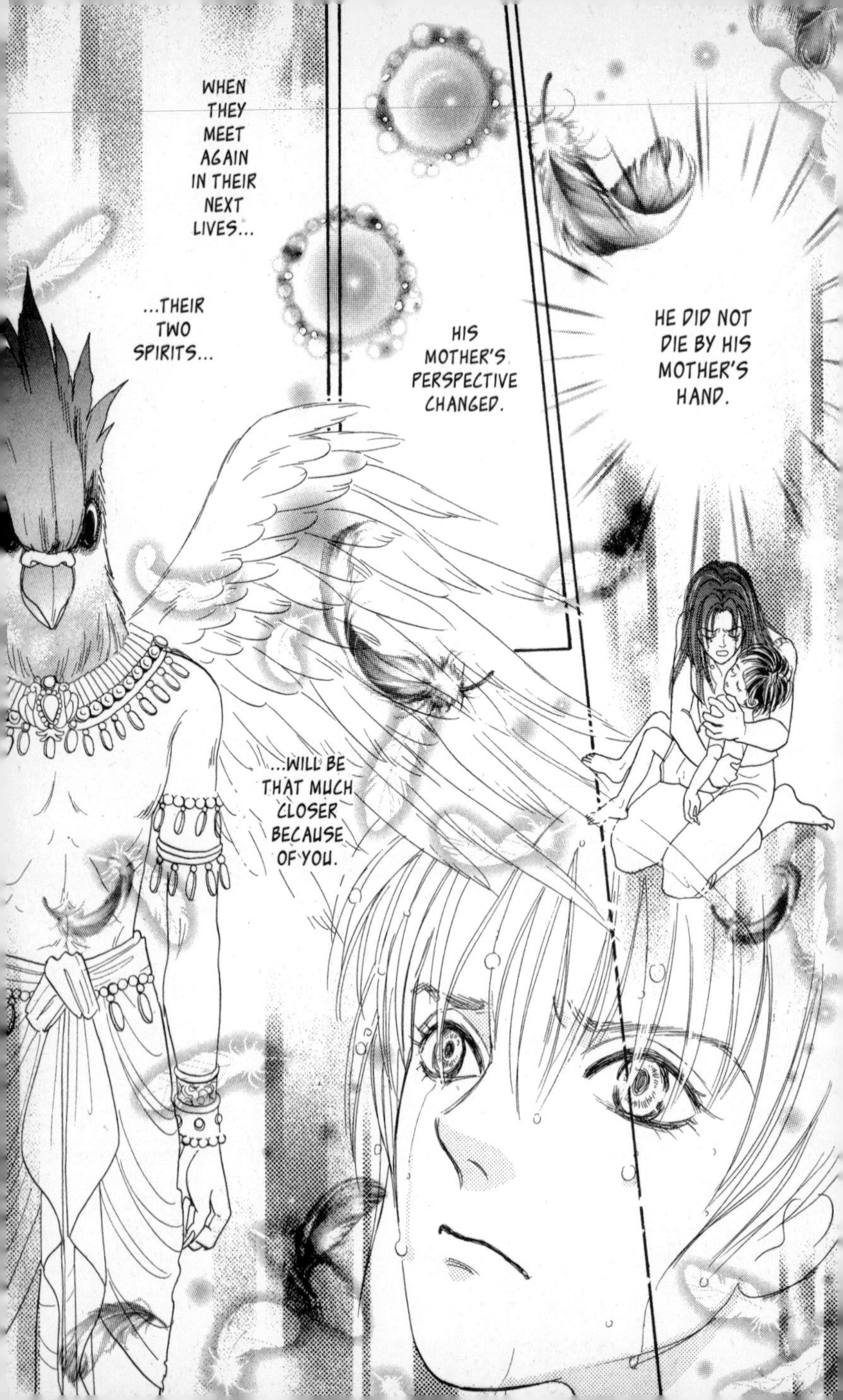
HE DID NOT DIE BY HIS MOTHER'S HAND.
HIS MOTHER'S PERSPECTIVE CHANGED.
WHEN THEY MEET AGAIN IN THEIR NEXT LIVES...
...THEIR TWO SPIRITS...
...WILL BE THAT MUCH CLOSER BECAUSE OF YOU.

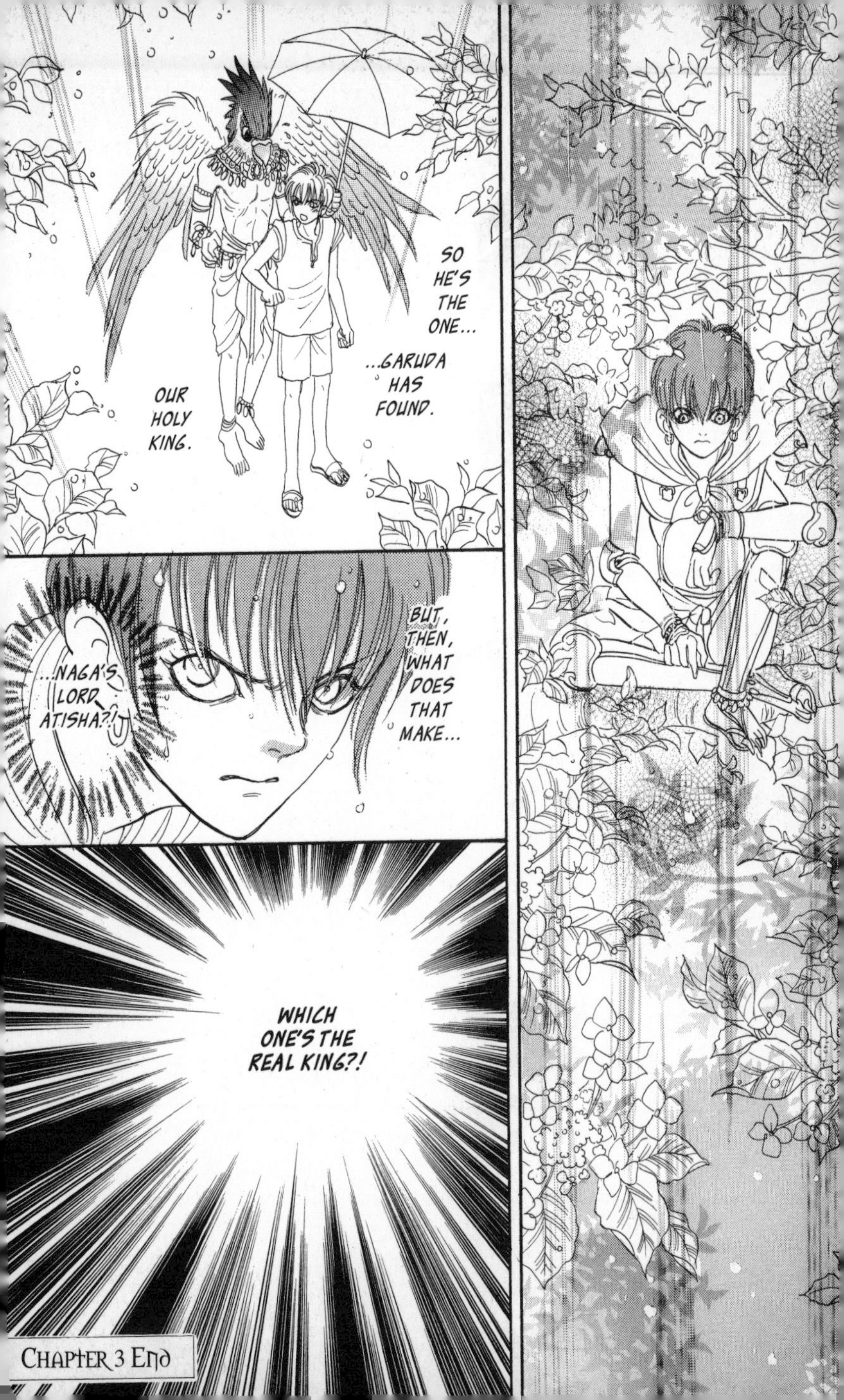
SO HE'S THE ONE...
...GARUDA HAS FOUND.
OUR HOLY KING.
BUT, THEN, WHAT DOES THAT MAKE...
...NAGA'S LORD ATISHA?!
WHICH ONE'S THE REAL KING?!
Chapter 3 End

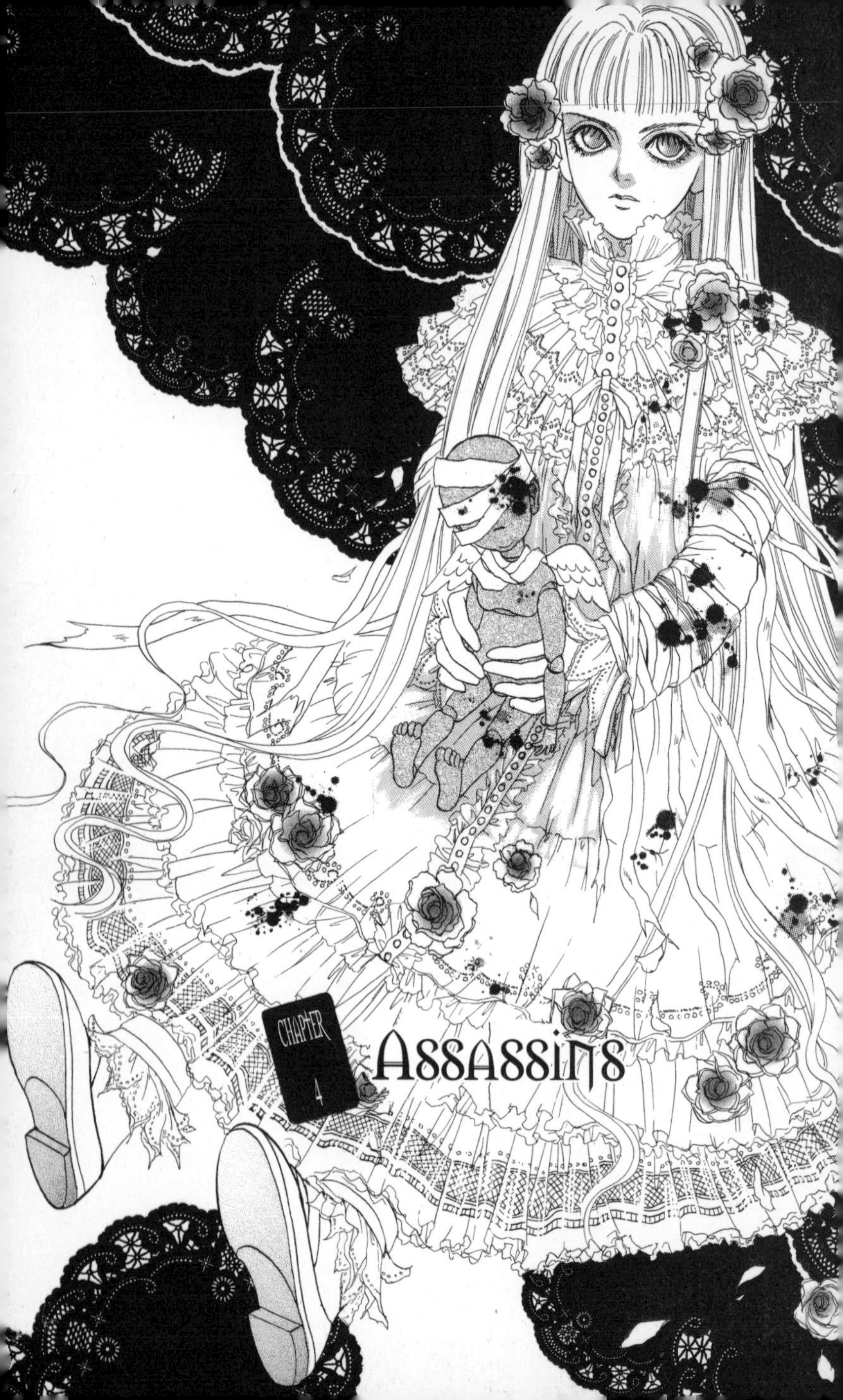
CHAPTER 4
Assassins

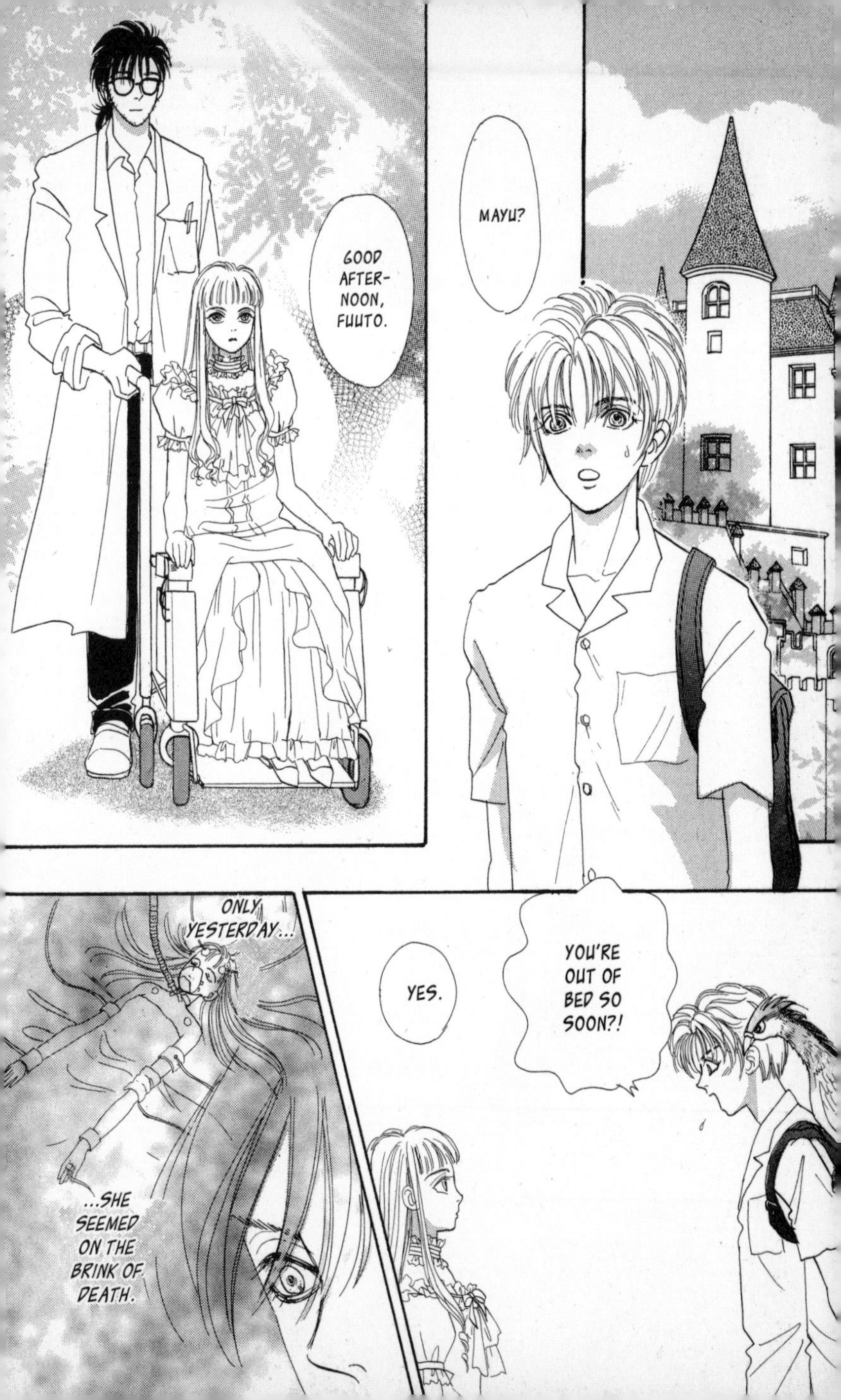
MAYU?
GOOD AFTER-NOON, FUUTO.
YOU'RE OUT OF BED SO SOON?!
YES.
ONLY YESTERDAY...
...SHE SEEMED ON THE BRINK OF DEATH.

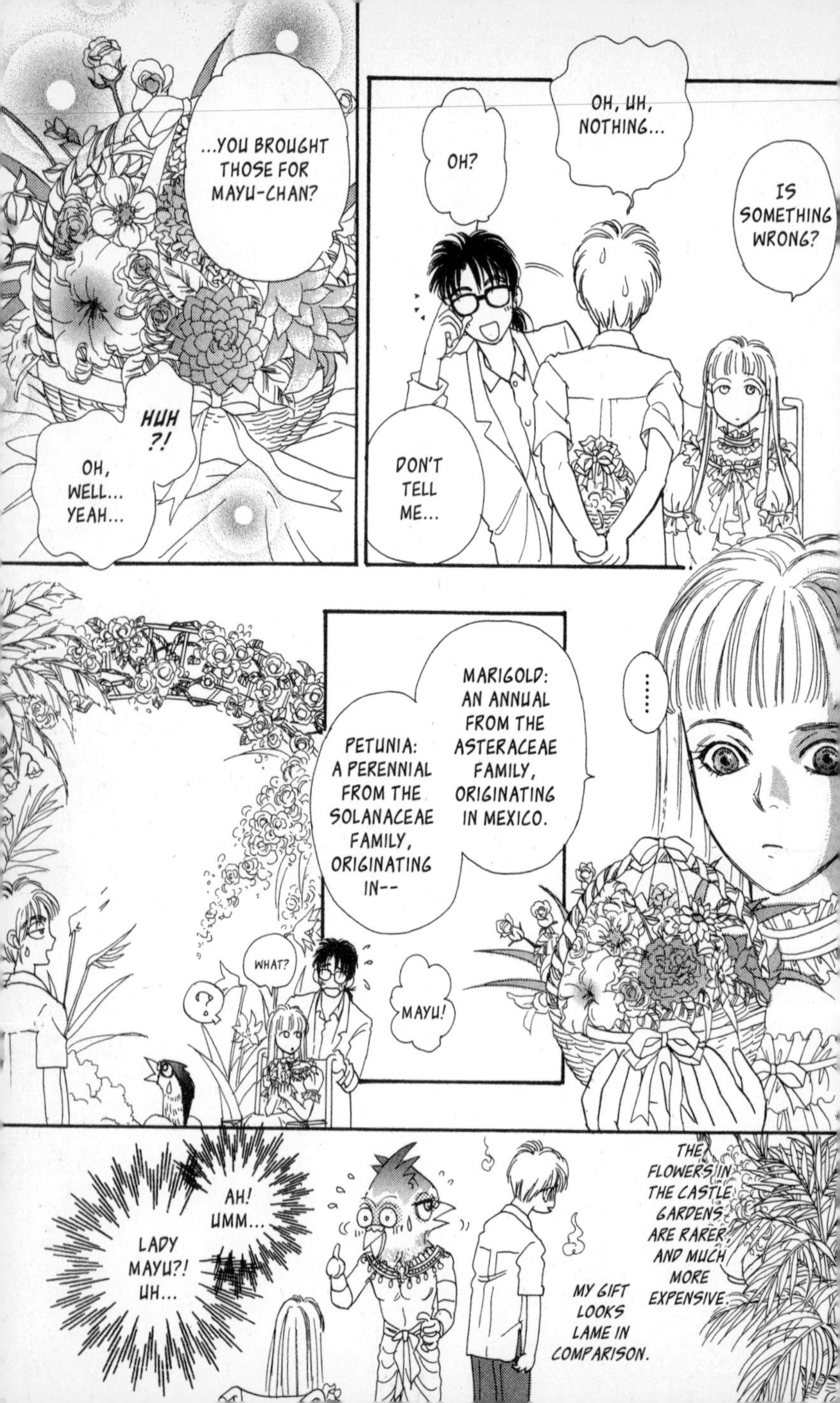
IS SOMETHING WRONG?
OH, UH, NOTHING...
OH?
DON'T TELL ME...
...YOU BROUGHT THOSE FOR MAYU-CHAN?
HUH?!
OH, WELL... YEAH...
......
MARIGOLD: AN ANNUAL FROM THE ASTERACEAE FAMILY, ORIGINATING IN MEXICO.
PETUNIA: A PERENNIAL FROM THE SOLANACEAE FAMILY, ORIGINATING IN--
MAYU!
WHAT?
?
THE FLOWERS IN THE CASTLE GARDENS ARE RARER AND MUCH MORE EXPENSIVE.
MY GIFT LOOKS LAME IN COMPARISON.
AH! UMM...
LADY MAYU?! UH...

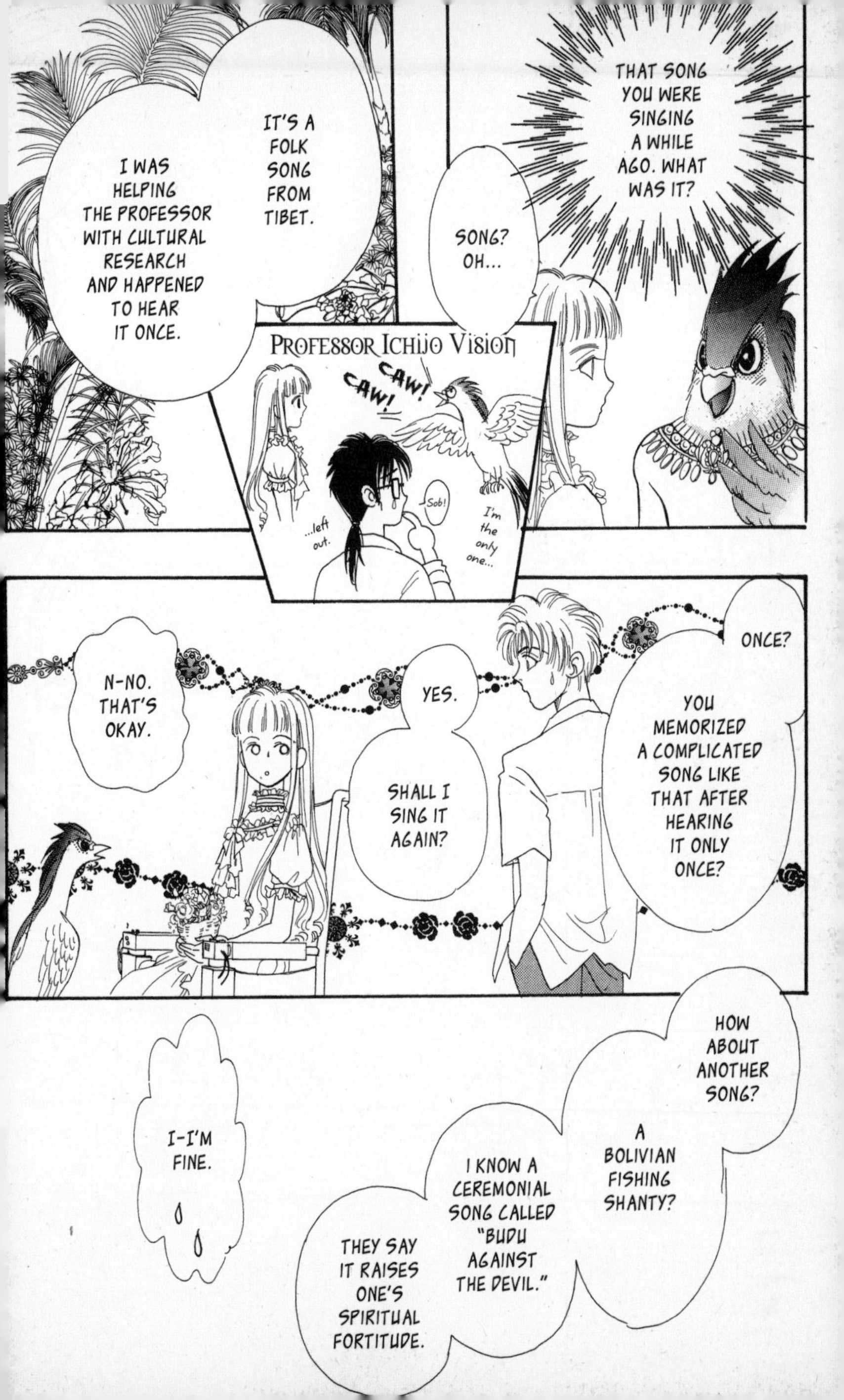
THAT SONG YOU WERE SINGING A WHILE AGO. WHAT WAS IT?
SONG? OH...
IT'S A FOLK SONG FROM TIBET.
I WAS HELPING THE PROFESSOR WITH CULTURAL RESEARCH AND HAPPENED TO HEAR IT ONCE.
PROFESSOR ICHIJO VISION
CAW! CAW!
I'm the only one...
Sob!
...left out.
ONCE?
YOU MEMORIZED A COMPLICATED SONG LIKE THAT AFTER HEARING IT ONLY ONCE?
YES.
SHALL I SING IT AGAIN?
N-NO. THAT'S OKAY.
HOW ABOUT ANOTHER SONG?
A BOLIVIAN FISHING SHANTY?
I KNOW A CEREMONIAL SONG CALLED "BUDU AGAINST THE DEVIL."
THEY SAY IT RAISES ONE'S SPIRITUAL FORTITUDE.
I-I'M FINE.

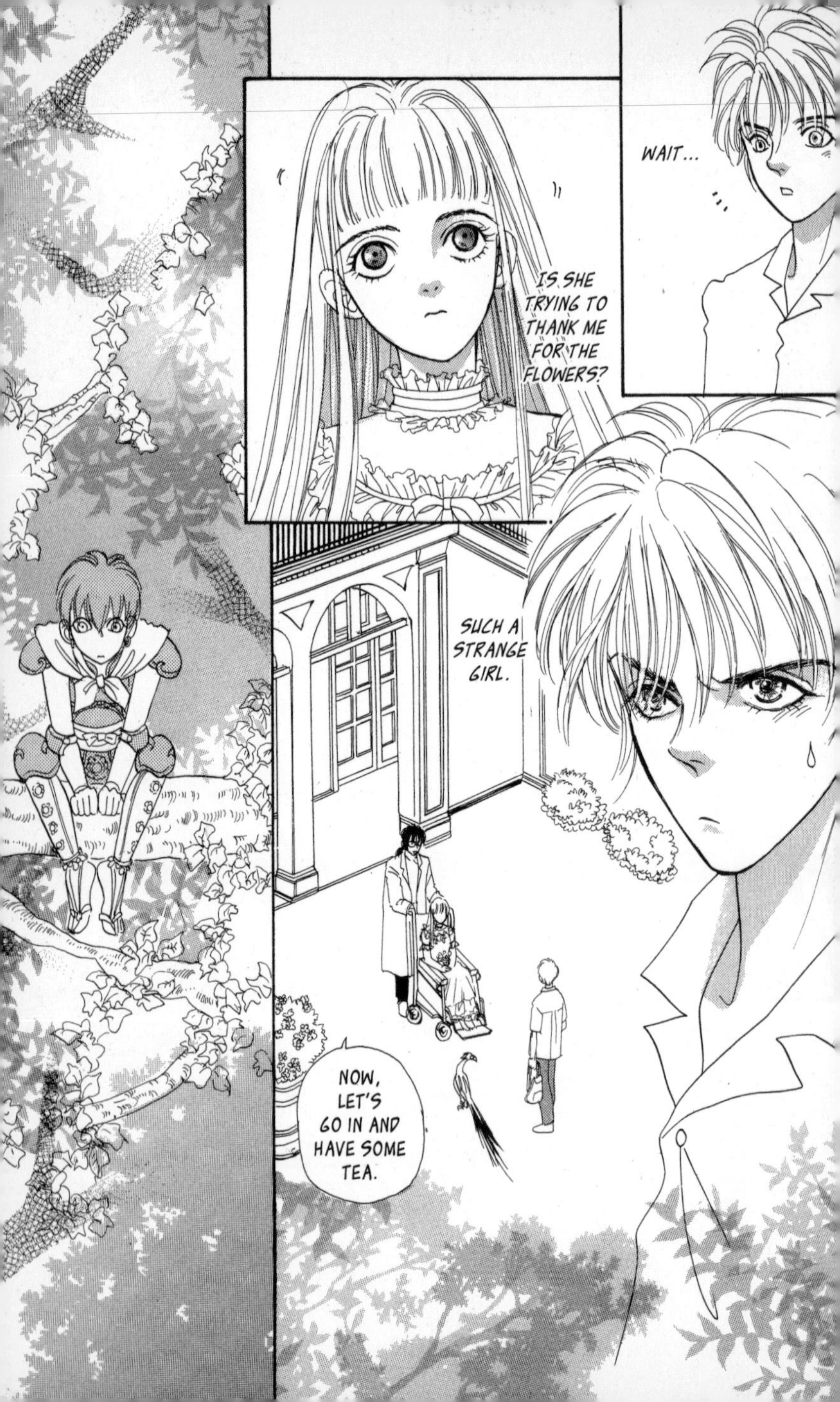
WAIT...
IS SHE TRYING TO THANK ME FOR THE FLOWERS?
SUCH A STRANGE GIRL.
NOW, LET'S GO IN AND HAVE SOME TEA.

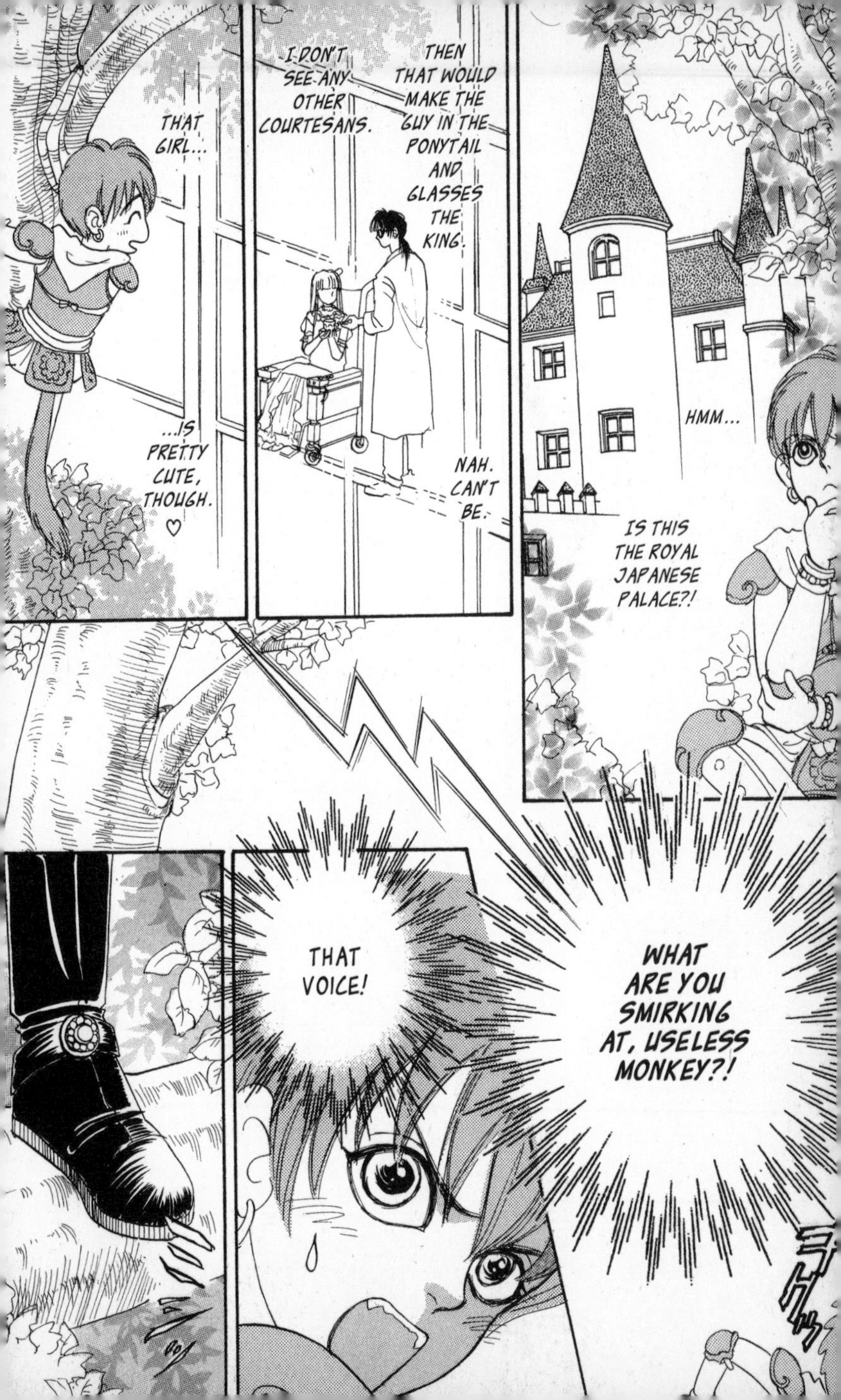
HMM...
IS THIS THE ROYAL JAPANESE PALACE?!
I DON'T SEE ANY OTHER COURTESANS.
THEN THAT WOULD MAKE THE GUY IN THE PONYTAIL AND GLASSES THE KING.
NAH. CAN'T BE.
THAT GIRL...
...IS PRETTY CUTE, THOUGH. ♡
WHAT ARE YOU SMIRKING AT, USELESS MONKEY?!
THAT VOICE!

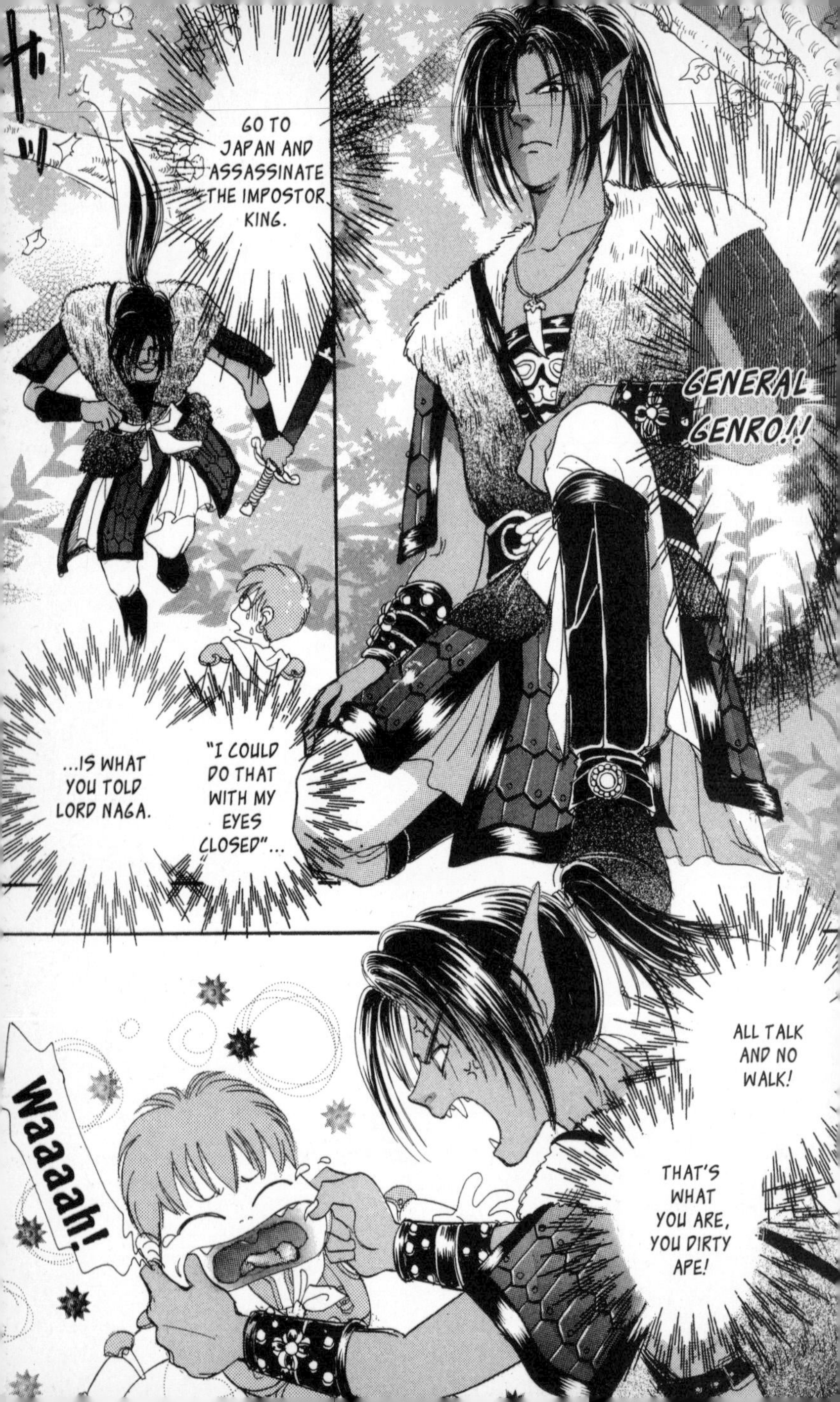
GENERAL GENRO!!
ザッ
GO TO JAPAN AND ASSASSINATE THE IMPOSTOR KING.
"I COULD DO THAT WITH MY EYES CLOSED"...
...IS WHAT YOU TOLD LORD NAGA.
ALL TALK AND NO WALK!
THAT'S WHAT YOU ARE, YOU DIRTY APE!
Waaaah!

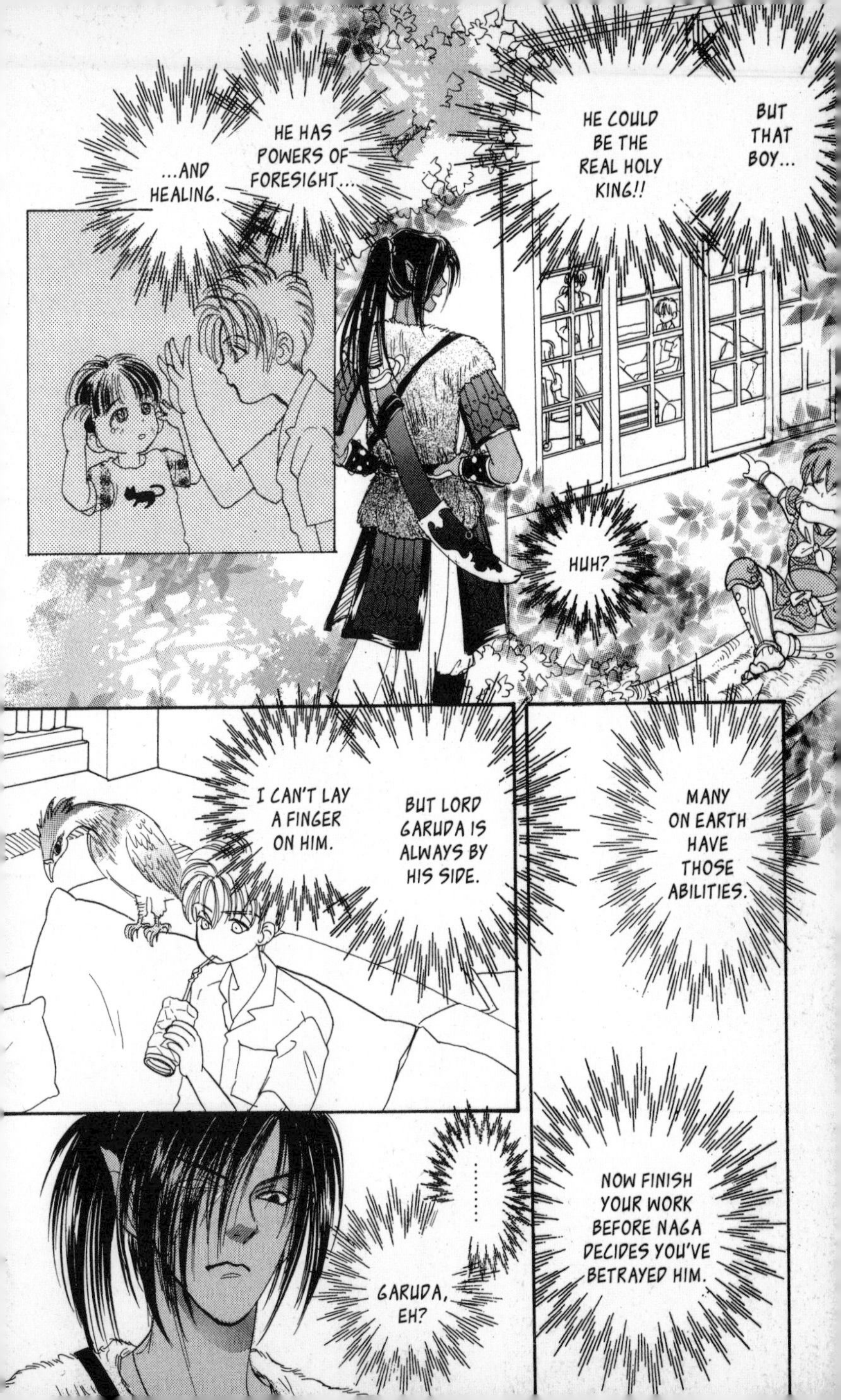
BUT THAT BOY...
HE COULD BE THE REAL HOLY KING!!
HE HAS POWERS OF FORESIGHT...
...AND HEALING.
HUH?
MANY ON EARTH HAVE THOSE ABILITIES.
NOW FINISH YOUR WORK BEFORE NAGA DECIDES YOU'VE BETRAYED HIM.
BUT LORD GARUDA IS ALWAYS BY HIS SIDE.
I CAN'T LAY A FINGER ON HIM.
......
GARUDA, EH?

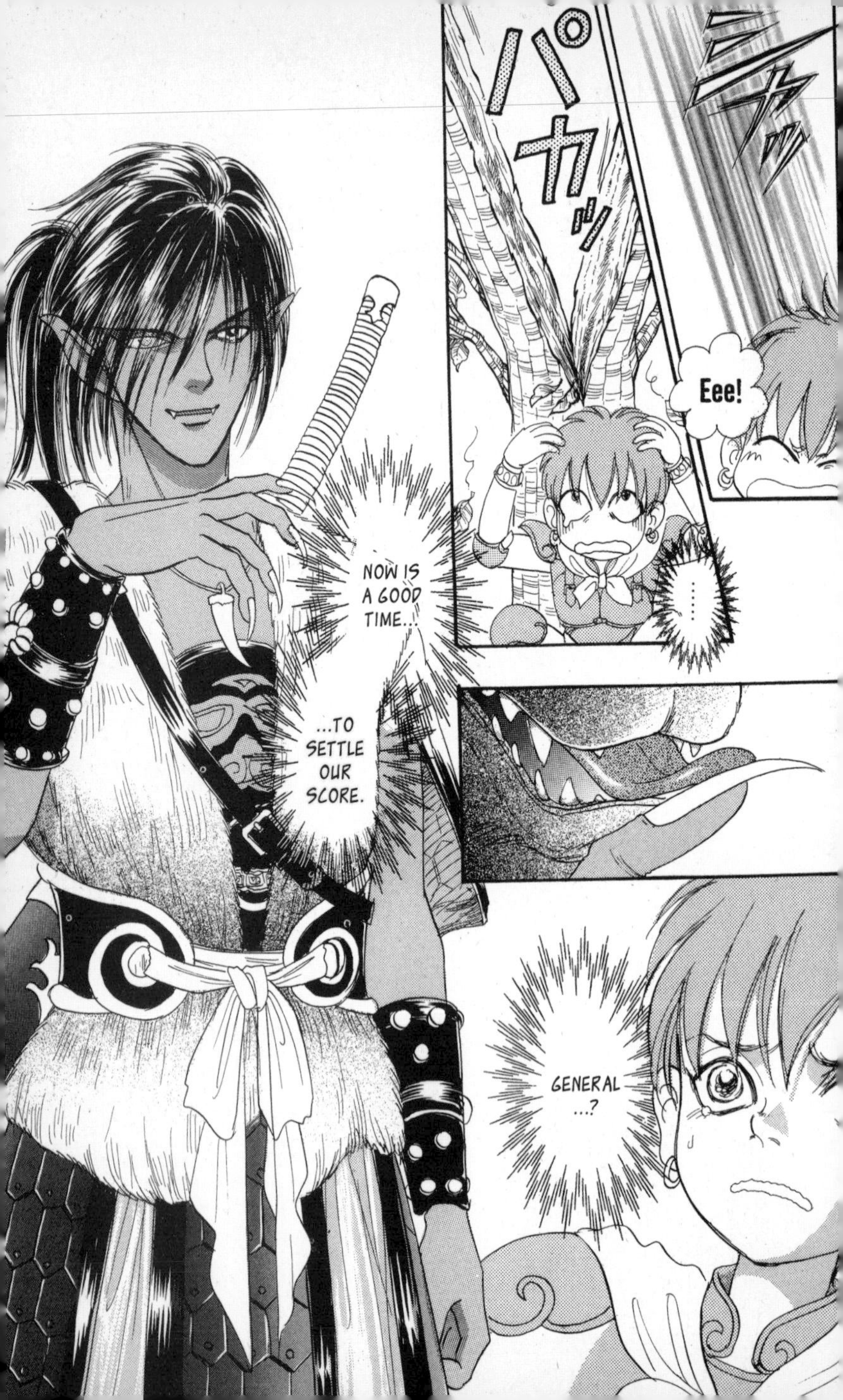
パカッ
Eee!
......
GENERAL ...?
NOW IS A GOOD TIME...
...TO SETTLE OUR SCORE.

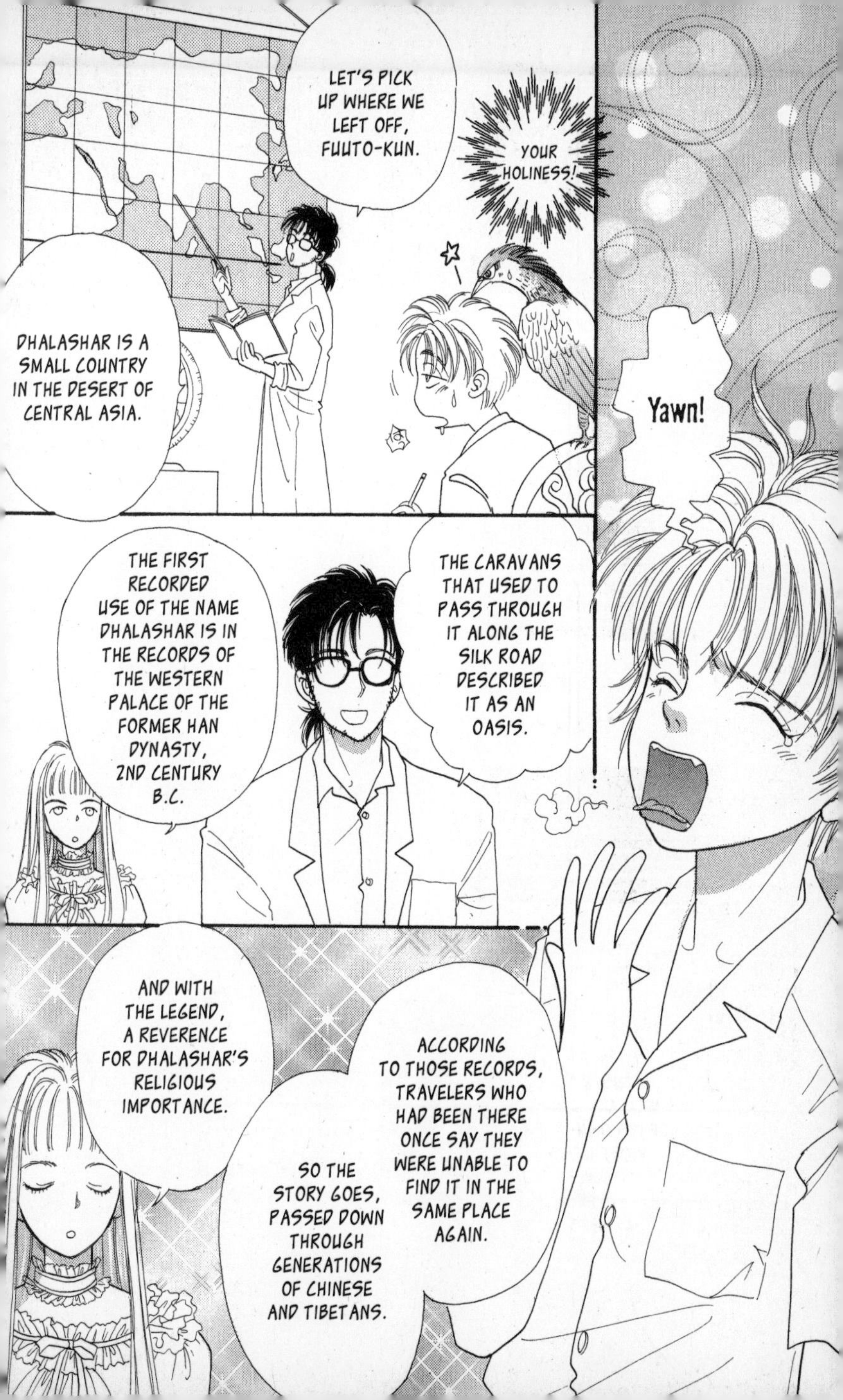
Yawn!
LET'S PICK UP WHERE WE LEFT OFF, FUUTO-KUN.
YOUR HOLINESS!
DHALASHAR IS A SMALL COUNTRY IN THE DESERT OF CENTRAL ASIA.
THE CARAVANS THAT USED TO PASS THROUGH IT ALONG THE SILK ROAD DESCRIBED IT AS AN OASIS.
THE FIRST RECORDED USE OF THE NAME DHALASHAR IS IN THE RECORDS OF THE WESTERN PALACE OF THE FORMER HAN DYNASTY, 2ND CENTURY B.C.
ACCORDING TO THOSE RECORDS, TRAVELERS WHO HAD BEEN THERE ONCE SAY THEY WERE UNABLE TO FIND IT IN THE SAME PLACE AGAIN.
SO THE STORY GOES, PASSED DOWN THROUGH GENERATIONS OF CHINESE AND TIBETANS.
AND WITH THE LEGEND, A REVERENCE FOR DHALASHAR'S RELIGIOUS IMPORTANCE.

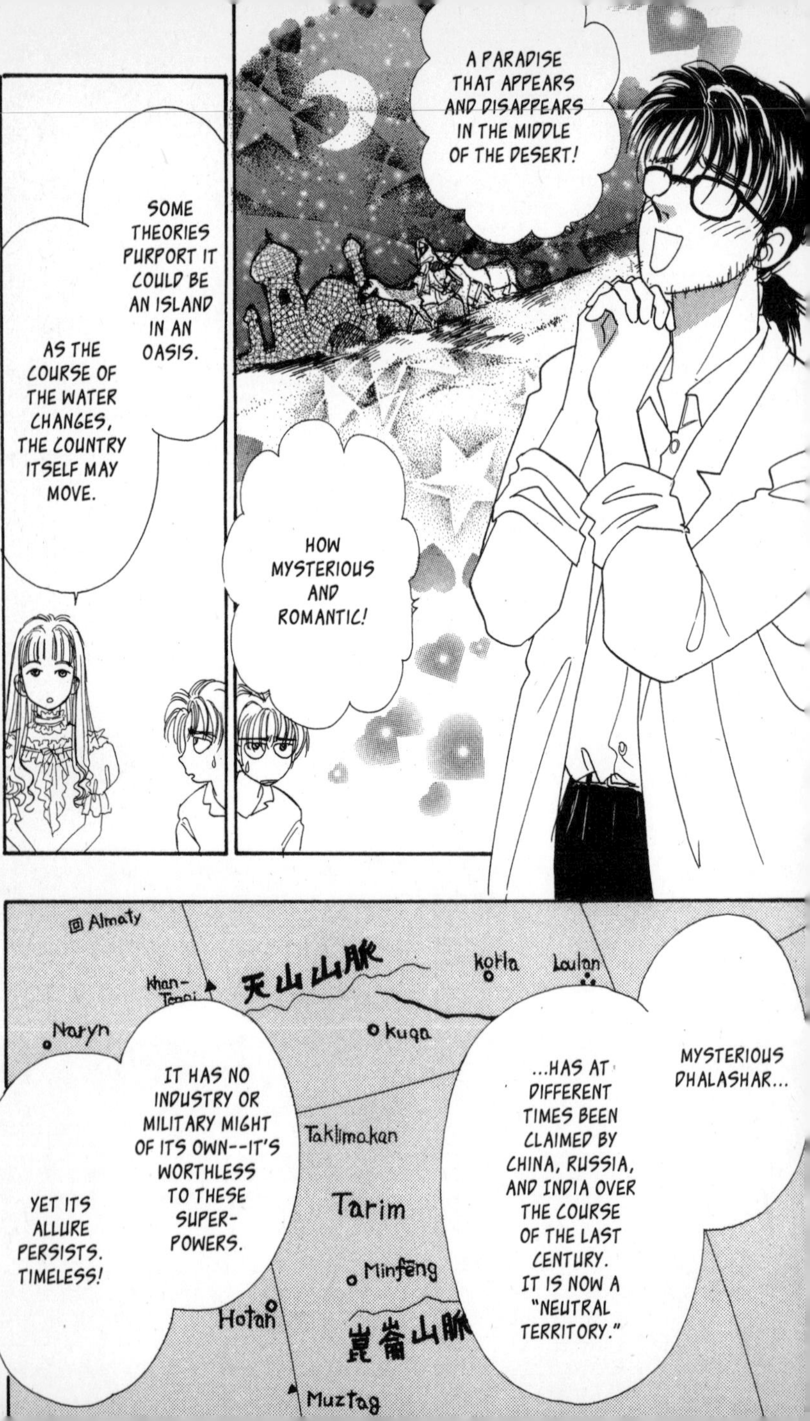
A PARADISE THAT APPEARS AND DISAPPEARS IN THE MIDDLE OF THE DESERT!
HOW MYSTERIOUS AND ROMANTIC!
SOME THEORIES PURPORT IT COULD BE AN ISLAND IN AN OASIS.
AS THE COURSE OF THE WATER CHANGES, THE COUNTRY ITSELF MAY MOVE.
MYSTERIOUS DHALASHAR...
...HAS AT DIFFERENT TIMES BEEN CLAIMED BY CHINA, RUSSIA, AND INDIA OVER THE COURSE OF THE LAST CENTURY. IT IS NOW A "NEUTRAL TERRITORY."
IT HAS NO INDUSTRY OR MILITARY MIGHT OF ITS OWN--IT'S WORTHLESS TO THESE SUPER-POWERS.
YET ITS ALLURE PERSISTS. TIMELESS!
Almaty
Korla
Loulan
天山山脈
Naryn
Kuqa
Taklimakan
Tarim
Minfeng
Hotan
崑崙山脈
Muztag

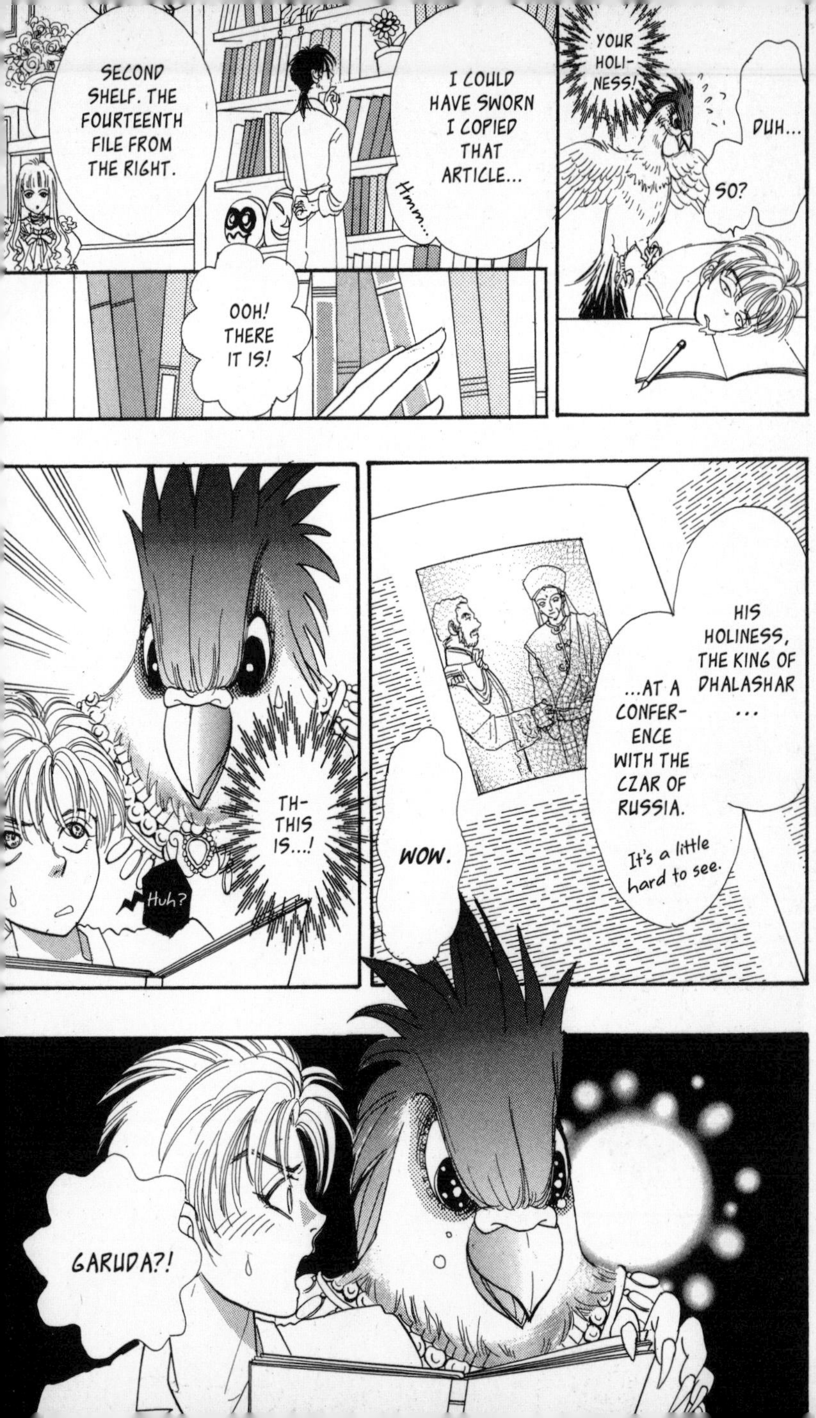

YOUR HOLI-NESS!
DUH...
SO?
I COULD HAVE SWORN I COPIED THAT ARTICLE...
Hmm...
SECOND SHELF. THE FOURTEENTH FILE FROM THE RIGHT.
OOH! THERE IT IS!
HIS HOLINESS, THE KING OF DHALASHAR...
...AT A CONFER-ENCE WITH THE CZAR OF RUSSIA.
It's a little hard to see.
WOW.
TH-THIS IS...!
Huh?
GARUDA?!

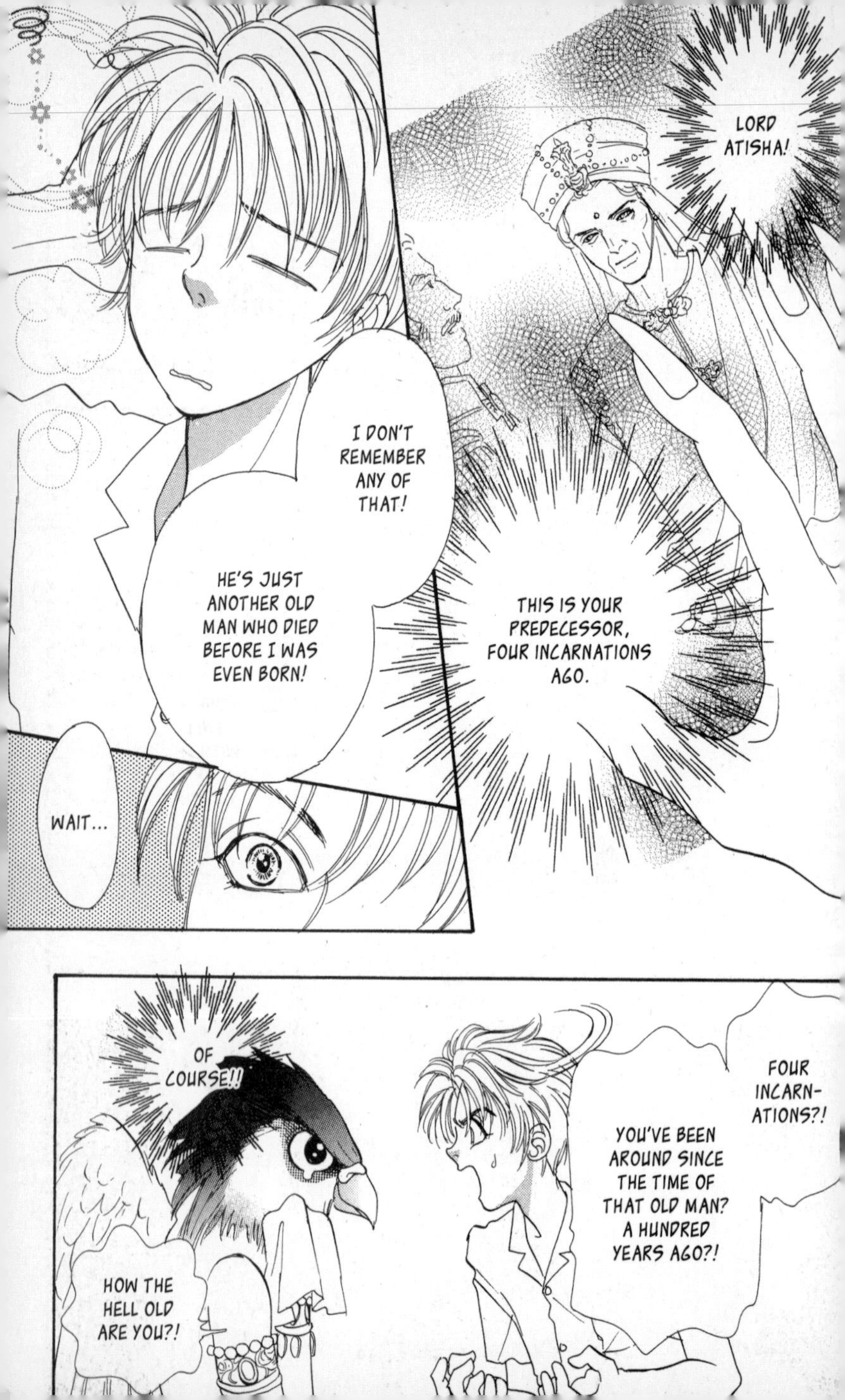
LORD ATISHA!
THIS IS YOUR PREDECESSOR, FOUR INCARNATIONS AGO.
I DON'T REMEMBER ANY OF THAT!
HE'S JUST ANOTHER OLD MAN WHO DIED BEFORE I WAS EVEN BORN!
WAIT...
FOUR INCARN-ATIONS?!
YOU'VE BEEN AROUND SINCE THE TIME OF THAT OLD MAN? A HUNDRED YEARS AGO?!
OF COURSE!!
HOW THE HELL OLD ARE YOU?!

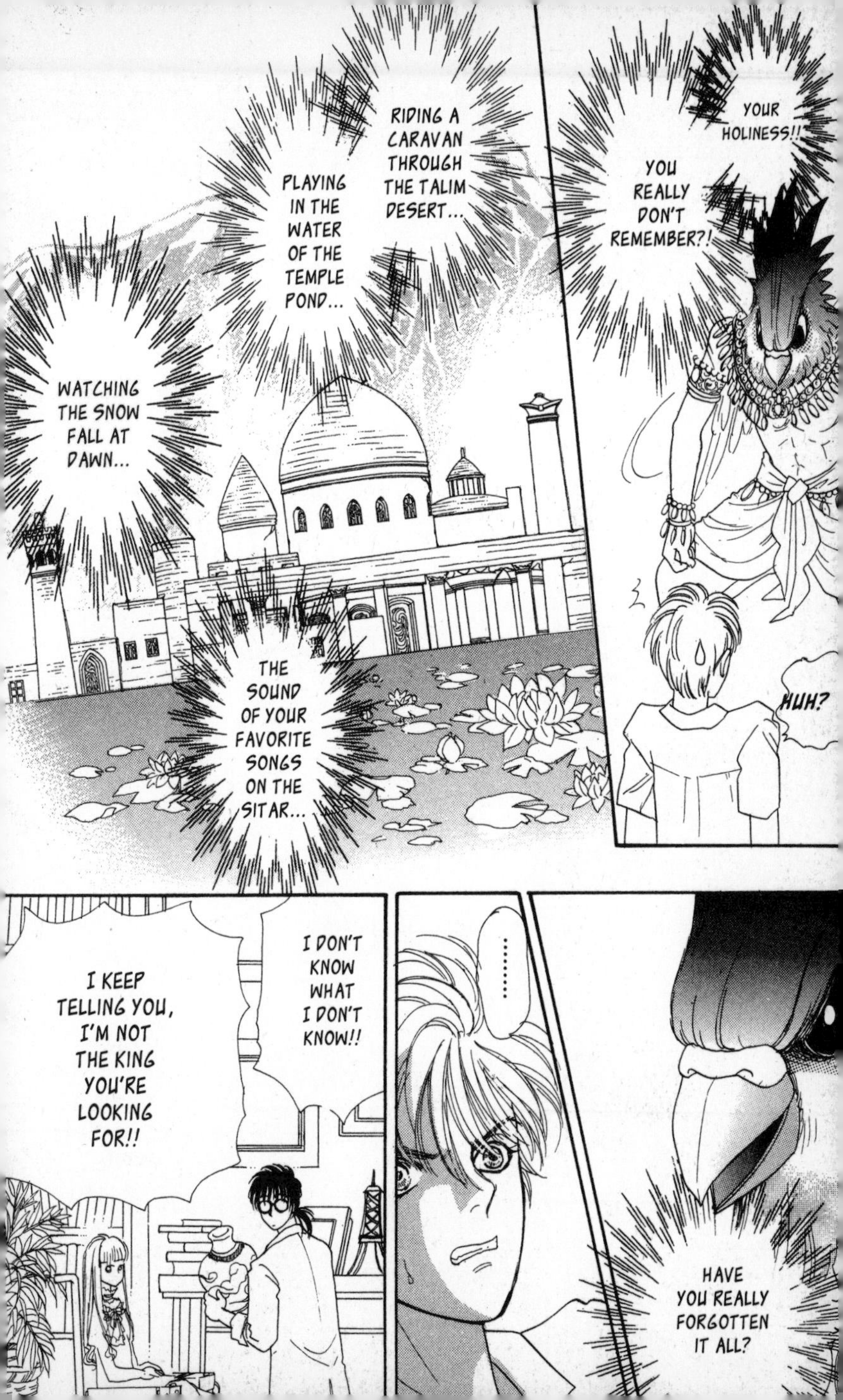

YOUR HOLINESS!!
YOU REALLY DON'T REMEMBER?!
HUH?
RIDING A CARAVAN THROUGH THE TALIM DESERT...
PLAYING IN THE WATER OF THE TEMPLE POND...
WATCHING THE SNOW FALL AT DAWN...
THE SOUND OF YOUR FAVORITE SONGS ON THE SITAR...
HAVE YOU REALLY FORGOTTEN IT ALL?
......
I DON'T KNOW WHAT I DON'T KNOW!!
I KEEP TELLING YOU, I'M NOT THE KING YOU'RE LOOKING FOR!!

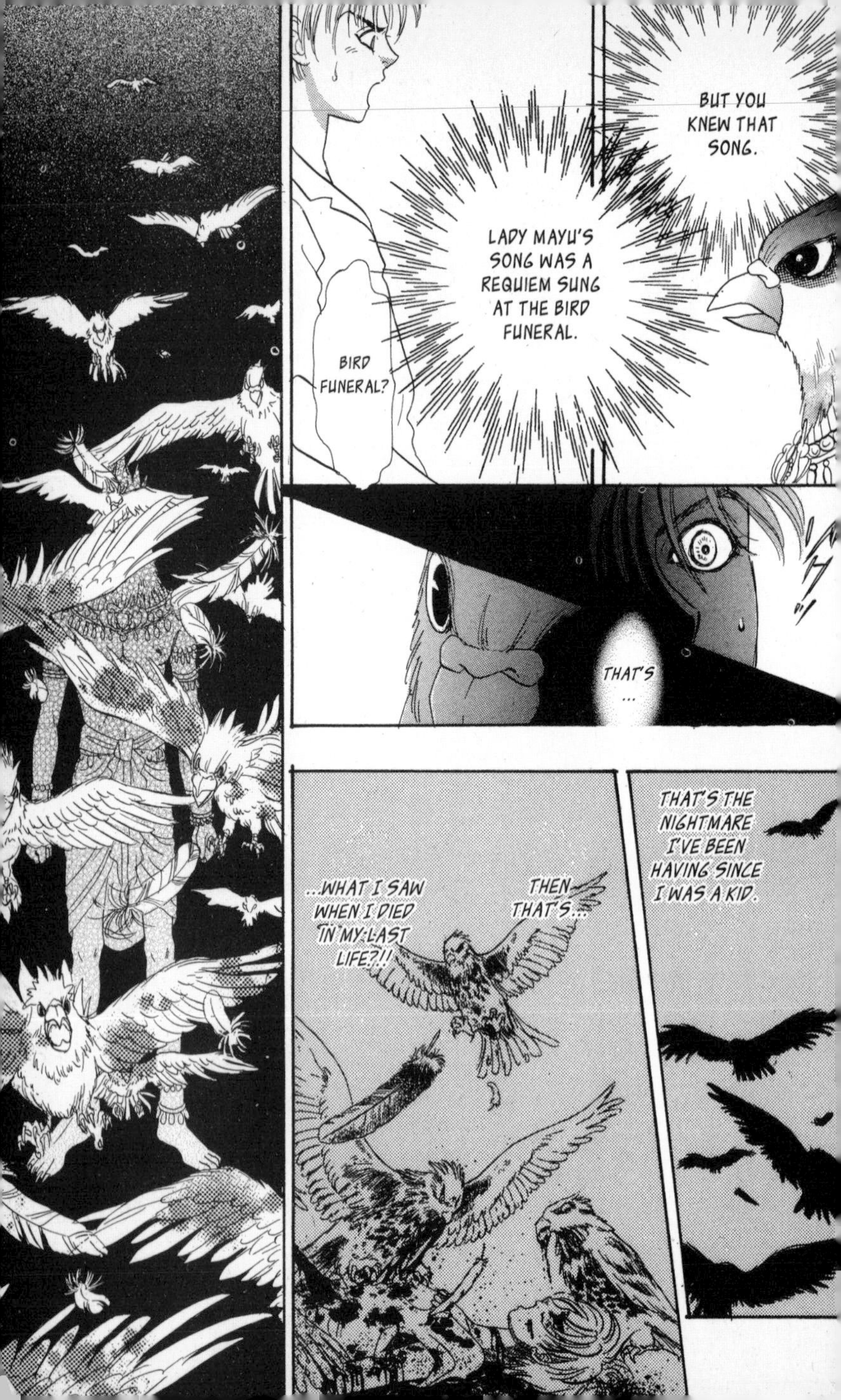
BUT YOU KNEW THAT SONG.
LADY MAYU'S SONG WAS A REQUIEM SUNG AT THE BIRD FUNERAL.
BIRD FUNERAL?
THAT'S ...
THAT'S THE NIGHTMARE I'VE BEEN HAVING SINCE I WAS A KID.
THEN THAT'S...
...WHAT I SAW WHEN I DIED IN MY LAST LIFE?!!

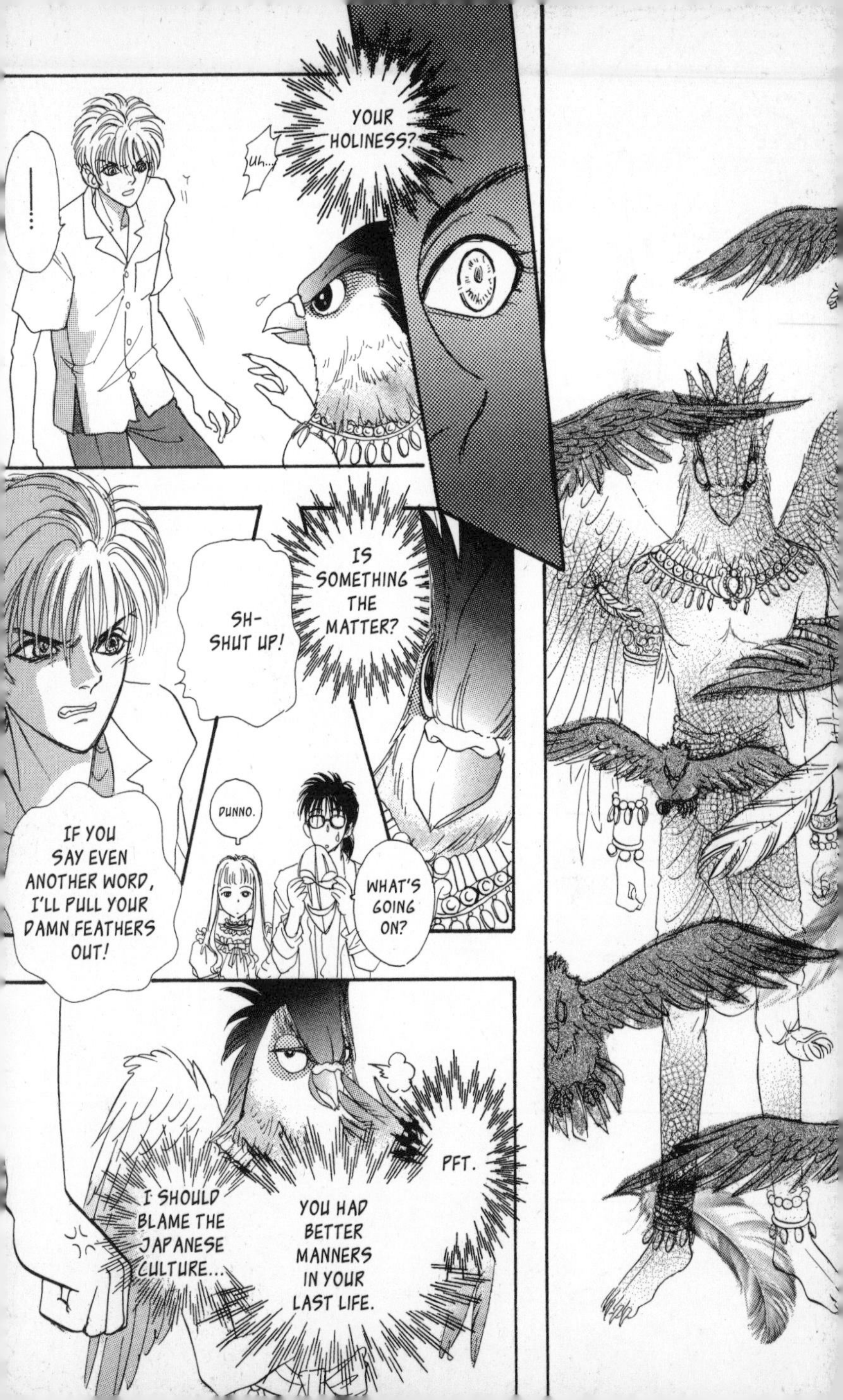
YOUR HOLINESS?
Uh...
!......
IS SOMETHING THE MATTER?
SH- SHUT UP!
WHAT'S GOING ON?
DUNNO.
IF YOU SAY EVEN ANOTHER WORD, I'LL PULL YOUR DAMN FEATHERS OUT!
PFT.
YOU HAD BETTER MANNERS IN YOUR LAST LIFE.
I SHOULD BLAME THE JAPANESE CULTURE...

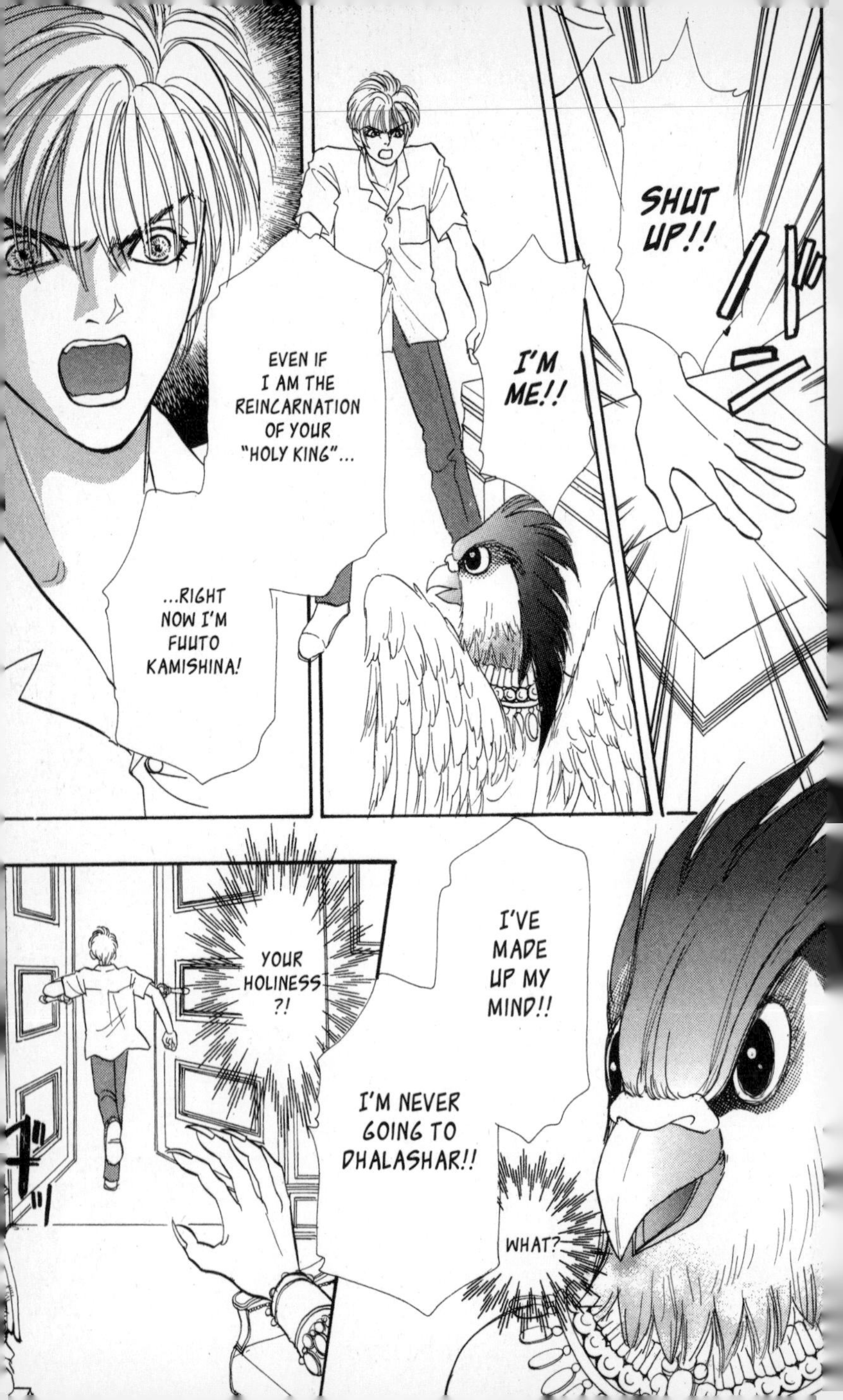
SHUT UP!!
I'M ME!!
EVEN IF I AM THE REINCARNATION OF YOUR "HOLY KING"...
...RIGHT NOW I'M FUUTO KAMISHINA!
I'VE MADE UP MY MIND!!
I'M NEVER GOING TO DHALASHAR!!
WHAT?
YOUR HOLINESS?!

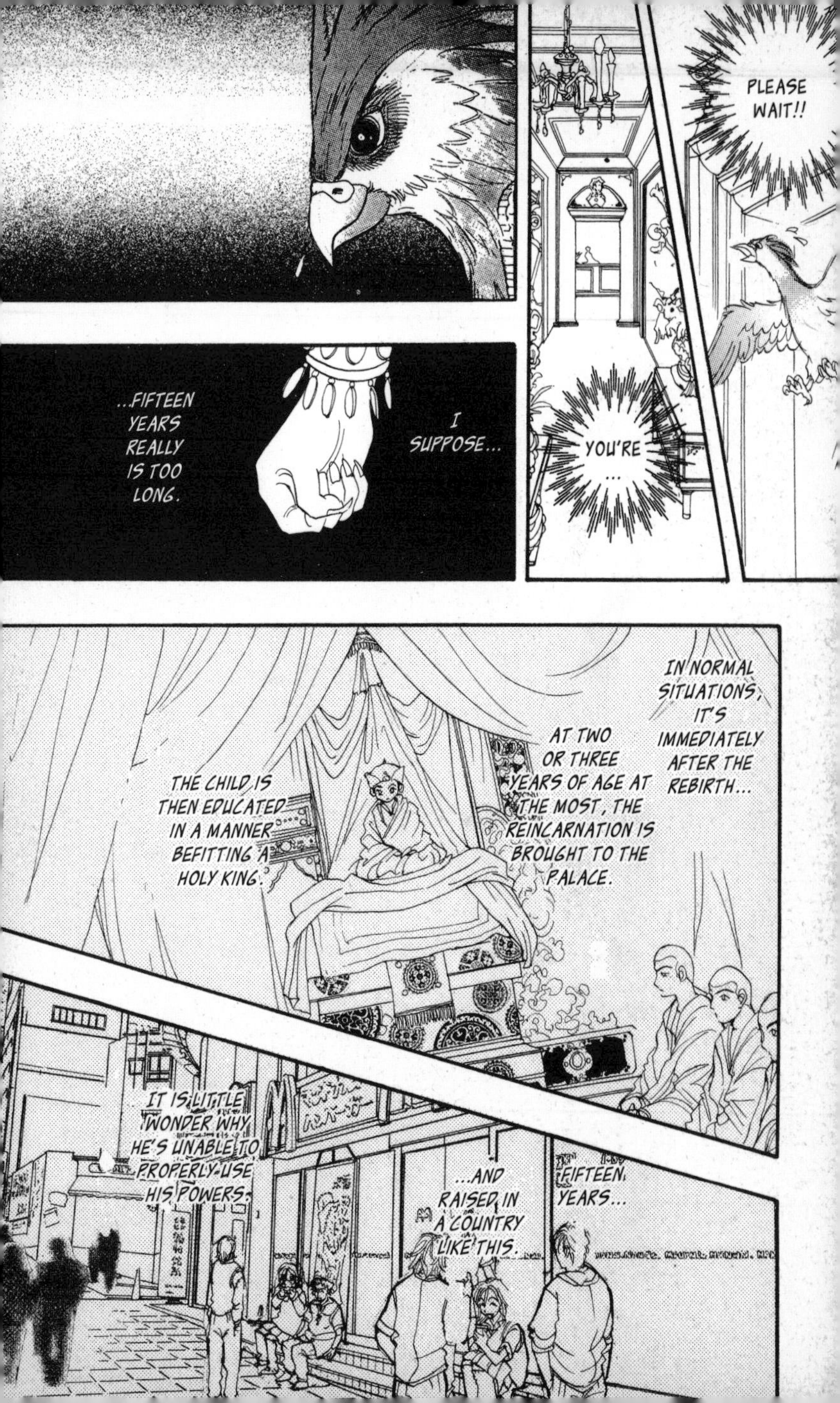
PLEASE WAIT!!
YOU'RE ...
I SUPPOSE...
...FIFTEEN YEARS REALLY IS TOO LONG.
IN NORMAL SITUATIONS, IT'S IMMEDIATELY AFTER THE REBIRTH...
AT TWO OR THREE YEARS OF AGE AT THE MOST, THE REINCARNATION IS BROUGHT TO THE PALACE.
THE CHILD IS THEN EDUCATED IN A MANNER BEFITTING A HOLY KING.
FIFTEEN YEARS...
...AND RAISED IN A COUNTRY LIKE THIS.
IT IS LITTLE WONDER WHY HE'S UNABLE TO PROPERLY USE HIS POWERS.

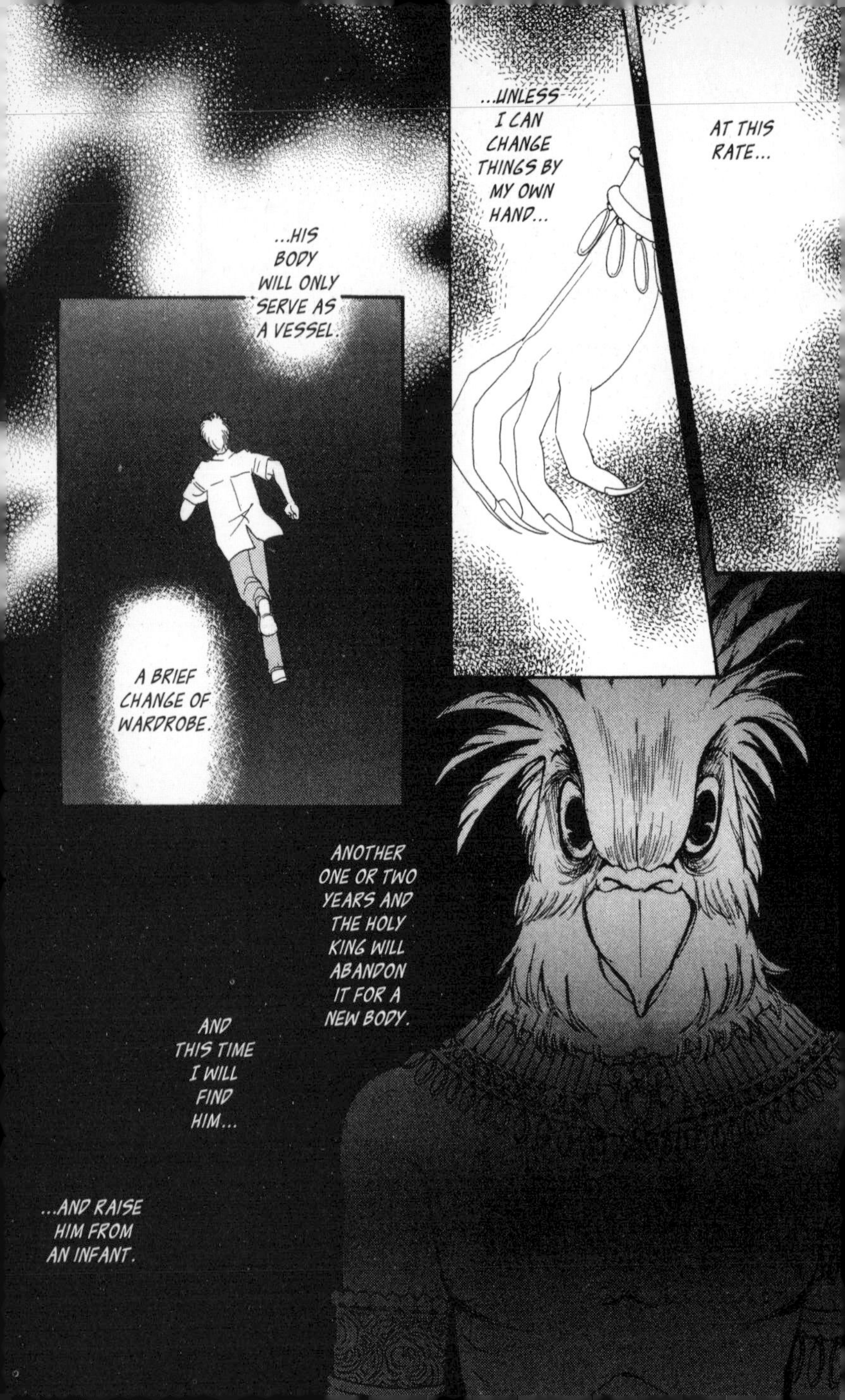
AT THIS RATE...
...UNLESS I CAN CHANGE THINGS BY MY OWN HAND...
...HIS BODY WILL ONLY SERVE AS A VESSEL.
A BRIEF CHANGE OF WARDROBE.
ANOTHER ONE OR TWO YEARS AND THE HOLY KING WILL ABANDON IT FOR A NEW BODY.
AND THIS TIME I WILL FIND HIM...
...AND RAISE HIM FROM AN INFANT.

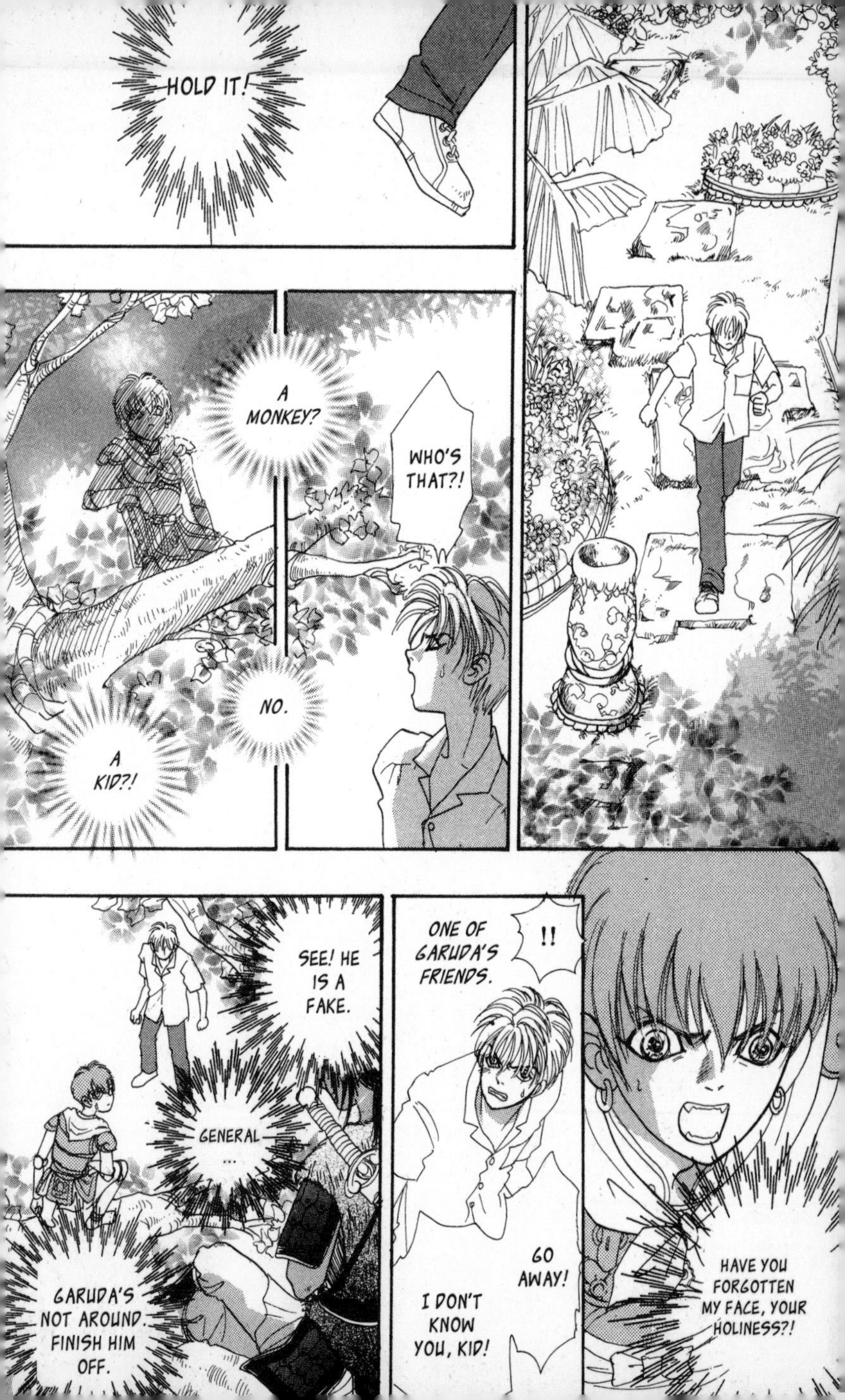
HOLD IT!
WHO'S THAT?!
A MONKEY?
NO.
A KID?!
HAVE YOU FORGOTTEN MY FACE, YOUR HOLINESS?!
!!
ONE OF GARUDA'S FRIENDS.
GO AWAY!
I DON'T KNOW YOU, KID!
SEE! HE IS A FAKE.
GENERAL ...
GARUDA'S NOT AROUND. FINISH HIM OFF.

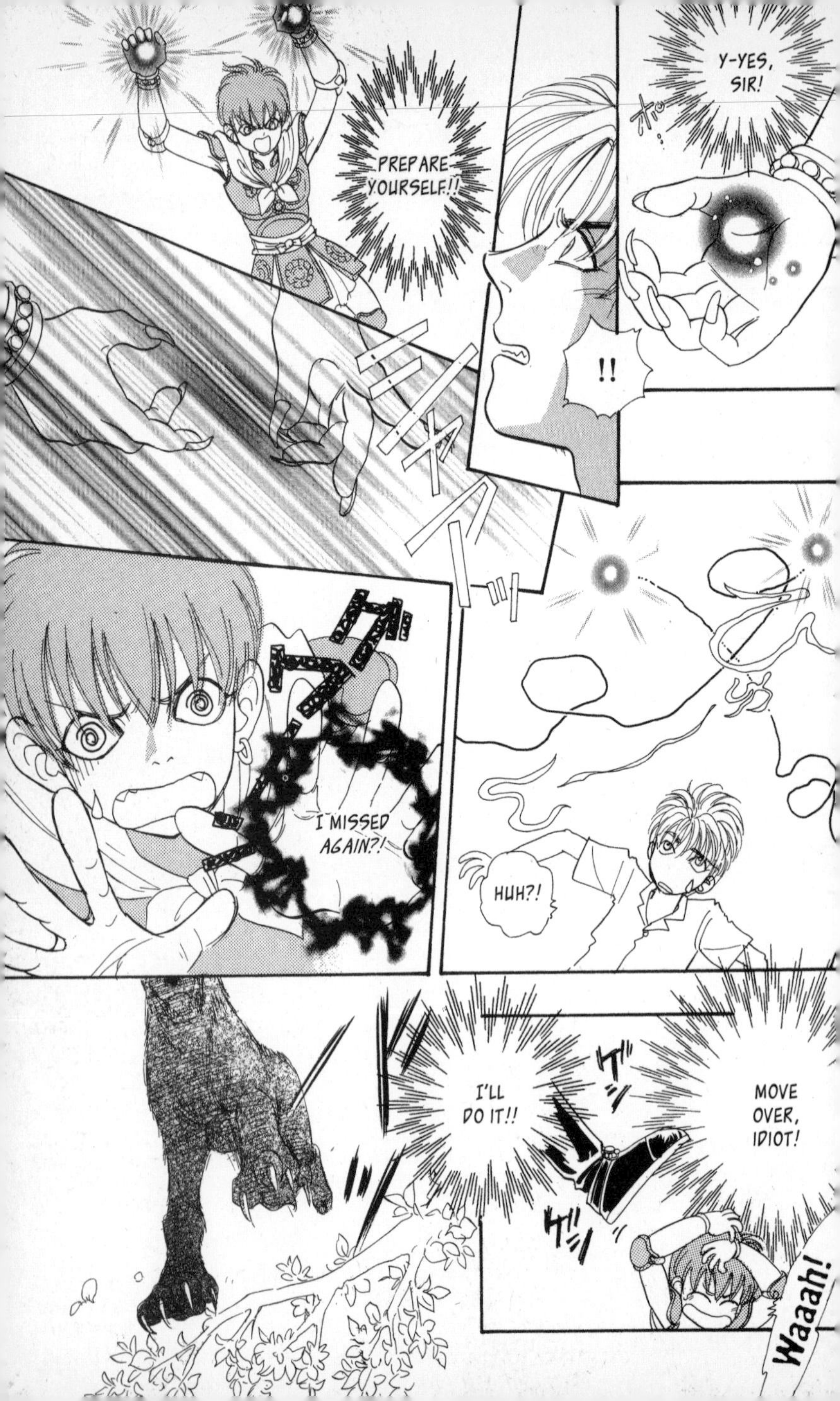
Y-YES, SIR!
!!
PREPARE YOURSELF!!
HUH?!
I MISSED AGAIN?!
MOVE OVER, IDIOT!
Waaah!
I'LL DO IT!!

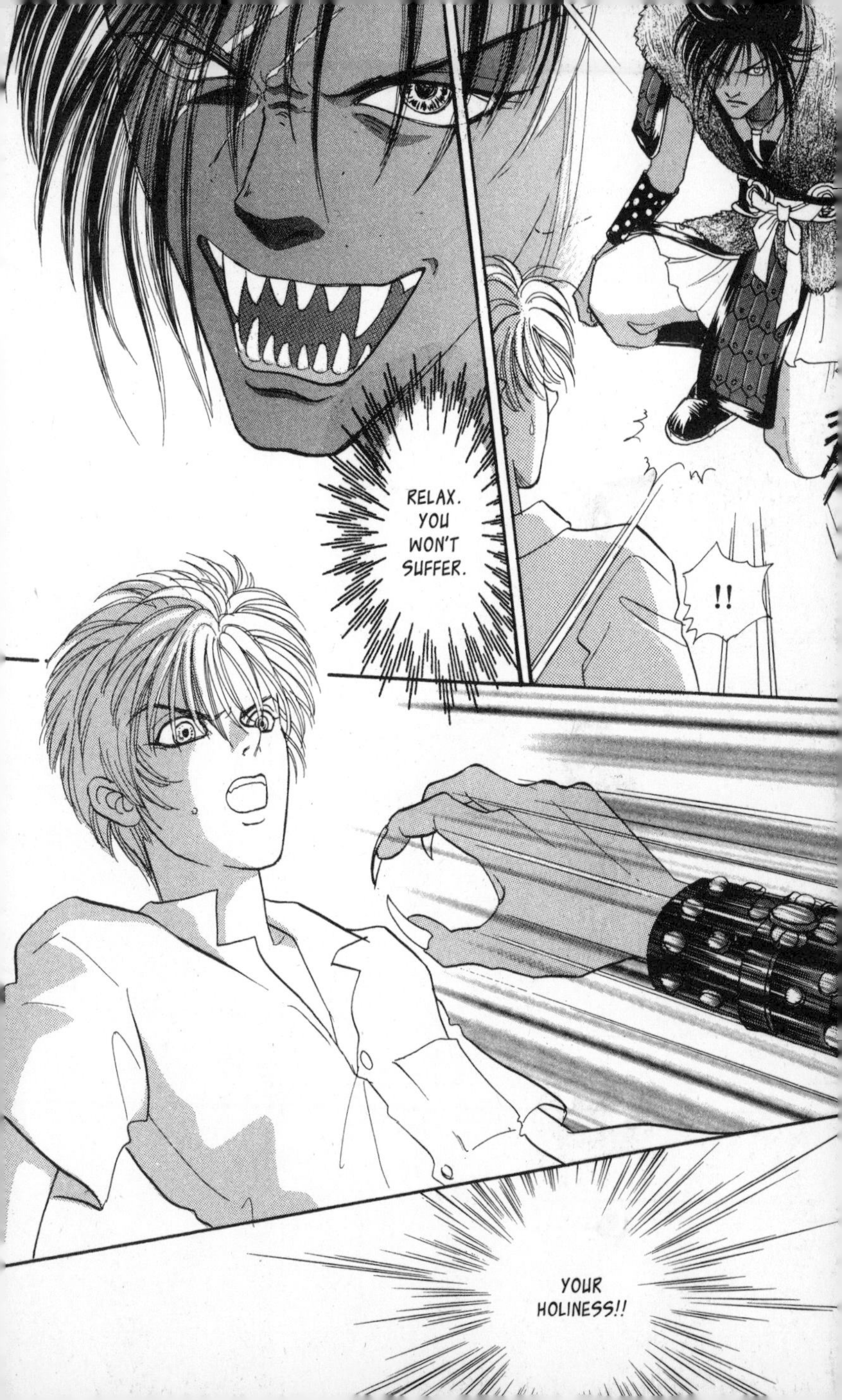
RELAX. YOU WON'T SUFFER.
!!
YOUR HOLINESS!!

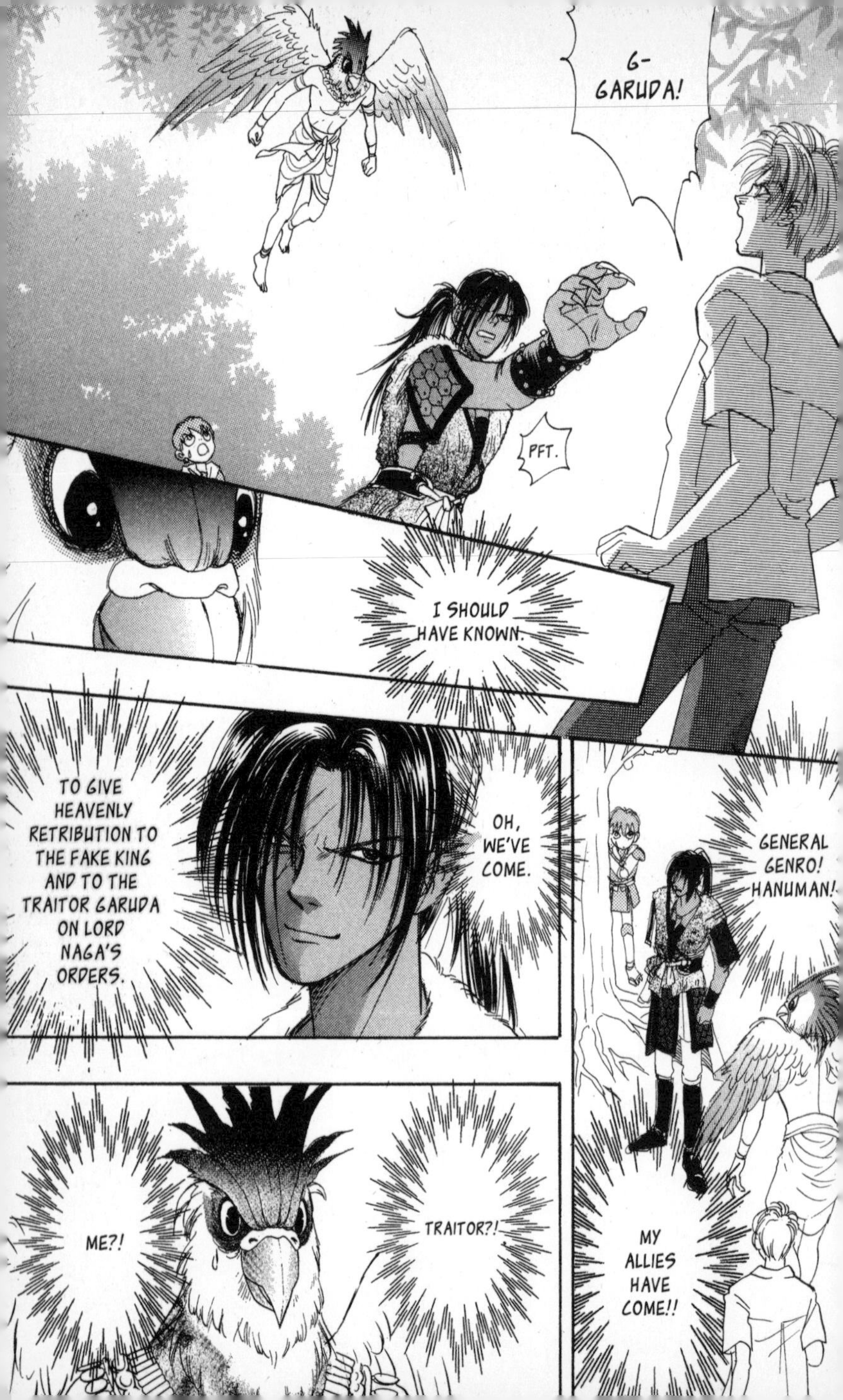
G-
GARUDA!
PFT.
I SHOULD HAVE KNOWN.
GENERAL GENRO! HANUMAN!
MY ALLIES HAVE COME!!
OH, WE'VE COME.
TO GIVE HEAVENLY RETRIBUTION TO THE FAKE KING AND TO THE TRAITOR GARUDA ON LORD NAGA'S ORDERS.
TRAITOR?!
ME?!

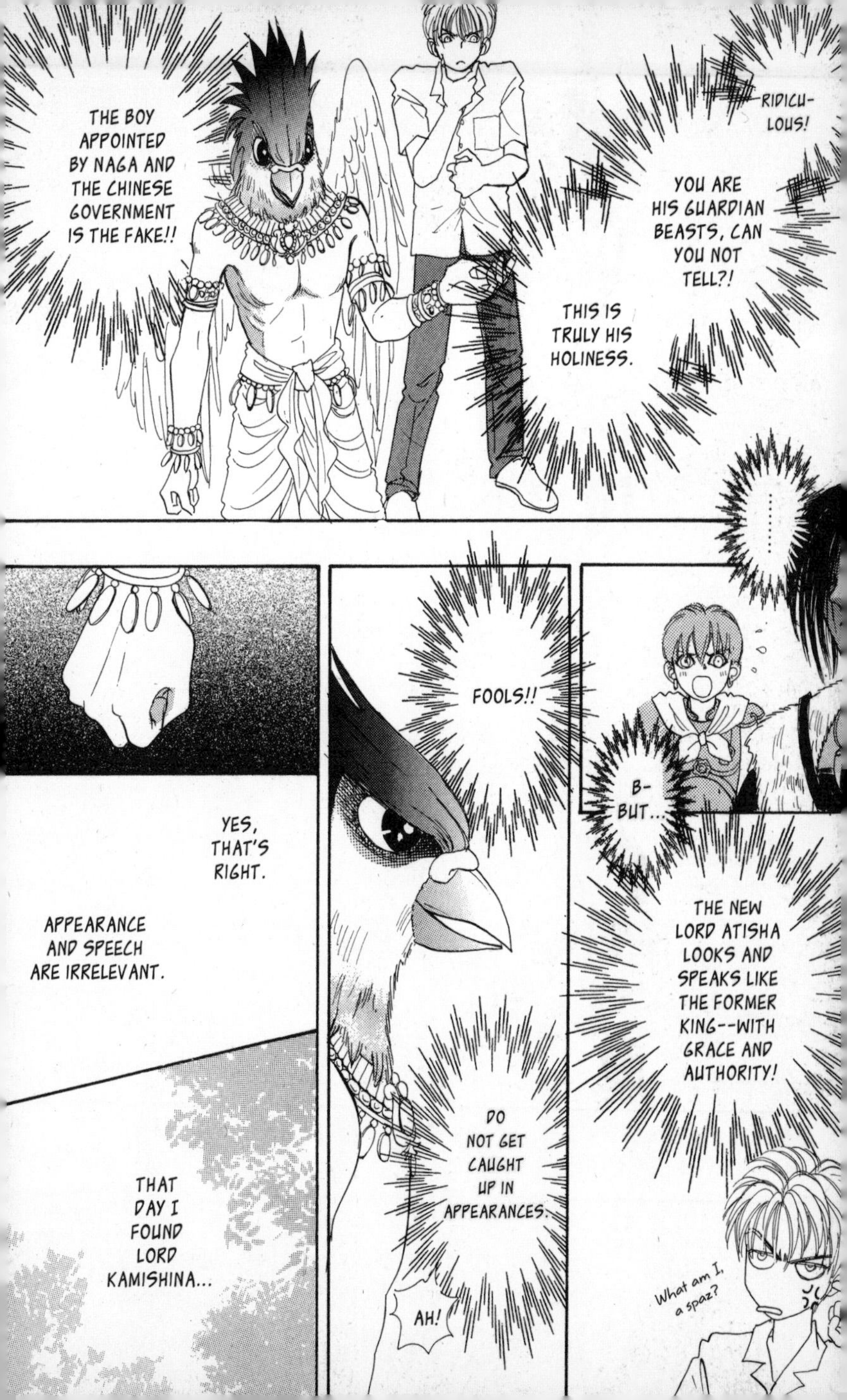
RIDICULOUS!
YOU ARE HIS GUARDIAN BEASTS, CAN YOU NOT TELL?!
THIS IS TRULY HIS HOLINESS.
THE BOY APPOINTED BY NAGA AND THE CHINESE GOVERNMENT IS THE FAKE!!
......
B-BUT...
THE NEW LORD ATISHA LOOKS AND SPEAKS LIKE THE FORMER KING--WITH GRACE AND AUTHORITY!
What am I, a spaz?
FOOLS!!
DO NOT GET CAUGHT UP IN APPEARANCES.
AH!
YES, THAT'S RIGHT.
APPEARANCE AND SPEECH ARE IRRELEVANT.
THAT DAY I FOUND LORD KAMISHINA...

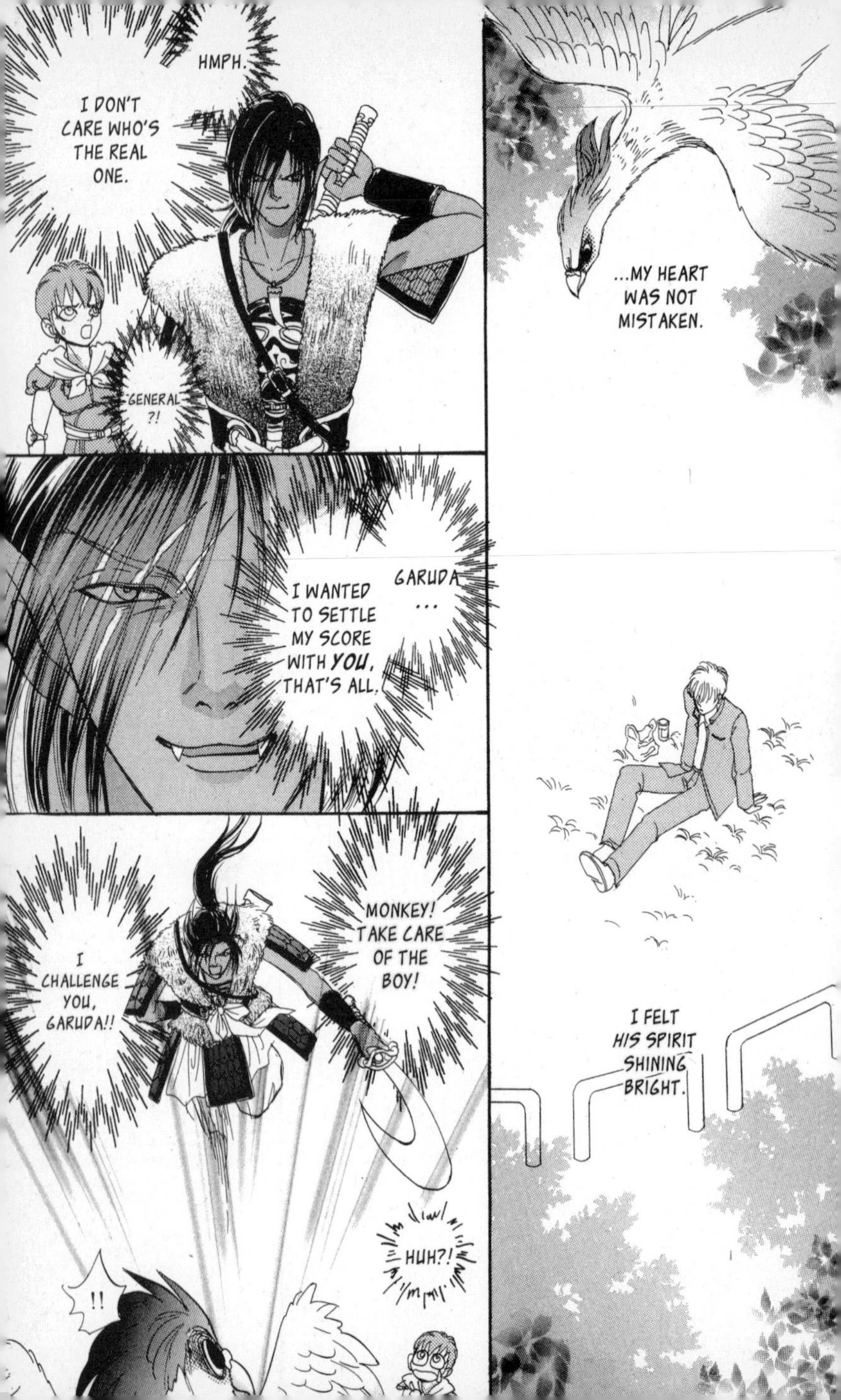
...MY HEART WAS NOT MISTAKEN.
I FELT HIS SPIRIT SHINING BRIGHT.
HMPH.
I DON'T CARE WHO'S THE REAL ONE.
GENERAL ?!
GARUDA ...
I WANTED TO SETTLE MY SCORE WITH *YOU*, THAT'S ALL.
MONKEY! TAKE CARE OF THE BOY!
I CHALLENGE YOU, GARUDA!!
HUH?!
!!

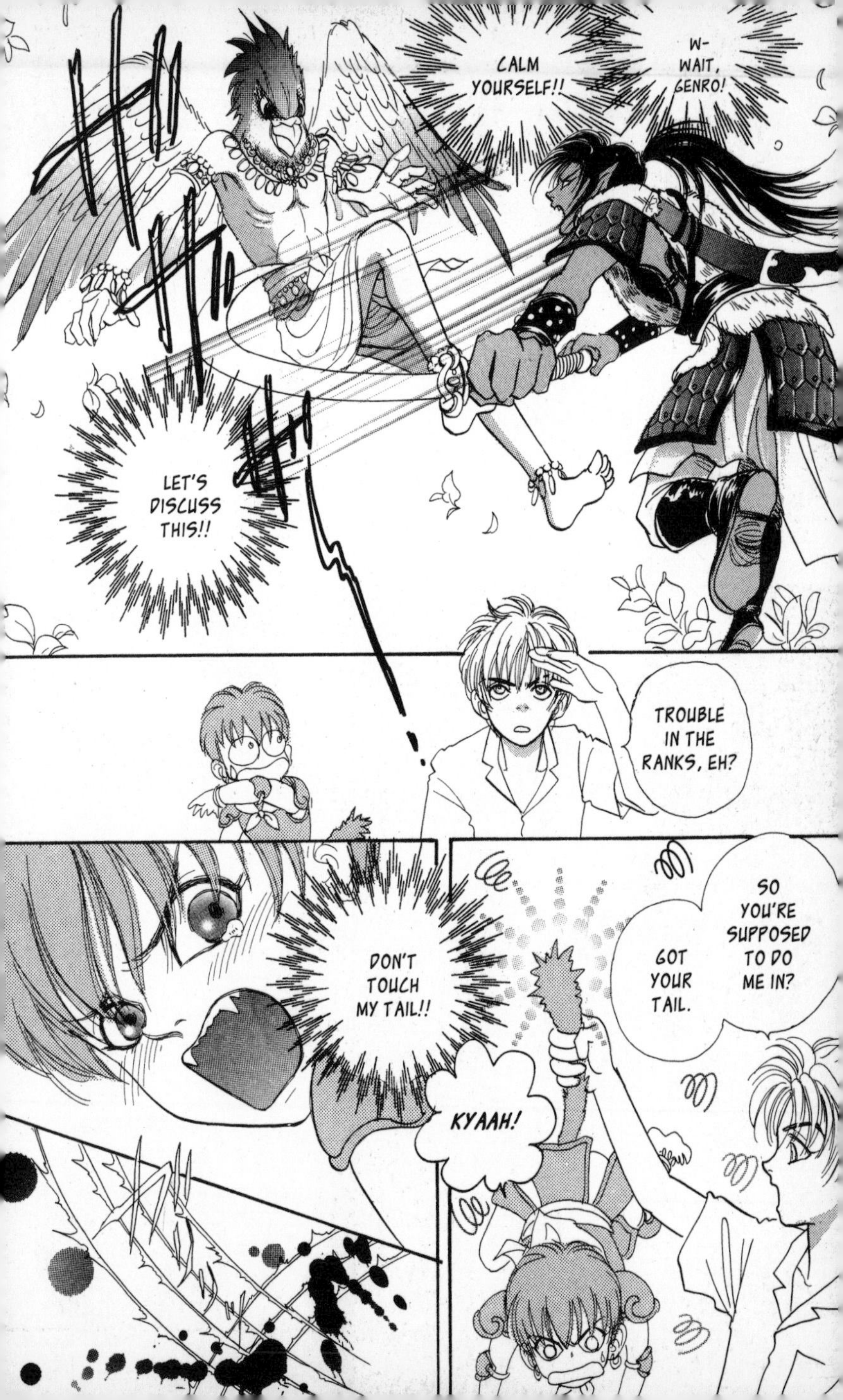
W- WAIT, GENRO!
CALM YOURSELF!!
LET'S DISCUSS THIS!!
TROUBLE IN THE RANKS, EH?
SO YOU'RE SUPPOSED TO DO ME IN?
GOT YOUR TAIL.
KYAAH!
DON'T TOUCH MY TAIL!!

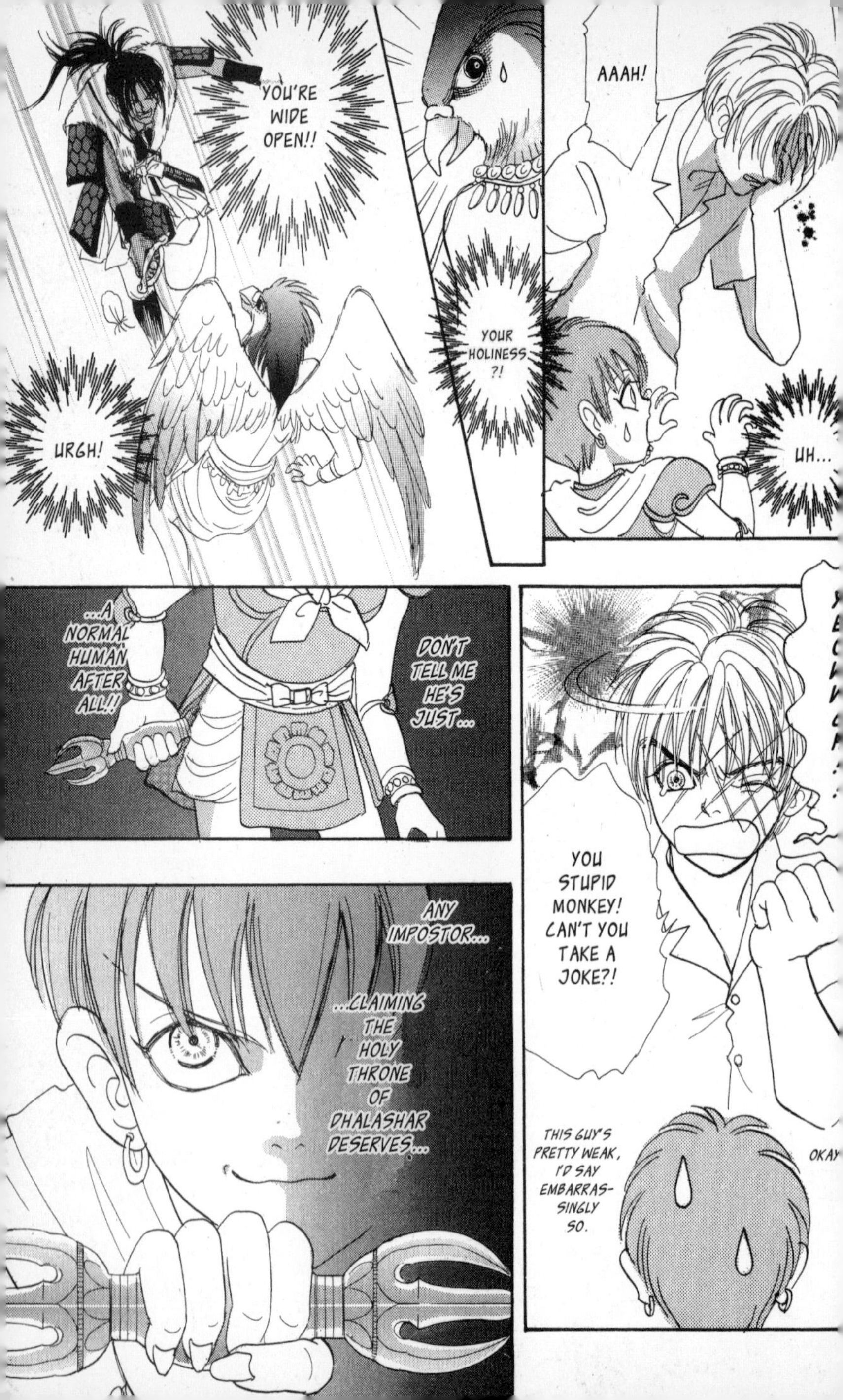
AAAH!
UH...
YOUR HOLINESS?!
YOU'RE WIDE OPEN!!
URGH!
YOU STUPID MONKEY! CAN'T YOU TAKE A JOKE?!
OKAY
THIS GUY'S PRETTY WEAK, I'D SAY EMBARRASSINGLY SO.
DON'T TELL ME HE'S JUST...
...A NORMAL HUMAN AFTER ALL!!
ANY IMPOSTOR...
...CLAIMING THE HOLY THRONE OF DHALASHAR DESERVES...

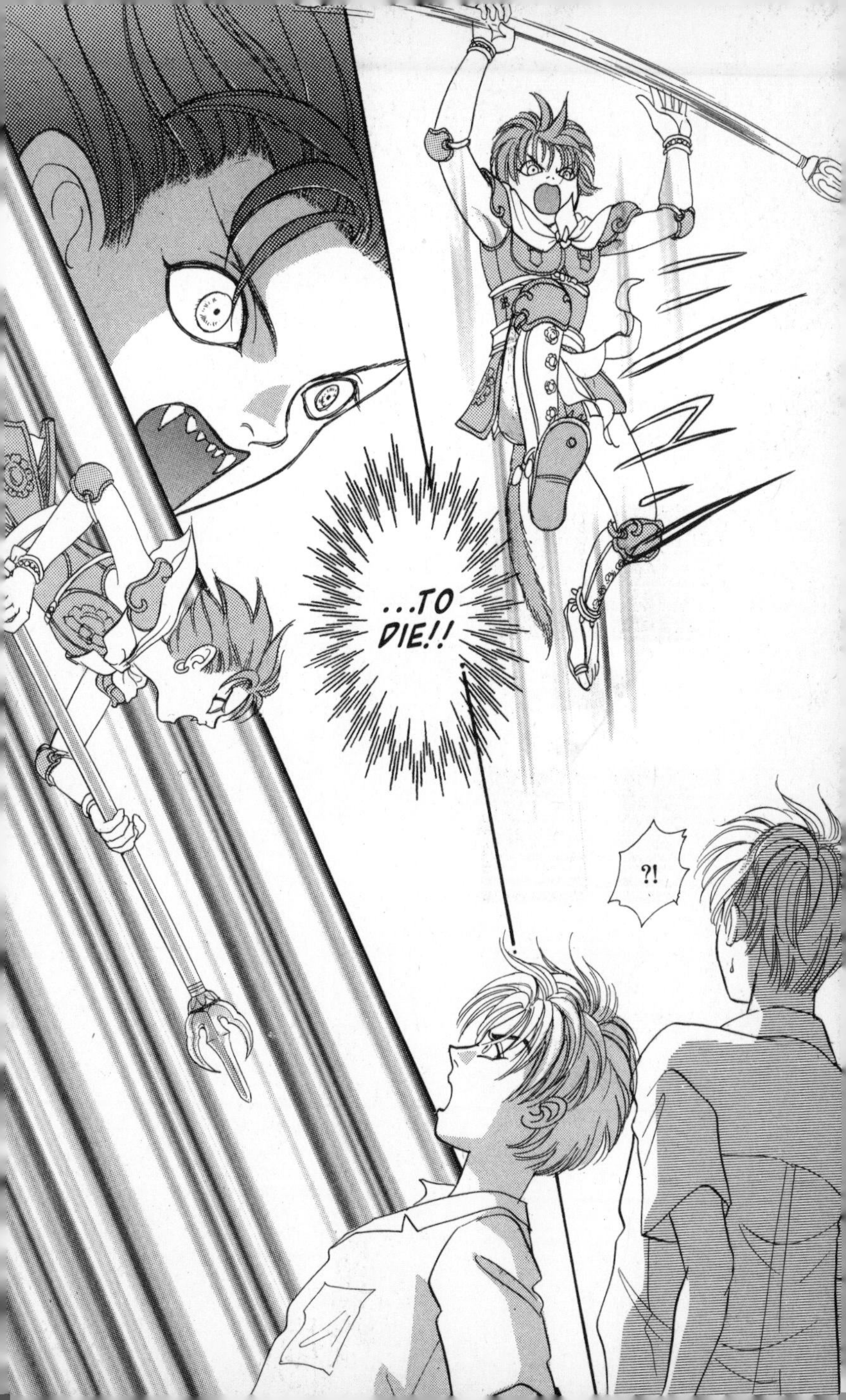
...TO DIE!!
?!

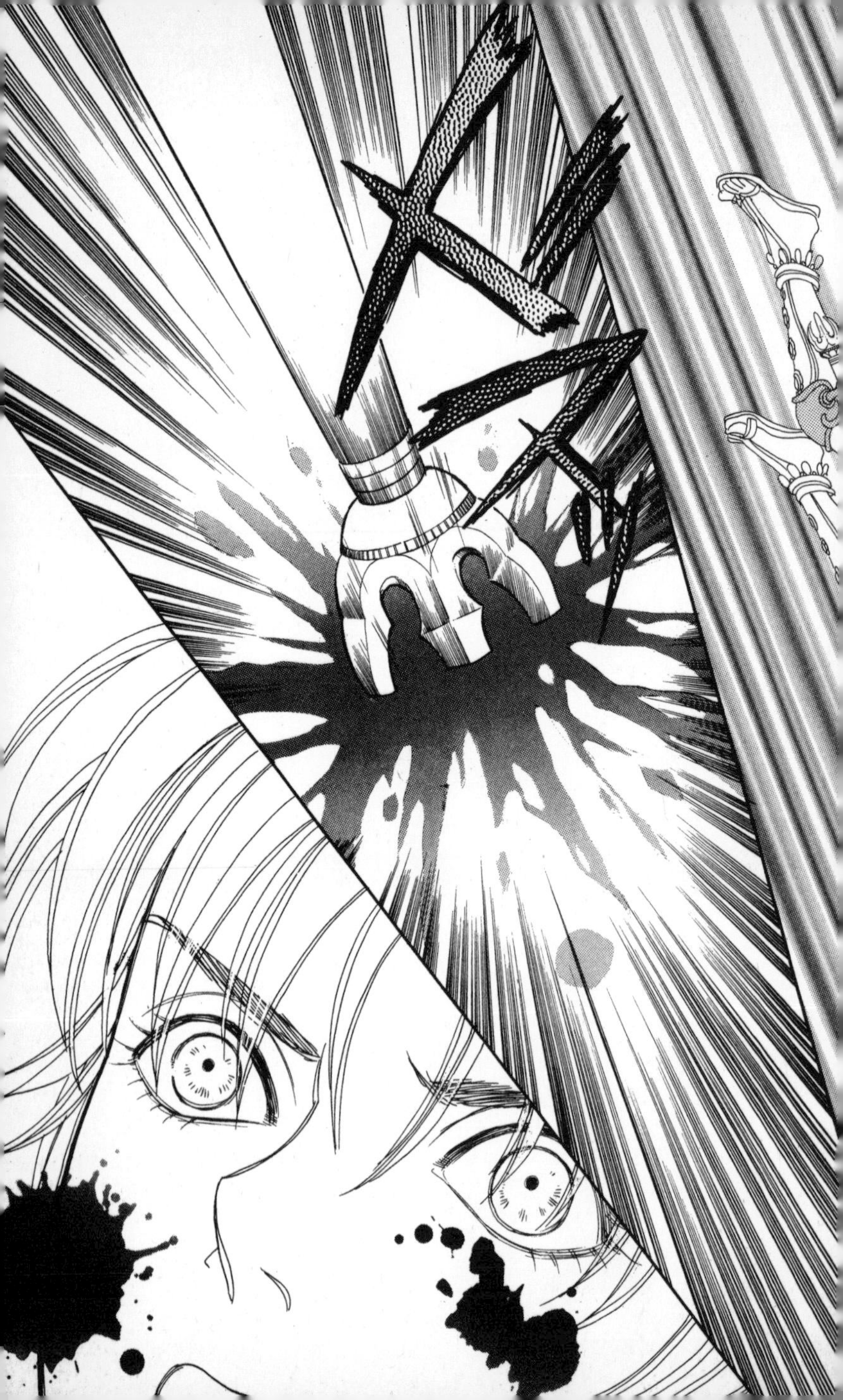

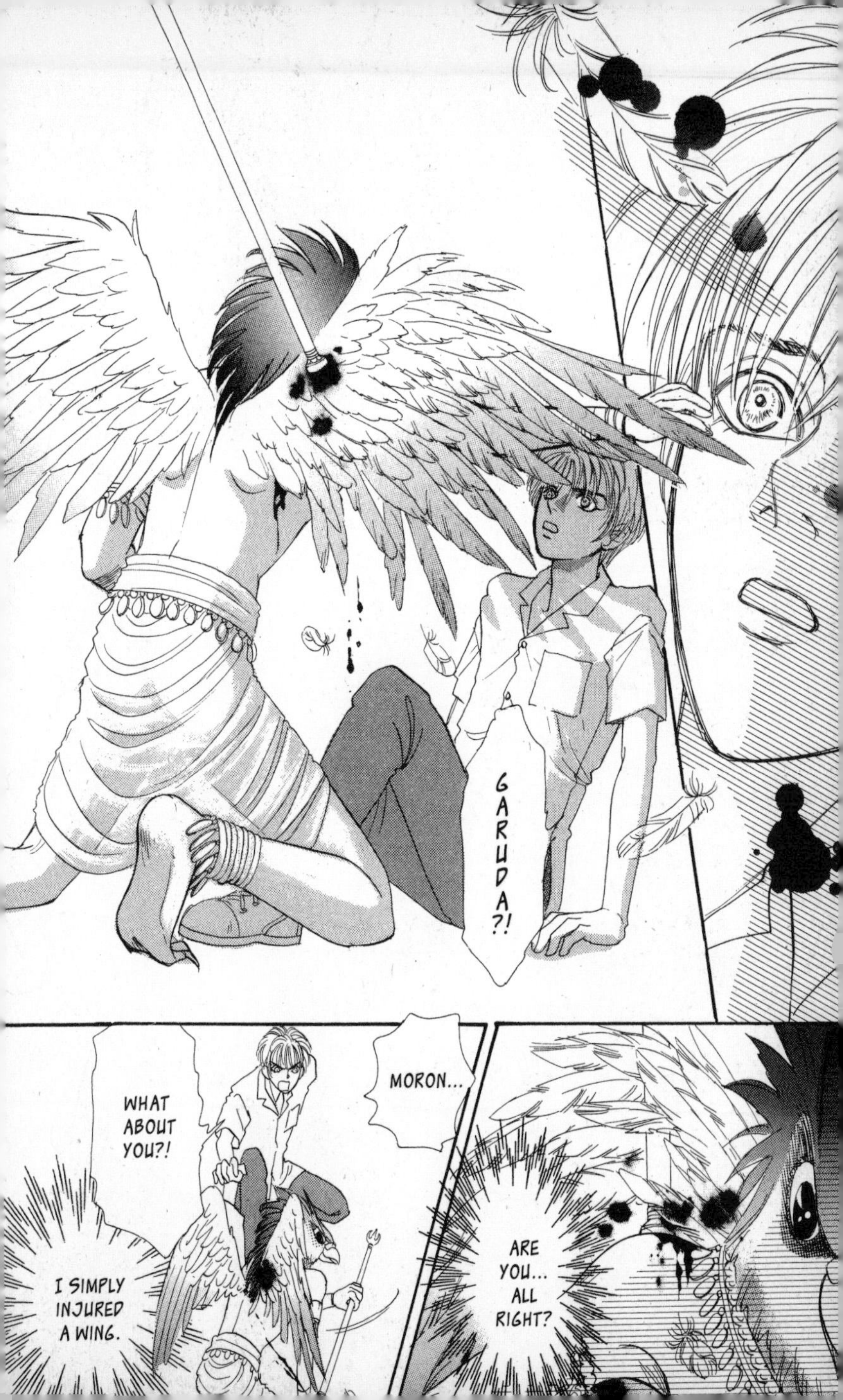
GARUDA?!
ARE YOU... ALL RIGHT?
MORON...
WHAT ABOUT YOU?!
I SIMPLY INJURED A WING.

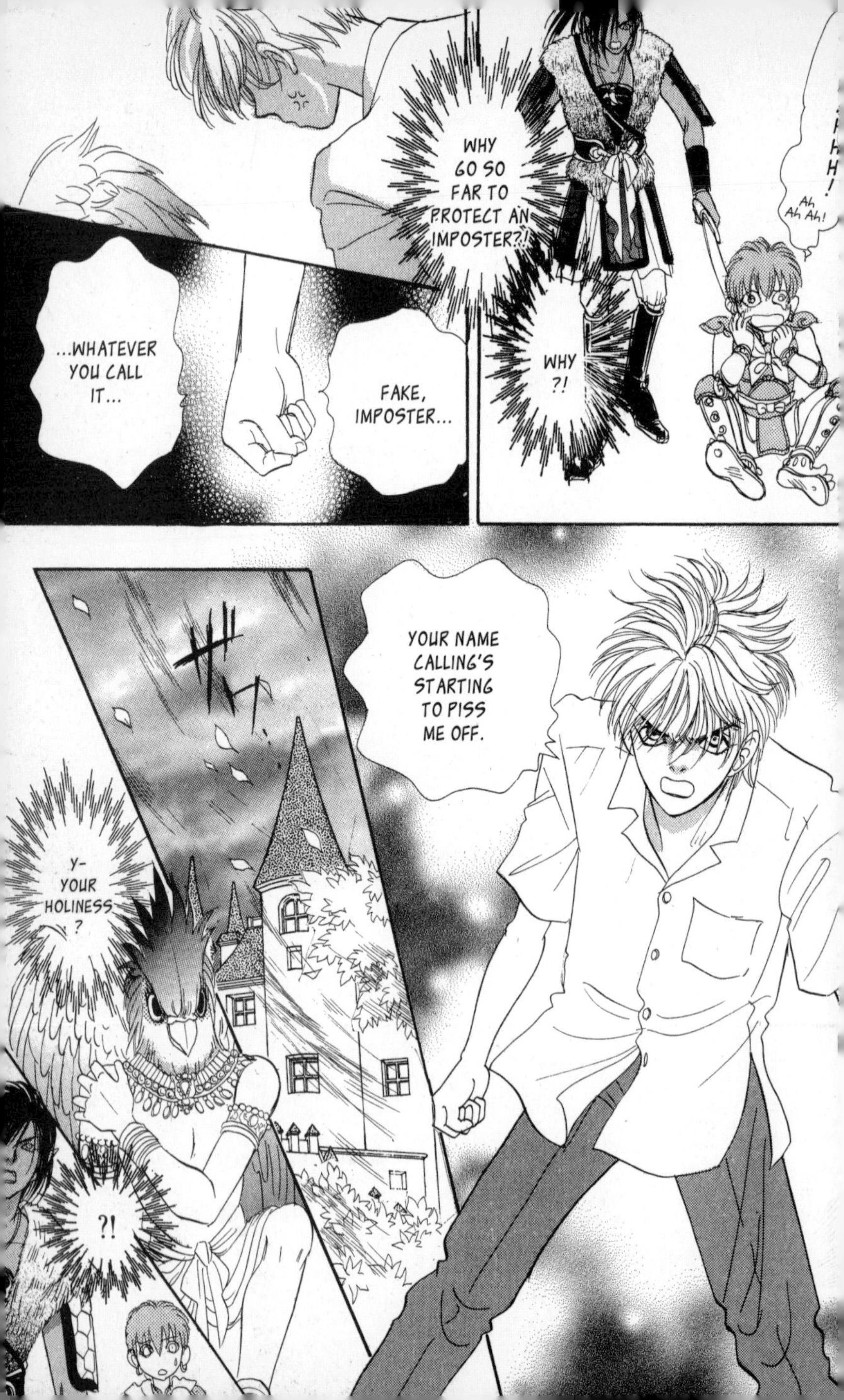
WHY GO SO FAR TO PROTECT AN IMPOSTER?!
WHY ?!
HHH!
Ah Ah Ah!
FAKE, IMPOSTER...
...WHATEVER YOU CALL IT...
YOUR NAME CALLING'S STARTING TO PISS ME OFF.
Y- YOUR HOLINESS ?
?!

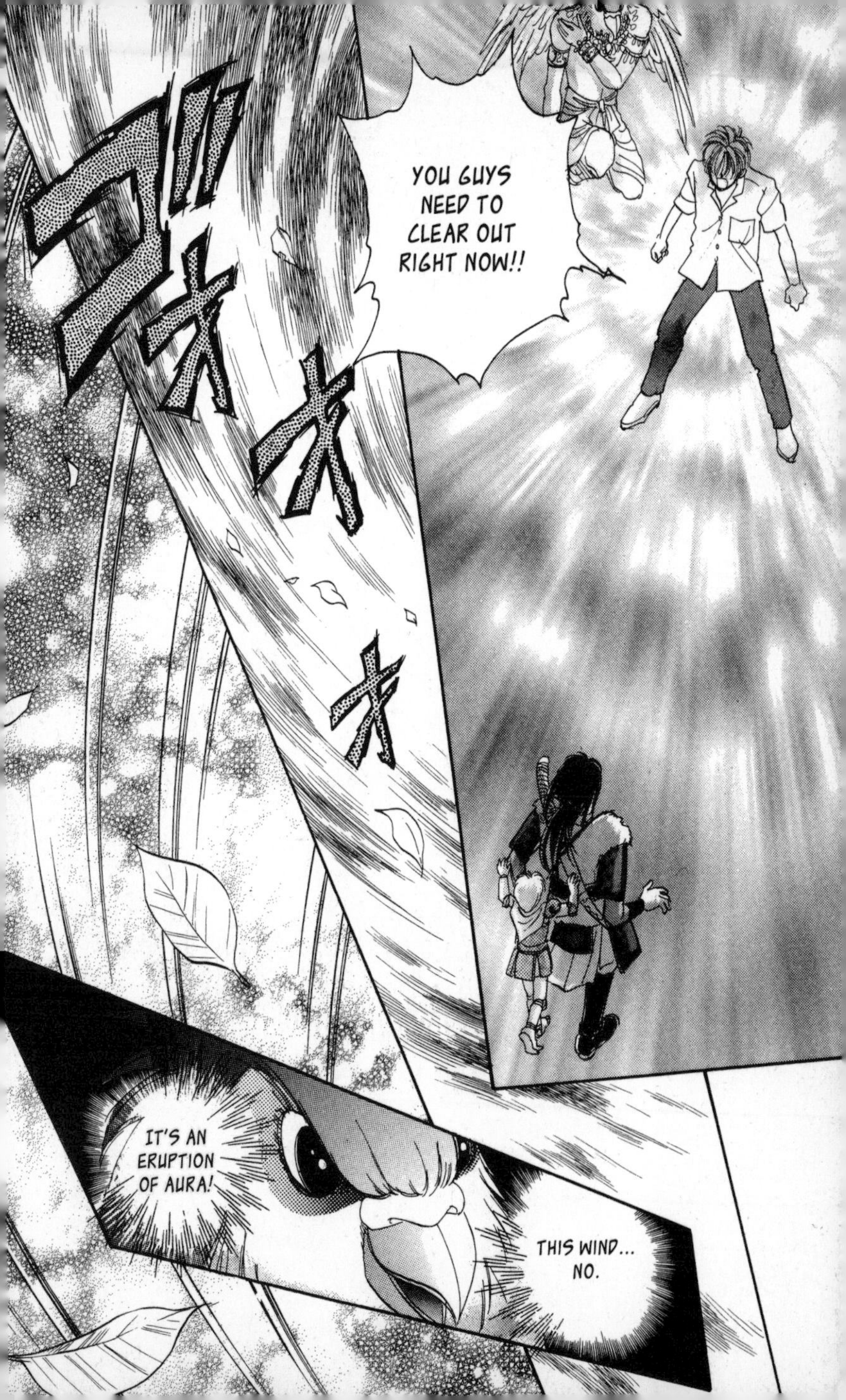
YOU GUYS NEED TO CLEAR OUT RIGHT NOW!!
ゴオオオ
THIS WIND... NO.
IT'S AN ERUPTION OF AURA!

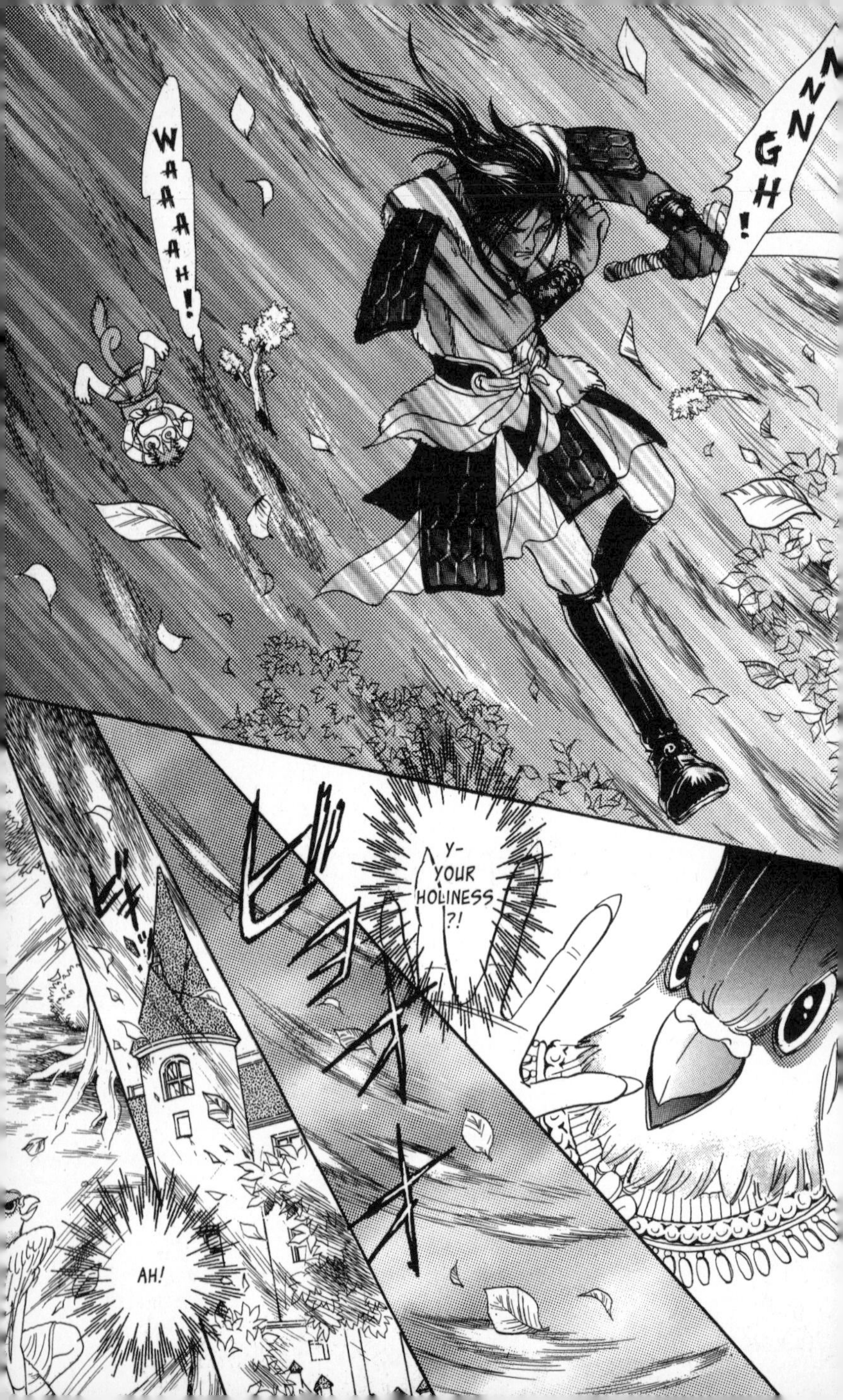
NNNGH!
WAAAAAH!
Y-YOUR HOLINESS?!
AH!

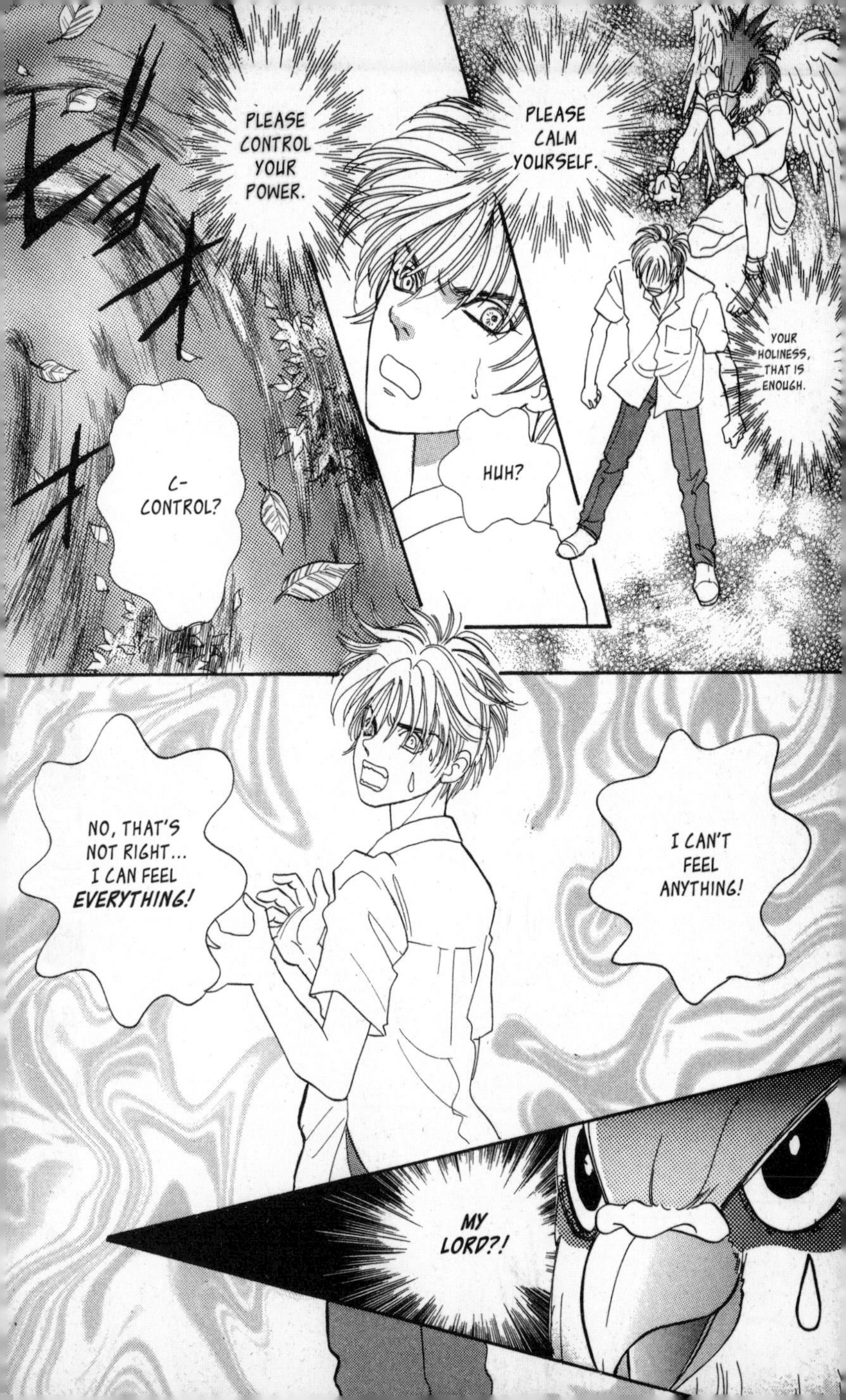
PLEASE CALM YOURSELF.
YOUR HOLINESS, THAT IS ENOUGH.
HUH?
PLEASE CONTROL YOUR POWER.
ビョオオ
C-CONTROL?
I CAN'T FEEL ANYTHING!
NO, THAT'S NOT RIGHT... I CAN FEEL **EVERYTHING!**
MY LORD?!

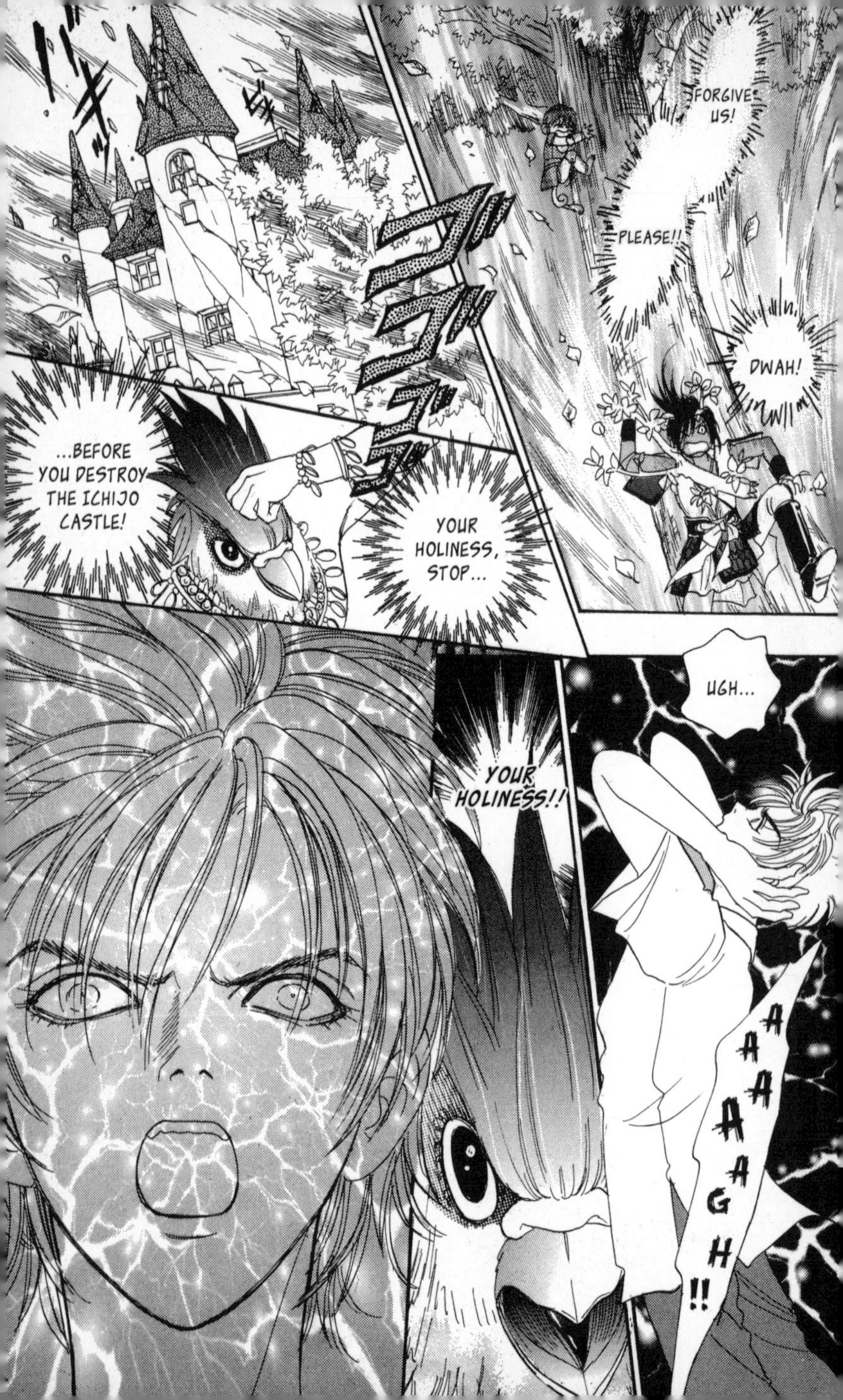

FORGIVE US!
PLEASE!!
DWAH!
YOUR HOLINESS, STOP...
...BEFORE YOU DESTROY THE ICHIJO CASTLE!
UGH...
AAAAAAGH!!
YOUR HOLINESS!!

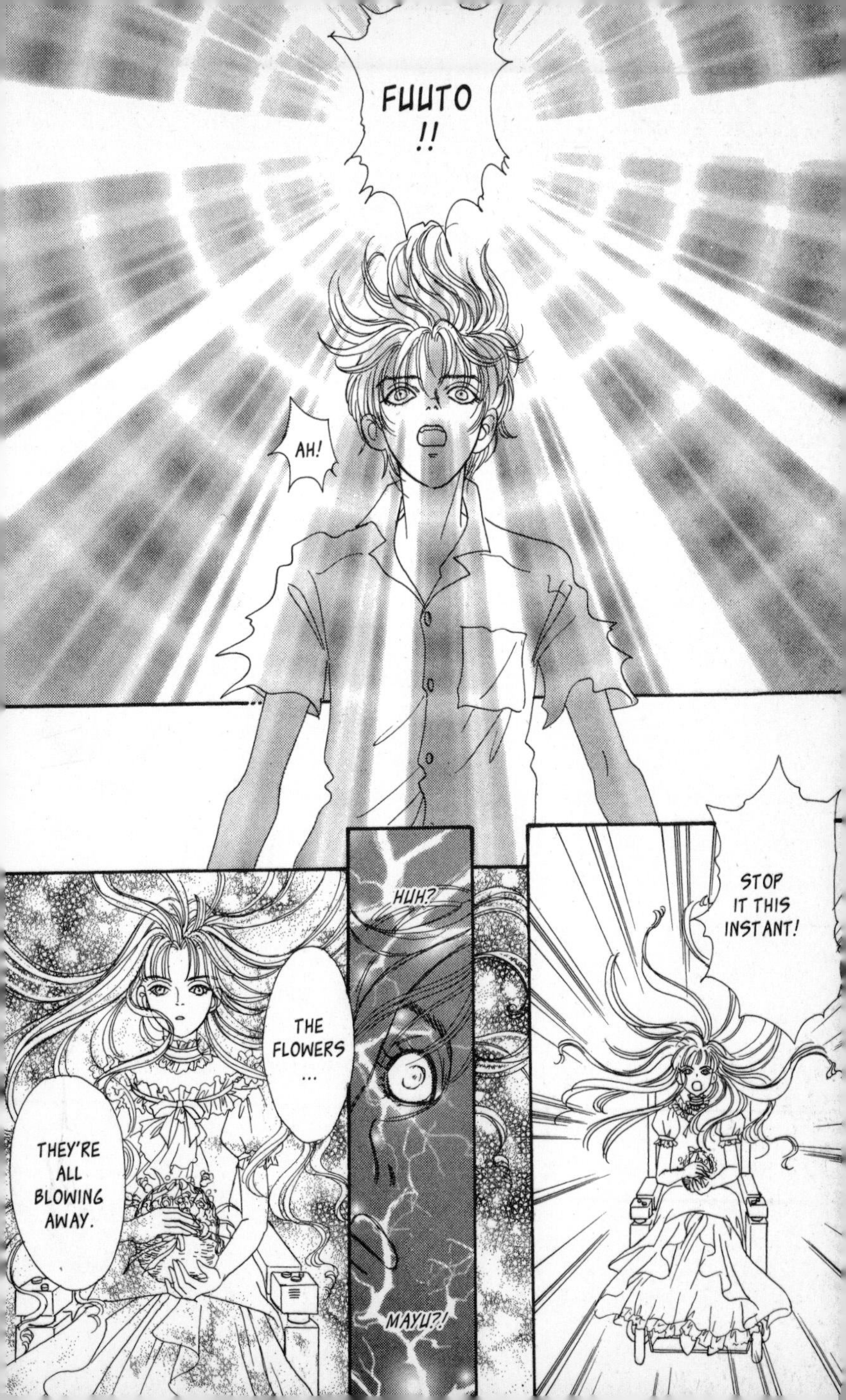
FUUTO !!
AH!
STOP IT THIS INSTANT!
HUH?
MAYU?!
THE FLOWERS ...
THEY'RE ALL BLOWING AWAY.

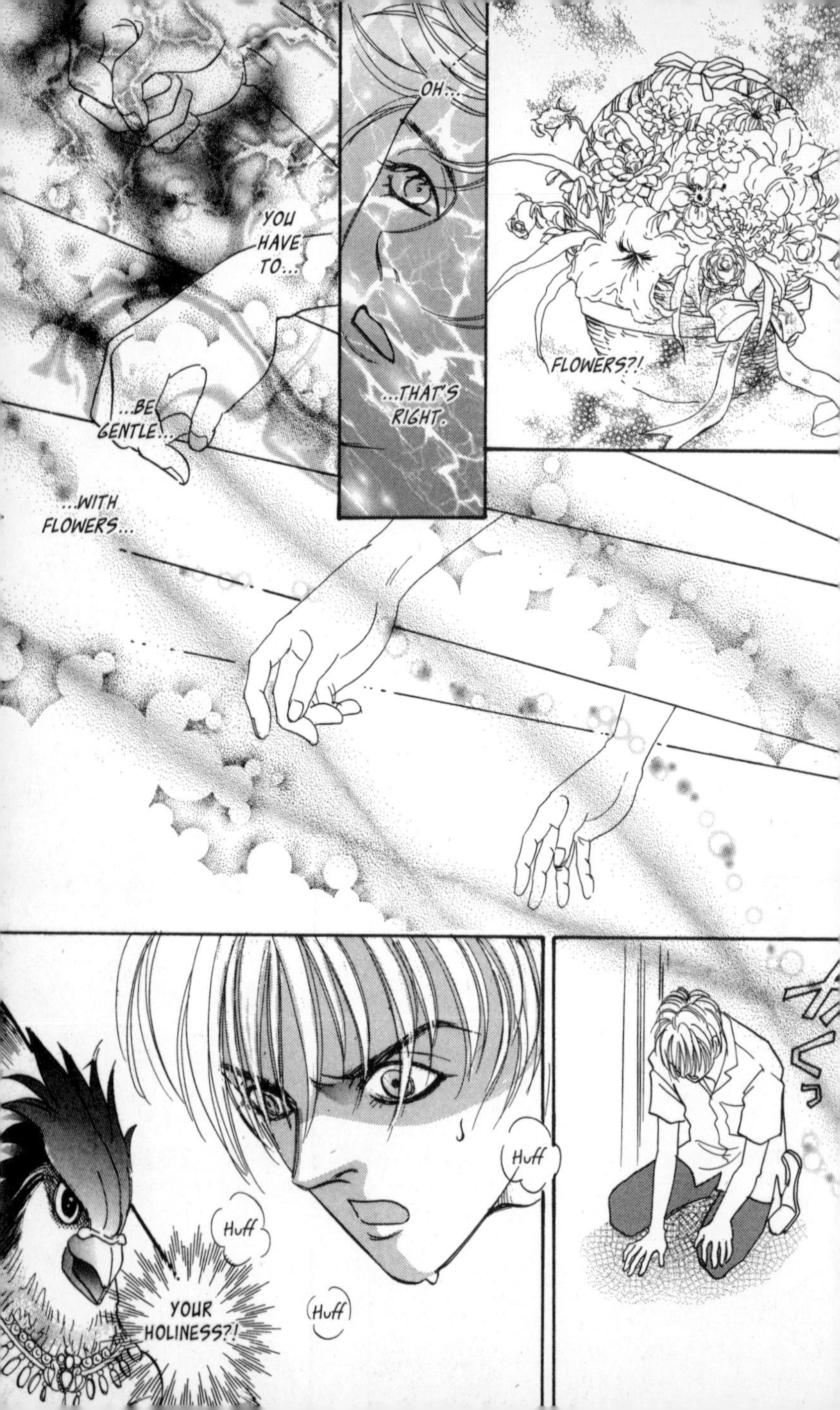
FLOWERS?!
OH...
...THAT'S RIGHT.
YOU HAVE TO...
...BE GENTLE...
...WITH FLOWERS...
Huff
Huff
YOUR HOLINESS?!
Huff

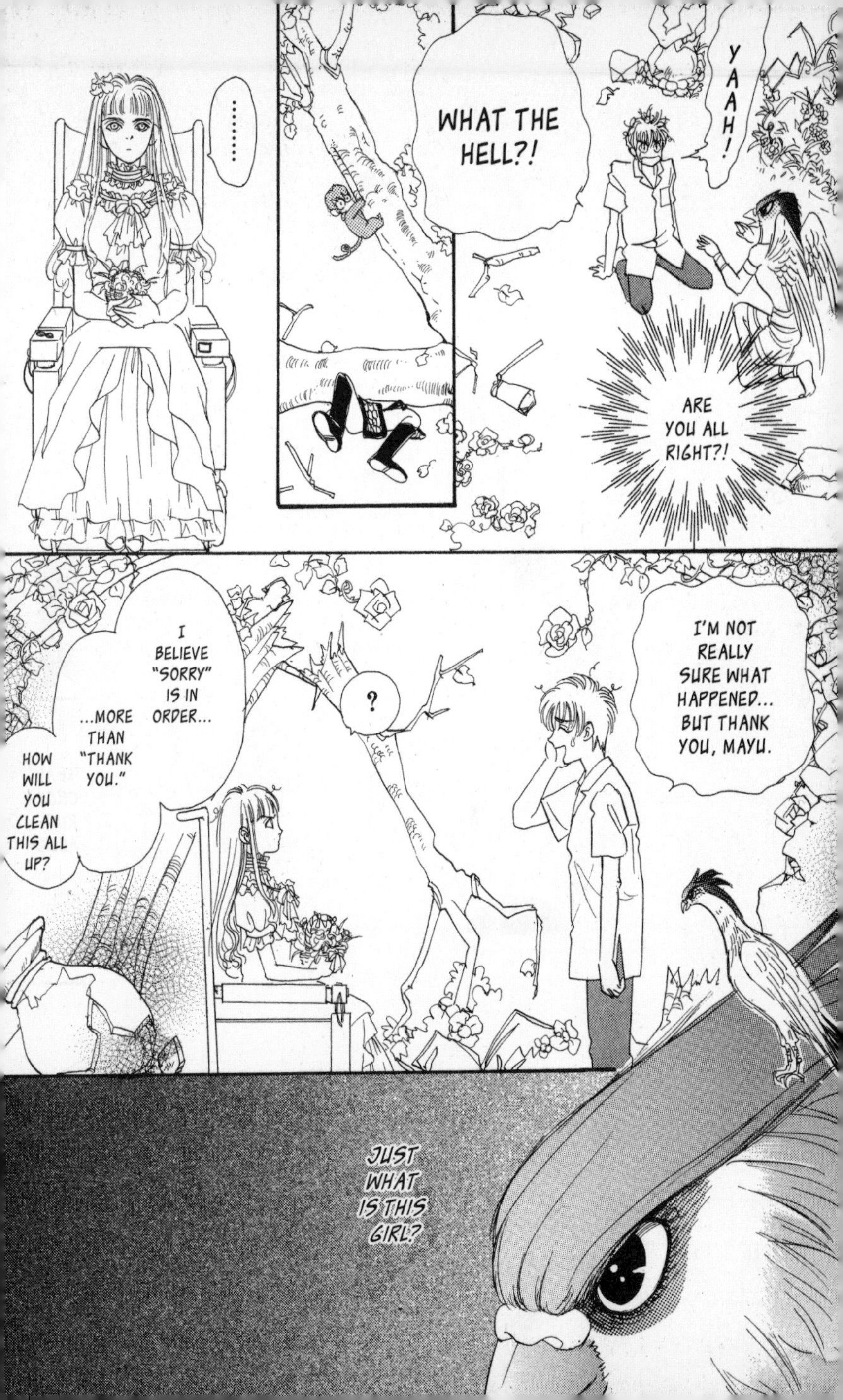
YAAH!
ARE YOU ALL RIGHT?!
WHAT THE HELL?!
....
I'M NOT REALLY SURE WHAT HAPPENED... BUT THANK YOU, MAYU.
?
I BELIEVE "SORRY" IS IN ORDER...
...MORE THAN "THANK YOU."
HOW WILL YOU CLEAN THIS ALL UP?
JUST WHAT IS THIS GIRL?

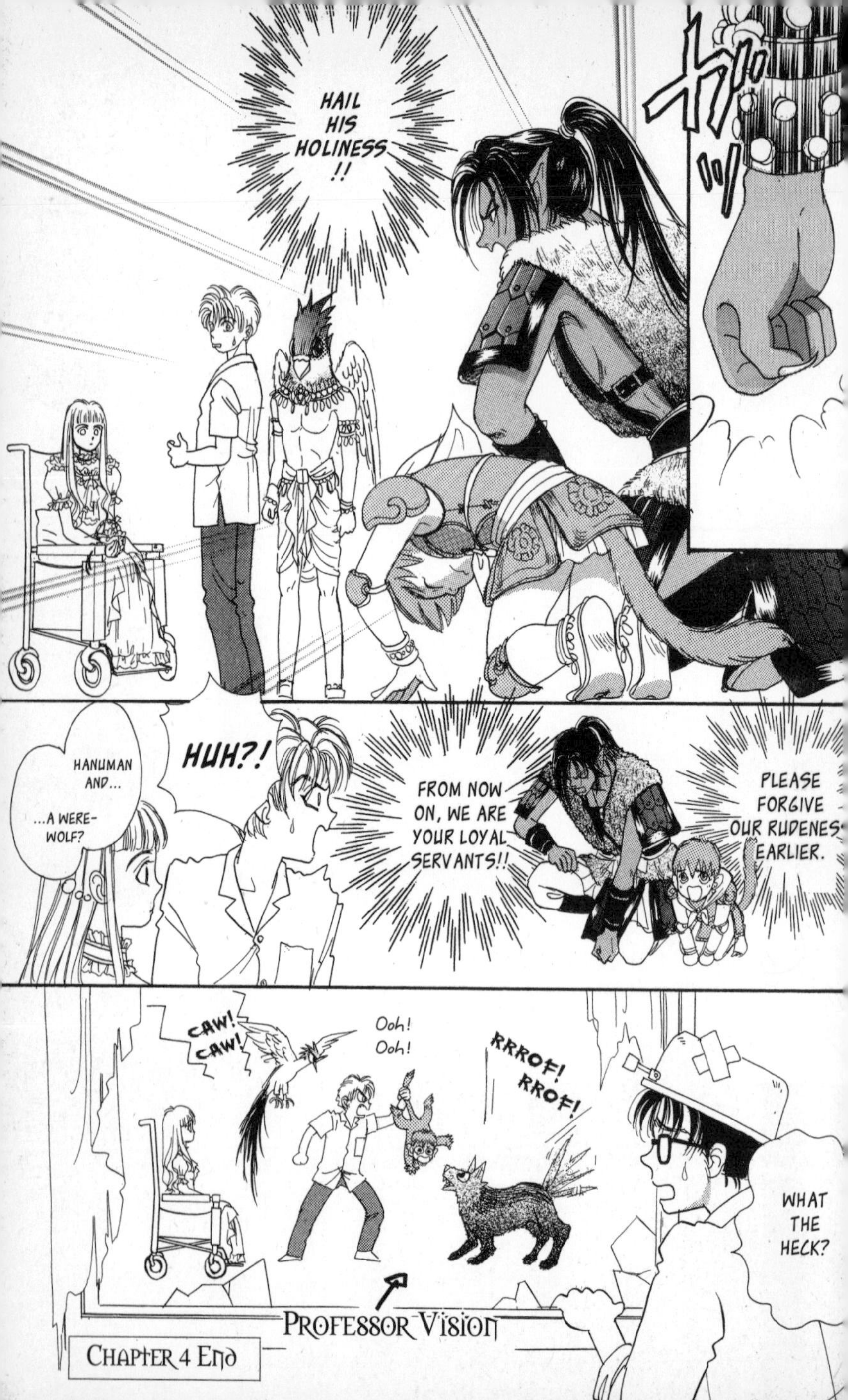
HAIL HIS HOLINESS!!
PLEASE FORGIVE OUR RUDENES EARLIER.
FROM NOW ON, WE ARE YOUR LOYAL SERVANTS!!
HUH?!
HANUMAN AND...
...A WERE-WOLF?
WHAT THE HECK?
RRROF! RROF!
Ooh! Ooh!
CAW! CAW!
PROFESSOR VISION
CHAPTER 4 END

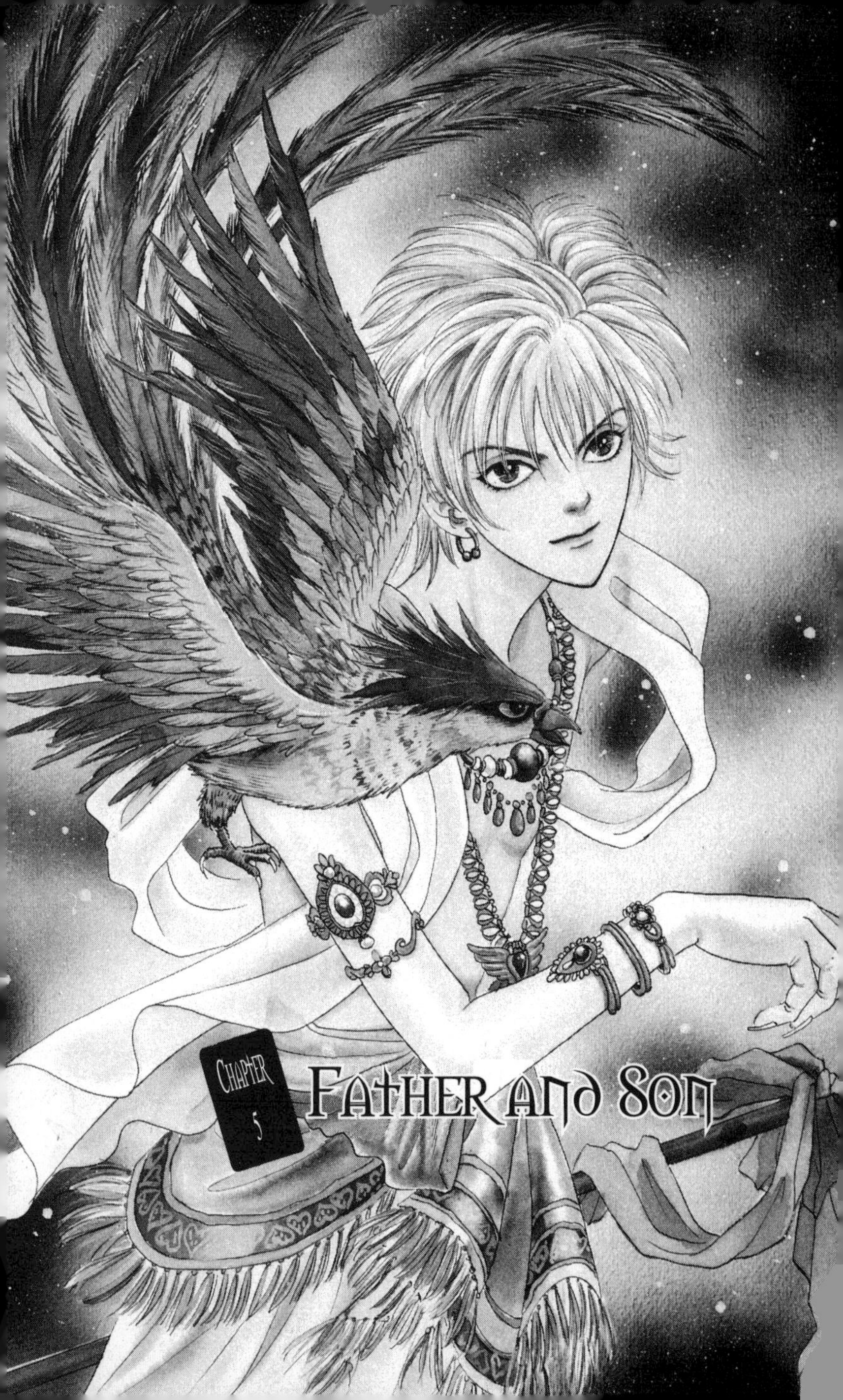
CHAPTER 5
FATHER AND SON

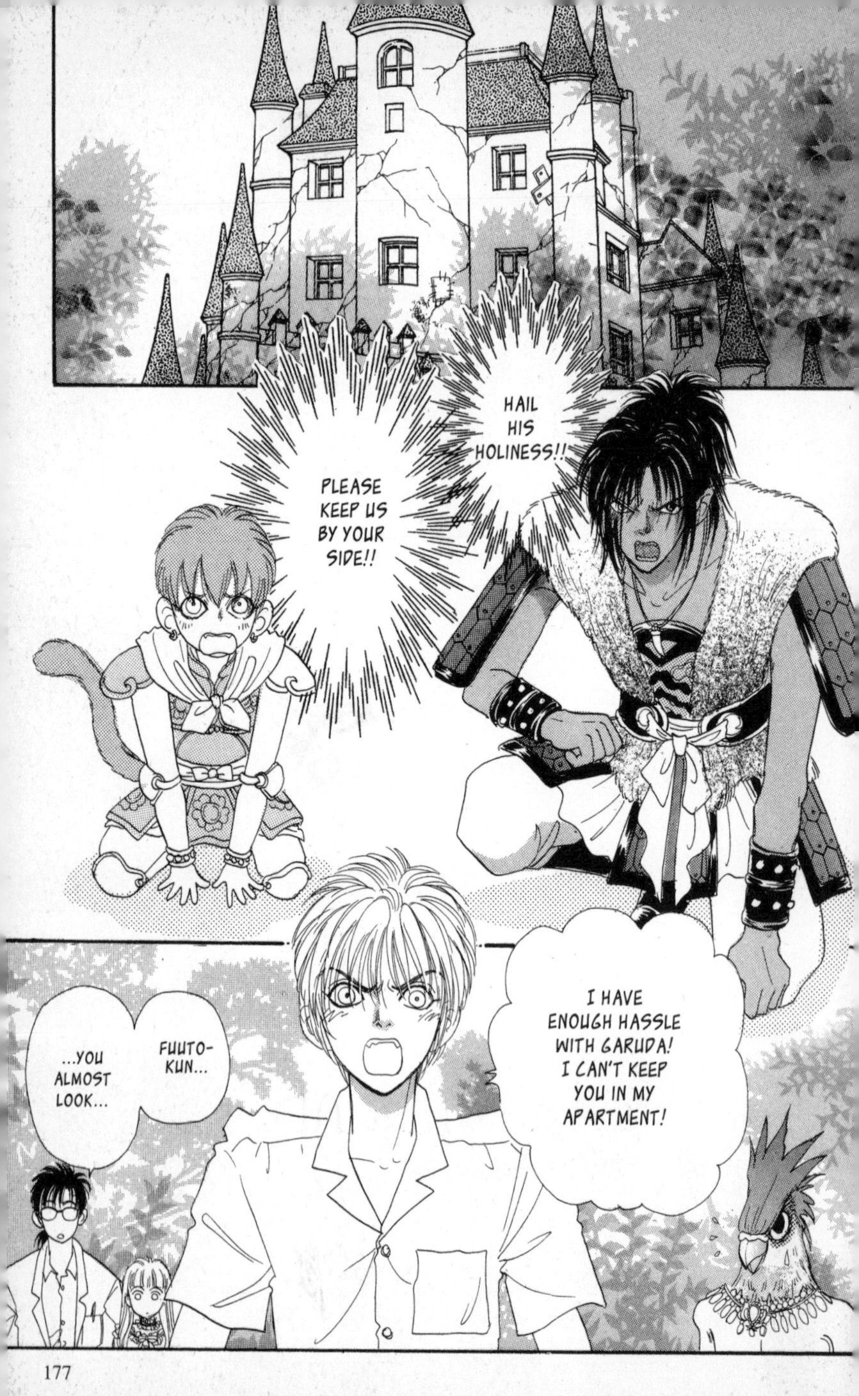
HAIL HIS HOLINESS!!
PLEASE KEEP US BY YOUR SIDE!!
I HAVE ENOUGH HASSLE WITH GARUDA! I CAN'T KEEP YOU IN MY APARTMENT!
FUUTO-KUN...
...YOU ALMOST LOOK...

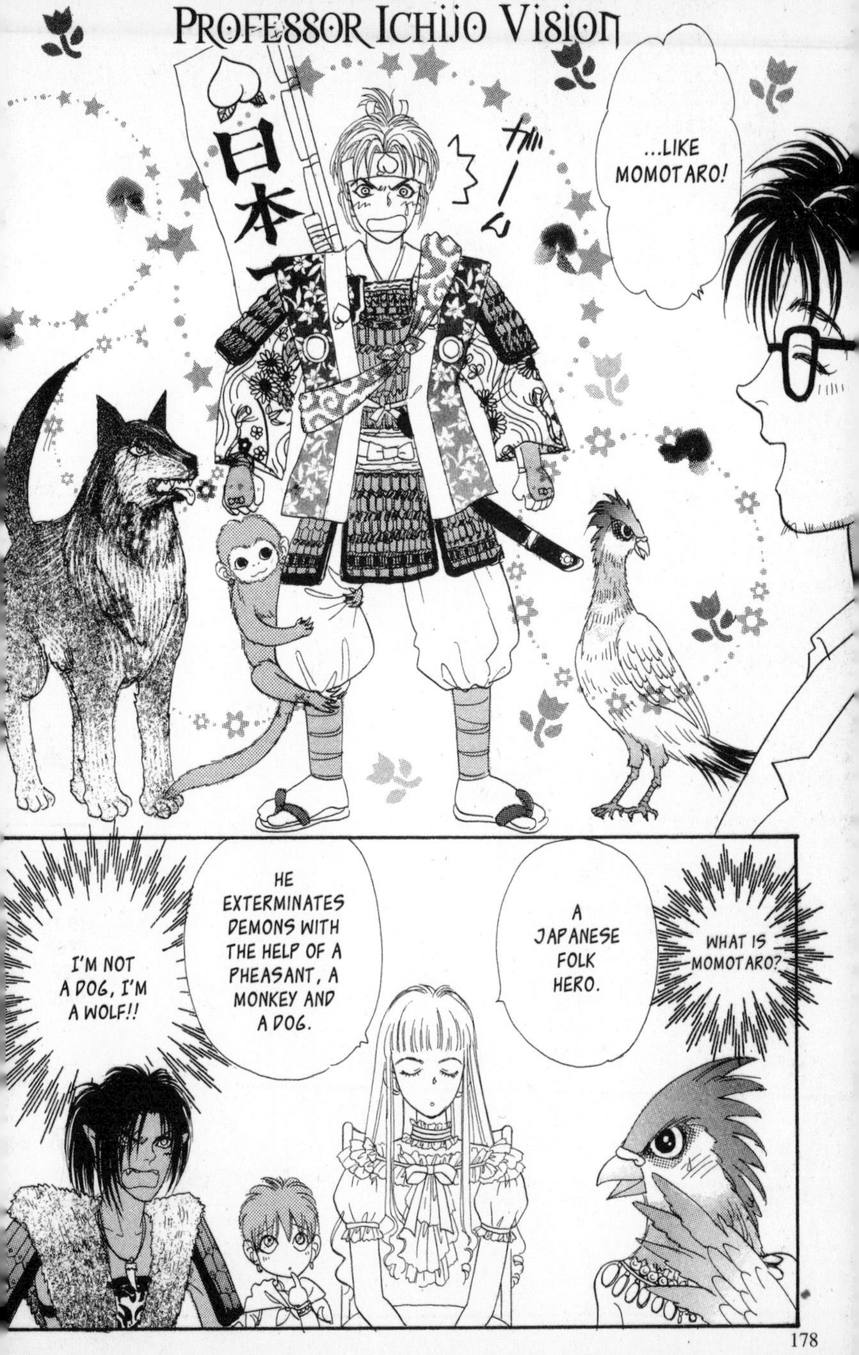
PROFESSOR ICHIJO VISION
...LIKE MOMOTARO!
ガーン
日本一
WHAT IS MOMOTARO?
A JAPANESE FOLK HERO.
HE EXTERMINATES DEMONS WITH THE HELP OF A PHEASANT, A MONKEY AND A DOG.
I'M NOT A DOG, I'M A WOLF!!

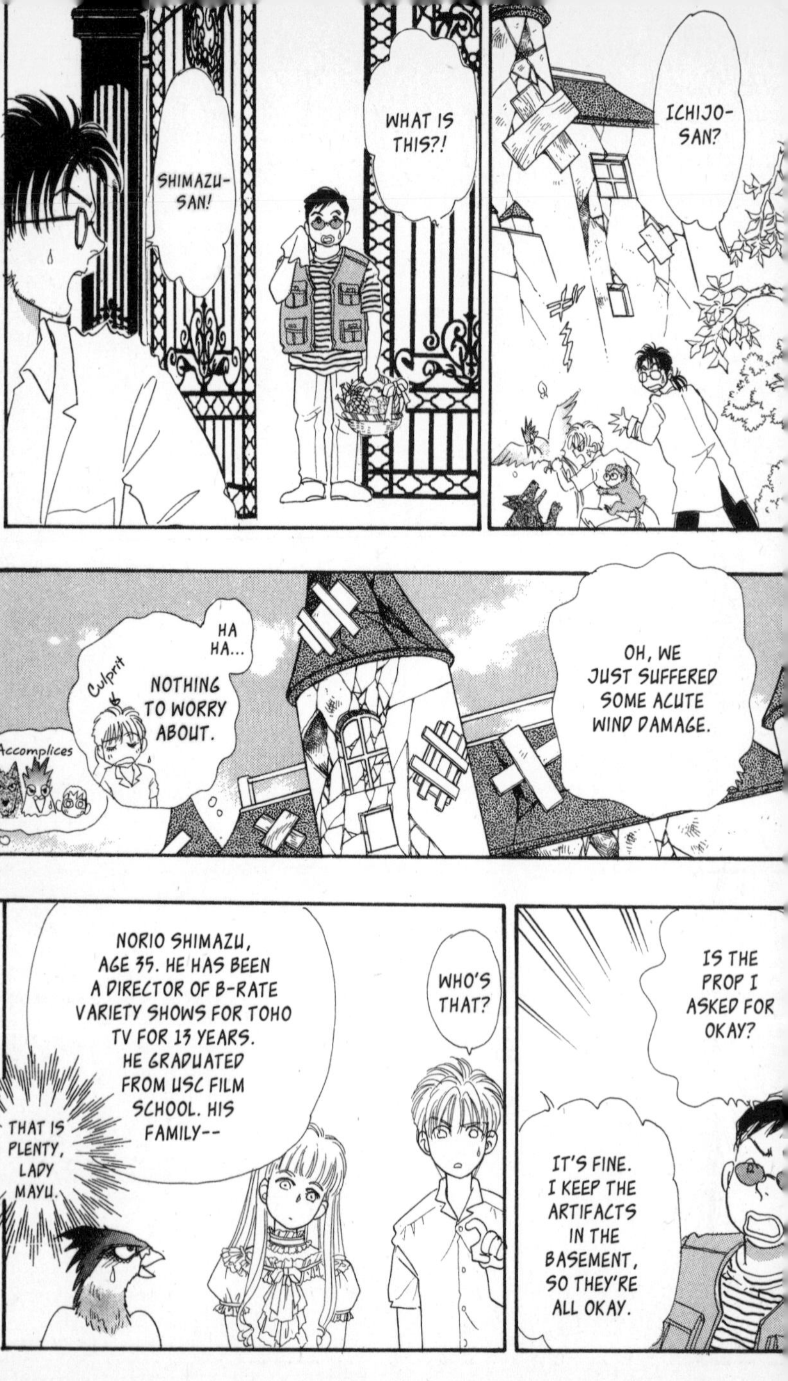
ICHIJO-SAN?
WHAT IS THIS?!
SHIMAZU-SAN!
OH, WE JUST SUFFERED SOME ACUTE WIND DAMAGE.
HA HA... NOTHING TO WORRY ABOUT.
Culprit
Accomplices
IS THE PROP I ASKED FOR OKAY?
IT'S FINE. I KEEP THE ARTIFACTS IN THE BASEMENT, SO THEY'RE ALL OKAY.
WHO'S THAT?
NORIO SHIMAZU, AGE 35. HE HAS BEEN A DIRECTOR OF B-RATE VARIETY SHOWS FOR TOHO TV FOR 13 YEARS. HE GRADUATED FROM USC FILM SCHOOL. HIS FAMILY--
THAT IS PLENTY, LADY MAYU.

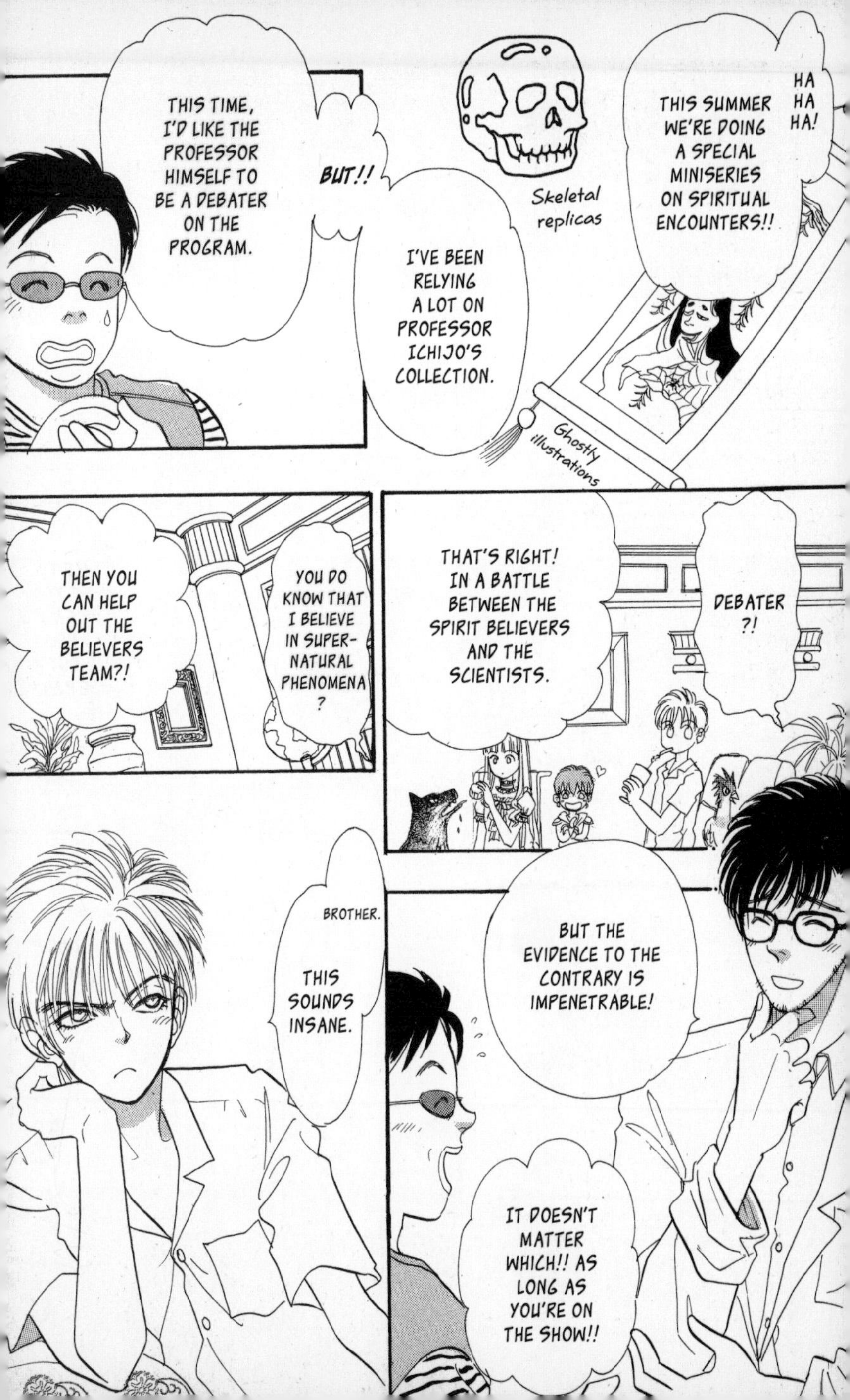
HA HA HA!
THIS SUMMER WE'RE DOING A SPECIAL MINISERIES ON SPIRITUAL ENCOUNTERS!!
Skeletal replicas
I'VE BEEN RELYING A LOT ON PROFESSOR ICHIJO'S COLLECTION.
Ghostly illustrations
BUT!!
THIS TIME, I'D LIKE THE PROFESSOR HIMSELF TO BE A DEBATER ON THE PROGRAM.
DEBATER ?!
THAT'S RIGHT! IN A BATTLE BETWEEN THE SPIRIT BELIEVERS AND THE SCIENTISTS.
YOU DO KNOW THAT I BELIEVE IN SUPER-NATURAL PHENOMENA ?
THEN YOU CAN HELP OUT THE BELIEVERS TEAM?!
BUT THE EVIDENCE TO THE CONTRARY IS IMPENETRABLE!
IT DOESN'T MATTER WHICH!! AS LONG AS YOU'RE ON THE SHOW!!
BROTHER.
THIS SOUNDS INSANE.

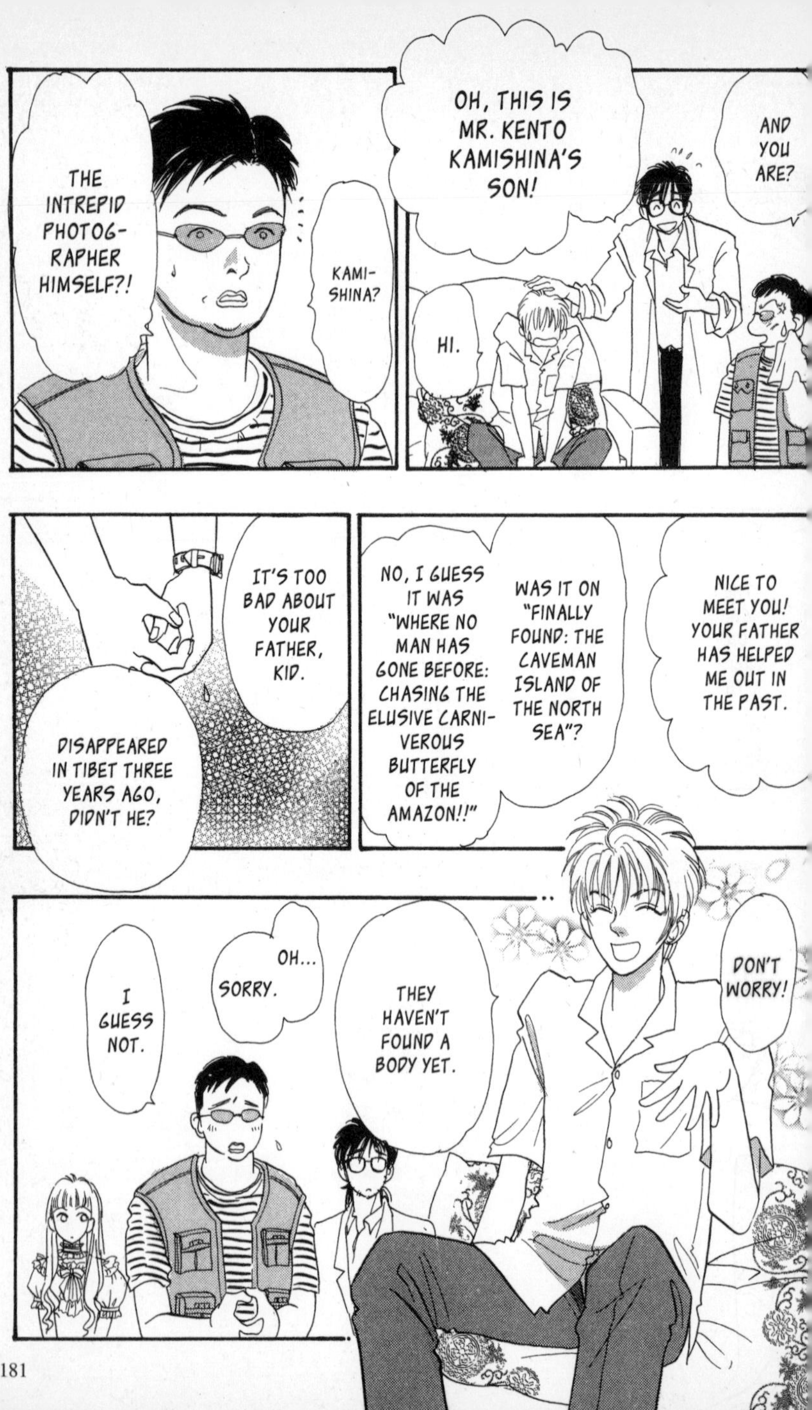
AND YOU ARE?
OH, THIS IS MR. KENTO KAMISHINA'S SON!
HI.
KAMI-SHINA?
THE INTREPID PHOTOG-RAPHER HIMSELF?!
NICE TO MEET YOU! YOUR FATHER HAS HELPED ME OUT IN THE PAST.
WAS IT ON "FINALLY FOUND: THE CAVEMAN ISLAND OF THE NORTH SEA"?
NO, I GUESS IT WAS "WHERE NO MAN HAS GONE BEFORE: CHASING THE ELUSIVE CARNI-VEROUS BUTTERFLY OF THE AMAZON!!"
IT'S TOO BAD ABOUT YOUR FATHER, KID.
DISAPPEARED IN TIBET THREE YEARS AGO, DIDN'T HE?
DON'T WORRY!
THEY HAVEN'T FOUND A BODY YET.
OH...
SORRY.
I GUESS NOT.

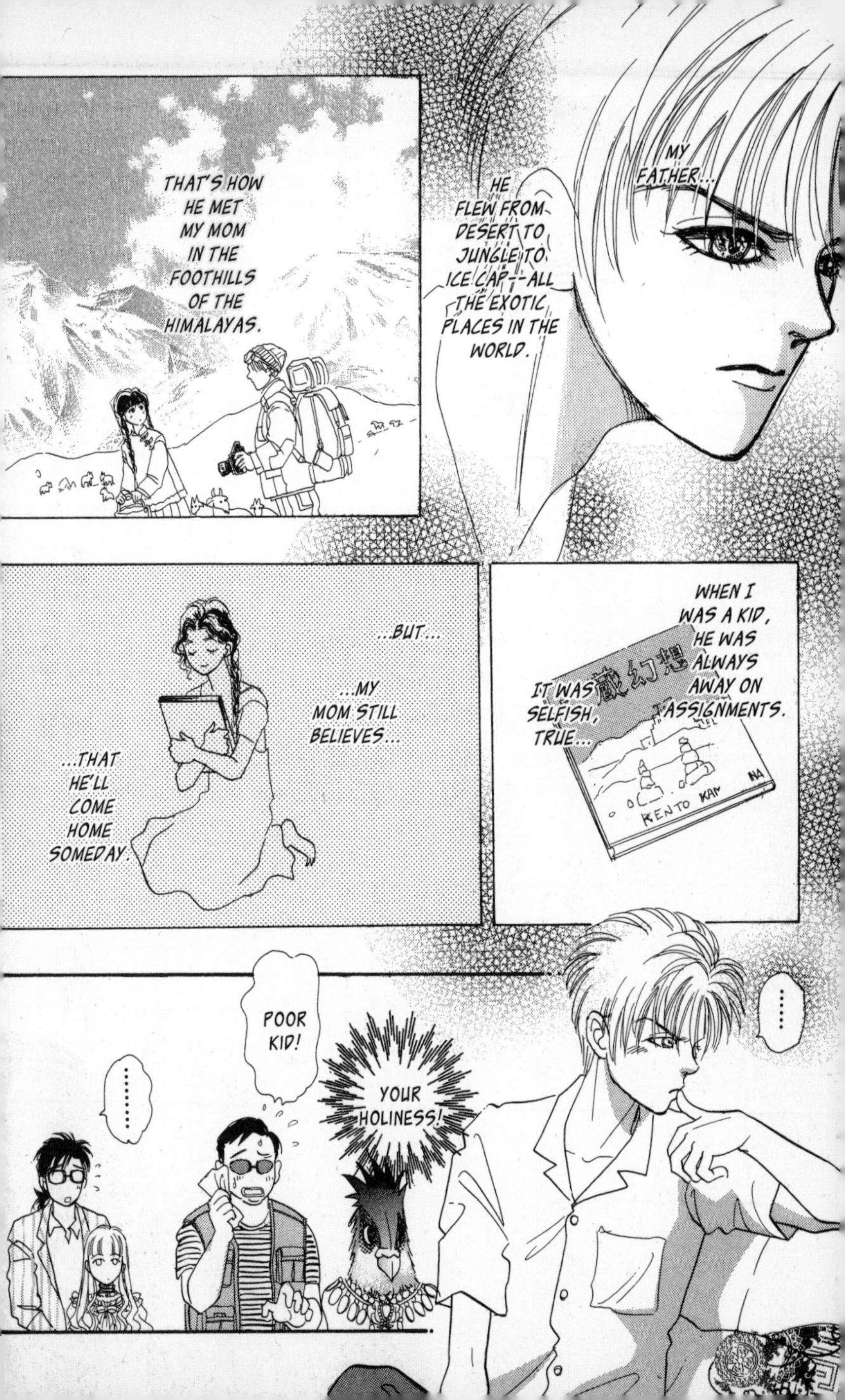
MY FATHER...
HE FLEW FROM DESERT TO JUNGLE TO ICE CAP--ALL THE EXOTIC PLACES IN THE WORLD.
THAT'S HOW HE MET MY MOM IN THE FOOTHILLS OF THE HIMALAYAS.
WHEN I WAS A KID, HE WAS ALWAYS AWAY ON ASSIGNMENTS.
IT WAS SELFISH, TRUE...
...BUT...
...MY MOM STILL BELIEVES...
...THAT HE'LL COME HOME SOMEDAY.
......
POOR KID!
YOUR HOLINESS!
......

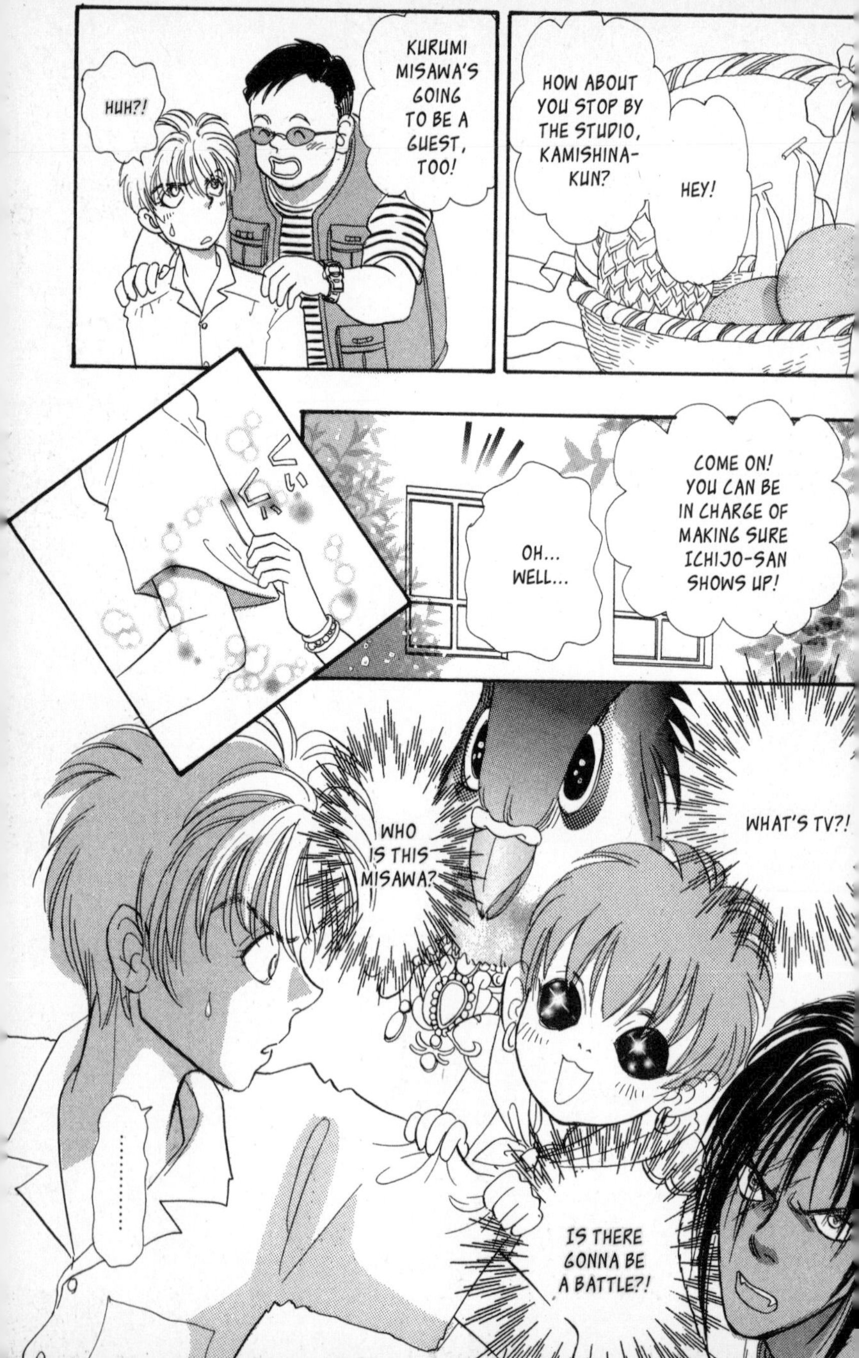
HEY!
HOW ABOUT YOU STOP BY THE STUDIO, KAMISHINA-KUN?
KURUMI MISAWA'S GOING TO BE A GUEST, TOO!
HUH?!
COME ON! YOU CAN BE IN CHARGE OF MAKING SURE ICHIJO-SAN SHOWS UP!
OH... WELL...
WHAT'S TV?!
WHO IS THIS MISAWA?
IS THERE GONNA BE A BATTLE?!
......

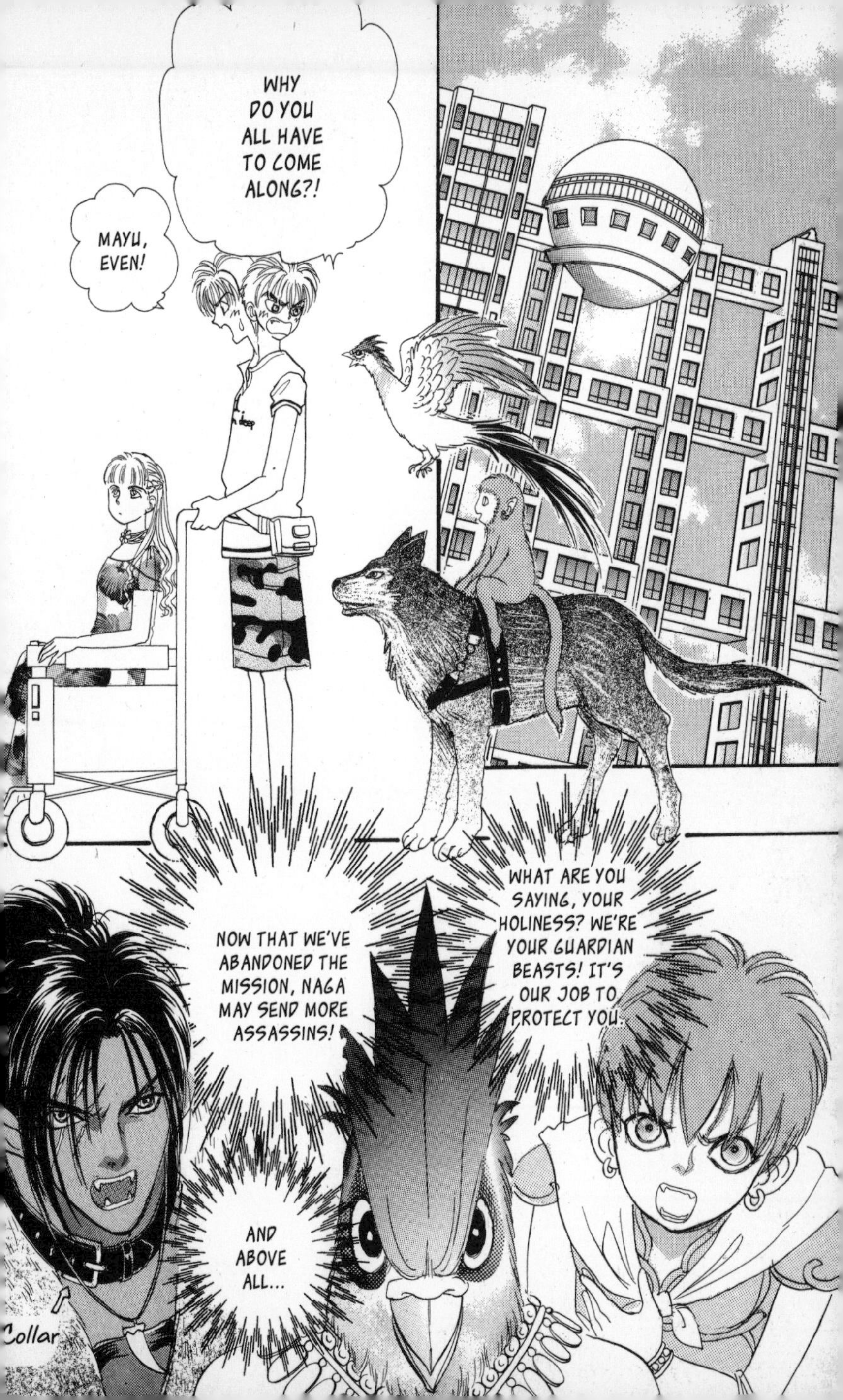
WHY DO YOU ALL HAVE TO COME ALONG?!
MAYU, EVEN!
WHAT ARE YOU SAYING, YOUR HOLINESS? WE'RE YOUR GUARDIAN BEASTS! IT'S OUR JOB TO PROTECT YOU.
NOW THAT WE'VE ABANDONED THE MISSION, NAGA MAY SEND MORE ASSASSINS!
AND ABOVE ALL...
Collar

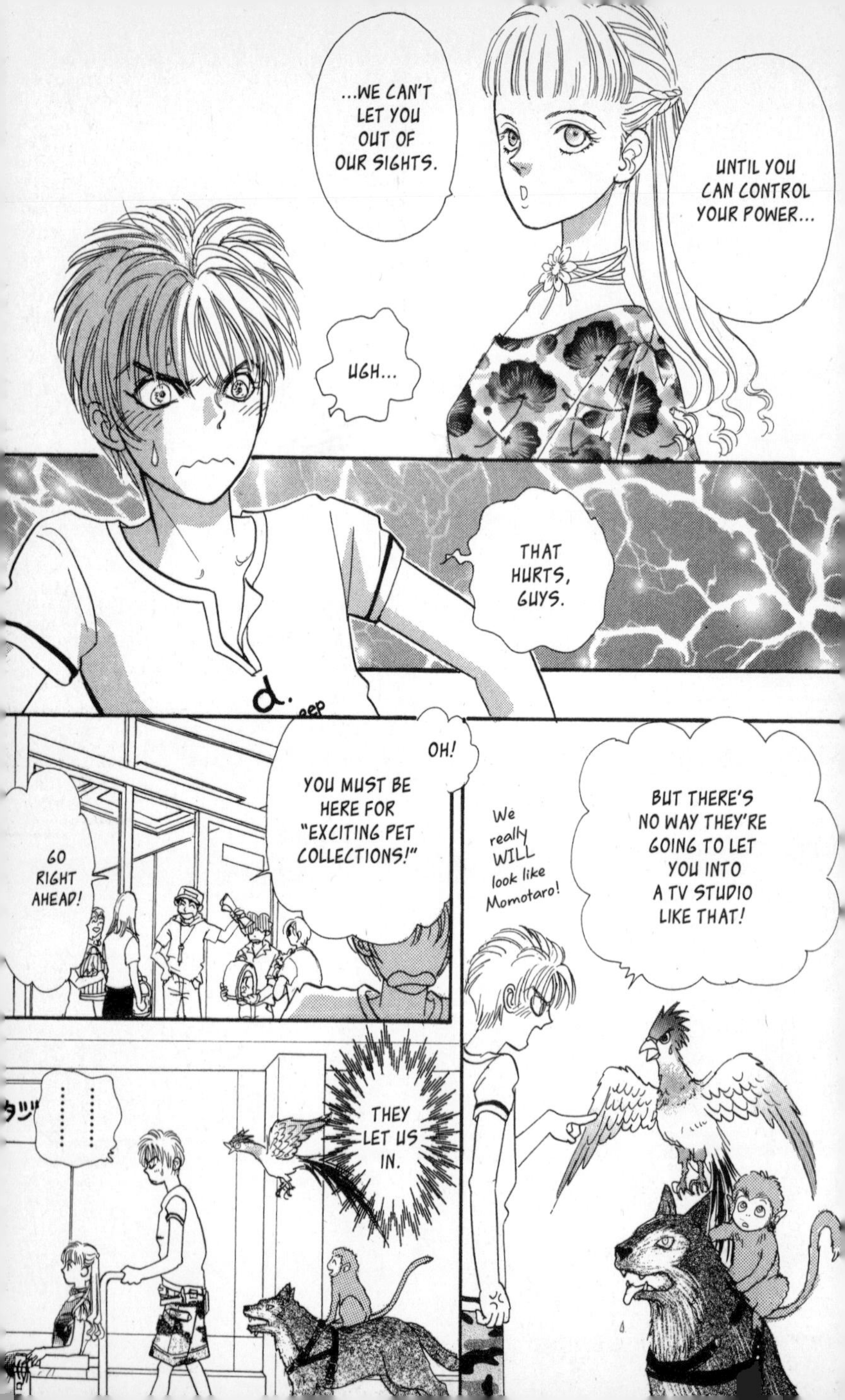
UNTIL YOU CAN CONTROL YOUR POWER...
...WE CAN'T LET YOU OUT OF OUR SIGHTS.
UGH...
THAT HURTS, GUYS.
BUT THERE'S NO WAY THEY'RE GOING TO LET YOU INTO A TV STUDIO LIKE THAT!
We really WILL look like Momotaro!
OH!
YOU MUST BE HERE FOR "EXCITING PET COLLECTIONS!"
GO RIGHT AHEAD!
THEY LET US IN.
......
......

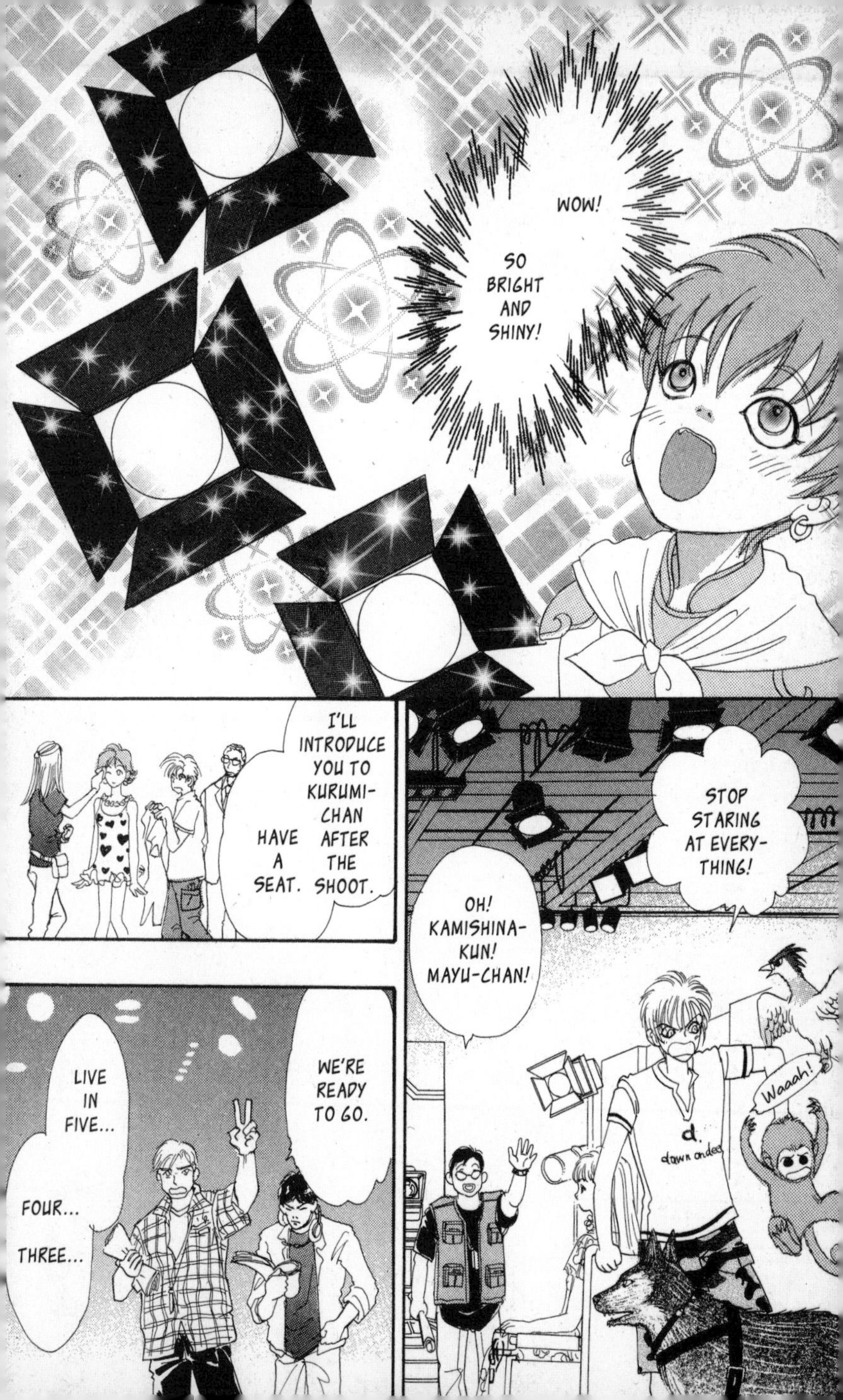
WOW!
SO BRIGHT AND SHINY!
STOP STARING AT EVERYTHING!
OH! KAMISHINA-KUN! MAYU-CHAN!
Waaah!
I'LL INTRODUCE YOU TO KURUMI-CHAN AFTER THE SHOOT. HAVE A SEAT.
WE'RE READY TO GO.
LIVE IN FIVE...
FOUR...
THREE...

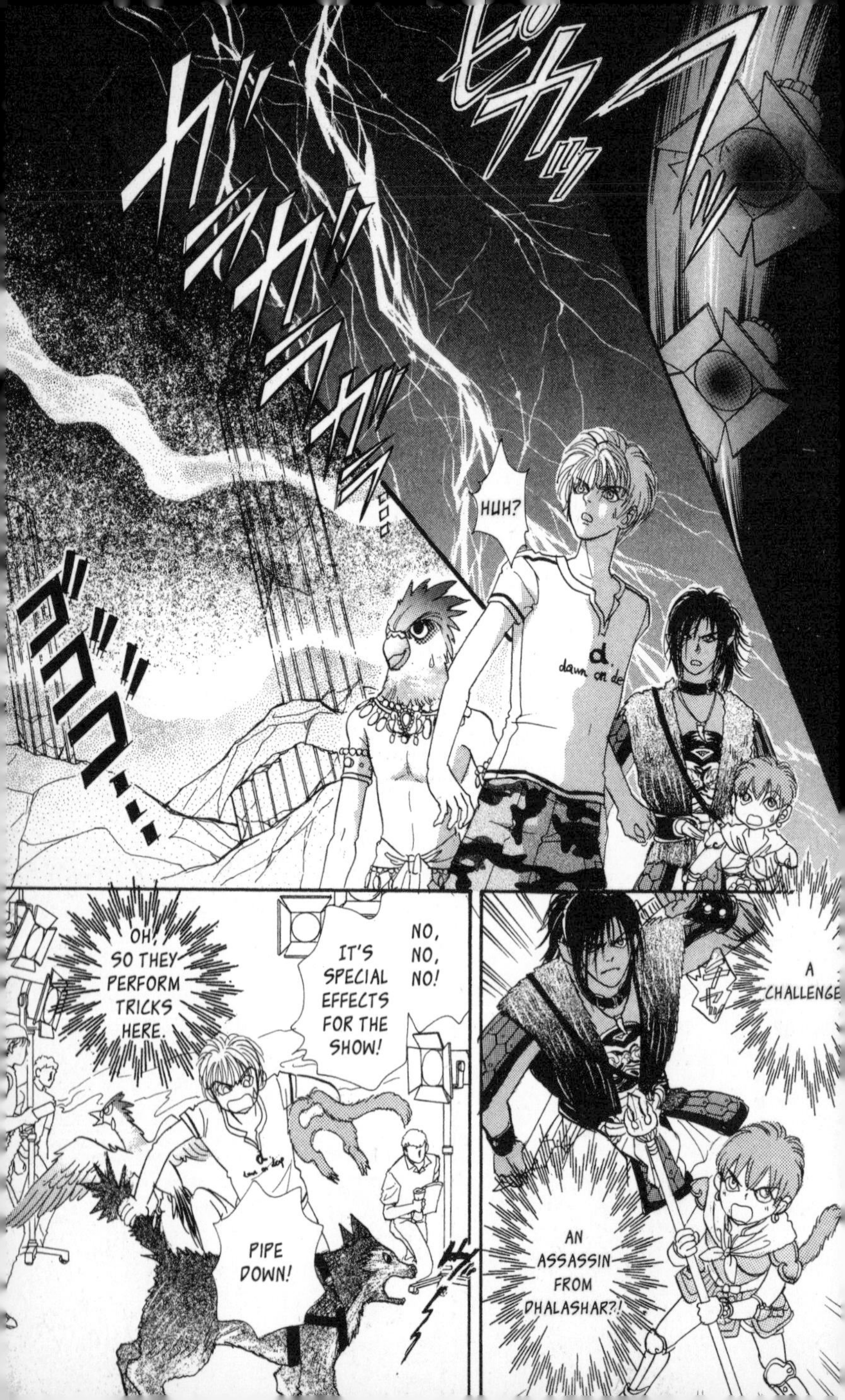
HUH?
A CHALLENGE
AN ASSASSIN FROM DHALASHAR?!
OH, SO THEY PERFORM TRICKS HERE.
NO, NO, NO!
IT'S SPECIAL EFFECTS FOR THE SHOW!
PIPE DOWN!

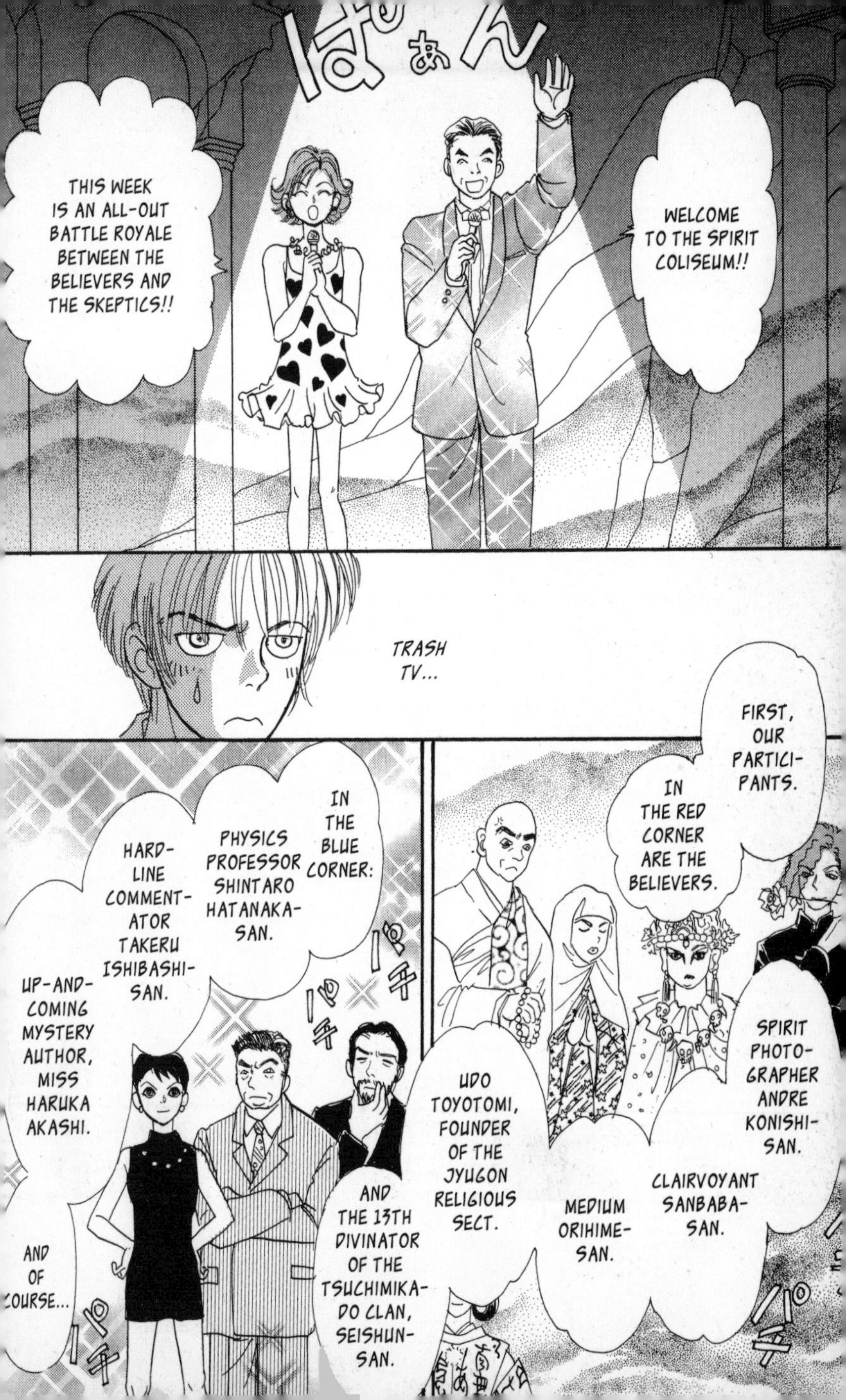
ぱぁん
WELCOME TO THE SPIRIT COLISEUM!!
THIS WEEK IS AN ALL-OUT BATTLE ROYALE BETWEEN THE BELIEVERS AND THE SKEPTICS!!
TRASH TV...
FIRST, OUR PARTICIPANTS.
IN THE RED CORNER ARE THE BELIEVERS.
SPIRIT PHOTOGRAPHER ANDRE KONISHI-SAN.
CLAIRVOYANT SANBABA-SAN.
MEDIUM ORIHIME-SAN.
UDO TOYOTOMI, FOUNDER OF THE JYUGON RELIGIOUS SECT.
AND THE 13TH DIVINATOR OF THE TSUCHIMIKADO CLAN, SEISHUN-SAN.
パチ
IN THE BLUE CORNER:
PHYSICS PROFESSOR SHINTARO HATANAKA-SAN.
HARD-LINE COMMENTATOR TAKERU ISHIBASHI-SAN.
UP-AND-COMING MYSTERY AUTHOR, MISS HARUKA AKASHI.
AND OF COURSE...
パチ
パチ
パチ

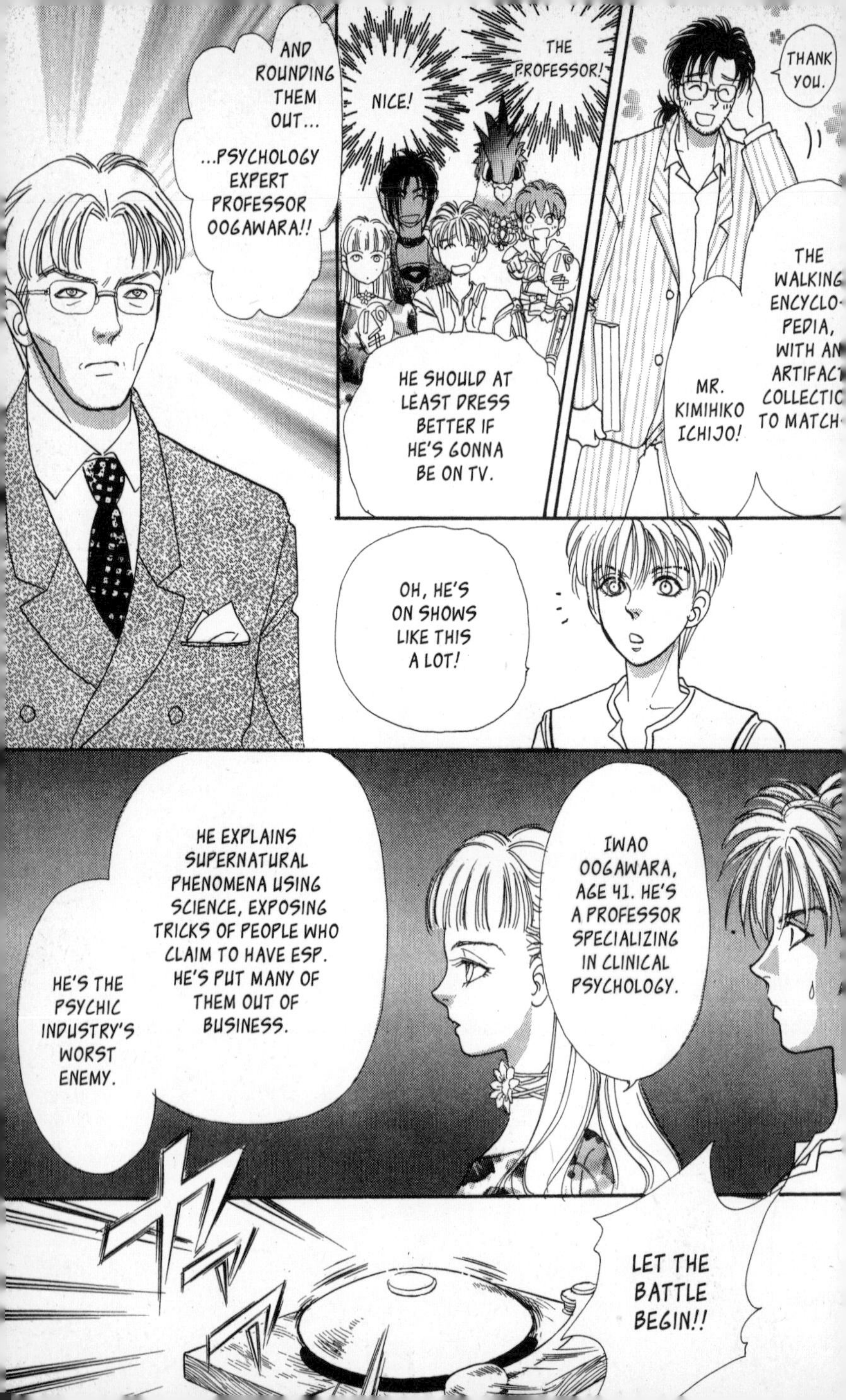
THE WALKING ENCYCLO-PEDIA, WITH AN ARTIFACT COLLECTIO TO MATCH-
MR. KIMIHIKO ICHIJO!
THANK YOU.
THE PROFESSOR!
NICE!
HE SHOULD AT LEAST DRESS BETTER IF HE'S GONNA BE ON TV.
OH, HE'S ON SHOWS LIKE THIS A LOT!
AND ROUNDING THEM OUT...
...PSYCHOLOGY EXPERT PROFESSOR OOGAWARA!!
IWAO OOGAWARA, AGE 41. HE'S A PROFESSOR SPECIALIZING IN CLINICAL PSYCHOLOGY.
HE EXPLAINS SUPERNATURAL PHENOMENA USING SCIENCE, EXPOSING TRICKS OF PEOPLE WHO CLAIM TO HAVE ESP. HE'S PUT MANY OF THEM OUT OF BUSINESS.
HE'S THE PSYCHIC INDUSTRY'S WORST ENEMY.
LET THE BATTLE BEGIN!!

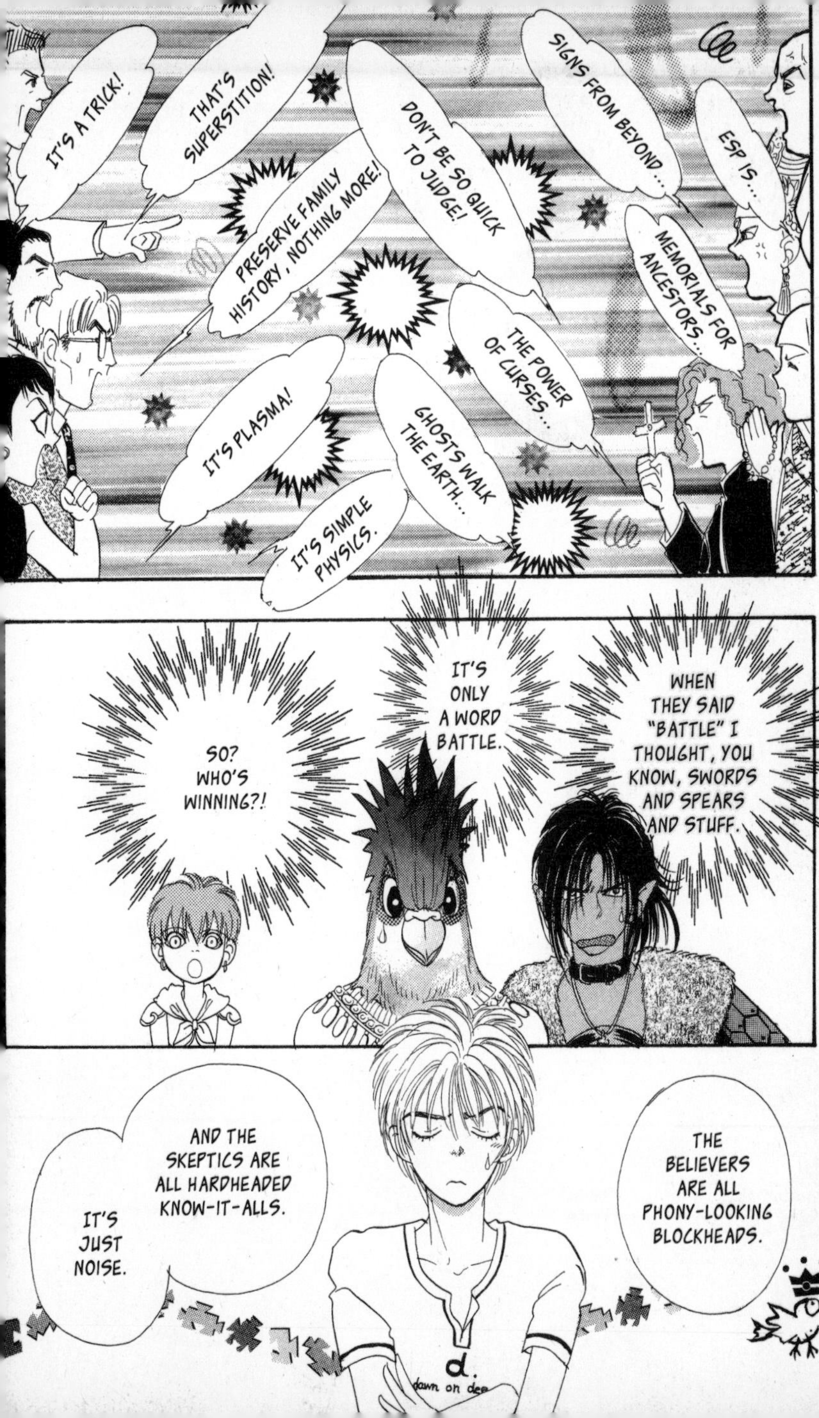
ESP IS...
SIGNS FROM BEYOND...
MEMORIALS FOR ANCESTORS...
DON'T BE SO QUICK TO JUDGE!
THE POWER OF CURSES...
GHOSTS WALK THE EARTH...
IT'S A TRICK!
THAT'S SUPERSTITION!
PRESERVE FAMILY HISTORY, NOTHING MORE!
IT'S PLASMA!
IT'S SIMPLE PHYSICS.
WHEN THEY SAID "BATTLE" I THOUGHT, YOU KNOW, SWORDS AND SPEARS AND STUFF.
IT'S ONLY A WORD BATTLE.
SO? WHO'S WINNING?!
THE BELIEVERS ARE ALL PHONY-LOOKING BLOCKHEADS.
AND THE SKEPTICS ARE ALL HARDHEADED KNOW-IT-ALLS.
IT'S JUST NOISE.
d. dawn on dee

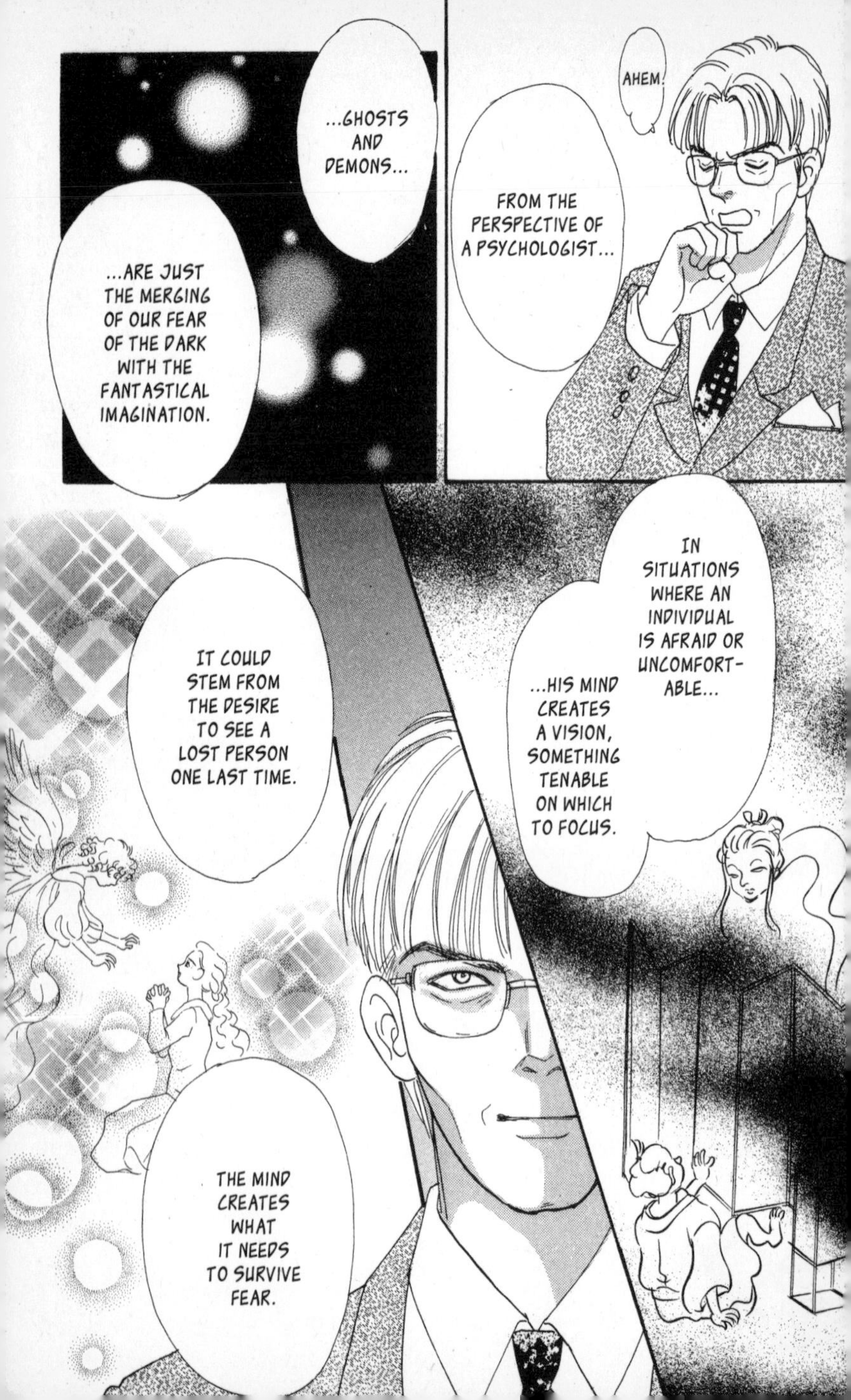
AHEM!
FROM THE PERSPECTIVE OF A PSYCHOLOGIST...
...GHOSTS AND DEMONS...
...ARE JUST THE MERGING OF OUR FEAR OF THE DARK WITH THE FANTASTICAL IMAGINATION.
IN SITUATIONS WHERE AN INDIVIDUAL IS AFRAID OR UNCOMFORT-ABLE...
...HIS MIND CREATES A VISION, SOMETHING TENABLE ON WHICH TO FOCUS.
IT COULD STEM FROM THE DESIRE TO SEE A LOST PERSON ONE LAST TIME.
THE MIND CREATES WHAT IT NEEDS TO SURVIVE FEAR.

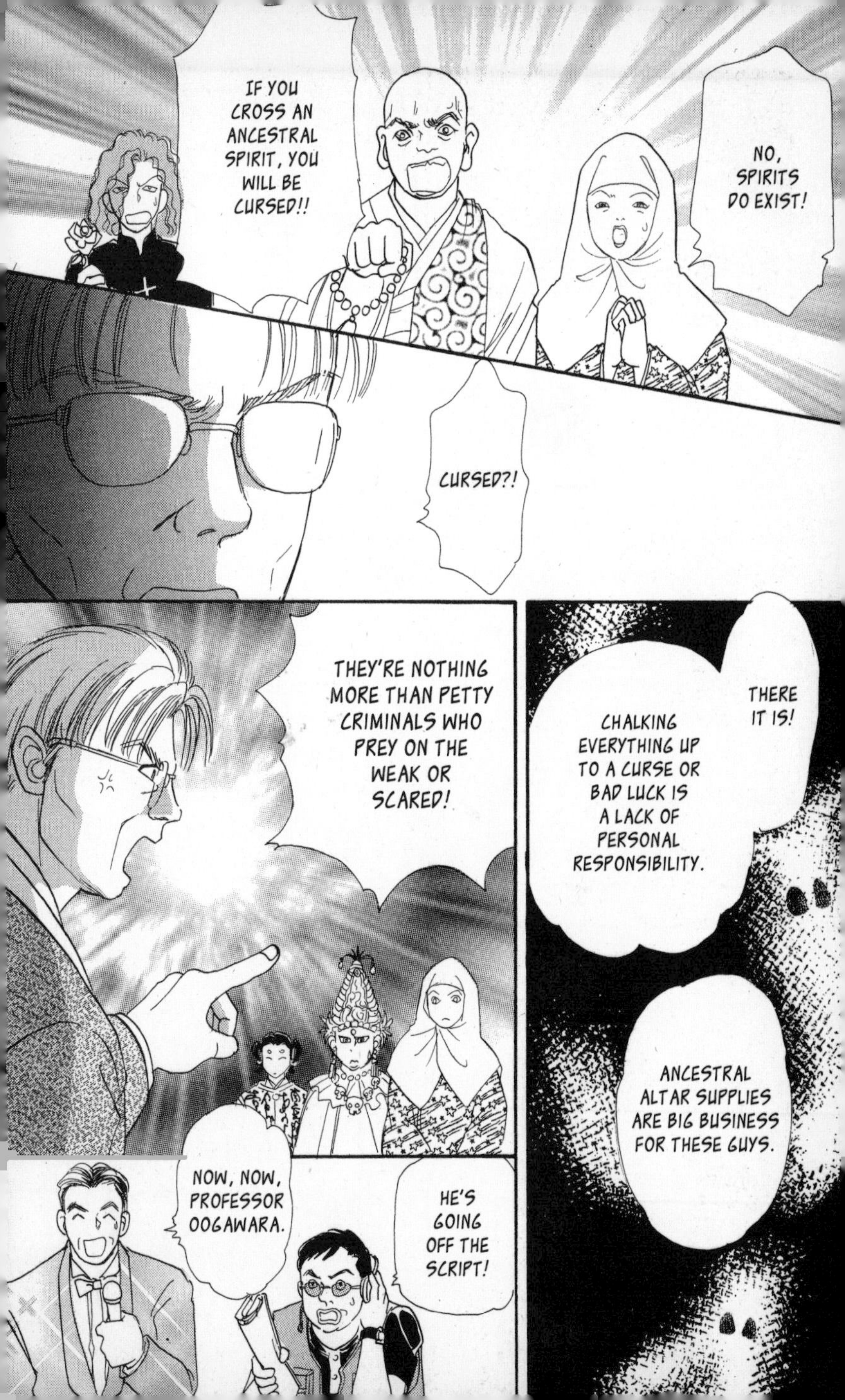
NO, SPIRITS DO EXIST!
IF YOU CROSS AN ANCESTRAL SPIRIT, YOU WILL BE CURSED!!
CURSED?!
THERE IT IS!
CHALKING EVERYTHING UP TO A CURSE OR BAD LUCK IS A LACK OF PERSONAL RESPONSIBILITY.
ANCESTRAL ALTAR SUPPLIES ARE BIG BUSINESS FOR THESE GUYS.
THEY'RE NOTHING MORE THAN PETTY CRIMINALS WHO PREY ON THE WEAK OR SCARED!
HE'S GOING OFF THE SCRIPT!
NOW, NOW, PROFESSOR OOGAWARA.

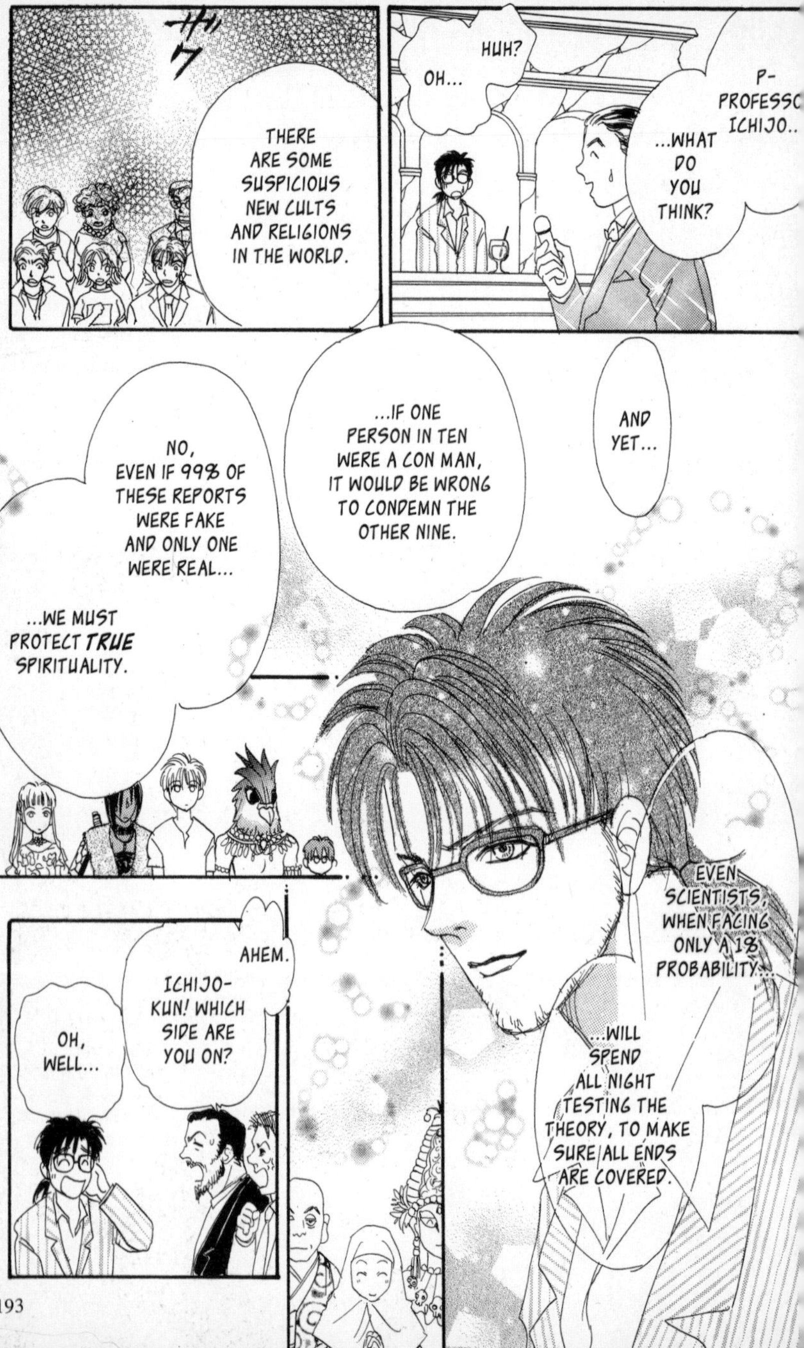
P- PROFESSC ICHIJO..
...WHAT DO YOU THINK?
HUH?
OH...
THERE ARE SOME SUSPICIOUS NEW CULTS AND RELIGIONS IN THE WORLD.
AND YET...
...IF ONE PERSON IN TEN WERE A CON MAN, IT WOULD BE WRONG TO CONDEMN THE OTHER NINE.
NO, EVEN IF 99% OF THESE REPORTS WERE FAKE AND ONLY ONE WERE REAL...
...WE MUST PROTECT **TRUE** SPIRITUALITY.
EVEN SCIENTISTS, WHEN FACING ONLY A 1% PROBABILITY...
...WILL SPEND ALL NIGHT TESTING THE THEORY, TO MAKE SURE ALL ENDS ARE COVERED.
AHEM.
ICHIJO-KUN! WHICH SIDE ARE YOU ON?
OH, WELL...

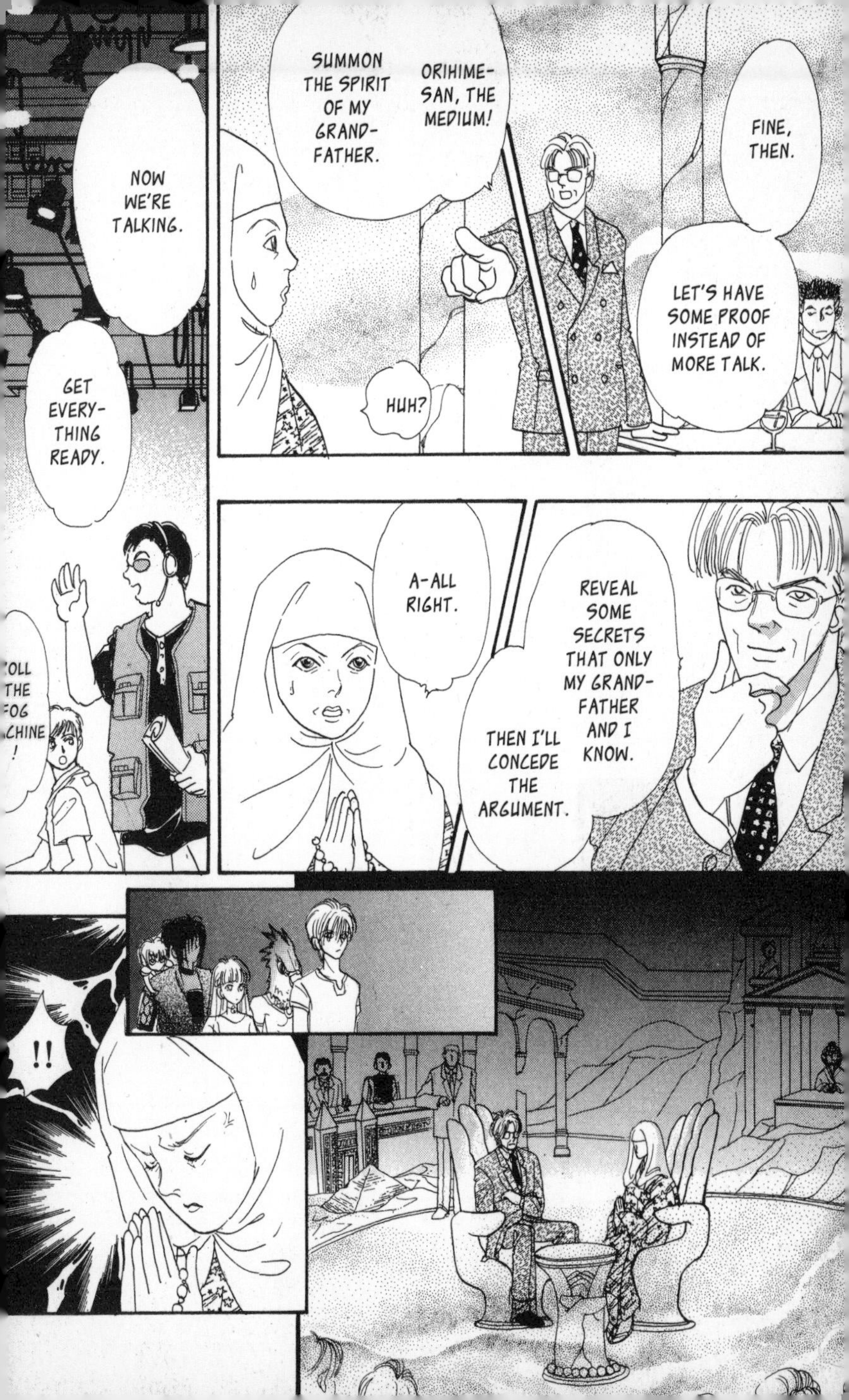
FINE, THEN.
LET'S HAVE SOME PROOF INSTEAD OF MORE TALK.
ORIHIME-SAN, THE MEDIUM!
SUMMON THE SPIRIT OF MY GRAND-FATHER.
HUH?
REVEAL SOME SECRETS THAT ONLY MY GRAND-FATHER AND I KNOW.
THEN I'LL CONCEDE THE ARGUMENT.
A-ALL RIGHT.
NOW WE'RE TALKING.
GET EVERY-THING READY.
ROLL THE FOG CHINE !
!!

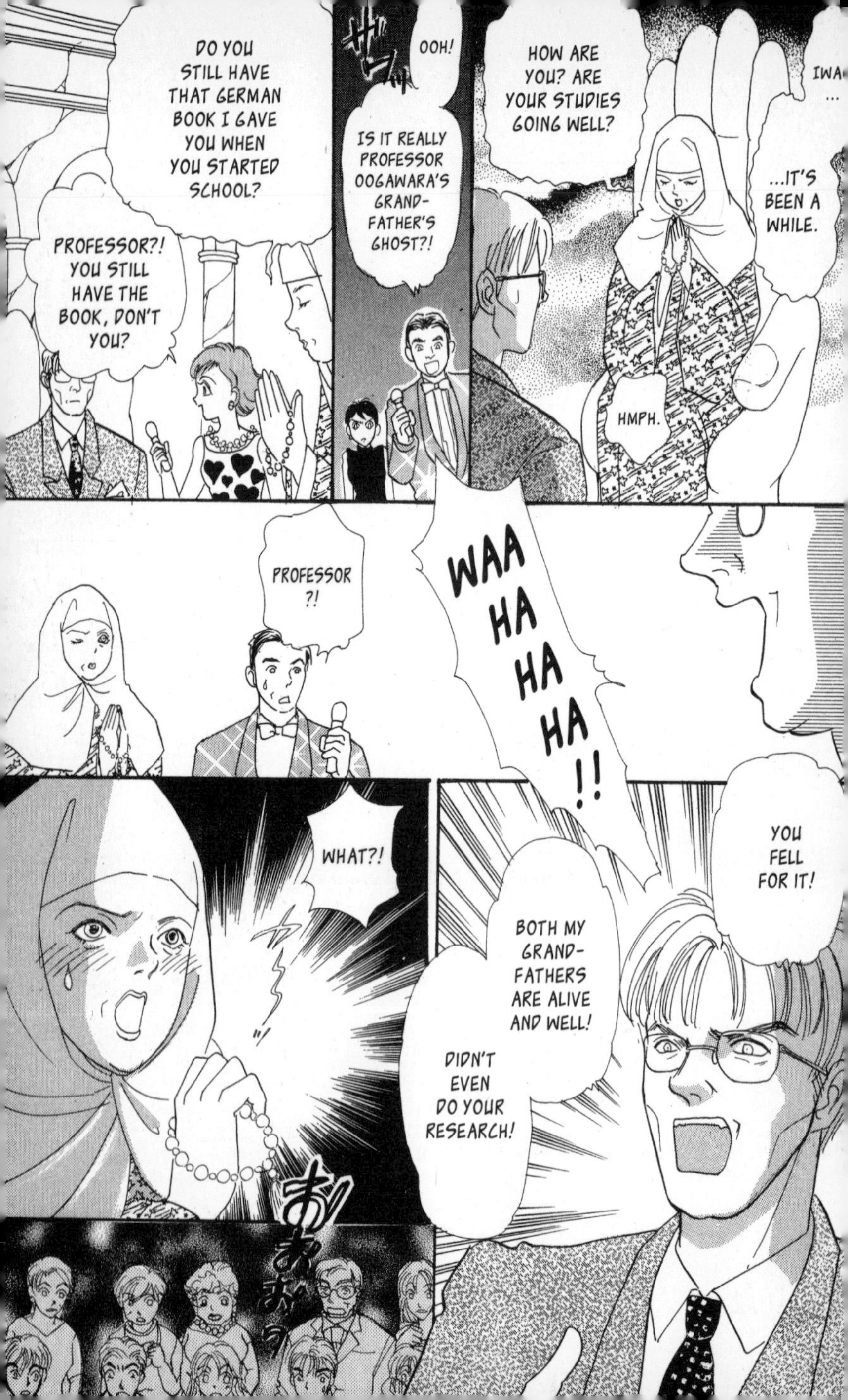
IWA...
HOW ARE YOU? ARE YOUR STUDIES GOING WELL?
...IT'S BEEN A WHILE.
HMPH.
OOH!
IS IT REALLY PROFESSOR OOGAWARA'S GRAND-FATHER'S GHOST?!
DO YOU STILL HAVE THAT GERMAN BOOK I GAVE YOU WHEN YOU STARTED SCHOOL?
PROFESSOR?! YOU STILL HAVE THE BOOK, DON'T YOU?
WAA HA HA HA HA!!
PROFESSOR?!
YOU FELL FOR IT!
BOTH MY GRAND-FATHERS ARE ALIVE AND WELL!
DIDN'T EVEN DO YOUR RESEARCH!
WHAT?!

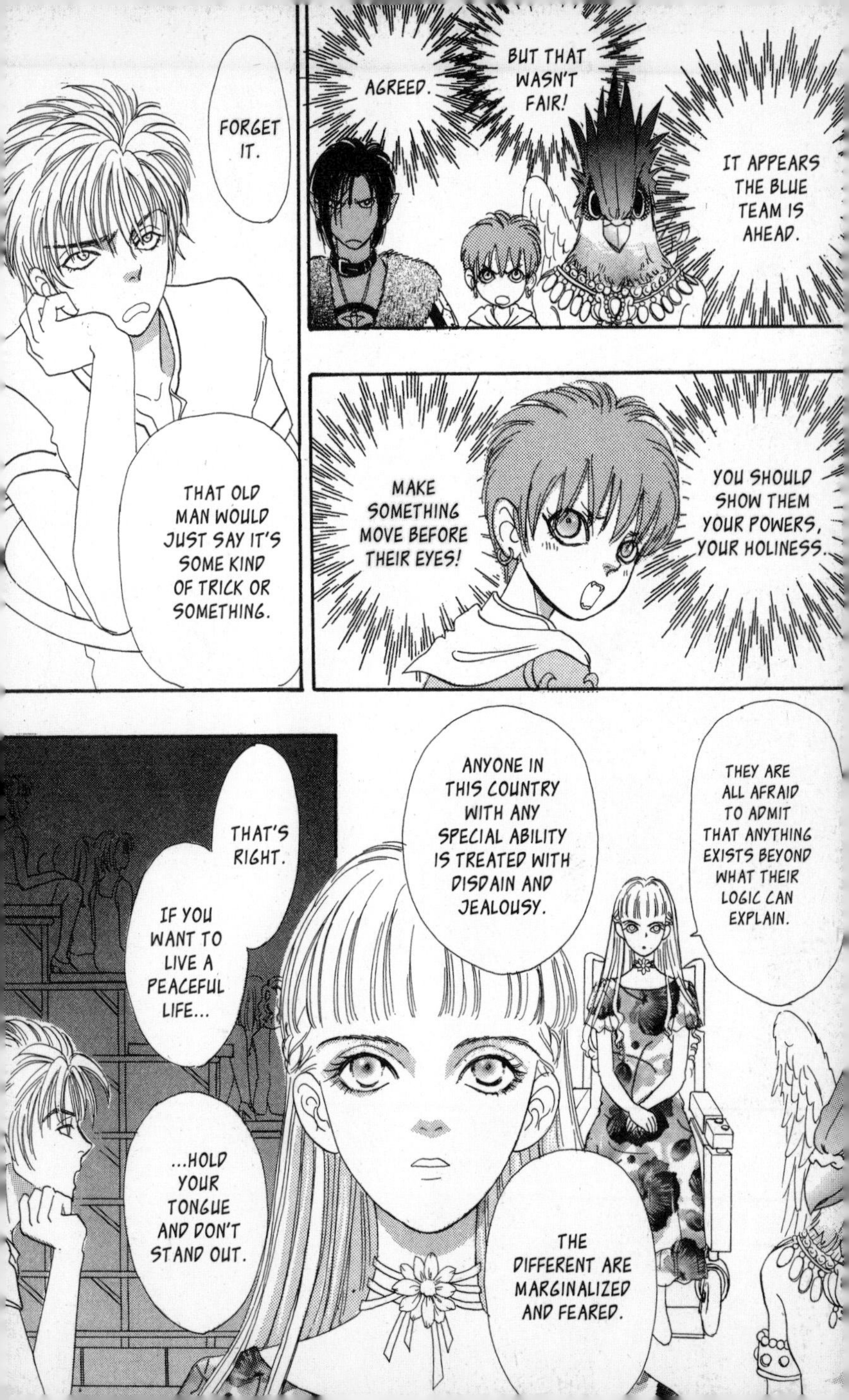
IT APPEARS THE BLUE TEAM IS AHEAD.
BUT THAT WASN'T FAIR!
AGREED.
YOU SHOULD SHOW THEM YOUR POWERS, YOUR HOLINESS.
MAKE SOMETHING MOVE BEFORE THEIR EYES!
FORGET IT.
THAT OLD MAN WOULD JUST SAY IT'S SOME KIND OF TRICK OR SOMETHING.
THEY ARE ALL AFRAID TO ADMIT THAT ANYTHING EXISTS BEYOND WHAT THEIR LOGIC CAN EXPLAIN.
ANYONE IN THIS COUNTRY WITH ANY SPECIAL ABILITY IS TREATED WITH DISDAIN AND JEALOUSY.
THE DIFFERENT ARE MARGINALIZED AND FEARED.
THAT'S RIGHT.
IF YOU WANT TO LIVE A PEACEFUL LIFE...
...HOLD YOUR TONGUE AND DON'T STAND OUT.

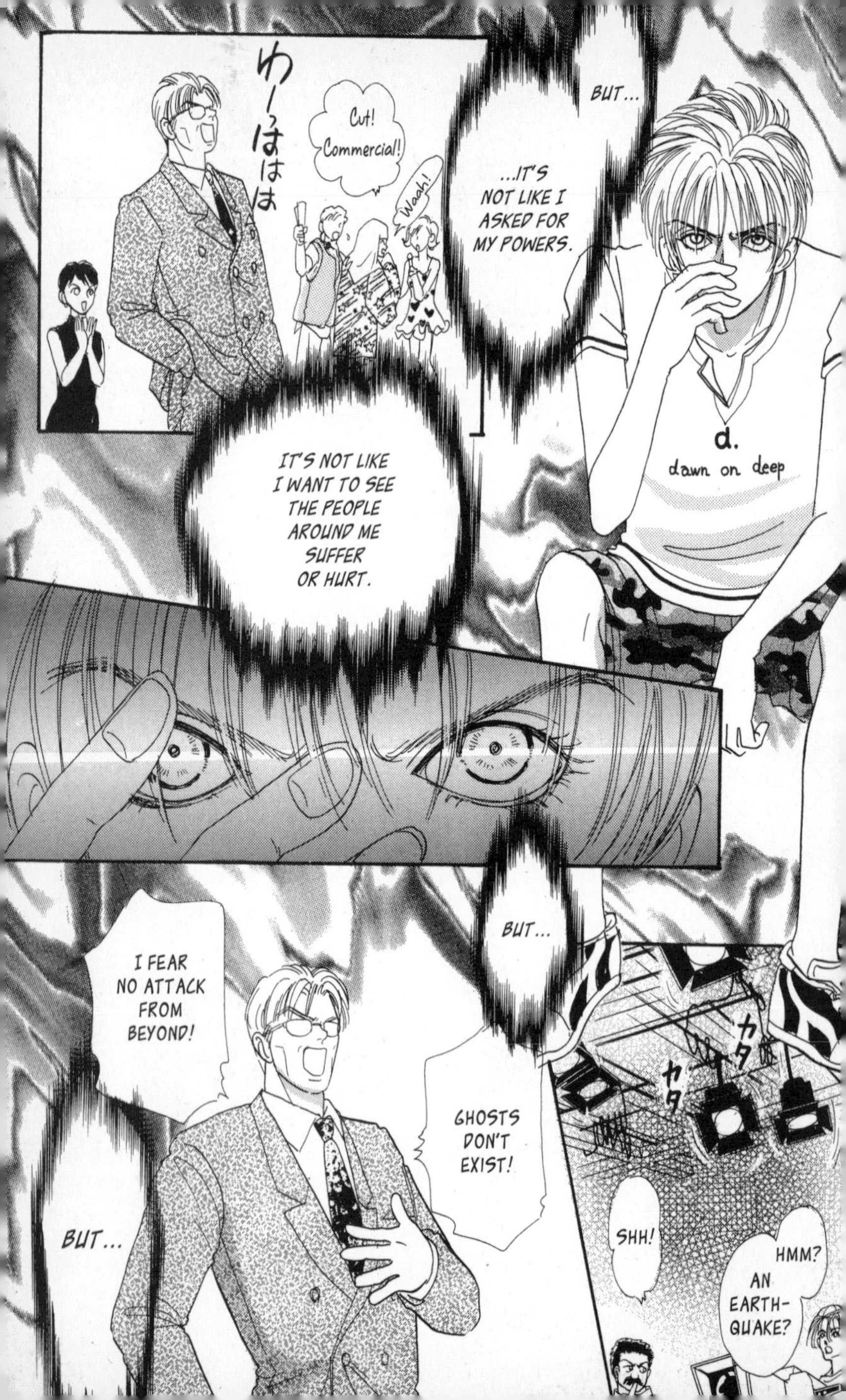

BUT...
...IT'S NOT LIKE I ASKED FOR MY POWERS.
わーっははは
Cut! Commercial!
Waah!
IT'S NOT LIKE I WANT TO SEE THE PEOPLE AROUND ME SUFFER OR HURT.
d. dawn on deep
BUT...
カタ
カタ
SHH!
HMM? AN EARTH-QUAKE?
I FEAR NO ATTACK FROM BEYOND!
GHOSTS DON'T EXIST!
BUT...

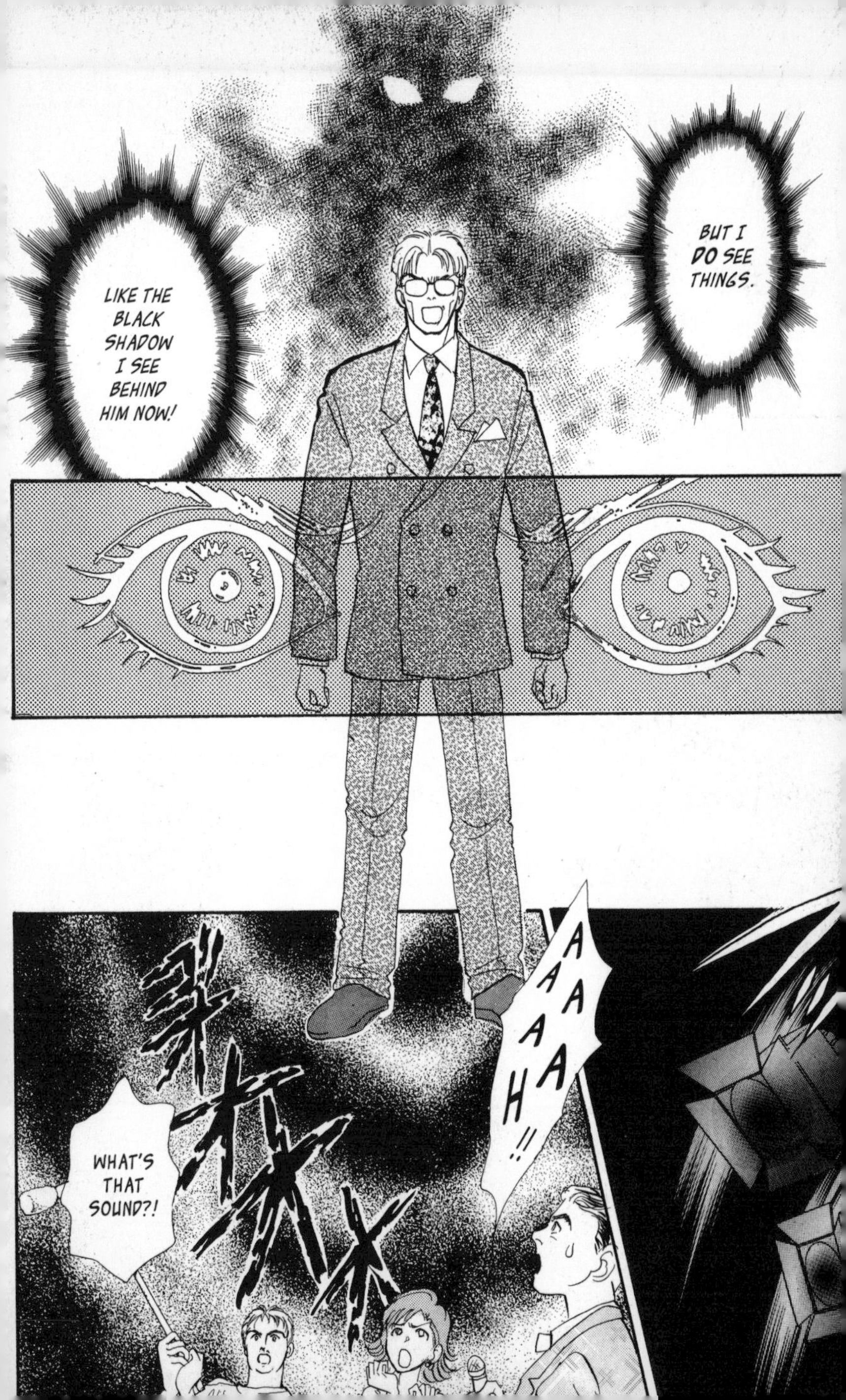
BUT I DO SEE THINGS.
LIKE THE BLACK SHADOW I SEE BEHIND HIM NOW!
AAAAAH!!
WHAT'S THAT SOUND?!

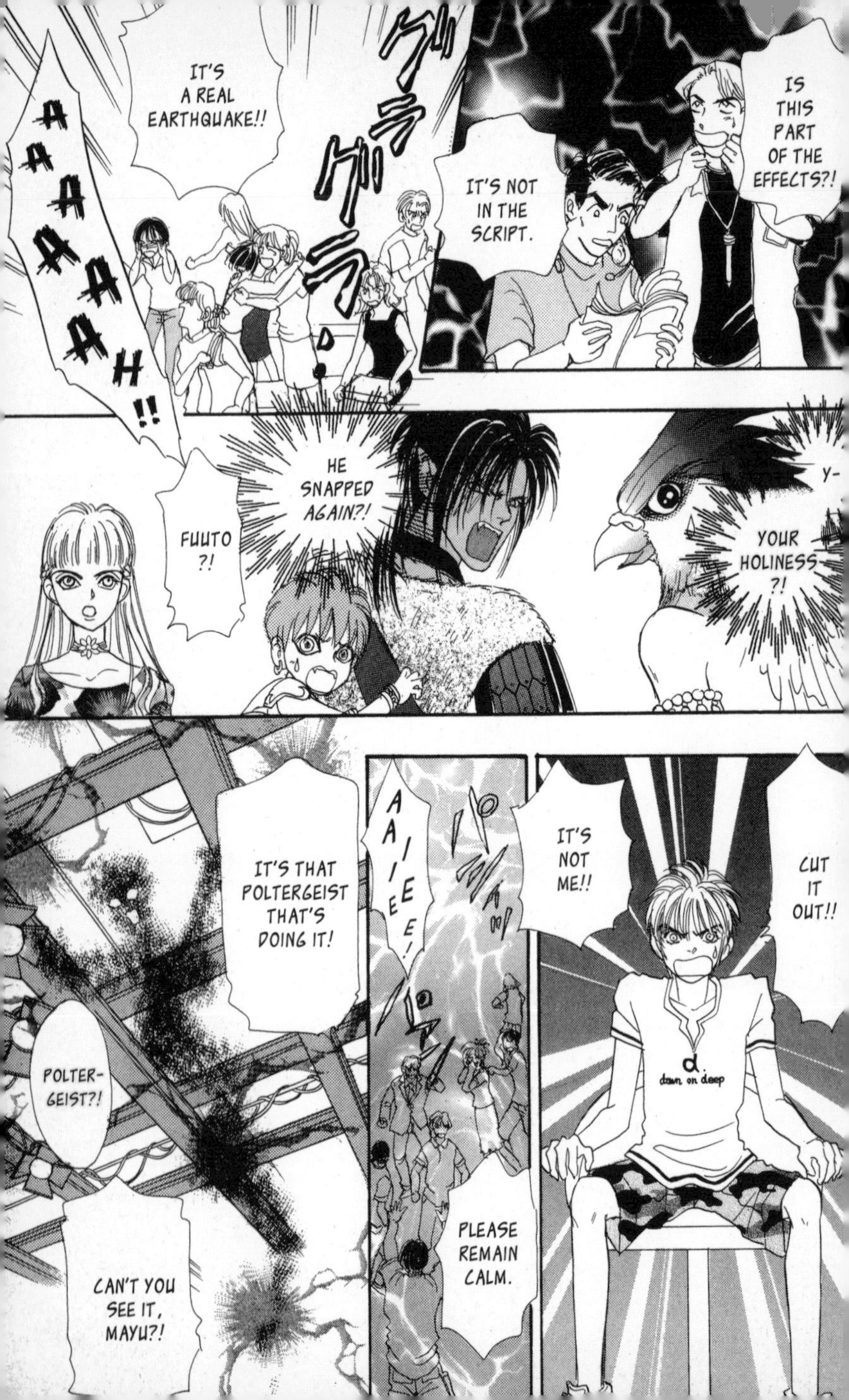
IS THIS PART OF THE EFFECTS?!
IT'S NOT IN THE SCRIPT.
IT'S A REAL EARTHQUAKE!!
AAAAAAH!!
Y-
YOUR HOLINESS?!
HE SNAPPED AGAIN?!
FUUTO?!
CUT IT OUT!!
IT'S NOT ME!!
AAIIEEE!
PLEASE REMAIN CALM.
IT'S THAT POLTERGEIST THAT'S DOING IT!
POLTER-GEIST?!
CAN'T YOU SEE IT, MAYU?!

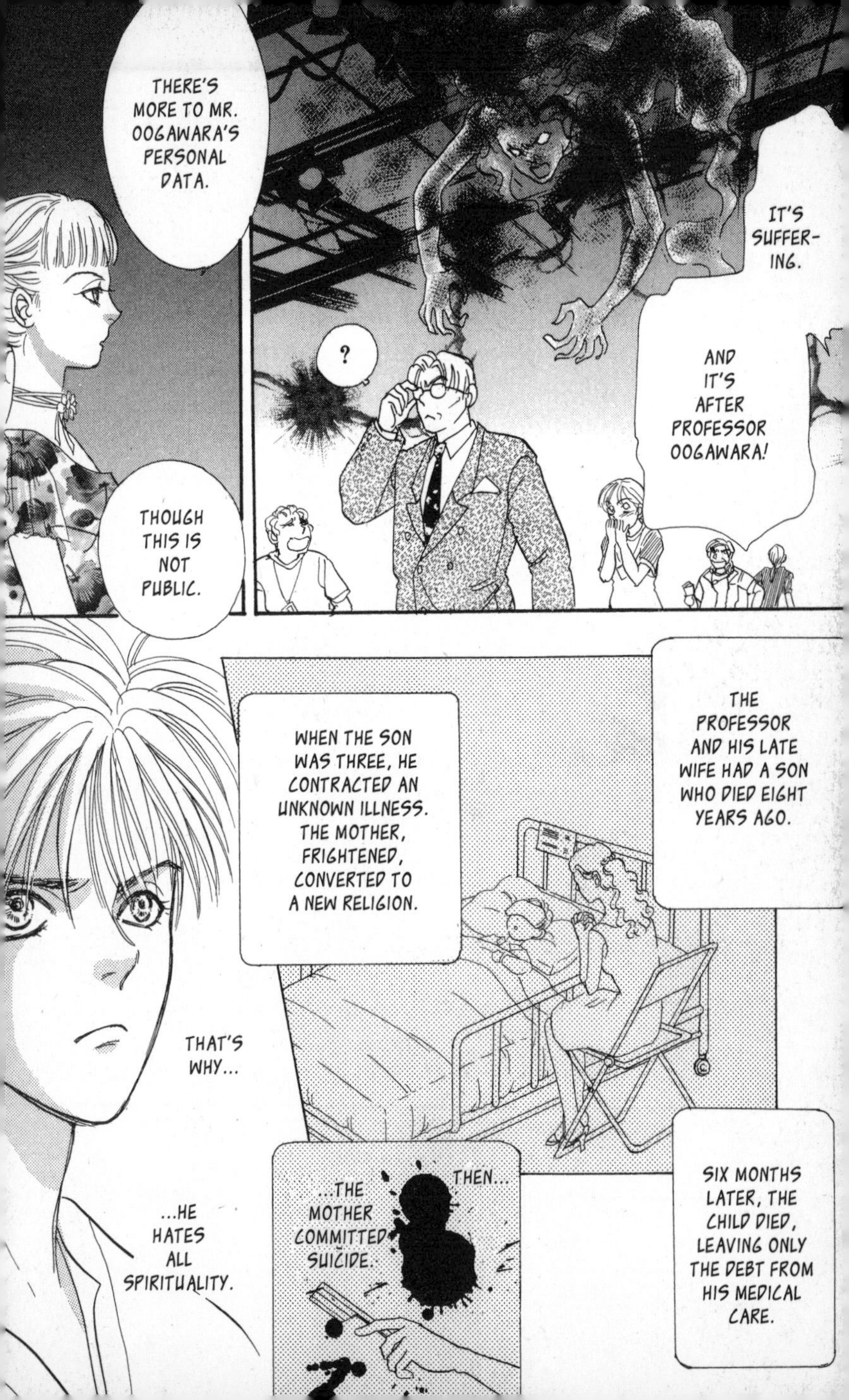
IT'S SUFFER-ING.
AND IT'S AFTER PROFESSOR OOGAWARA!
?
THERE'S MORE TO MR. OOGAWARA'S PERSONAL DATA.
THOUGH THIS IS NOT PUBLIC.
THE PROFESSOR AND HIS LATE WIFE HAD A SON WHO DIED EIGHT YEARS AGO.
WHEN THE SON WAS THREE, HE CONTRACTED AN UNKNOWN ILLNESS. THE MOTHER, FRIGHTENED, CONVERTED TO A NEW RELIGION.
SIX MONTHS LATER, THE CHILD DIED, LEAVING ONLY THE DEBT FROM HIS MEDICAL CARE.
THEN...
...THE MOTHER COMMITTED SUICIDE.
THAT'S WHY...
...HE HATES ALL SPIRITUALITY.

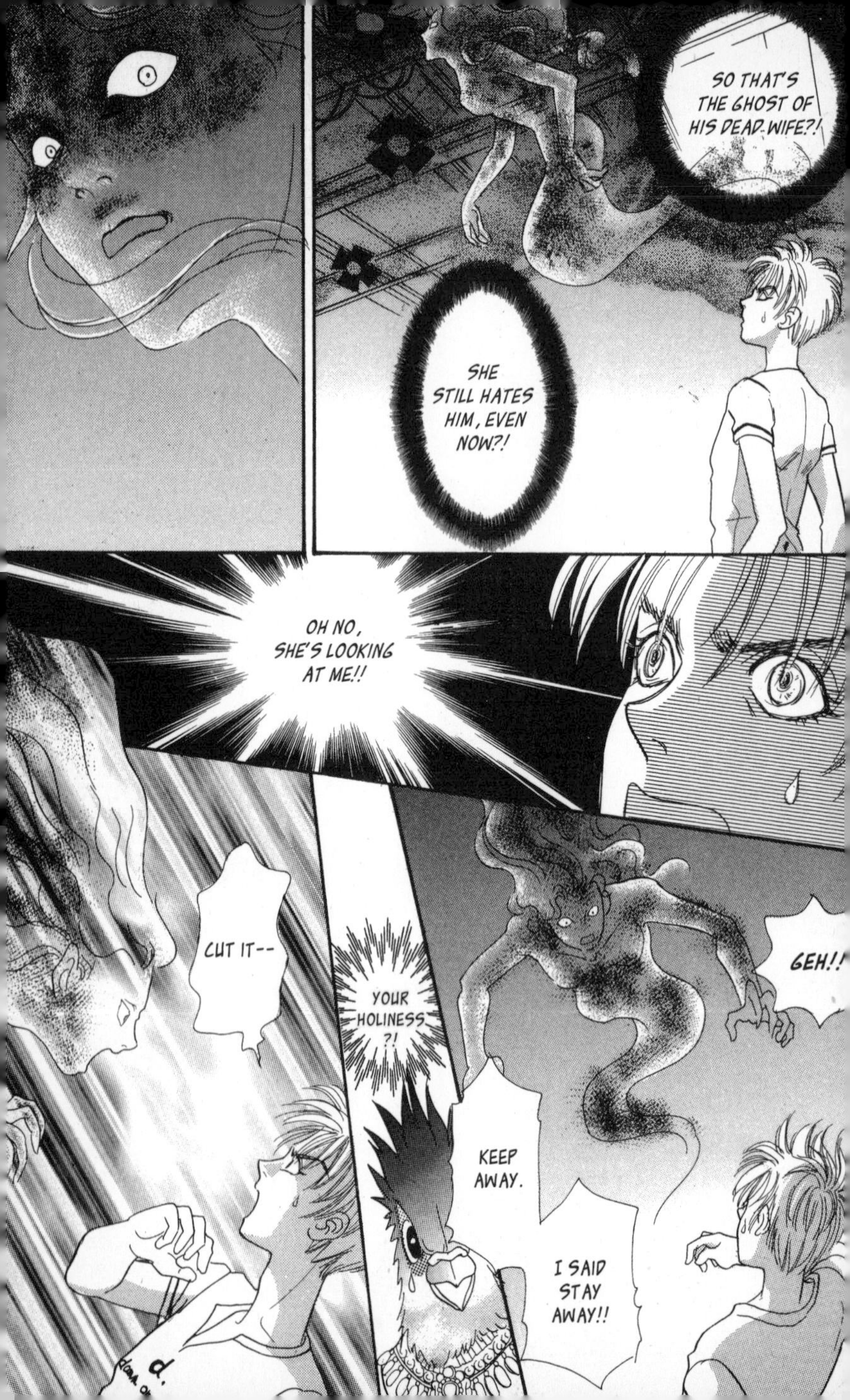
SO THAT'S THE GHOST OF HIS DEAD WIFE?!
SHE STILL HATES HIM, EVEN NOW?!
OH NO, SHE'S LOOKING AT ME!!
GEH!!
KEEP AWAY.
I SAID STAY AWAY!!
YOUR HOLINESS?!
CUT IT--

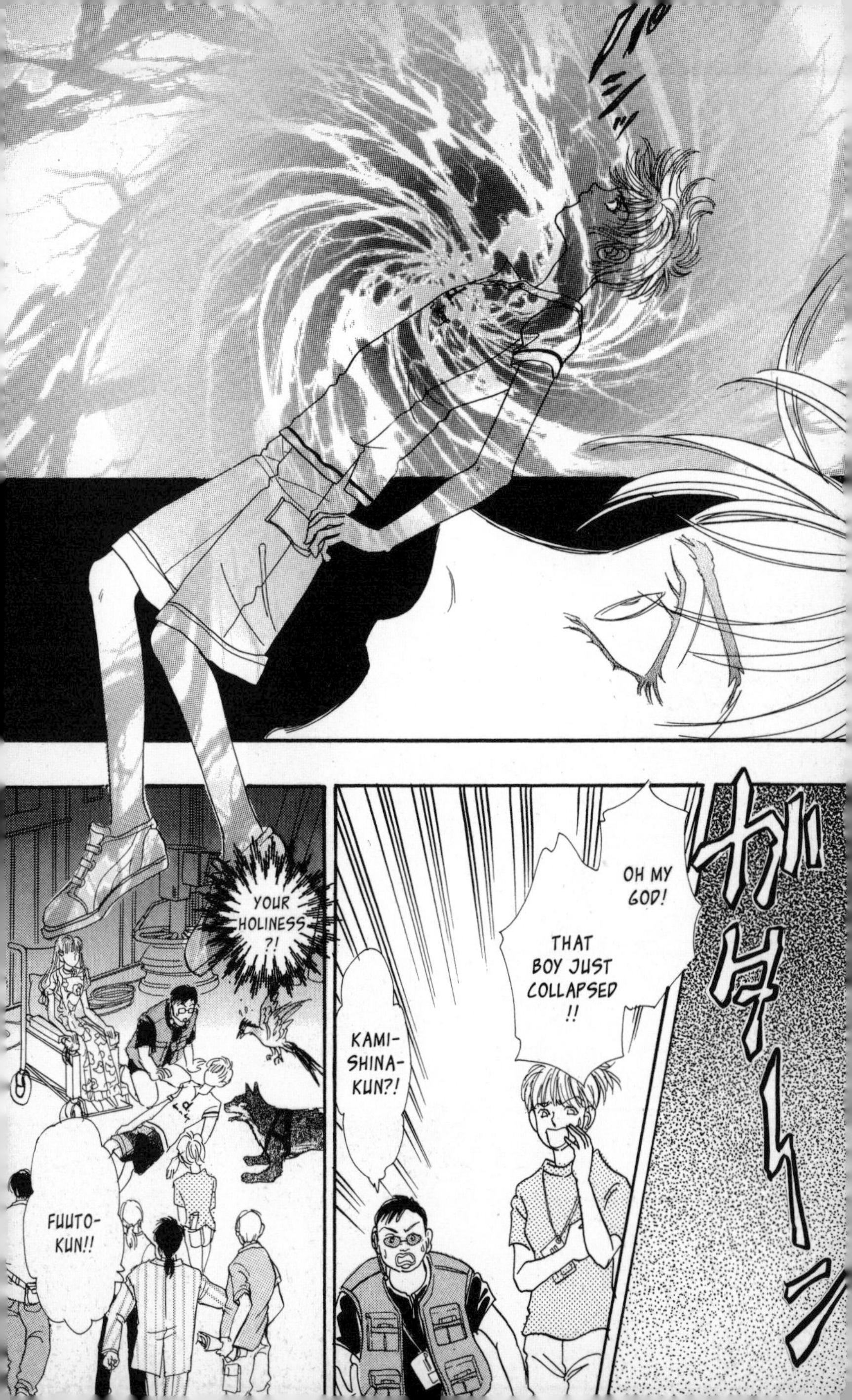
OH MY GOD!
THAT BOY JUST COLLAPSED !!
KAMI-SHINA-KUN?!
YOUR HOLINESS ?!
FUUTO-KUN!!

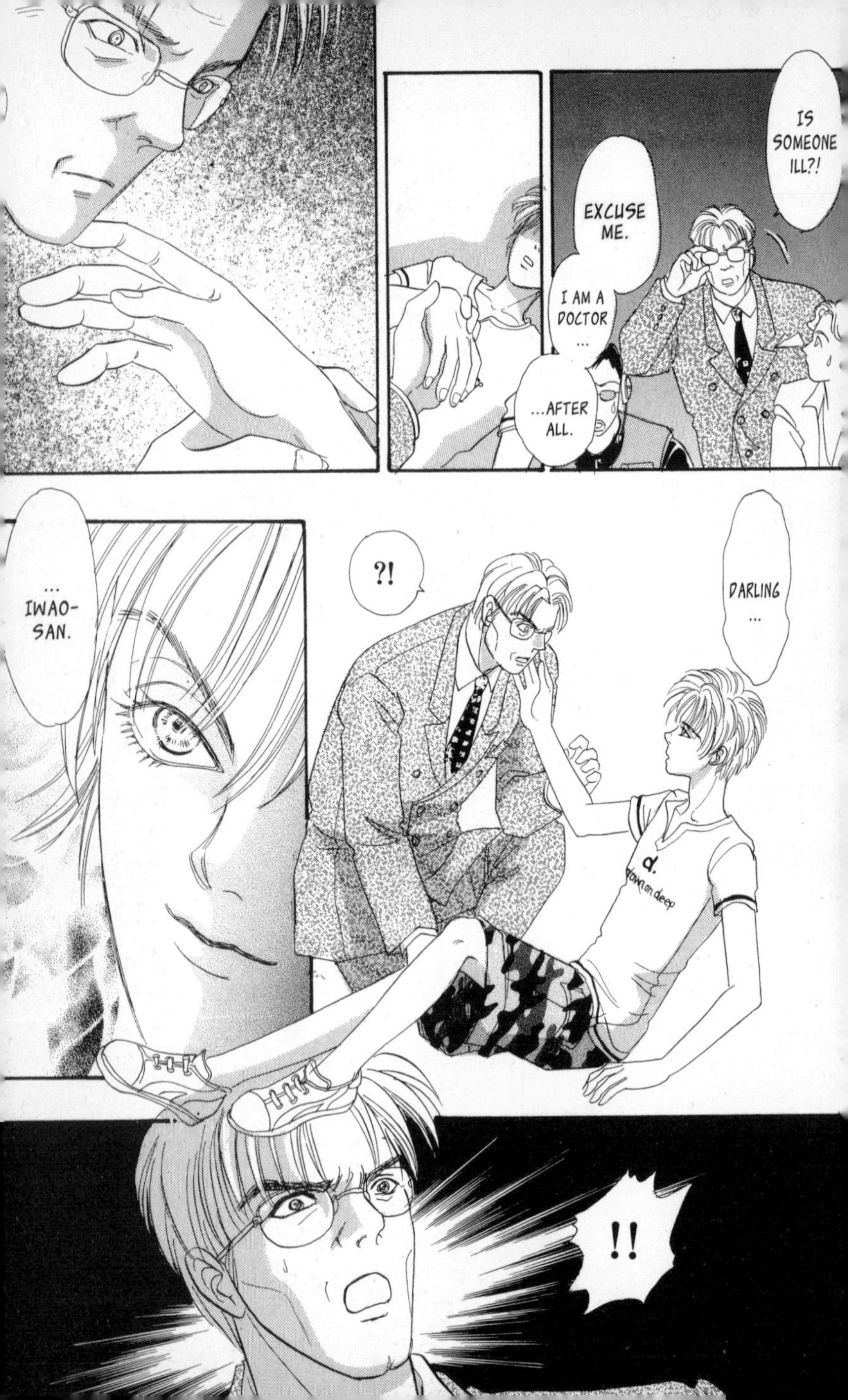
IS SOMEONE ILL?!
EXCUSE ME.
I AM A DOCTOR ...
...AFTER ALL.
DARLING ...
?!
... IWAO-SAN.
!!

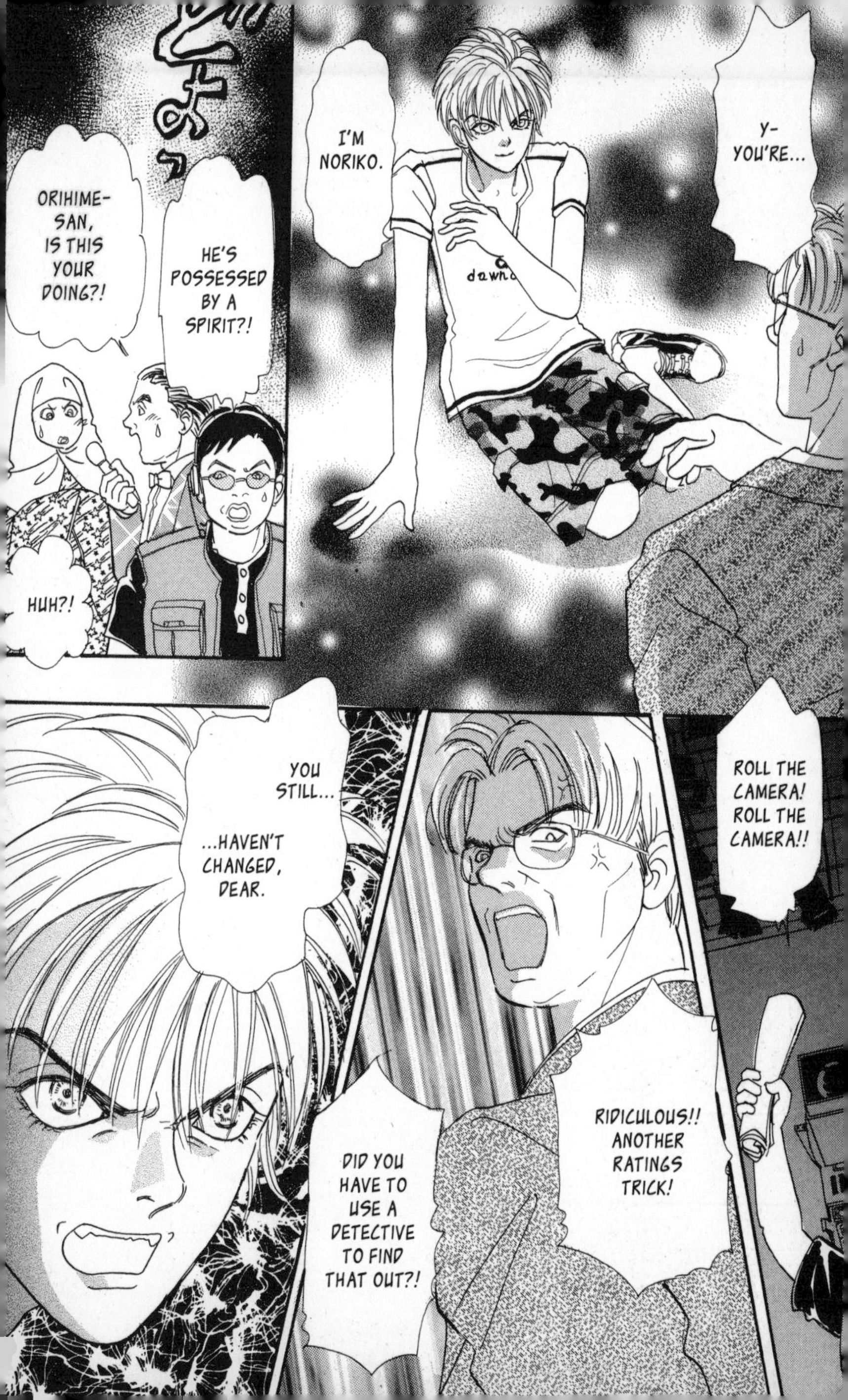
Y- YOU'RE...
I'M NORIKO.
HE'S POSSESSED BY A SPIRIT?!
ORIHIME-SAN, IS THIS YOUR DOING?!
HUH?!
ROLL THE CAMERA! ROLL THE CAMERA!!
RIDICULOUS!! ANOTHER RATINGS TRICK!
YOU STILL...
...HAVEN'T CHANGED, DEAR.
DID YOU HAVE TO USE A DETECTIVE TO FIND THAT OUT?!

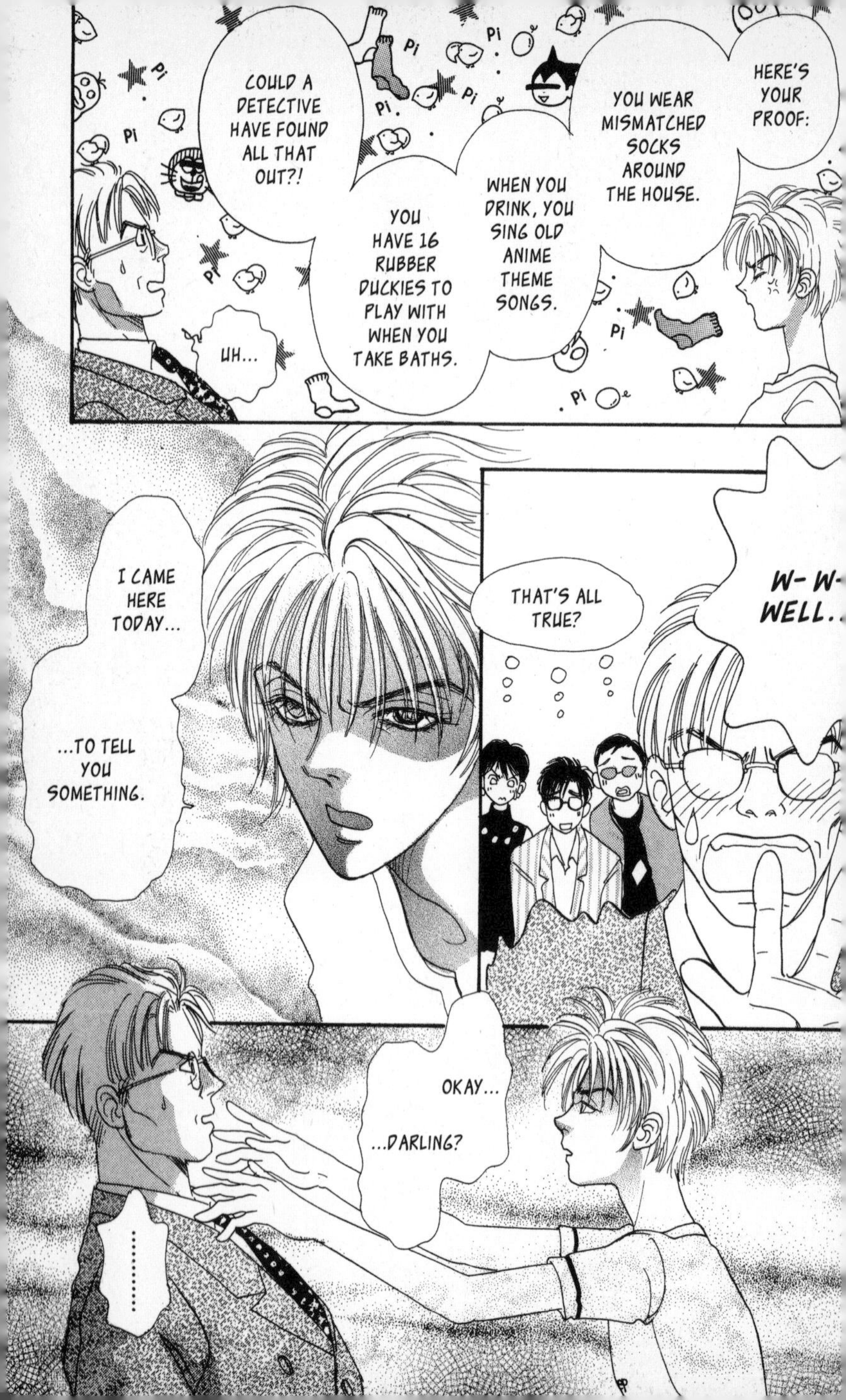
HERE'S YOUR PROOF:
YOU WEAR MISMATCHED SOCKS AROUND THE HOUSE.
WHEN YOU DRINK, YOU SING OLD ANIME THEME SONGS.
YOU HAVE 16 RUBBER DUCKIES TO PLAY WITH WHEN YOU TAKE BATHS.
COULD A DETECTIVE HAVE FOUND ALL THAT OUT?!
UH...
W- W- WELL...
THAT'S ALL TRUE?
I CAME HERE TODAY...
...TO TELL YOU SOMETHING.
OKAY...
...DARLING?
......

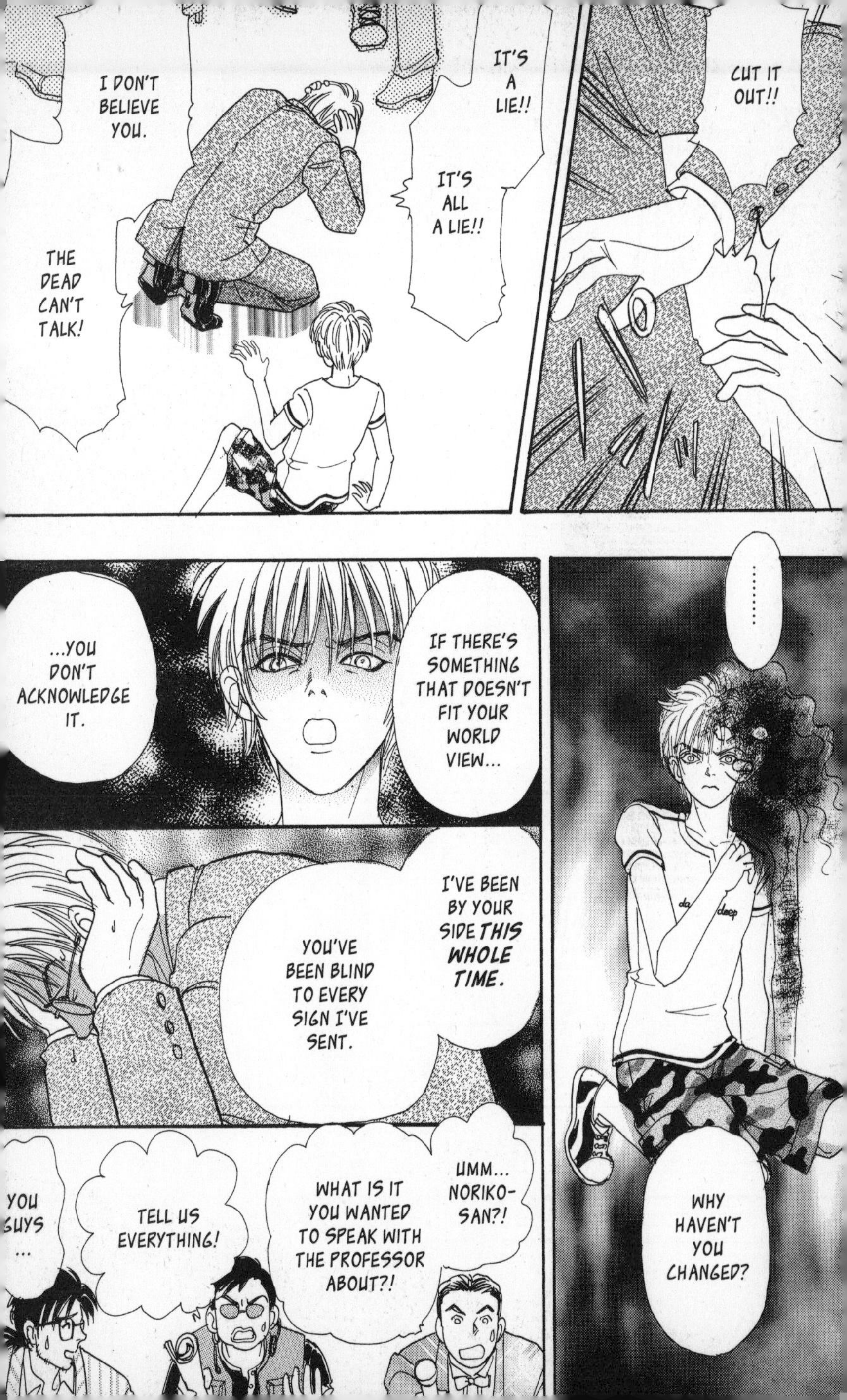
CUT IT OUT!!
IT'S A LIE!!
IT'S ALL A LIE!!
I DON'T BELIEVE YOU.
THE DEAD CAN'T TALK!
......
WHY HAVEN'T YOU CHANGED?
IF THERE'S SOMETHING THAT DOESN'T FIT YOUR WORLD VIEW...
...YOU DON'T ACKNOWLEDGE IT.
I'VE BEEN BY YOUR SIDE THIS WHOLE TIME.
YOU'VE BEEN BLIND TO EVERY SIGN I'VE SENT.
UMM... NORIKO-SAN?!
WHAT IS IT YOU WANTED TO SPEAK WITH THE PROFESSOR ABOUT?!
TELL US EVERYTHING!
YOU GUYS ...

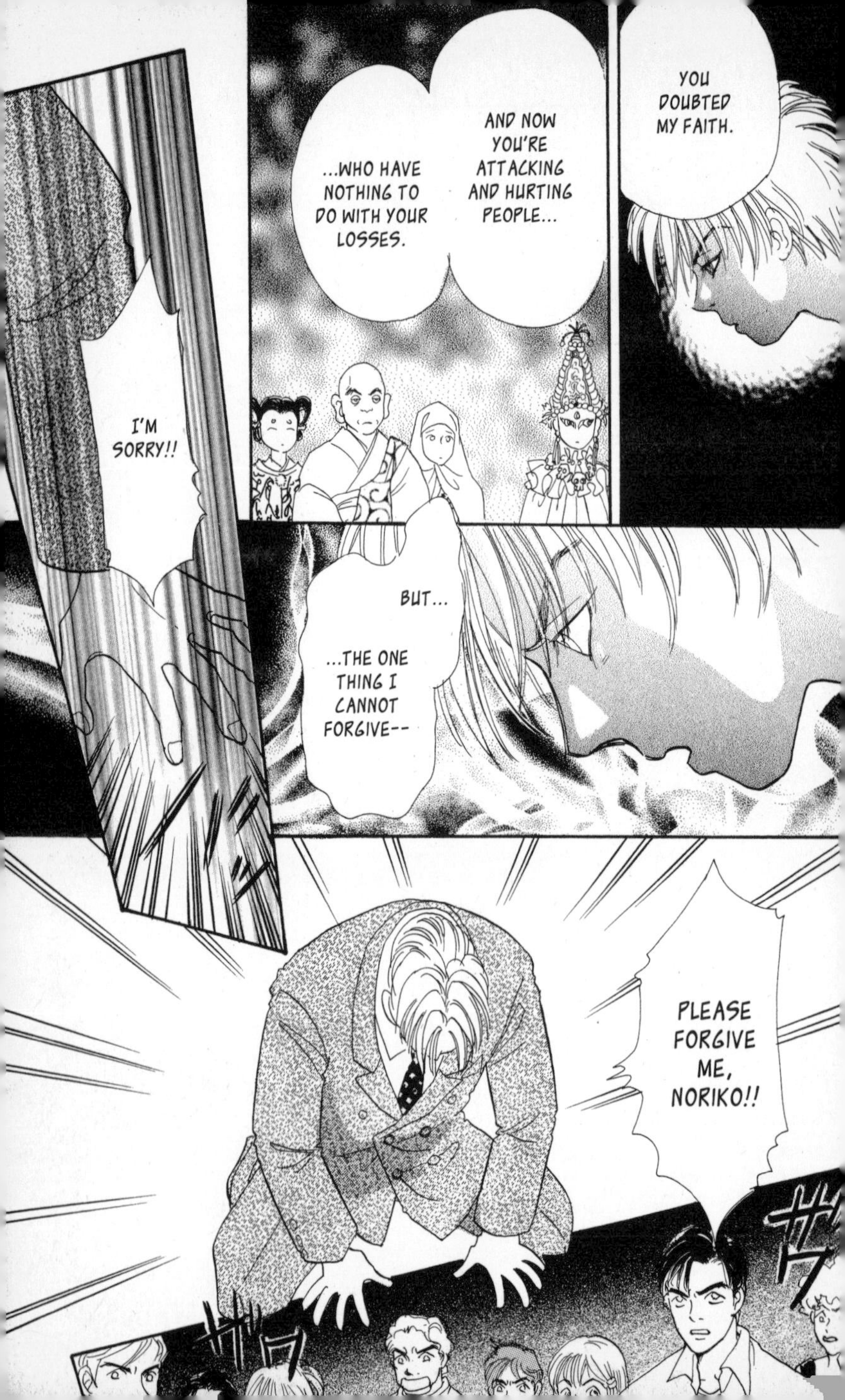
YOU DOUBTED MY FAITH.
AND NOW YOU'RE ATTACKING AND HURTING PEOPLE...
...WHO HAVE NOTHING TO DO WITH YOUR LOSSES.
BUT...
...THE ONE THING I CANNOT FORGIVE--
I'M SORRY!!
PLEASE FORGIVE ME, NORIKO!!

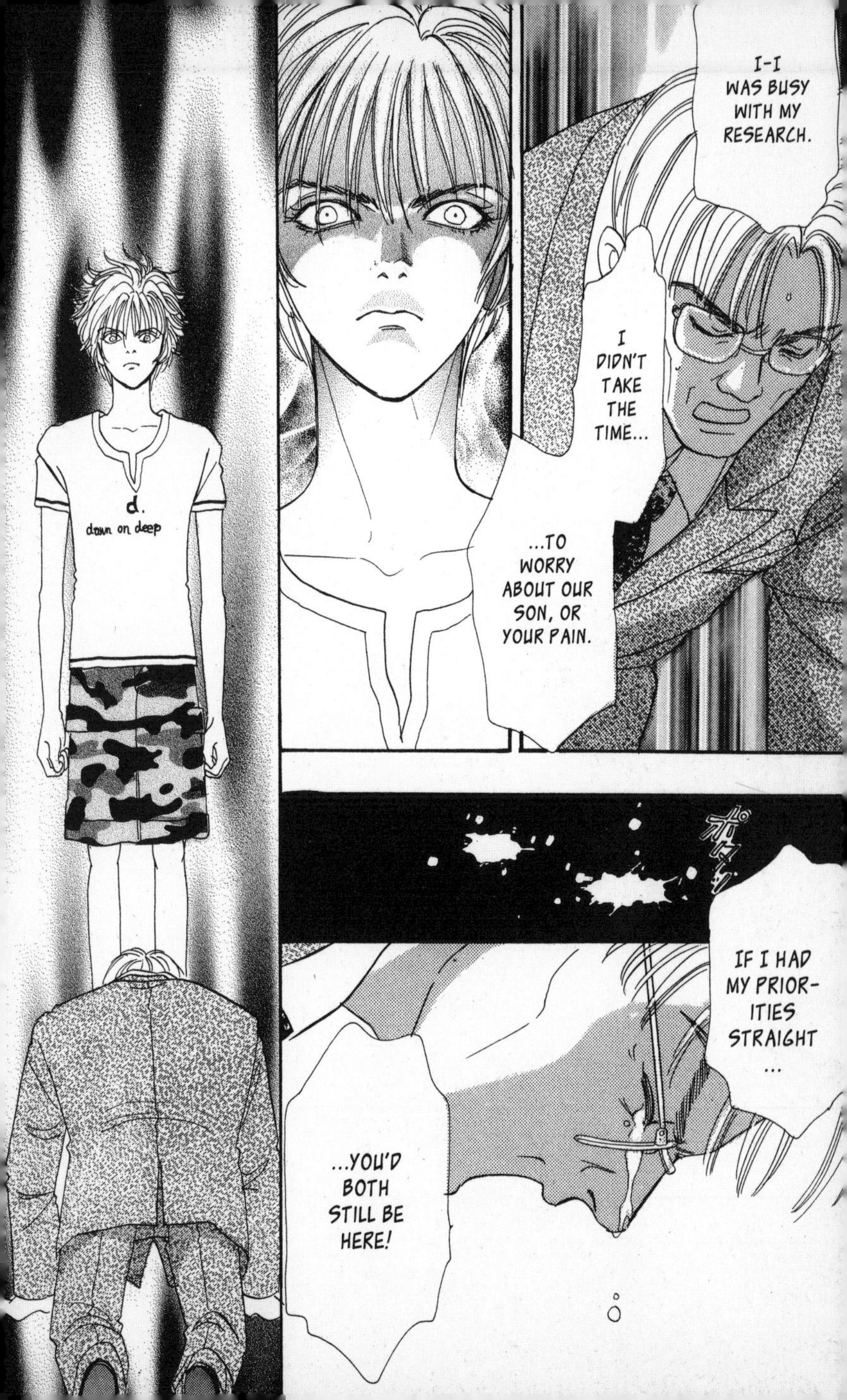
I-I WAS BUSY WITH MY RESEARCH.
I DIDN'T TAKE THE TIME...
...TO WORRY ABOUT OUR SON, OR YOUR PAIN.
IF I HAD MY PRIOR-ITIES STRAIGHT...
...YOU'D BOTH STILL BE HERE!
d.
down on deep

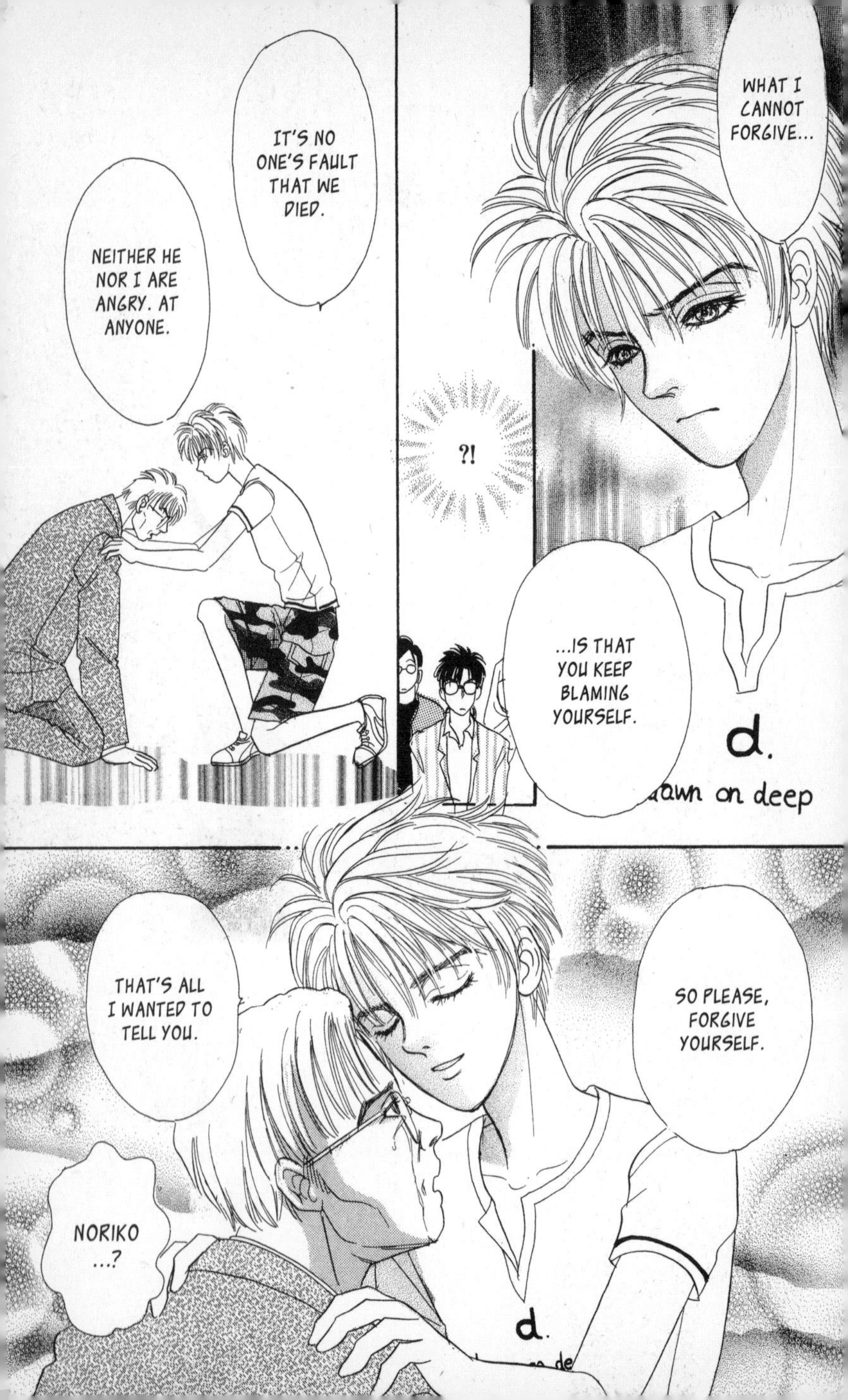

WHAT I CANNOT FORGIVE...
?!
...IS THAT YOU KEEP BLAMING YOURSELF.
IT'S NO ONE'S FAULT THAT WE DIED.
NEITHER HE NOR I ARE ANGRY. AT ANYONE.
SO PLEASE, FORGIVE YOURSELF.
THAT'S ALL I WANTED TO TELL YOU.
NORIKO ...?

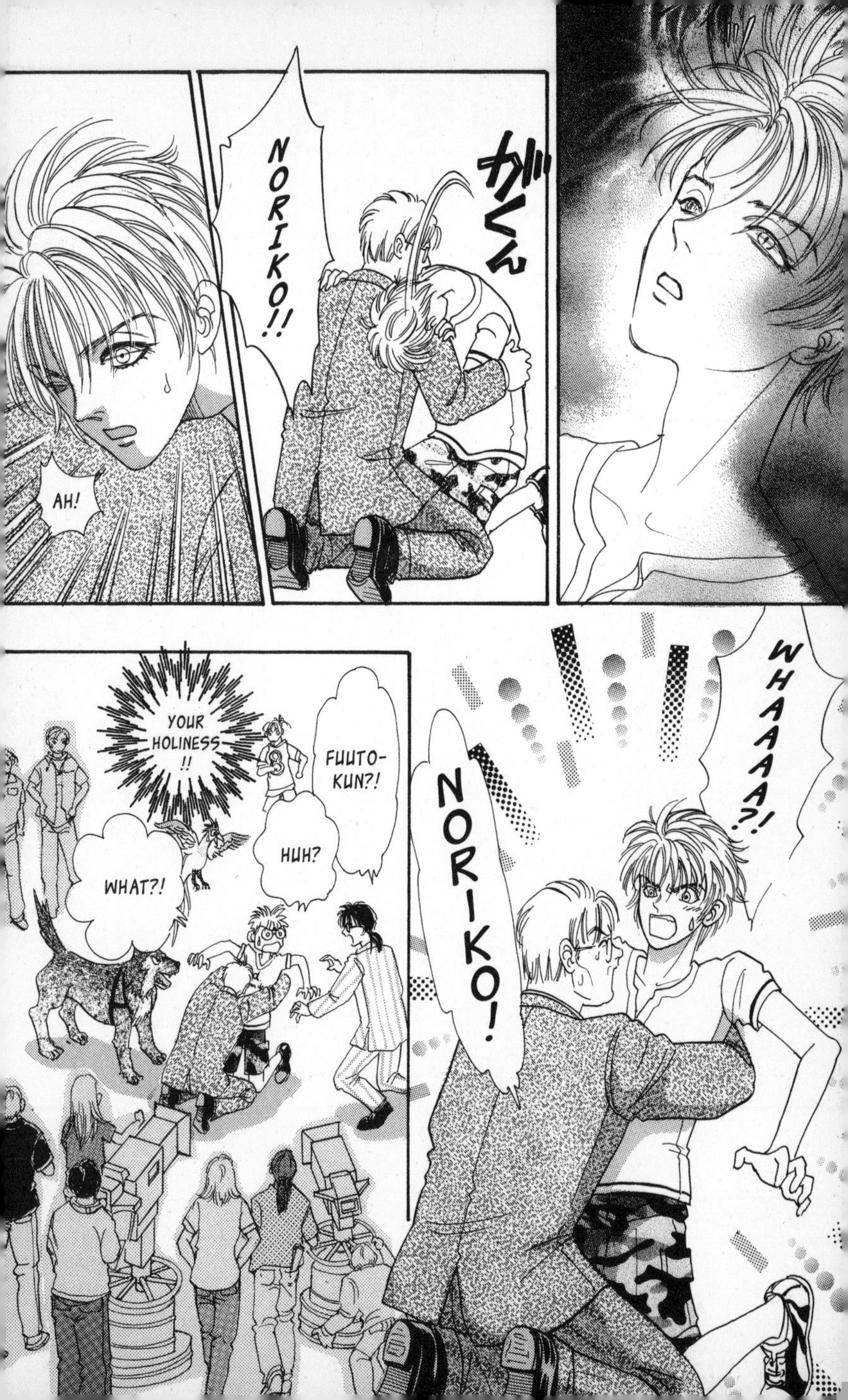
がくん
NORIKO!!
AH!
WHAAAAA?!
NORIKO!
FUUTO-KUN?!
YOUR HOLINESS !!
HUH?
WHAT?!

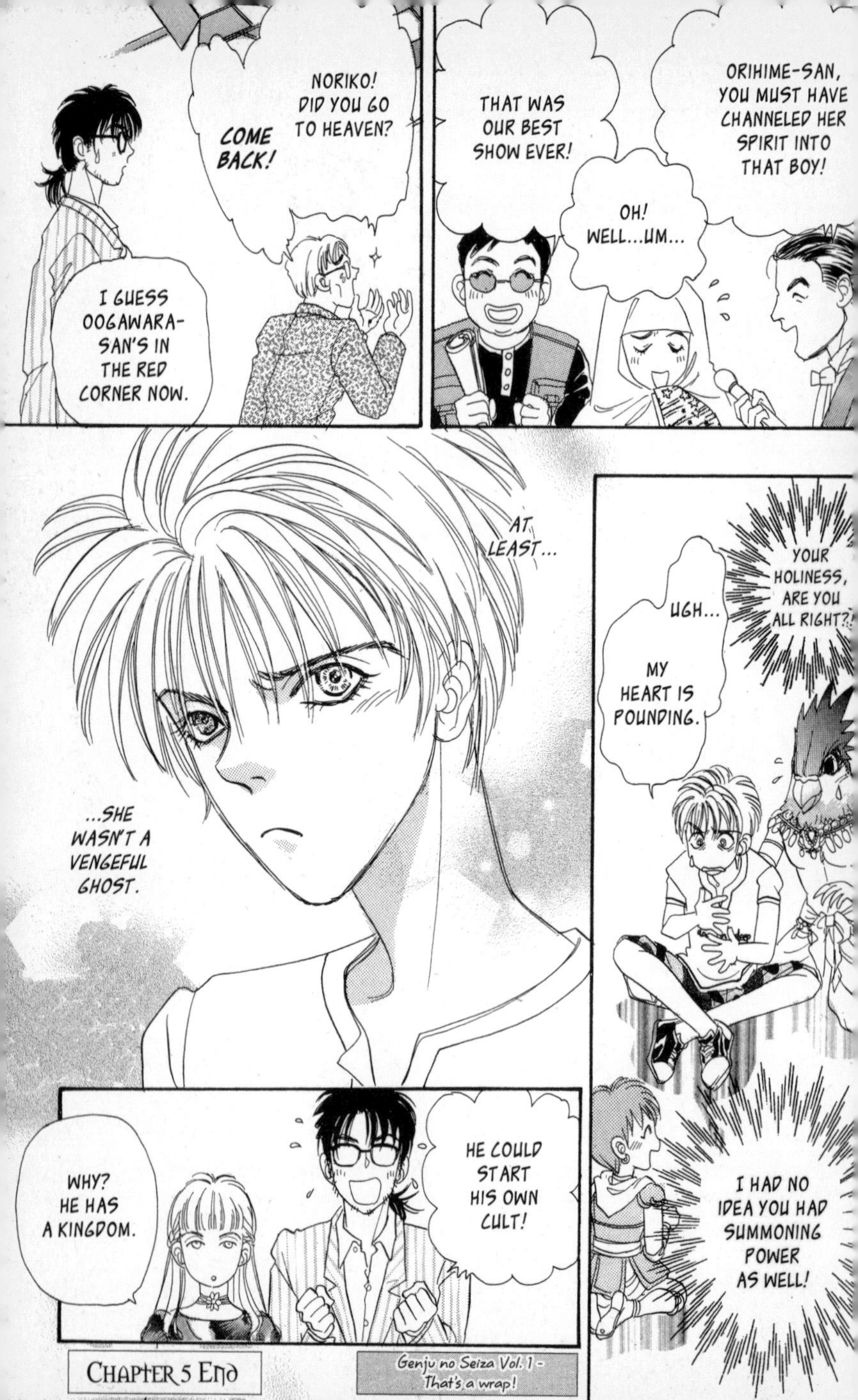
ORIHIME-SAN, YOU MUST HAVE CHANNELED HER SPIRIT INTO THAT BOY!
THAT WAS OUR BEST SHOW EVER!
OH! WELL...UM...
NORIKO! DID YOU GO TO HEAVEN?
COME BACK!
I GUESS OOGAWARA-SAN'S IN THE RED CORNER NOW.
YOUR HOLINESS, ARE YOU ALL RIGHT?!
UGH...
MY HEART IS POUNDING.
I HAD NO IDEA YOU HAD SUMMONING POWER AS WELL!
AT LEAST...
...SHE WASN'T A VENGEFUL GHOST.
HE COULD START HIS OWN CULT!
WHY? HE HAS A KINGDOM.

Chapter 5 End

Genju no Seiza Vol. 1 - That's a wrap!

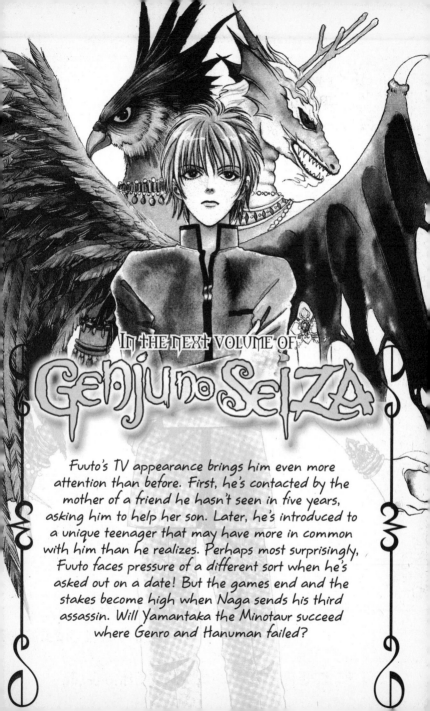

In THE NEXT VOLUME OF

Genju no Seiza

Fuuto's TV appearance brings him even more attention than before. First, he's contacted by the mother of a friend he hasn't seen in five years, asking him to help her son. Later, he's introduced to a unique teenager that may have more in common with him than he realizes. Perhaps most surprisingly, Fuuto faces pressure of a different sort when he's asked out on a date! But the games end and the stakes become high when Naga sends his third assassin. Will Yamantaka the Minotaur succeed where Genro and Hanuman failed?

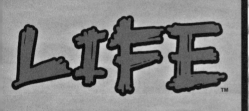
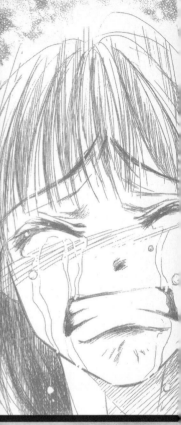
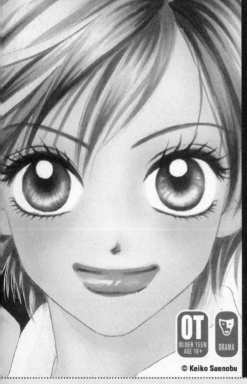

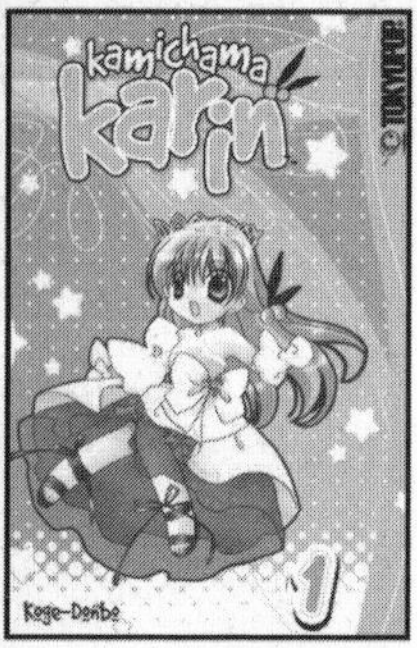
kamichama karin
TOKYOPOP
Koge-Donbo
1

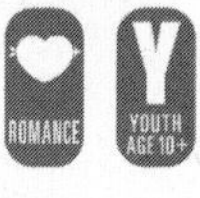
ROMANCE
Y
YOUTH AGE 10+

KAMICHAMA KARIN

BY KOGE-DONBO

This one was a surprise. I mean, I knew Koge-Donbo drew insanely cute characters, but I had no idea a magical girl story could be so darn clever. *Kamichama Karin* manages to lampoon everything about the genre, from plushie-like mascots to character archetypes to weapons that appear from the blue! And you gotta love Karin, the airheaded heroine who takes guff from no one and screams "I AM GOD!" as her battle cry. In short, if you are looking for a shiny new manga with a knack for hilarity and a penchant for accessories, I say look no further.

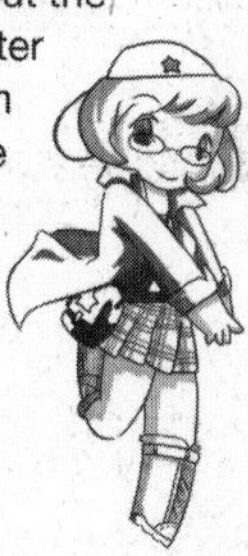

~Carol Fox, Editor

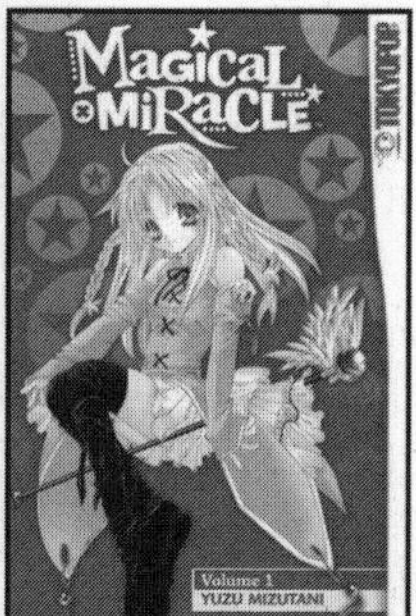
Magical Miracle
TOKYOPOP
Volume 1
YUZU MIZUTANI

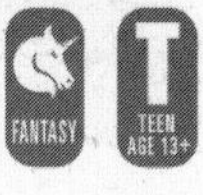
FANTASY
T
TEEN AGE 13+

MAGICAL X MIRACLE

BY YUZÙ MIZUTANI

Magical X Miracle is a quirky—yet uplifting—tale of gender-bending mistaken identity! When a young girl must masquerade as a great wizard, she not only finds the strength to save an entire kingdom...but, ironically, she just might just find herself, too. Yuzu Mizutani's art is remarkably adorable, but it also has a dark, sophisticated edge.

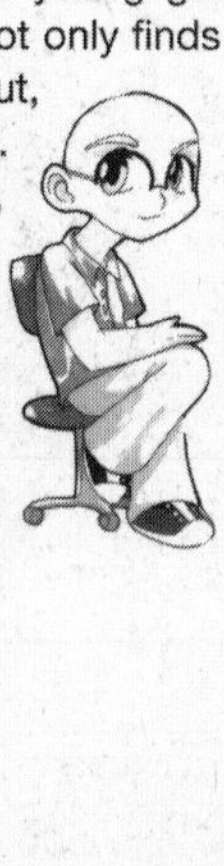

~Paul Morrissey, Editor

STOP

This is the back of the book.
You wouldn't want to spoil a great ending!

This book is printed "manga-style," in the authentic Japanese right-to-left format. Since none of the artwork has been flipped or altered, readers get to experience the story just as the creator intended. You've been asking for it, so TOKYOPOP® delivered: authentic, hot-off-the-press, and far more fun!

DIRECTIONS

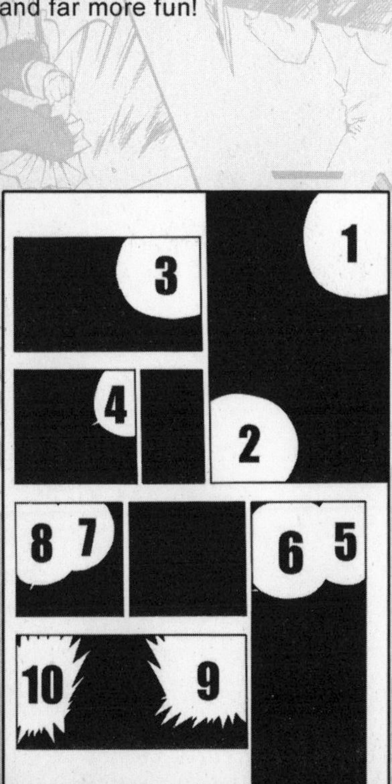
1
2
3
4
5
6
7
8
9
10

If this is your first time reading manga-style, here's a quick guide to help you understand how it works.

It's easy... just start in the top right panel and follow the numbers. Have fun, and look for more 100% authentic manga from TOKYOPOP®!

100% AUTHENTIC MANGA

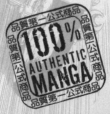